SHAKESPEARE IN STAGES

The history of Shakespearean performance is very well served at its two extremes, with a number of volumes providing a valuable historical overview of the subject and others concentrating on the performance history of a particular play. However, no individual volume provides an in-depth consideration of the stage histories of a number of plays, chosen for their particular significance within specific cultural contexts. *Shakespeare in Stages* addresses this gap. The original case studies explore significant anglophone performances of the plays, as well as ideas about 'Shakespeare', through the changing prisms of three different cultural factors that have proved influential in the way Shakespeare is staged: notions of authenticity, attitudes towards sex and gender, and questions of identity. Ranging from the sixteenth to the twenty-first centuries and examining productions of plays in Britain, the USA, Canada, Australia, and South Africa, the studies focus attention on the complex interaction between particular plays, issues, events, and periods, carefully linking changing perceptions of the meanings of Shakespeare's plays both to particular theatre practices and to specific social, cultural, and political forces.

CHRISTINE DYMKOWSKI is Professor of Drama and Theatre History at Royal Holloway, University of London.

CHRISTIE CARSON is Senior Lecturer in the English Department at Royal Holloway, University of London.

SHAKESPEARE IN STAGES

New Theatre Histories

EDITED BY

CHRISTINE DYMKOWSKI AND
CHRISTIE CARSON

CAMBRIDGE
UNIVERSITY PRESS

CAMBRIDGE UNIVERSITY PRESS
Cambridge, New York, Melbourne, Madrid, Cape Town,
Singapore, São Paulo, Delhi, Tokyo, Mexico City

Cambridge University Press
The Edinburgh Building, Cambridge CB2 8RU, UK

Published in the United States of America by Cambridge University Press, New York

www.cambridge.org
Information on this title: www.cambridge.org/9780521884792

First published 2010

A catalogue record for this publication is available from the British Library

Library of Congress Cataloguing in Publication data
Shakespeare in stages: new theatre histories / [edited by]
Christine Dymkowski, Christie Carson.
p.   cm.
ISBN 978-0-521-88479-2 (hardback)
1. Shakespeare, William, 1564–1616–Stage history. 2. Shakespeare, William,
1564–1616–Dramatic production. I. Dymkowski,
Christine, 1950– II. Carson, Christie. III. Title.
PR3091.S3635   2010
792.9′5–dc22

ISBN 978-0-521-88479-2 Hardback

*In loving memory of my mother, Helen Papula Dymkowski,
and of my grandparents, Ilja Bobak and Jan Papula,
Stanisława Klimkowska and Władysław Dymek
(later Dymkowski) – C.D.*

*To Lynne, Mark, Anna, and Cameron Rickards with thanks
for all of their love, laughter, and support – C.C.*

Contents

Illustrations

Notes on contributors

Christopher Baugh is Professor of Theatre at the University of Hull. As professional scenographer he has worked in Bristol, California, Oregon, Manchester, London, and with the Abbey Theatre, Dublin, winning a New York Drama Critics' Tony Award for the 'best staged play' (*The Borstal Boy*). He was resident scenographer with Mecklenburgh Opera (1987–97), winning the Prudential Award for Opera. He has written *Garrick and Loutherbourg* (1990); 'Stage Design from Loutherbourg to Poel', *The Cambridge History of British Theatre*, Vol. II, ed. Joseph Donohue (2004); 'Philippe de Loutherbourg: Technology-driven entertainment and spectacle in the late eighteenth century', *Huntington Library Quarterly* (2007); and 'Scenography and Technology 1737–1843', *The Cambridge Companion to British Theatre, 1737–1843*, ed. J. Moody and D. O'Quinn (2007). His *Theatre, Performance and Technology: The development of scenography in the 20th century* (2005) was nominated in 2007 by the United States Institute of Theatre Technology (USITT) for a Golden Pen Award.

Susan Bennett is University Professor in the Department of English, University of Calgary, Canada. She is widely published in theatre studies across a variety of periods and performance genres. One of her current research projects involves an anonymous manuscript drama from the 1640s, working with an international team of scholars to explore textual, critical, and performance approaches to the play.

Christie Carson is a senior lecturer in the Department of English at Royal Holloway, University of London; she previously worked as an institutional research fellow in the Department of Drama and Theatre at Royal Holloway from 1996 to 2003. She is the co-editor of *The Cambridge*

King Lear CD-ROM: Text and Performance Archive (2000) and the Principal Investigator of the AHRB-funded research project *Designing Shakespeare: An Audio-Visual Archive, 1960–2000*, which documents the performance history of Shakespeare in Stratford and London. She has published widely on the subject of contemporary performance and the influence of digital technology on audience interaction and research practices, including articles for *Shakespeare Survey* and *Performance Research*. Most recently she has edited *Shakespeare's Globe: A Theatrical Experiment* with Farah Karim-Cooper (Cambridge University Press, 2008).

Neil Carson is an emeritus professor of English at the University of Guelph, Canada. He has published books on Canadian, American, and British drama and stage history, among them an analysis of the chief source of our knowledge of Elizabethan stage practice: *A Companion to Henslowe's Diary* (Cambridge University Press, 1988, 2005). Before entering the calmer waters of academe, Professor Carson worked for some years in the professional theatre in Canada, including four seasons at the fledgling Stratford Shakespeare Festival; he played a small role in Guthrie's *Richard III*.

Christine Dymkowski is Professor of Drama and Theatre History in the Department of Drama and Theatre, Royal Holloway, University of London. She is the author of *Harley Granville Barker: A Preface to Modern Shakespeare* (1986), the theatre history edition of *The Tempest* in the Shakespeare in Production series (Cambridge University Press, 2000), and ' "Ancient [and Modern] Gower": Presenting Shakespeare's *Pericles*', *The Narrator, the Expositor and the Prompter in European Medieval Theatre*, ed. Philip Butterworth (2007); she is also Theatre History editor of Andrew Gurr's New Variorum *Tempest* team. In addition to her work on Shakespeare, she has written numerous articles and papers on Lena Ashwell, Edith Craig, Cicely Hamilton, Susan Glaspell, Caryl Churchill, Sarah Daniels, and Timberlake Wertenbaker, as well as introductions to thirteen plays by Eugene O'Neill (1991–5).

Kate Flaherty is an ARC Linkage Postdoctoral Fellow in the Department of English, University of Sydney, Australia. She is currently writing her first book, *Ours as We Play It: Australia Plays Shakespeare into the New Millennium*, which examines cultural and imaginative intersections brought to light through performance of Shakespeare's plays in contemporary Australia. Her role in the collaborative research project, Shakespeare Reloaded, extends this focus to the context of tertiary education, exploring the history, theory, and practice of Shakespeare as a university subject.

Penny Gay, until her recent retirement, held a personal chair in English Literature and Drama at the University of Sydney, Australia. Her principal publications are *As She Likes It: Shakespeare's Unruly Women* (1994), *Jane Austen and the Theatre* (Cambridge University Press, 2002), *The Cambridge Introduction to Shakespeare's Comedies* (2008), and editions of *The Merchant of Venice* (1995) and *Twelfth Night* (updated edition, Cambridge University Press, 2003). She has published articles on contemporary Shakespearean performance and is currently working on a project on post-modernism in Shakespearean production, as well as pursuing interests in eighteenth-century theatre.

Lynette Goddard is a senior lecturer in drama and theatre at Royal Holloway, University of London. Her research interests include contemporary black British theatre, black productions of Shakespeare and other canonical playwrights, and the politics and practice of integrated casting. She has published widely on black women's theatre, including the monograph *Staging Black Feminisms: Identity, Politics, Performance* (2007) and articles in *Companion to Black British Culture* (2002), *The Cambridge Companion to the Actress* (2007), and *Contemporary Theatre Review*. She is currently working on a book about black playwriting in the first decade of the twenty-first century.

Andrew Gurr is Professor Emeritus at the University of Reading and former Director of Research at the Shakespeare Globe Centre, London. While at the Globe he spent twenty years chairing the committee that identified the Globe's shape and structure. His academic books include *The Shakespearean Stage 1574–1642*, now in its fourth edition, *Playgoing in Shakespeare's London*, now in its third, *The Shakespearian Playing Companies*, *The Shakespeare Company 1594–1642*, and most recently *Shakespeare's Opposites: The Admiral's Men 1594–1625*, a history of the company that performed at the Rose and the Fortune. He has edited several Renaissance plays, including Shakespeare's *Richard II*, *Henry V*, and the Quarto *Henry V* for the Cambridge Shakespeare editions, and is currently editing *The Tempest* for the New Variorum. He is a trustee of the Rose Theatre Trust.

Farah Karim-Cooper is Head of Courses and Research in Globe Education, oversees all research activities at Shakespeare's Globe, and chairs the Globe Architecture Research Group. She is also a visiting research fellow of King's College London and co-convenes the Globe/King's MA in Shakespearean Studies: Text and Playhouse. In addition to articles and essays, she has written *Cosmetics in Shakespearean and Renaissance Drama* (2006) and co-edited *Shakespeare's Globe: A Theatrical Experiment* (Cambridge University Press, 2008).

Jan McDonald, FRSE, FRSAMD, is Professor Emerita in the Department of Theatre Studies, University of Glasgow; she also holds the posts of Honorary Professorial Research Fellow and Dean of Faculties. Her research interests are primarily in the theatre and drama of nineteenth-century British theatre, with publications on the independent stage societies of the 1890s, the Royal Court Theatre (1904–7), and the work of George Bernard Shaw and Harley Granville Barker. She has also written on contemporary Scottish women dramatists.

Elaine M. McGirr is a senior lecturer in English and drama at Royal Holloway, University of London. Her main area of research is the interconnecting worlds of the stage and the page in the long eighteenth century, with a particular focus on the ways in which history, both literary and national, was rewritten and re-inscribed throughout the century. She has published on the novels of Samuel Richardson and Aphra Behn, on the process of British self-fashioning through the use and abuses of stock characters, and on the rewriting of rebellion as farce on the London stage in 1745. She has recently published *The Heroic Mode and Political Crisis, 1660–1745* (2009) and is currently researching the art and times of Colley Cibber.

Lucy Munro is a senior lecturer in English at Keele University. Her publications include *Children of the Queen's Revels: A Jacobean Theatre Repertory* (Cambridge University Press, 2005), editions of Shakespeare's *Pericles* and Sharpham's *The Fleer*, and essays on subjects including *Coriolanus*, female pirates, Irish tragicomedy, and children in film versions of *Richard III*. She is a contributing editor to forthcoming editions of the plays of James Shirley and Richard Brome, and her current projects include a book-length study provisionally titled *The English Archaic: Materialising the Past in Early Modern Literature and Culture*.

Brian Pearce teaches drama and theatre studies at Durban University of Technology and was appointed Associate Professor in 2001. He is also a research associate in both the Centre for Systems Research at Durban University of Technology and the Institute for the Study of English in Africa at Rhodes University. He was the editor of *Shakespeare in Southern Africa* from 2000 to 2008.

Fiona Ritchie is an assistant professor of drama and theatre in the English Department at McGill University, Montreal, Canada. She has published several articles on women and Shakespeare in the eighteenth century and is currently working on a monograph on the part played by women in the process of Shakespeare's canonisation as English national poet. She is also co-editing a collection of essays on eighteenth-century Shakespeare.

Abigail Rokison began her career as a professional actor, training at LAMDA and working in theatre, film, and television. Following a degree with the Open University, undertaken whilst acting, she went on to take an MA in 'Shakespeare: Text and Playhouse' at the Globe Theatre/King's College London. She completed her PhD in the English faculty at Cambridge University in 2006, after which she became lecturer in English and drama in the Education Faculty in Cambridge. In November 2008 she was elected to the board of trustees of the British Shakespeare Association. She has contributed articles to the journal *Shakespeare* and transcriptions to the Malone Society Collections. Her book *Shakespearean Verse Speaking* is forthcoming with Cambridge University Press.

Elizabeth Schafer is Professor of Drama and Theatre Studies at Royal Holloway, University of London. Her main publications include *MsDirecting Shakespeare: Women Direct Shakespeare* and the Cambridge Shakespeare in Production volumes on *The Taming of the Shrew* and *Twelfth Night*; she is also co-author of *Ben Jonson and Theatre*. Her *Lilian Baylis: A Biography*, was shortlisted for the Theatre Book Prize 2006. Currently she is editing *The City Wit* for the online edition of the works of Richard Brome and co-editing an issue of *Contemporary Theatre Review* entitled 'Unsettling Shakespeare'.

Acknowledgements

We are very grateful to Sarah Stanton for her constructive help and support in developing this project and to Joanne Hill for her meticulous, sensitive, and efficient copy-editing. We also thank the Departments of Drama and Theatre and of English, Royal Holloway, University of London, for research allowances that defrayed the cost of illustrations and of compilation of the index.

Introduction

Christine Dymkowski and Christie Carson

At the moment, the history of Shakespearean performance is very well served at its two extremes. A number of volumes, such as *The Cambridge Companion to Shakespeare on Stage* and *The Oxford Illustrated History of Shakespeare on Stage*, offer a valuable historical overview of the subject, while series like Cambridge's Shakespeare in Production, Manchester's Shakespeare in Performance, and Arden's Shakespeare at Stratford concentrate on the performance history of a particular play. However, no individual volume or series offers an in-depth consideration of the stage histories of a number of plays, chosen for their particular significance within specific cultural contexts.

The present book, *Shakespeare in Stages: New Theatre Histories*, aims to address this gap, steering a course between the Scylla of homogenising generalisation on the one hand and the Charybdis of eclectic and unrelated essays on the other. The original case studies that comprise the volume explore significant anglophone performances of particular plays, as well as ideas about 'Shakespeare', through the changing prisms of three different cultural factors that have proved influential in the way Shakespeare is staged: notions of authenticity, attitudes towards sex and gender, and questions of identity. Ranging from the sixteenth to the twenty-first centuries and examining productions of plays in Britain, the USA, Canada, Australia, and South Africa, the studies focus attention on the complex interaction between particular plays, issues, events, and periods, carefully linking changing perceptions of the meanings of Shakespeare's plays not only to particular theatre practices but also to specific social, cultural, and political forces.

The first part of the volume, 'Notions of authenticity', focuses on the complex idea of authenticity and its influence on how Shakespeare's plays have been understood and performed. Andrew Gurr explores current understandings of Renaissance theatre spaces and the ways in which they shaped original performances of the plays. Elaine McGirr, through a study of Cibber's adaptation of *King John*, investigates the complex realities underlying eighteenth-century bardolatry, literary reputation, Shakespearean adaptations, and Whig politics. Lucy Munro, examining William Poel's 'inauthentic' 1931 *Coriolanus* and setting it within the context of his other productions, highlights changes in his theories and methods that other commentators usually overlook. Neil Carson, focusing on *Richard III*, examines the effects of Tyrone Guthrie's experiments in 1953 with a practicable Elizabethan stage in Stratford, Ontario. Abigail Rokison, comparing the work of Shakespeare's Globe and Edward Hall's Propeller with special reference to 21st-century productions of *Twelfth Night* by both companies, considers alternative approaches to the issue of 'authenticity'.

The second section, 'Attitudes towards sex and gender', first looks at the presentation of women on the Shakespearean stage and then concentrates on how changing attitudes towards them, not only within the theatre profession but also within society, have subsequently opened up new meanings for Shakespeare's plays in performance. Farah Karim-Cooper examines the relationship between the early modern cultural ideal of beauty and the enactment of beautiful women on the Renaissance stage, a relationship further complicated by the practice of using boys to portray women. Fiona Ritchie, exploring the work of Hannah Pritchard and Catherine Clive during the 1740–1 theatrical season, establishes the artistic, cultural, and economic power of the Shakespearean actress in the mid-eighteenth century, redressing the usual bias towards Garrick as Shakespeare's populariser. Jan McDonald's essay on *The Winter's Tale* examines the ways in which nineteenth-century women writers and actors appropriated the play's women characters to challenge or to reinforce prevalent ideologies of gender. Elizabeth Schafer, unpicking critical dismissal of Lydia Lopokova's performance as Olivia in Tyrone Guthrie's 1933 Old Vic production of *Twelfth Night*, offers three alternative readings, situating it within a theatrical lesbian genealogy, an understanding of the Vic-Wells community, and theatrical management practices. Christine Dymkowski explores the shifts in attitudes towards gender, sexuality, and the relationship between the individual and the state that have made *Measure for Measure* especially resonant with English audiences in a variety of theatrical interpretations since the 1970s.

The final section, 'Questions of identity', focuses on how Shakespeare has been used in the past and continues to be used today to help to formulate local and national identity; it highlights how location – cultural as well geographical – can shape the interpretation, presentation, and reception of Shakespeare's plays. Christopher Baugh considers how scenographic tropes of spectacle and of antiquarianism became crucial to the staging of Shakespeare during the late eighteenth and early nineteenth centuries, ultimately playing an important role in the development of national identity and the birth of a national theatre. Susan Bennett looks at how and what Shakespeare means in a very local context, with particular reference to early twentieth-century and contemporary performances of Shakespeare in rural Montana. Kate Flaherty and Penny Gay investigate why *A Midsummer Night's Dream* was Australia's most popular play between 1988 and 1998 and examine how five recent productions made the play meaningful for Australian audiences, addressing questions of the 'cultural cringe', post-colonialism, and the particular concept of 'play' in Australian culture. Lynette Goddard looks at 'Binglish' Shakespeare, focusing particularly on the shifting race and gender dynamics in Yvonne Brewster's 1997 production of *Othello* for Talawa. Brian Pearce examines how British directors, attempting to make Shakespeare relevant within post-apartheid South Africa, can sometimes invert their intended meanings through unfamiliarity with the country's historical context and traditions of performance.

Christie Carson concludes the volume by addressing the role of Shakespeare in building identity through education, examining the work of the education departments of the Royal Shakespeare Company (RSC) and of Shakespeare's Globe. In so doing, she again raises the question that all of the other essays ask either implicitly or explicitly: when we respond to a performance, when we try to understand its context, when we decode its meanings, when we feel it addresses or reflects or ignores our concerns, who are 'we'? Meanings are multiple, dependent on answers to that question. For that reason, we, the editors and contributors, do not offer a general narrative overview of the history of how Shakespeare has been presented on stage, but 'thick descriptions' of the many ways in which particular plays have created local meanings in specific places, periods, and communities: a plurality of new theatre histories that document – even celebrate – temporal, geographic, and cultural complexity.

Christine Dymkowski
Christie Carson

PART I

Notions of authenticity

CHAPTER I

The move indoors

Andrew Gurr

Over the last five hundred years there have been many changes in the character of theatre venues in England. The range is wide, from the out-door bowl on a hillside on the flanks of Shrewsbury where schoolboys staged their shows in the sixteenth century, or the inns that offered either their galleried yards or great rooms upstairs, to the proscenium-arched stages and theatres-in-the-round of this century. Theatre venues are always changing, and playwriting changes with them. Every performance event differs too. The venue may be the same, but the actors and audience will always brew their own distinct chemistry. It is never easy to identify the elements stirred into those brews, but it should not be impossible to see how the physical character of any particular building used for a play affects the nature of the performance staged in it. For the decades up to Shakespeare's time, transient venues at guildhalls, schoolrooms, and churches used by itinerant bands of players were the norm. Between 1575 and 1609 in London, however, we can see the basis of modern theatre developing, and audiences made their key choice of the forms that came to dominate English theatre thereafter. For nearly seventy years from 1576 till 1642 the choice between indoor and outdoor venues was in the bal-ance. It seems appropriate that a book devoted to the ways in which the social and cultural experiences and expectations of an audience inflect the meanings of a play should begin with a look at how the decision to prefer the indoor venues was initially made and how that preference helped to shape the writing and reception of the plays themselves.

Theatre audiences are always affected by the auditorium they occupy. An outdoor setting, whether for a play or a sporting event, prompts the feeling that you are a member of a crowd gathered for the same purpose, responding to what is offered you in ways influenced by the other reac-tions you hear or see or feel around you. On the other hand, in the con-finement of an enclosed space where you feel comfortably freed from any effect of weather and have your own passive sitting space, you can much more easily feel yourself an individual, separate from the others around you, conscious of your identity as a free and perhaps sceptical observer of the events you have paid to witness. That is particularly the case when you sit in the dark. Outdoor arenas have the feeling of being public spaces, whereas an indoor hall offers an intimacy more like that of a private house or a venue designed for at most a small and intimate community. The dark helps you to feel private and passive, like an eavesdropper. For something like thirty years in the Shakespearean period, after the distinction became a false one, they used to call indoor playhouses 'private' while the outdoor theatres were called 'public' venues. Jacobean and Caroline playgoers paid money to attend plays at either kind of venue, but publishers and others continued to insist that the hall playhouses were private or exclusive, in deliberate contrast to the common nature of the outdoor venues. These terms echo the different feelings activated by the two types of venue. When playgoing gentry attended a play of the Shakespeare company's in the summer while the company abandoned its superior playhouse the Blackfriars for the sordidly 'public' Globe, their choice entailed a calculated acceptance of the more populist and lower-class environment.[1]

A seated audience at an indoor venue is always likely to behave more politely and to be more docile and passive in its responses than an audience that is on its feet surrounding the stage that the actors are walking on. When you add to the difference between the inherent dispositions of the two kinds of audience the fact that access to small indoor venues is always likely to cost their customers much more than for large arenas open to the sky, the division between the two kinds of behaviour patterns intensifies. The groundlings who got to know their Shakespeare at the outdoor Globe had a quite different mindset from those who later came to enjoy his plays at the indoor Blackfriars. And since all the theatres built after 1660 cater for only the indoor and more passive kind of audience, that difference is significant.

At one end of the social spectrum in early modern England, the rich had ample experience of enjoying plays staged at indoor venues. The court always held its entertainments late at night, with only candles to illuminate the intimate event. That made it clearly distinct from public events, whether indoors or out. They were always performed in the afternoons,

---

[1] Several comments from the time express surprise when large numbers of gentry appeared at the Globe, as they did for *A Game at Chess* in 1624 and *The Late Lancashire Witches* in 1635. For a survey of the general picture, see Gurr, *Playgoing* 89–94; note the citations in Appendix 2, 148, 191 and 211.

the indoor playhouses making use of such daylight as their high windows provided to supplement the candelabra suspended across the stage and auditorium.[2] Every courtier at a royal performance, too, knew, prized, and flaunted his or her individuality, whether as an English aristocrat and dignitary, as a senior prelate or court officer, or as an ambassador for one of the eminent European countries. In utter contrast, the crowds of '*Rables, Apple-wives* and Chimney-boyes'[3] who attended the open-air venues in the 1630s well knew how anonymous they were individually amongst the jostling hordes similarly dressed that they stood and reacted with.

Such a difference and its impact on the range of playgoers in playhouse venues was a feature of the vast social divisions in early modern England throughout Shakespeare's time. Today we have to look into the fragments of evidence – the passing remarks by Grub Street writers, gossipy anecdotes about scandals, and incidental references by would-be poets of the time – to identify what effects the two distinct types of theatre venue had on the hordes of Londoners who attended plays up to 1642. As with any broad social distinctions, generalisations are easy but they soon become more of a vague assertion than a clinical conclusion. Since the distinction between the open-air playhouses like the Globe and the fashionable indoor halls like the Blackfriars started the long process of popular playgoing that still features in London's nightlife, it is useful to look carefully at the key elements of English society that generated the difference between the two types, and that eventually determined the complete triumph of the indoor over the outdoor kind of playhouse for the subsequent centuries.

London's first theatres, both those with outdoor and those with indoor stages, opened over a remarkably short span of time in 1575 and 1576. The two types continued in use till the general closure of 1642, except for the decade of the 1590s, when no indoor theatres were allowed for commercial use.[4] The huge stages of the open-air amphitheatres were distinct from the indoor stages chiefly in their much larger size and the pair of massive stage posts that upheld the 'shadow' or 'cover' protecting the stage and the players from London's rain and snow. The indoor or hall stages needed no stage posts, and the much smaller capacity of their stages was restricted even further during performances by the presence of up to fifteen gallants who sat round the flanks of the stage itself. Such eminences paid to watch the plays sitting on stools at both sides, in front of the flanking stage

[2] For a careful and thorough analysis of the effect of candlelight in these auditoria, see Graves.
[3] See Gurr, *Playgoing* 298–9 (Appendix 2, reference 212).
[4] Civic opposition to all playing was at its strongest in this decade and led to a ban on playing in city inns; see Gurr, 'Henry Carey'.

boxes, or across the line by the tiring-house doors at the back of the stage. As a result of this radical difference in stage capacity, access to daylight, and the intrusion on stage of the gallants at the indoor playhouses, we usually assume that the presentation of plays on these two kinds of stage was quite distinct. But it may be that the key differences came more from the character of the two types of auditorium and the consequent behaviour patterns of their occupants than on the different stages.

The assumption that several decades of writing for the indoor stages up to 1642 created a social as well as a practical differentiation in what was written for the two types of playhouse is now generally accepted. So is the assumption that it led to the demise of Shakespearean, meaning open-air, staging at the Globe in London. But the story can be nothing like so simple or so directly a sequence of cause and effect as that. The evidence for the changes that developed in the early forms of staging and in performance through the Jacobean and Caroline periods needs some careful sorting out.

At a conference some years ago I tried to use the evidence about where each play was first staged to make a fairly comprehensive survey of the differences between plays written for the indoor and those for the outdoor playhouses once the King's Men started using both types of playhouse after 1608.[5] In broad terms I looked at all the plays that could be identified as written specifically either for an indoor or for an outdoor venue, and also at those known to be performed at both types of venue. Characteristic of its time, this account concluded in general terms that, while we cannot easily generalise, on the whole the companies using the outdoor playhouses preferred to stage plays with battles and noisy sword-and-buckler fights, whereas the companies at the indoor playhouses favoured smaller-scale duels with rapiers and emphasised wit-play rather than sword-play. That conclusion took the question into the equally broad and even more specious territory of the so-called 'citizen' plays like *The Spanish Tragedy* and *Tamburlaine*, both of which Jonson said in 1614 were out of date but which persisted at the outdoor playhouses, the Fortune and the Red Bull, all the way until 1642. The question of how far this dismissive characterisation of the 'outdoor' plays for the citizenry was more than a transient vogue and the dismissals a manifestation of the literary snobbery inherent in Jonson and others needs further consideration here. Who besides Jonson said they were old-fashioned, and what companies at what playhouses were characterised in this way?

---

[5] See Gurr, 'Playing'.

In recent years the prime mover of the idea that the Red Bull and the Fortune were mocked as 'citizen' playhouses, full of loud speeches and louder swordfights, was Gerald Eades Bentley. In the seven volumes of his *Jacobean and Caroline Stage* he regularly downrated the Red Bull and the Fortune in comparison with the other playhouses, because he thought they were characterised by a lower quality of repertory. In Volume VI (1968), he added to his account of the Red Bull ten pages (238–47) under the heading 'The reputation of the "Red Bull"', which is full of evidence about how, he asserted, from 1610 onwards, 'As the Curtain falls into disuse, the Red Bull reigns supreme in ignominy.' This lower status he thought was effected by the artisan and apprentice audiences that frequented the Red Bull in particular (he found fewer condescending references to the Fortune). It was also Bentley who argued that the acquisition of Beaumont and Fletcher's services from the boy company who had been using the Blackfriars was the Shakespeare company's attempt to get new plays from writers familiar with Blackfriars tastes, and that Shakespeare's later plays were all designed for the indoor venue.[6] This theory, which has to ignore Shakespeare's creation of *Pericles* in 1606 or 1607 and its appearance in that and subsequent years at the Globe, has been seriously challenged. Bentley's idea that the Red Bull and the Fortune were lower-class theatre venues and that they were rated as bad because of their loud-mouthed playing of bad verse, on the other hand, has undergone a less drastic reconsideration.

It needs one. Much of Bentley's evidence comes from contemporary assertions that the Red Bull and Fortune players spoke particularly loudly, with wide mouths that resonated in their open-air space. In a history of the playing companies published in 1996, I set out a chart of how the companies used both indoor and outdoor playhouses through the 1630s.[7] It looks like Table 1.

The first two playhouses listed were indoor venues, the other two outdoor. The company names as abbreviated here are QH = Queen Henrietta's Men, BB = Beeston's Boys, KR = King's Revels, PC2 = Prince Charles's (II), Boh = King and Queen of Bohemia's, Rev = Red Bull (Revels). The King and Queen of Bohemia's Men were dispersed in 1631, chiefly to supply a group of leaders for the new Prince Charles's Men set up in that year. The King's Revels Men, set up at the indoor Salisbury Court when it was opened in 1629, moved to the open-air

[6] Bentley, 'Shakespeare'.
[7] The chart appears in *Shakespearian Playing Companies* 138 and in *Playgoing* 94.

Table 1 *Use of playhouses, 1626–40*

YEAR	1626	1629	1631	1634	1637	1640
COMPANIES						
Cockpit	QH	QH	QH	QH	BB	BB
Salisbury Court	–	KR	PC2	KR	QH	QH
Fortune	Boh	Boh	KR	Rev	Rev	PC2
Red Bull	Rev	Rev	Rev	PC2	PC2	Rev

Fortune two years later and went back to the indoor venue three years after that; they disappeared in the long plague closure of 1637, when Queen Henrietta's, dispossessed of the Cockpit, replaced them at the Salisbury Court. Christopher Beeston set up his young company, known as Beeston's Boys though it had a core of six adult players, after the plague closure and gave them the Cockpit. Queen Henrietta's and Beeston's Boys were the only companies to play exclusively at indoor venues. The Red Bull Revels company played consistently at the outdoor venues, switching from the Red Bull to the Fortune for six years in the middle, while the young Prince Charles's company replaced them at the Red Bull from 1634 to 1640. In all, the Prince Charles's company used three playhouses, one indoors and two outdoors, over their ten or more years of playing. The King's Revels also used both an indoor and an outdoor venue. There is little sign in all this that the well-trumpeted social distinctions between the indoor and the outdoor venues, especially the claim that the outdoor players had loud voices and wide mouths, had much relevance to the companies that used them. Nor, since Prince Charles's and the King's Revels companies must have taken their own plays with them to their diverse venues, can their repertories have been much influenced by the kind of venue they used.

Bentley's stories of wide-mouthed players shouting their verses in the face of genteel derision may fit the evident practice of companies regularly switching between the two kinds of venue. But the evidence that the companies could so easily switch their venues from indoor to outdoor gives little direct support to the sneers. Nor does the story of the Shakespeare company shifting its venue from one to the other each year. It may well be that the venues themselves rather than any predisposition of the playing companies were what generated the distinction. Much, perhaps too much, debate has been caused by James Shirley's prologue to *The Doubtful Heir*, written and performed in Dublin by 1638 and taken up by the King's Men in 1640.

Shirley's prologue apologised for its being staged at the Globe, when, he says, 'Our Author did not calculate his Play / For this Meridian'. He excuses the absence of what he identifies as the Globe audience's usual preferences:

> No shews, no frisk, and what you most delight in,
> (Grave understanders) here's no Target fighting
> Upon the Stage, all work for cutlers barrd,
> No Bawd'ry, nor no Ballads.

This was specific mockery of what the groundlings, the 'grave' customers standing around the Globe's stage, were thought to have expected. Instead his play asked them to think themselves in the 'Black-friers pit'. Moreover, he hoped that the players appearing on the much bigger Globe stage would not disconcert the audience by speaking too quietly, and that the latter, 'Because we have no heart to break our lungs, / Will pardon our vast Scene'.[8] Shirley may have been echoing what he had heard about the reputation of the Red Bull and Fortune players. He clearly did not expect the King's Men to change their voices to suit the outdoor venue. The Shakespeare company's practices at their two venues evidently did not conform to Bentley's assumptions. The difference may have been in the audiences rather than on the stage.

The story of how the leading adult playing company added a smaller indoor venue for the winter to their huge outdoor venue is generally seen as starting in 1608, when Richard Burbage retrieved the Blackfriars playhouse from Henry Evans, who had leased it for his boy company since 1600. In fact it began in 1594, when the Chamberlain's Men were founded. In the first autumn of their work at the Globe's predecessor, the Theatre, they got their patron to ask the Lord Mayor of London for permission to act at the Cross Keys inn through the winter. The Cross Keys was an indoor venue in the city used before by several members of the new company. When the Lord Mayor refused, the owner of the Theatre, James Burbage, built the Blackfriars in a 'liberty' precinct near St Paul's. Then and for the next few years, however, the local residents stopped them from using it. In 1600 it was leased out to a boy company, who ran it for the next eight years. It was not until the long plague closure of 1608–9 that Richard Burbage, who inherited the Blackfriars from his father while his elder brother got the open-air Theatre, and who was now leader of what had become the King's Men, not only took control of it, but was allowed to use it for the first time for performances by his company of adult players. He immediately

---

[8] The full prologue is analysed at greater length in *Playgoing* 221–3.

distributed shares in his new/old theatre to those of his fellow players who already had shares in the Globe. From then on the company used the open-air Globe between May and October and the Blackfriars through the winter months.

As a newly authorised member of the 'duopoly', the two companies that shared the Privy Council's authority to perform around London, the Shakespeare company clearly had their own view of what London should get from them in the complex politics of professional playing in London, caught though they were in the manoeuvres between the two Privy Councillors who set up the duopoly and the mayor's opposition to all playing. Their enthusiasm for an indoor venue in winter was evidently not shared by the other duopoly company, the Admiral's Men, since they stayed at the Rose and its successor the Fortune throughout the thirty-two years of their existence. More will be said about what determined their choice later.

Once the King's Men started using it, the Blackfriars soon became the favoured resort for a rich and upmarket clientele. Summer was when the aristocracy went to live in their country mansions, and the law courts were in recess. Summer was the time when the great halls of the nobility were warmest and most hospitable. Recurrent epidemics of plague were at their worst in the warmer months, when it seemed wise, if you could afford it, to avoid the contagion of London's crowds. Winter was when the King and court occupied their riverside palaces, and Whitehall was at its busiest trying to run the country. Winter was when countrymen came to London to have their lawsuits heard.

The two types of playhouse had remarkably different features. One surprising element in the plan the Shakespeare company held to for so long is how ready they were to switch plays written for the Globe to the Blackfriars. Since they had a ready-made and familiar repertory at the Globe, and since they were well practised at taking their plays to different venues, including the royal court and great houses in the country, it is not surprising that they expected to fit into the new venue without too much trouble. But there is also the surprise, and the question, of how readily they switched plays written specifically for the Blackfriars to the Globe. And behind that is the question of how reliable is Bentley's identification of the Fortune and Red Bull as 'citizen' playhouses, distinct in their audience and their plays from those staged at the indoor playhouses.

Some of the Blackfriars features were an instant asset. Above all, the King's Men took on a pre-existing major feature of the Blackfriars by re-engaging the 'broken consort' of musicians who were used to playing for the

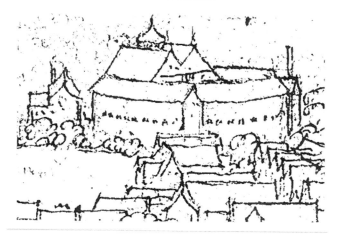

1. A pencil drawing of the exterior of the second Globe, by Wenceslas Hollar
in the 1630s.

boy company. Their contribution to the staging of plays was immediately
apparent in Shakespeare's *The Tempest*, with its use of background music and
its emphasis on songs, the music for some of them written for the occasion.[9]

The real distinction of playing indoors is evident in the shape of two plays
written for the Blackfriars, *The Tempest* and *The Duchess of Malfi*. It has been
argued, usually unconvincingly, that most of Shakespeare's late plays, even
Coriolanus, were written with the Blackfriars in mind. The one play that
there is no doubt he wrote for the indoor playhouse with its consort of musicians is *The Tempest*. Not only does it have off stage orchestral music integrated into the story, but it is the only play of Shakespeare's possessing an
act break where the same two characters who end one act re-enter to start
the next. Act breaks were a necessary feature of the indoor playhouses, evident in all the boy company plays of the early 1600s written for Paul's and
the Blackfriars, in order to keep the interior lighting under control. They
seem to have lasted for roughly two minutes, filled with offstage music,[10]

---

[9] The work of the Blackfriars consort is evident in *The Knight of the Burning Pestle*, written in
1607 for the Blackfriars Boy company. While its chief singer, Merrythought, uses snatches from
popular ballads, three songs, notably the central motif-song, ''Tis mirth that fills the veins with
blood', were designed as 'composer's pieces', verses set to music by professionals for boys to sing,
probably with a string accompaniment. For *The Tempest*, music for two songs composed by
Robert Johnson, lutenist to King James, survives in early manuscript versions, as does the setting for one song from *The Duchess of Malfi*. See Lindley, Appendix 1.

[10] The most positive evidence for the time an inter-act break was expected to take is the final one
in *The Knight of the Burning Pestle*. It was filled by the apprentice Rafe, who delivers a rhyming

2. The Blackfriars, seen from Hollar's 'Long View' printed in 1644. It is under the long roof south-east of the church tower, with two chimneys or turrets rising from its centre.

while theatre hands trimmed the candles around the stage and auditorium. In *The Tempest* Prospero and Ariel close Act 4 by hunting the clowns off stage together, and they open Act 5 with Prospero's formal entry dressed for his invocation, 'Ye elves of hill, brooks, standing dales [...]', accompanied by Ariel.

The Tempest was a peculiar product in any case. Distinctive in its single story, with only a parodic sub-plot to stretch its range, it conforms remarkably well to the three classical unities of action, place, and time.

maylord's speech lasting 36 lines, taking about two minutes. A reference from a play manuscript some years later suggests that a single longer interval was added in the 1630s.

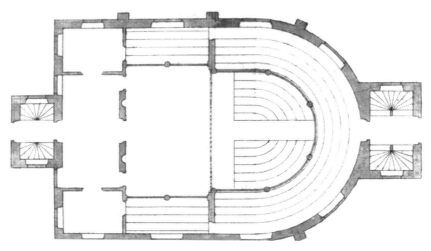

3. The ground plan of a building designed by Inigo Jones, possibly modelled on the Blackfriars, with which it shares many features. The original is in the library of Worcester College, Oxford.

Indeed, Prospero's comments on the play action's timing are marked throughout, giving it in all no more than the three hours of a normal play in performance. Such ostensible realism stands in such obvious contrast to *The Winter's Tale*, with its story covering sixteen years and its travels from Sicily to the sea-coast of Bohemia, that we can distinguish such features of *The Tempest* as part of a private game, probably played with Ben Jonson.[11] The evidence that it was designed for the Blackfriars lies in its practical features, chiefly the use of act breaks and offstage music.

In a previous article on *The Tempest*, I did suggest that Shakespeare may have designed his opening scene mischievously, with the intention of giving the Blackfriars audience a deliberate shock. Its all-seated playgoers were accustomed to being welcomed by music from the resident consort. In later years under the King's Men they even seem to have greeted newcomers with special tunes. Bulstrode Whitelocke reported of the 1630s that he composed an air that became known as 'Whitelocke's coranto'. The Blackfriars musicians performed it and would strike it up whenever he arrived for a play (Burney II: 299). So the first audiences at *The Tempest* would have been already well comforted by the consort's orchestral harmonies when the play

---

[11] For other likely features of this game, see Gurr, 'Who is Lovewit? What is he?'

opened. The sudden roaring, the shrieks of the master's whistle, the mari-
ners hauling on ropes and rushing on and off stage, the confusion of offstage noises, and the general uproar of the opening would have startled any
crowd sitting in comfortable expectation. Prospero's subsequent reassurance
to Miranda that all the melodrama of the storm was done and controlled
through his magic then served merely to emphasise the game of art controlling nature that the play was broaching. That opening shock was an element in the design of a cleverly innovatory Blackfriars play.

As befitted its emphasis on art ruling nature, *The Tempest*'s music
remains silent after the pre-play harmonies until in the second scene Ariel
enters leading Ferdinand. As an invisible sea-nymph, he plays what was
probably a lute while he sings two songs. The consort in the music room
over the stage provides him with an accompaniment, including a 'Burthen'
or refrain line, since Ferdinand asks 'Where shold this Musick be? I'th
aire, or th'earth?'[12] Ariel's subsequent appearances are similarly marked
by offstage music, notably at 2.1 when he arouses Gonzalo to the danger
from the plotters, and at 3.2 when he mocks the clowns by playing their
own tune on a clown's 'Tabor and Pipe'. In 3.1, the scene where Prospero
bewitches the king and the others, and Ariel appears scarily as a harpy, the
stage directions call for 'Solemne and strange Musicke', and then thunder
followed by 'soft Musicke'. The same phrase is used again for the music
accompanying the masque in 4.1. Shakespeare made the Blackfriars consort's offstage music a new means of augmenting stage spectacle.

Not many other features of *The Tempest*'s staging show particularly distinctive signs of its being purely a Blackfriars play. It makes no use of the
Globe's stage posts, but nor do most of the other plays Shakespeare wrote. It
uses the three kinds of stage entrance that it shared with the Globe, the wide
central opening behind a cloth of arras and the two doors on each flank.
The notorious reference to Prospero 'on the top' has been thought to indicate
some distinctive feature of the Blackfriars at a level above the stage balcony
where Prospero could have shown himself, while Ariel dangled somewhere
below him dressed as a harpy, suspended over the banquet table with its
reversible lid. This 'top' is a stage direction whose wording is shared only
with *1 Henry VI*, an early play which might have been staged at the Theatre,
the Globe's precursor, but not at the Blackfriars.[13] The term is extraneous,
certainly in its use for Prospero in *The Tempest*. It does not appear in any

---

[12] All quotations from *The Tempest* are taken from the First Folio edition.
[13] While it is just possible that the text of *1 Henry VI*, not printed until the Folio of 1623, contains
alterations made after the company acquired the Blackfriars, it seems highly unlikely that the
coincidence of the term 'top' comes from any modifications that might have been made to set it

other play written for the Blackfriars. We know that Ralph Crane, the scribe from whose copy the Folio play was printed, seems to have elaborated some of the stage directions in this play for the reader, such as when we are told that, when Ariel appears suspended as a harpy, 'with a quient device the Banquet vanishes' from the table beneath him. The one reference to the 'top', which occurs in the same scene, 3.3, may also have come from Ralph Crane's attempt at explaining the staging as well as he could.

After some years apprenticed to the Henslowe stable of collaborative writers, John Webster in 1610–11 wrote his first solo play, *The White Devil*, for the Queen's Men at the Red Bull. Webster's resentment at the play's first staging appears in the letter he wrote to go with its publication. He grumbled that 'it was acted, in so dull a time of Winter, presented in so open and blacke a Theater, that it wanted (that which is the onely grace and setting out of a Tragedy) a full and understanding Auditory'. The Red Bull was indeed an 'open' playhouse, and in winter the usual value of the light provided by an open-air site was less evident than on a summer's afternoon. But Webster merged the dull time and the dull auditory and reacted by taking his next tragedy to the Blackfriars. The Globe, the King's Men's equivalent to the Red Bull, was out of action between the fire of 29 June 1613 that destroyed it and the opening of the second Globe, rebuilt on the same site, by June of the following year. So while Webster was finishing his play the Blackfriars was the only venue available to the King's Men. Yet, with its candlelight and only secondary daylight from the high windows, the indoor playhouse was definitely a darker place than the open-air Red Bull. For tragedies it could become blacker still, as Dekker once noted. He has a reference in *The Seven deadlie Sinns of London* (1606), aptly enough in the chapter on 'Candle-light', about how 'all the City lookt like a private Play-house, when the windowes are clapt downe, as if some Nocturnal, or dismall Tragedy were presently to be acted'. That was the first indication that variable lighting could be used in any theatre in England.

The glitter of candlelight in a general aura of darkness is thought by critics today to give a peculiarly apposite atmosphere to *The Duchess*. Whether we think Webster wanted the Blackfriars for that reason depends in part on how one reads the epistle to his previously published play. It should be borne in mind, however, that, while both of the plays studied here show signs that they were primarily intended for the indoor venue,

out for the company's new venue, like the Folio *Midsummer Night's Dream*'s stage direction for the lovers to '*sleepe all the Act*' at the end of Act 3 – i.e., through the musical act break. The battles that *1 Henry VI* makes such extensive use of identify it as the kind of play least likely to have been transferred indoors.

The Tempest possibly and *The Duchess of Malfi* certainly also appeared subsequently at the Globe. When Webster got *The Duchess* published in 1624, its title page specified that it had been acted at the Globe as well as the Blackfriars: 'privatly, at the Black-friers, and publiquely at the Globe, By the Kings Majesties Servants'. The claim that playing at the Blackfriars was 'private', or non-commercial, whereas the Globe gave 'public' or paid-for performances, was a relic of the social snobbery that elevated the indoor venues over the Red Bull and the Globe, by their claim to be available only to 'private' or invited audiences, a manifest untruth. But *The Duchess* was one of a number of King's Men's plays published in the 1620s that claimed to have been staged at both of the company's venues. The Blackfriars did not prevail over the Globe with publishers till the 1630s.

The Duchess's text has other signs showing that Webster did design his play for the Blackfriars. The five acts are distinct in time from each other, as a musical act break between each of them would affirm. As in *The Tempest*, most of its music was played off stage and suited the work of the Blackfriars consort.[14] The madmen who sing 'to a dismall kind of Musique' had offstage accompaniment, as most likely had Bosola for his dirge, which was printed in italics in the original edition. The scene with the wax effigies in 4.1 and the colourful dumbshow of 3.4 might have been staged equally well at either kind of venue. Even the echo scene, 5.3, might be staged equally easily at the Globe or the Blackfriars. Few scenes demand a large number of characters on stage at once. None requires bigger crowds than any in *The Tempest*, even with all the comings and goings of that play's frenetic opening, which resembles the opening scene of *The Duchess* in the number of its entrances and exits.

The success of the Blackfriars and its music is shown most strongly in the long career of William Davenant. Having written a number of plays for the King's Men's indoor playhouse from 1629 onwards, ten years later, in March 1639, he secured a patent from the King for a grand new indoor theatre in Fleet Street. It was designed specifically to give shows involving music and dancing. His scheme was a grandiose one. He planned to build what by the standards of the existing indoor playhouses was a very large structure, on a site measuring forty yards by forty, more than twice the size of the Blackfriars.[15] He was licensed to use it for not only 'Action', the then-

[14] See the note by Peter Walls on Webster's use of music in this play, in Gunby *et al.* 708. Walls thinks the Robert Johnson who composed for *The Tempest* was also the most likely author of 'O let us howle', the song that opens the masque of madmen in 4.2, and perhaps other music for the play's songs and other musical moments.
[15] The licence, which has the only known specifications about the theatre, is reprinted in Bentley, *Jacobean and Caroline Stage* VI: 305–6.

traditional form of staging plays, but for 'musical Presentments, Scenes, Dancing and the like'. The stage had to accommodate not merely a consort of musicians but enough space for both scenic shows and dances. Davenant did not realise this ambition – the licence was withdrawn that October – and he was forced to postpone his ambition for a more operatic kind of performance for another twenty years, towards the end of the Interregnum, when he set up *The Siege of Rhodes* as an opera (a new name he used in order to free his productions from the opprobrium and hazards that mere 'plays' still suffered from).

When after the Restoration in 1660 Davenant joined the new duopoly of playing companies alongside William Killigrew, he began to use scenic staging as soon as he could get a proscenium-arch stage. From then on, he augmented the old repertory with songs and music in operatic mode. Over the next ten years he produced drastic rewrites of Shakespeare's *Tempest* and many other plays, adding song, dance, and scenic spectacles as well as female actors. From this time on, the new scenic stage ruled all of England's theatre. By then the indoor venues were the only mode, with their quieter, passive audiences, so much more convenient for the impresarios than the active and more vigorously responsive groundlings of the Globe and the Red Bull.

WORKS CITED

Bentley, G. E. 'Shakespeare and the Blackfriars Theatre'. *Shakespeare Survey* 1 (1948): 38–50.

The Jacobean and Caroline Stage. 7 vols. Oxford: Oxford University Press, 1942–68.

Burney, Charles. *A General History of Music from the Earliest Ages to the Present Period.* 2 vols. London, 1782–9.

Graves, R. B. *Lighting the Shakespearean Stage, 1567–1642.* Carbondale and Edwardsville: Southern Illinois University Press, 1999.

Gunby, David, David Carnegie, Antony Hammond, and Doreen DelVecchio, eds. *The Works of John Webster.* Vol. 1. Cambridge: Cambridge University Press, 1995.

Gurr, Andrew. 'Henry Carey's Peculiar Letter'. *Shakespeare Quarterly* 56 (2005): 51–75.

Playgoing in Shakespeare's London. 3rd edn. Cambridge: Cambridge University Press, 2004.

'Playing in Amphitheatres and Playing in Hall Theatres'. *Elizabethan Theatre* 13 (1994): 27–62.

The Shakespearian Playing Companies. Oxford: Oxford University Press, 1996.

'Who is Lovewit? What is he?' *Ben Jonson and Theatre: Performance, Practice and Theory.* Ed. Richard Cave, Elizabeth Schafer, and Brian Woolland. London: Routledge, 1999. 5–19.

Lindley, David, ed. *The Tempest.* The New Cambridge Shakespeare. Cambridge: Cambridge University Press, 2002.

CHAPTER 2

Whig heroics: Shakespeare, Cibber, and the troublesome King John

Elaine M. McGirr

In 1700, at the beginning of his career, Colley Cibber tried his hand at adapting Shakespeare. The result, *Richard III*, was wildly successful – despite some initial difficulties with political readings of the first act[1] – and seemed to confirm the young actor-playwright's reputation as a dramatist.[2] At the close of his career, Cibber, now not only an established actor, playwright, and theatre manager, but also Poet Laureate, returned to Shakespeare, but with a very different result. His radical adaptation of Shakespeare's *King John*, re-titled *Papal Tyranny in the Reign of King John*, did not enjoy anything like the success of his *Richard III* and has gone down in history as 'a deserved failure,' a 'wretched version,' and 'an alteration for the worse' (Cibber, *Apology* iv; Salmon n.p.; Waith 193). Most analyses of Shakespearean adaptation agree with this condemnation or ignore *Papal Tyranny* altogether – for instance, while Michael Dobson relegates discussion of the play itself to a footnote, it is 'denounced' on three separate occasions (10, 28, 176). When *Papal Tyranny* is discussed, its supposed failure is used to support the comforting and familiar narrative of the rise of bardolatry and the decline of adaptation.[3] *Papal Tyranny* is made to fail so that 'real' Shakespeare might live.

---

[1] The Master of the Revels 'expung'd the whole First Act without sparing a Line of it [... because] the Distresses of King *Henry the Sixth*, who is kill'd by *Richard* in the first Act, would put weak People too much in mind of King *James*, then living in *France* [...] tho' this first Act was at last recovered, and made the Play whole agen' (Cibber, *Apology* 152).

[2] Cibber's *Richard III* was not only a repertory staple throughout the eighteenth and nineteenth centuries, but also went through thirty-three editions in the eighteenth century alone, according to the *English Short Title Catalogue* (*ESTC*). John Kemble's version, which follows Cibber's nearly word-for-word, enjoyed a further three editions in the early nineteenth century. Many of Cibber's alterations remained in acting texts well into the twentieth century, the most notable perhaps being Lawrence Olivier's film version of 1955.

[3] So, for instance, Jean Marsden glosses over the play with the inaccurate claim that 'the mid-eighteenth century marked the end of sweeping alteration, and from 1737 until the end of the century the only playwright who attempted to create a radically new adaptation was Colley Cibber, with the ill-fated *Papal Tyranny*' (86).

But the rise of an authentic Shakespeare against the tide of adaptations is a problematic narrative, and the fate of *Papal Tyranny* does not offer the clear-cut evidence needed to support an argument for bardolatry. Cibber's last adaptation was not the spectacular failure so often reported, and the problems it did have had less to do with adaptation than with personal and partisan conflicts, for both the play and its author suggested uncomfortable and unpopular analogies to the very ideologies they opposed. Cibber, despite being a fervent supporter of the revolution principles and the official poet of the Whig ministry, was easily and often cast as an absolutist in the Stuart mode, while *Papal Tyranny*'s complicated plot could be read as a critique rather than a celebration of the Glorious Revolution that ousted James II and of the Hanoverian Succession that excluded the Stuarts from the British crown. Cibber, like Shakespeare, used English history to articulate the present; like Shakespeare as well, the resulting play was bigger than the immediate parallel. Audiences used to drawing patriotic lessons from history plays were left somewhat befuddled by *Papal Tyranny*, a state of mind shared by most modern readers.

First, while Cibber's last adaptation did not enjoy the longevity of his first effort, it cannot be classed as a failure, deserved or otherwise. It enjoyed an impressive run of twelve nights and saw three print editions in 1745 alone.[4] By comparison, David Garrick's rival production of the 'authentic' *King John* lasted only nine nights.[5] Far from demonstrating audience exhaustion with radical adaptation, this success suggests that mid-eighteenth-century audiences still preferred adaptations to the so-called authentic, a supposition borne out by the mid-century's raft of new adaptations and the continued popularity of earlier ones.[6] In other words, claims that *Papal Tyranny* marked the end of Shakespearean adaptation are simply wrong. As George Branam noted, 'The production of alterations throughout the rest of the century [after 1745] was steady and the volume was considerably greater than in the earlier period' (10). Nor was this preference limited to common tastes: Shakespeare's

---

[4] Avery, *London Stage* and *ESTC*. New plays were considered successful if they ran for more than three successive nights.

[5] With author's benefits (which could earn the author as much as £200) coming every three nights, the difference between nine and twelve is significant. Garrick's version of the play is also an adaptation, albeit less radical than Cibber's. Garrick cut nearly 900 lines, mostly from the first and fifth acts (Pedicord 445).

[6] New adaptations were not limited by type or genre. They included main pieces, ballad operas, and afterpieces. A sample includes *The Comedy of Errors*, re-titled *See If You Like It* (anon., 1734); *Marina*, an adaptation of *Pericles* (Lillo, 1738); *As You Like It* (Carrington, 1739); *Romeo and Juliet* (T. Cibber, 1744; Garrick, 1748); *Pyramus and Thisbe: a mock opera* (Lampe, 1745); *Cymbeline* (Hawkins, 1759; Garrick, 1761); and several versions and elements of *The Winter's Tale* (Morgan, 1754; Garrick, 1756; Colman, 1777).

biggest cheerleaders were themselves guilty of either adapting his plays or preferring adaptations to the Bard they sought to memorialise. Garrick, for all his praise, adapted nine plays, including a radical rewrite of *Hamlet* in 1772.[7] Samuel Johnson felt that the catastrophe in Nahum Tate's altered *King Lear* was preferable to Shakespeare's. And while he was happy to profess Shakespeare's genius, he also considered the Bard's affection for word play not just an aesthetic blot but evidence of moral failing. In Johnson's view, 'A quibble, poor and barren as it is, gave him such delight that he was content to purchase it, by the sacrifice of reason, propriety, and truth. A Quibble was to him the fatal Cleopatra for which he lost the world, and was content to lose it' (74). Shakespeare's 'beauties' were legion and his genius unquestioned, but when it came to details, even his greatest admirers admitted that there was room for improvement in plot, language, and moral application.

If *Papal Tyranny* was not a failure, and Shakespeare was considered to require improvement, then why is Cibber's play remembered and recorded as both failure and sacrilege? This chapter will investigate both why the story of *Papal Tyranny*'s failure has been so much exaggerated and how it interrogates modern and eighteenth-century assumptions about authentic Shakespeare. I suggest that Cibber's appropriation of Shakespeare and King John challenged assumptions about both English history and literature by splitting the entwined narratives of Whig history and bardolatry.[8]

Papal Tyranny's prolonged birth pangs make it unique among mid-century adaptations. Unlike the 1744 *Romeo and Juliet* adapted by Cibber's son Theophilus (and readapted by Garrick in 1748), *Papal Tyranny* was initially formed to please audiences of the 1720s, not the 1740s. Cibber first turned to *King John* as a theatrical response to the partisan and Jacobite upheavals of 1722, just as he had successfully adapted Molière's *Tartuffe*

---

[7] *Macbeth* (1744); *Romeo and Juliet* (1748); *The Taming of the Shrew* (1754); *A Midsummer's Night Dream* (1755); *The Winter's Tale* (1756); *King Lear* (1756); *The Tempest* (1756); *Cymbeline* (Hawkins, 1759; Garrick, 1761); *Hamlet* (1772). Garrick also offered a version of *Antony and Cleopatra* in 1758, but, as it is unclear whether he was adapting Shakespeare or Dryden, it is not included in the canon. Likewise, his adaptation of *King John* is considered 'so slight' that it is also excluded (Pedicord 443). He also composed a Shakespearean harlequinade and the spectacular that was the Shakespeare Jubilee.

[8] Whig history offered a teleological reading of English history progressing to the present and confirming Whig ideology in the process. History plays, especially Shakespeare's, were used to legitimate and naturalise Whig history, teaching audiences how to understand the past and appreciate the present. The only problem was that the Whigs were themselves in disagreement about both past and present. The party split in the early 1720s between those who supported Robert Walpole, the first Prime Minister, and those who opposed him.

into his *Non-Juror* in the wake of the failed 1715 Jacobite Rebellion. But while *The Non-Juror* (1717) was a success with theatregoers and brought Cibber to the attention of up-and-coming Whig politicians like Robert Walpole, it also inspired enmity, particularly among Tory writers like the Scriblerians (Pope, Gay, Arbuthnot, and Swift) and the branch of the Whig party that would become the Opposition (most vociferously represented by Fielding). In his *Apology*, Cibber identifies the success of *The Non-Juror* as the beginning of his troubles and suggests that the out-of-favour and disaffected thought that attacking the messenger was safer than publicly owning themselves 'Enemies of the Government' by hissing a patriotic play: 'as it was then probable that I might write again, they knew it would not be long before they might with more Security give Loose to their Spleen, and make up Accounts with me. And to do them Justice, in every Play I afterwards produced, they paid me the Balance' (*Apology* 282–3). Cibber's lack of subtlety with *The Non-Juror* marked him for life, and those who were forced to hold their tongues in 1717 were eager to hiss his plays in performance and attack them in print, although his earlier pre-Walpole comedies remained popular. Savvy enough to see which way the wind was blowing (and secure in his Ministerial favour), Cibber shelved *Papal Tyranny*, choosing instead to complete and adapt a comedy by John Vanbrugh. The resulting play, *The Provok'd Husband* (1728), was one of Cibber's biggest successes, despite the concerted attacks of his political enemies. In this case, Cibber had the last laugh, for the play was 'acted twenty-eight Nights together' (*Apology* 284).[9] As Cibber himself acknowledged, the play owed its initial success to Vanbrugh's name and the popular Anne Oldfield's outstanding performance as Mrs Townley; indeed, in order to foster its success, Cibber kept himself to the periphery, assigning himself the minor role of the country bumpkin Wronghead, placing Vanbrugh's name above his on the title page, and singing both Vanbrugh's and Oldfield's praises in the prefatory materials. Acknowledging the strength of the clique aligned against him, Cibber attempted no full-length play other than *The Provok'd Husband* after *Papal Tyranny*.[10]

---

[9] The 'powerful Party' aligned against the play included Fielding and Nathanial Mist, the editor of the anti-Walpole weekly *Mist's Journal*. The paper for 13 January 1728 attacks Cibber's completion of Vanbrugh's *A Trip to London* as 'a most [...] barbarous [...] Murder [...] upon a posthumous Child of the late Sir John Vanbroog [*sic*]' and encourages audiences to hiss or stay away (qtd in Avery, *London Stage* Part 2, II: 954).

[10] In 1729, Cibber wrote *The Rival Queans*, a line-by-line burlesque of Lee's heroic drama *The Rival Queens*. That year also saw the production and publication of two ballad-opera afterpieces: *Love*

But Cibber was not prepared to give up without a fight. He returned to *Papal Tyranny* in 1736, but with no more success. The Templars, who had 'long since passed condemnation on the entire Cibber tribe', gave out notice (supposedly acting under Henry Fielding's orders) that they would hiss the play unheard (Genest 146). Fearing a riot, Cibber preferred his managerial role to his authorial and pulled the play, 'even though rehearsals had been completed and new scenes painted' (Scouten 1: clxx). Cibber waited nine years before making another attempt, and then only his staunch loyalty to the Hanoverian court and his sense that the Jacobite threat was best fought through the performance of Whig history could coax him out of retirement and back into the theatre. Cibber's Whig tub-thumping begins in the Prologue, where he calls attention to the Jacobite crisis by pretending to deny it:

> These dire disasters, this religious Rage,
> That shames our Annals, may become the Stage.
> [..]
> At least this Pleasure from the View may flow,
> That long! long distant were those Scenes of Woe!
> And as such Chains no more these Realms annoy,
> Applaud the Liberty you now enjoy. (ll. 45–6, 48–51)

And, as had been the case with *The Non-Juror*, 'happy was it for this Play, that the very Subject was its Protection' (*Apology* 282). Papal tyranny suddenly seemed real and threatening, and a play dramatising its ineffectualness and celebrating 'Liberty' was sure to be 'receiv'd with those honest cordial Applauses, which *English* Auditors I foresaw would be naturally warm'd to' (epistle dedicatory to *Papal Tyranny* v).

The blatant topicality may account for its initial success, for the Jacobite Rebellion of 1745 was a serious enough threat to the Hanoverian throne to unite the fractured Whig party under a common banner. Henry Fielding turned from sniping at the Ministry to broadside attacks on 'the Devil, the Pope, and the Pretender', the unholy trinity of foreign threats exposed in his dialogic pamphlet of the same name. A similar national accord existed in 1700 when Cibber premiered his *Richard III*: the disastrous reign of James II was still a living memory, ensuring that all England was at least outwardly supportive of the Revolution that ousted him. In the 1720s and 1730s, however, national politics were more fractured because less divided. The well-documented rise of Robert Walpole and the Whig ascendancy

---

in a Riddle and *Damon and Phillida*. Both of these productions were responses to Gay's *The Beggar's Opera* (1728).

meant Britain was effectually a single-party state, but this situation was no more stable than was London with only one official theatre. Just as rebellions and defections split the theatrical world, Walpole's reign split the Whig party into Ministerial and Opposition camps: Cibber, an advocate for theatrical monopoly, was firmly in the Ministerial camp.

Indeed, during the 1720s and 1730s, Cibber, that first minister of the stage, functioned as a handy analogue for Walpole, the first minister of the state (just as Dryden had been made to stand in for James II). Both Walpole and Cibber were routinely charged with abuses of patronage and exploiting their positions for the improvement of their families. But as Walpole's real power carried with it the threat of real repercussions, it was much safer to lambaste Cibber in his stead. John Dennis accused Cibber of preferring absolute power and arbitrary reign, and Fielding, along with other Opposition figures, routinely attacked 'the great man' as a tyrant, a usurper, and an absolute, arbitrary ruler.[11] As Cibber puts it, 'that celebrated Author Mr. *Mist* [...] scarce ever fail'd of passing some of his Party Compliments upon me: The State, and the Stage, were his frequent Parallels, and the Minister, and *Minheer Keiber* the Menager, were as constantly droll'd upon' (*Apology* 283). Both Cibber and Walpole are accused of having absolutist tendencies and of taking into their own hands power that should belong to their betters (to 'real poets' in Cibber's case, the King and Parliament in Walpole's) to the detriment and endangerment of both state and stage.

Calling Cibber's Whiggery into question, as Dennis does, seems unwarranted. His loyalty to the Hanoverian house and Walpole ministry may have had pragmatic elements, but it was too consistent, too thorough, to have been mere lip-service to a paymaster. He was writing plays with Whig tropes as early as 1700 (*Richard III, Xerxes*), and his 1713 *Cinna's Conspiracy* offers a Whig heroics to rival that of Addison's *Cato*, which replaced it in the Drury Lane repertory. His version of *King John* offers a complex articulation of several facets of Whig ideology, including the privileging of legal over hereditary succession, the preference for plain speech and common sense over baroque circumlocution, and the juxtaposition of British liberty with continental slavery. Perhaps what offended

---

[11] Dennis claims that Cibber's selfishness was so gross that it was impossible for him to be truly loyal to a 'good and gracious King'. Instead, 'He must be for Absolute Power in his Heart; and would do his Business best in an Arbitrary Reign. He must be qualify'd for consummate Villany and would be a rare Tool for a Tyrant' (Dennis 16). For instance, Fielding seduced Charlotte Charke to the Haymarket and convinced her to perform a parody of her father in the role of Lord Place, a satire on both Cibber and Walpole (Shevelow 16).

his Whig opponents so much was that Cibber, tainted with his own and Walpole's reputations, assumed the right to write Whig history, even before receiving the Laureateship in 1730. Furthermore, Cibber's grasp of and belief in Whig principles may have been sound, but his performance of them gave cause for concern.

His supposed similarity to Walpole was not the only factor that made Cibber unattractive to his opponents at both ends of the political spectrum. It is vital to stress that the critical denigration of Cibber's plays, especially the serious plays, is for the most part a continuation of the attacks made by Cibber's political enemies. But there is also the point that Cibber was writing to please the town, rather than Mount Parnassus. Cibber's plays are about stagecraft, not poetry: they play, rather than read. In this, he is not dissimilar to Shadwell, whose politics annoyed Dryden and whose humours-style comedies were written to be seen, as opposed to Dryden's witty comedies, which were designed to be read. That Cibber's theatrical nous improved plays for performance is clear – even his enemies granted him that. And while Cibber's serious plays other than *Richard III* may not be remembered today, he was not an incompetent tragedian, either as poet or performer. But his tragedy was not to everyone's taste. In tragedy, as in his comedies, Cibber played to his strengths. His were not the lofty sentiments or grand manner that could inspire awe: pity was more in his line. Cibber knew how to move an audience, and the power of his performances, perhaps coupled with a perceived weakness of the play in print, made Cibber's articulation of Whiggery dangerous on multiple fronts and obnoxious to both Tories/Jacobites and Opposition Whigs. Cibber's version of Whig history may have played well, but ideologically it was problematic at best. Instead of composing a new heroic, Cibber tried to discredit Tory/Jacobite tropes through feminisation, domestication, and burlesque. Instead of creating a positive alternative to the huffing heroes of the Stuart stage, he highlighted the pathetic victims of their tyranny; thus, his *Richard III* was a rousing success because his Richard III is clearly a villain and his victims, from Anne and Elizabeth to the princes in the Tower – who were initially murdered on stage – inspire sympathy.

Without a positive alternative to the Stuart articulation of heroism, the strutting warrior and lover of heroic drama remained an admirable character, and the frequent parodies ironically kept him in view, a complaint Samuel Richardson made in *Clarissa*.[12] Without a serious rival, this

---

[12] See Elaine McGirr, 'Why Lovelace Must Die', *Novel* 37.1/2 (2004): 1–22.

performance of Stuart absolutism continued to reign on stage and in the popular imagination. Furthermore, Cibber himself, washed-out, bandy-legged, and weedy-voiced, was hardly the ideal embodiment of a new model of heroism. And if his physique were not bad enough, his further association with his signature roles Foppington and Richard III made him an even less desirable author of Whig cultural identity. Foppington, after all, was a half-ironic imitation of Restoration rakery/foppery who combined *arriviste* arrogance with performative failure, and Cibber's Richard III was the century's tyrant *par excellence*, the very embodiment of twisted and dangerous ambition. While both roles did offer critiques of the Restoration rake-hero and absolutist king, both were also dangerously close to the negative characterisations of Walpole and Cibber himself. Even more threateningly, the reliance on Restoration/Jacobite tropes ensured they played on as trace or ghost elements in the Hanoverian age. Instead of erasing or rewriting the past, Cibber's feminised and debased variations reminded audiences of the original's attractions.

Papal Tyranny brings all of these problems together: its historical lessons cannot so easily be reduced to moral certainties as *Richard III*'s can, and Cibber's strengths in pathos and ridicule seem to cut against the heroic reading of John he wants to promote. Tarred with Cibber's reputation long before audiences had a chance to evaluate it for themselves, it arguably only received a hearing in 1745 because personal and partisan opposition to Cibber had declined with his retirement and Walpole's fall. While sincere and consistent in its Whig principles, it is, like all of Cibber's plays, also spectacular, pathetic, and feminised: tactics that worked well in his earlier efforts which all focused on villains and victims, but are far more complex in a play with a putative male hero. Cibber's title change suggests his strategy of shifting attention away from the positive actions of King John to the dastardly actions of Catholic France and Rome, but effacing John from his own history raises more problems than it resolves.

Cibber did not publish any early versions of his final adaptation and does not discuss it in his *Apology*, making it impossible to determine exactly what changes he made when and how radically he altered his alteration between 1723 and 1745. In an open letter of 1736, Cibber claims to have completed the adaptation 'above Ten Years since', suggesting the play did not undergo substantial revisions (Avery, 'Cibber' 273–4). The emphasis on the twinned threats of France and Rome was certainly not inserted as anti-Jacobite propaganda in 1745, for it was advertised under the title *Papal Tyranny in the Reign of King John* in 1736. Furthermore, the speed with which the play was readied for performance suggests that

Cibber did not tinker with it much to prepare it for 1745. Internal evidence further supports a hypothesis that *Papal Tyranny* was more or less complete in the 1720s and merely dusted off for its long-delayed premiere.

Cibber's adaptation of *King John* contains what Jean Marsden has identified as the main features of all radical adaptations: pathetic women, politics, and unambiguous language (16–46). As was common in early eighteenth-century adaptations, many of his alterations were designed to improve or create female roles. Thus, while John himself is the titular hero, Cibber chose to concentrate on John's rivals Constance and Arthur, whom he rewrites as a breeches role, a part perhaps intended for his daughter Charlotte, but eventually played by his granddaughter Jenny. Both Arthur and Constance are pathetic, sentimental characters in the style of early eighteenth-century she-tragedies. Their tearful suffering is intended to melt audiences and balance the 'fiery' actions of the male characters. This neo-classical balance might have been good stagecraft, but it created several problems for audiences trying to interpret Cibber's historical lesson. The expanded stage time and affective power given to John's rival claimants seriously undercut his claims to legitimate authority and created several problems for audiences attempting to read topically. On the one hand, John is clearly meant to be read as a stand-in for George II, the defender of English liberties against the machinations of France, Rome, and the discredited Jacobites. But, at the same time, a Jacobite reading is also available, for John also appears to be the cruel usurper of lovely Arthur's birthright, a *de facto* ruler using his ill-gotten power to crush a rival with a better claim to the throne.

Difficulties of interpretation are conflated with critiques of Shakespearean adaptation: in a 1745 response to the play, Cibber is attacked for the style of his adaptation, for that style seems to pervert the historical Shakespeare's historical 'truth' – a Whig history of the Magna Carta. The anonymous author of *A Letter to Mr. Cibber* castigates Cibber not for adaptation per se, but for his old-fashioned tastes, tastes that lead to the valorisation of Constance and Arthur at the expense of King John. Cibber is presented not as a violator of authentic Shakespeare, but rather as a theatrical has-been who is stuck in the past and unaware of new trends. This stylistic failure makes Cibber a faulty historian and a bad Whig. Dramaturgy and historical lesson go hand-in-hand, for Cibber's aesthetic choices seem to cut against his dramatic intent. 'Instead therefore of *torturing Shakespear* into *Rule* and Dramatick Law,' the anonymous critic begs, 'let his *Clinches, False Wit,* &c. be the Objects of Amendment' (*Letter* 11). Neo-classicism, here presented as 'reducing' Shakespeare to rule, and deriving as much from French as classical sources, was the method of an earlier generation of adaptors (*Letter* 9). By mid-century, tastes were already beginning to shift in favour of Romantic rough-ness and native barbarisms: 'corrections' like Cibber's are therefore both unfashionable and un-English. Shakespeare's rough vernacular was pref-erable to Cibber's Frenchified *politesse*.

Cibber's aesthetic choices are thus not only old-fashioned, but also suspiciously French, aligning him with the Catholic enemy he played – Cibber took the role of the papal legate Pandulph – rather than the English hero he had written. But it is Cibber's transformation of Constance from a fiery queen to a politely sentimental tragedienne that the *Letter* holds up as the epitome of his mistaken line of correction. Far from improving Shakespeare, the author claims, the domestication of Constance dimin-ishes both character and play, for '*Constance* is a Character design'd to be *outragious* and *violent* in *Grief*, not *soft and pathetick*'; hers is a character 'above the *wet Eye* or *broken Voice*', the common tropes of she-tragedy (18, 20). Cibber's mid-century critic devotes nearly a third of the entire *Letter* to a side-by-side *examen* of Cibber's changes to Constance's char-acter and speeches, concluding 'It is plain then from these Quotations, that *Constance* is a Character of *Fire* throughout! *Great* and *Impetuous* in ev'ry Thing! [...] What Reason, Dear *Colley*, to alter this Character?' (25). Cibber has reduced a noble queen into a 'whimp'rer' who is 'so *witty* in her *Sorrow*, so *polite* in her *Reproaches*' that the critic finds himself ques-tioning her humanity: he feels that a woman attending her son's funeral should not be capable of 'talking [...] a thousand Tropes and Figures cull'd from the richest Images of the most luxuriant Fancy' (28, 33). Not only is Cibber's Constance out of style, she seems unnatural and her pas-sions inconsistent. In fact, the author of *A Letter* identifies a general lack of consistency – or an interpretive ambiguity – running throughout the play. He reminds Cibber that Shakespeare's lack of 'fire' was his supposed provocation in taking on *King John*,[13] yet he has devoted much of his energy to creating she-tragedy and pathetic tableaux like Arthur's funeral procession. In *Papal Tyranny*, pathetic tears are juxtaposed with incen-diary rhetoric and, for Cibber's critic at least, the tears quench the fire.

---

[13] 'In all the historical Plays of *Shakespear* there is scarce any Fact, that might better have employed his Genius, than the flaming Contest between his insolent *Holiness* and *King John*. This is so remarkable a Passage in our Histories, that it seems surprising our *Shakespear* should have taken no more fire at it [...] It was this Coldness then [...] that first incited me to inspirit his King *John* with a Resentment that justly might become an *English* Monarch, and to paint the intoxicated Tyranny of *Rome* in its Proper Colours' (Cibber, epistle dedicatory to *Papal Tyranny* ii).

Ultimately, this is a larger problem than violating the unities: it creates a problem of interpretation.

The interpretive difficulties facing readers and audiences are exacerbated by Cibber's refusal to acknowledge any such ambiguity. Cibber claims in his epistle dedicatory to be restoring Shakespeare's history of *King John* to its rightful place: the pantheon of Whig heroes and histories already occupied by the *Henriad*. Cibber's new title points to his revision of history: instead of the dynastic crisis dramatised in Shakespeare's play, Cibber's play is less about the troublesome reign of King John and more about England's ongoing resistance to papal tyranny – a parable for the Jacobite Rebellion and a celebration of Whig principles. Cibber's main plot shifts dramatic interest away from King John's submission to the barons in favour of his refusal to submit to the Pope, making John a prototypical Georgian (Protestant) hero. In this reading, signing the Magna Carta becomes further evidence of his Whiggish desire to enthrone English liberties, and his assumption of the throne a legitimate succession and protection of England from the machinations of her real enemies, France and Rome.

Cibber works hard to make John the hero in Act 1, where he draws a parallel between John's accession and the Act of Succession and argues that legal succession is more important than mere hereditary claims, a clear dig at Jacobite pretensions. John, not Arthur, is the 'successor approv'd' who was 'adopted' and 'by the general States confirm'd'.[14] John, like George or William, is King by 'a Nation's Act', not mere accident of birth. Shakespeare offers a much weaker presentation of John's claim, merely posing the vexed question 'Doth not the crown of England prove the King?' (2.1.273). For Jacobites, the answer to that was a resounding 'no'. Cibber is careful to present John as not just the *de facto* but also the *de jure* ruler. Arthur has no legitimate claim on the throne: a Young Pretender figure, he is being used by France and Rome to promote their own interests.

However, Cibber's stagecraft complicates this neat political parallel. Not only is John's heroic identification unstable, but, unlike most stage

---

[14] PHILIP: What Crime alleg'd has set aside young *Arthur*?
              Can Treason, Lunacy of tainted Blood,
              Be once pretended in this Youth's Disfavour?
        JOHN: Prevaricating Claim, is Courdelion's Will,
              That gave his Crown to us, of no Validity?
              Are we not there his Successor approv'd?
              Adopted? by the general States confirm'd?
              And is a Nation's Act responsible to thee? (1.1.170–7)

pretenders, Arthur is not a clear figure of ridicule. Having Arthur played by a girl transforms the Young Pretender from a dangerous would-be-usurper into an idol whose passive suffering inspires heartfelt tears, not derisive laughter. Even within the play, Arthur is made admirable, if ill-advised. S/he may not have a legitimate claim on the throne, but s/he is a heroically tragic figure who more resembles the attractive princes in the Tower than the risible Perkin Warbeck. By giving the part to the attractive, young, and popular Jenny, Cibber ensures that Arthur is played as an innocent, not a Pretender. Hubert cannot bring himself to kill him/her, and the barons take up Arthur as their rallying cry. Moreover, Arthur's tragic death and funeral are presented as pathetic tableaux – hardly the treatment appropriate for a stand-in for Charles Edward Stuart.

Nor, despite all of Cibber's careful stage-setting in the first act, is King John the stable hero of the piece. He may be the legitimate monarch, but he shares too many traits with the evil Richard III, such as boundless ambition and nephew-displacing, to be simply the defender of England against France and Rome. In John, Cibber was faced with a king at religious variance with his subjects and accused of tyranny by his barons, for which everyone would have read Parliament. In this reading, John looks suspiciously like a Stuart absolutist or another unattractive portrait of the 'absolute' and now disgraced Walpole, instead of the fiery defender of the (Protestant) faith and protector of English liberties. Indeed, by Act 4, King John looks so much like a Stuart absolutist attempting to impose his will on the barons/Parliament that he, not Arthur, seems to be the Pretender figure. The Dauphin crows:

> King John, but from what Cause alarm'd, they say not
> Struck all his Tents for Sudden secret March:
> Northward he still sets on, and flies 'fore us;
> Yet we at last shall force him to a Stand,
> Though to the hindermost Orcades we hunt him! (4.1.47–51)

King John, like Charles Edward Stuart, is presented as fleeing north and skulking about the highlands; no longer the rightful king appointed, John is a king without subjects, a tyrant, and a rebel. However, Whig heroics return in Act 5, when, after having been treacherously poisoned, King John uses the very last of his strength to sign the Magna Carta and enshrine 'traditional English liberties' – that familiar Whig slogan – into law. John slides uneasily from hero to potential usurper and back to hero again; his reign is both tragic and triumphant. The troublesome reign of King John might have been a remarkable passage in our histories, but it is also too complex to be easily flattened out into dramatic history, Whig or otherwise. A play with no clear hero, and in which everyone is a bit of a Bastard, cannot claim unity either of fable or of character. It has no rousing nationalist message and is ultimately too ambiguous to function as successful propaganda. After the immediacy of the Jacobite threat faded, *Papal Tyranny* could not function as positive Whig history, unlike Cibber's *Richard III*, whose clear villains and victors continued to rouse patriotic – Whig – enthusiasm.

The anonymous critic's attack on Cibber's 'reduction' of Shakespeare begs the question of authenticity. By offering side-by-side comparisons of Cibber's and Shakespeare's poetry, the author of *A Letter* seems to suggest that revision and adaptation are no longer acceptable, a claim that modern critics have been only too happy to endorse. Yet adaptation is not here the issue, for while Cibber's choices are systematically denounced, the author is quick to admit that '[o]ther instances might be produced to shew, where *Shakespear* might admit, with great Beauty and Propriety, of strong Alterations, nay Amendments' (12). The author of *A Letter* does, however, make several tacit assumptions about Shakespeare, assumptions that were new in the eighteenth century but have become so ingrained in modern times as to become invisible. For him, Shakespeare is a poet, not a playwright, and he therefore limits his critique to textual comparison. The tongue-in-cheek *Letter* opens 'I should not have delay'd so long making you my Acknowledgments for the great Pleasure I have receiv'd from your *Transformation of King* JOHN, but that I was willing to see the Copy, that I might at the same Time point out the particular Passages that have afforded me [...] so much Wonder and Delight' (5–6). The anonymous author goes on to feign confusion about Cibber's choices, particularly with regard to Arthur. Arthur's speech, 'The mote beneath I've fathom'd with a line, / And find its depth proportion'd to my stature' (5.1.6–7), is met with mock-incredulity 'But as you have not ascertain'd the *Depth*, otherwise than by his *Stature*, and have left us in the Dark, as to either, we can draw no positive Inference' (40). Audiences, who the opening of *A Letter* informs us included its author, would have had no difficulty judging either the depth of the imagined moat or the stature of the personated prince: not only did Jenny Cibber's physical presence supply the necessary information, the lines demand audiences view her closely and appreciate her 'stature', or at least her legs. Cibber's text is part of a performative display. Publication of the text was withheld until *Papal Tyranny* made it to the stage: it was designed to reinforce and remind readers of performance, not to be read as a 'heap of poetry' (*Apology* 318). The author of *A Letter* maliciously reduces Cibber's tragedy to the words on the page in order to render it absurd. He denies theatricality altogether in an attempt to prove that the then-Poet Laureate was no poet.

This is the line most frequently taken up by modern critics. Reading *Papal Tyranny* with its complex, shifting parallel and its unapologetic preference for theatricality over poetry, it is easy to denounce it as 'wretched'. *Papal Tyranny* is further injured in literary history because it is Colley Cibber's, and Cibber, like King John, sits awkwardly in the pantheon of heroes, both literary and Whig. Despite his many successes, innovations, and talent, Cibber has been mercilessly reduced to the figure he cuts in the biting – and partisan – satires of Pope and Fielding. He is cast as an anti-heroic figure, personally ridiculous and politically suspect. The King of Dunces is not a figure to be taken seriously, we are assured, so his plays can be safely ignored and forgotten. As several recent studies of the rise of Shakespeare attest, bardolatry was not just a nationalist but a Whig enterprise.[15] Shakespeare is the representative of 'real' English identity, politics, and poetry. Through the efforts of his apologists, especially Garrick, he is made into a Georgian hero. There is simply no room for Cibberian softness, for self-parody or pathetic tableaux in the new Shakespeare story.

WORKS CITED

Anon. *A Letter to Colley Cibber, Esq; On His Transformation of King John.* London, 1745. *Eighteenth-Century Collections Online* (ECCO). British Library. http://galenet.galegroup.com, accessed 4 May 2008.

Avery, Emmet L. 'Cibber, *King John*, and the Students of the Law'. *Modern Language Notes* 53.4 (1938): 272–5.

Avery, Emmet L., ed. and intro. *The London Stage 1660–1800: a Calendar of Plays, Entertainments, & Afterpieces, Together with Casts, Box-Receipts, and Contemporary Comment, Part 2: 1700–1729.* 2 vols. Carbondale: Southern Illinois University Press, 1961.

Babcock, R. W. 'The Attack of the Late Eighteenth-Century on Alterations of Shakespeare's Plays'. *Modern Language Notes* 45.7 (1930): 446–51.

Branam, George. *Eighteenth-Century Adaptations of Shakespearean Tragedy.* Berkeley and Los Angeles: University of California Press, 1956.

Cibber, Colley. *Apology for the Life of Colley Cibber, Esquire.* 1740. Ed. and intro. B. R. S. Fone. Ann Arbor: University of Michigan Press, 1968.

Papal Tyranny in the Reign of King John. London, 1745.

---

[15] Dobson offers the best and most sustained analysis of this meta-narrative, but see also Marsden; Babcock; Robert Hume, 'Before the Bard: "Shakespeare" in Early Eighteenth-Century London'. *ELH* 64.1 (1997): 41–75; and Grace Ioppolo, '"Old" and "New" Revisionists: Shakespeare's Eighteenth-Century Editors'. *Huntington Library Quarterly* 52.3 (1989): 347–61.

Dennis, John. *The Characters and Conduct of Sir John Edgar, and His Three Deputy-Governours. During the Administration of the Late Separate Ministry.* London, 1720. *Eighteenth-Century Collections Online* (ECCO). British Library. http://galenet.galegroup.com, accessed 4 May 2008.

Dobson, Michael. *The Making of the National Poet: Shakespeare, Adaptation, and Authorship, 1660–1769.* 1992. Rpt. Oxford: Clarendon Paperbacks, 2001.

Fielding, Henry. *A Dialogue Between the Devil, the Pope, and the Pretender.* London, 1745.

Genest, John. *History of the Drama and Stage in England from 1660 to 1830.* Vol. IV. Bath, 1832.

Johnson, Samuel, ed. *The Plays of William Shakespeare.* 8 vols. London, 1765.

Kemble, John. *Shakespeare's King John; Revised by J.P. Kemble; and now published as it is performed at the Theatres Royal.* London, 1814.

Marsden, Jean. *The Re-Imagined Text: Shakespeare, Adaptation, and Eighteenth-Century Literary Theory.* Lexington: University of Kentucky Press, 1995.

Pedicord, Harry William. 'Garrick Produces "King John"'. *Theatre Journal* 34.4 (1984): 441–9.

Salmon, Eric. 'Cibber, Colley (1671–1757)'. *Oxford Dictionary of National Biography.* Oxford University Press, Sept. 2004; online edn Jan. 2008. www.oxforddnb.com/view/article/5416, accessed 4 May 2008.

Scouten, Arthur H., ed. and intro. *The London Stage, 1660–1800: a Calendar of Plays, Entertainments, & Afterpieces, Together with Casts, Box-Receipts, and Contemporary Comment, Part 3: 1729–1747.* 2 vols. Carbondale: Southern Illinois University Press, 1961.

Shakespeare, William. *The Life and Death of King John. The Oxford Shakespeare: The Complete Works.* Ed. Stanley Wells and Gary Taylor. Oxford: Clarendon Press, 1988. 397–424.

Shevelow, Kathryn. *Charlotte.* New York: Henry Holt, 2005.

Waith, Eugene. 'King John and the Drama of History'. *Shakespeare Quarterly* 29.2 (1979): 192–211.

CHAPTER 3

Coriolanus *and the (in)authenticities of William Poel's platform stage*

Lucy Munro

On 12 May 1931 *Coriolanus* was performed at the Chelsea Palace Theatre. In the following day's papers, reviewers commented on the radical revisions to the text, which was, according to *The Times*, 'almost completely altered' ('Chelsea Palace' 14). In addition, the costumes mixed different periods, encompassing a lionskin, Roman armour, Napoleonic military costume, and pre-Raphaelite dress. Radical treatment of the text was a familiar feature of nineteenth-century Shakespearean performance, and eclectic costuming was to become a fixture of the later twentieth-century stage, but neither has been generally associated with William Poel, the director of this production.

Poel's production of *Coriolanus* has often been viewed as eccentric, which was a common assessment of his methods, and as inauthentic, which was not. Robert Speaight, who played Coriolanus, saw it as a perverse example of Poel's 'wilfulness' (*William Poel* 255), while John Ripley, in his stage history of *Coriolanus*, accuses Poel of dereliction of duty: 'Having managed after a half a century to convince his theatrical colleagues that Shakespeare's texts deserved respect, he now proceeded to flout his most cherished principles, all the while using supposititious scholarship to justify pure whimsey' (261). Scholars have often examined Poel's *Coriolanus* in isolation or have compared it with his 1890s productions, and have judged it as failing to match up to Poel's own standards of authenticity. Others have overlooked changes in Poel's theories and methods. For instance, in his otherwise excellent account of Poel's career and influence in *The Shakespeare Revolution*, J. L. Styan quotes approvingly from the theatre critic Ivor Brown's assessment of Poel's impact (47–63), but in applying it to the whole of Poel's career he elides the fact that Brown was writing on the subject of Poel's activities in the late 1920s, which were – as *Coriolanus* suggests – rather different from their predecessors.

As Rinda F. Lundstrom valuably demonstrates in her account of Poel's various productions of *Hamlet*, Poel's ideas and practices did not remain static, and it is problematic to measure a production of 1931 against theories advanced half a century earlier.[1] In addition, scholars have rarely examined Poel's Shakespearean productions in the context of his frequent stagings of non-Shakespearean plays – an approach that provides an alternative perspective both on Poel's Shakespearean productions and on his notions of authenticity.[2] My intention in this chapter is therefore to examine Poel's *Coriolanus* in the light of his other post-Edwardian projects and, in particular, a series of 'platform-stage' productions staged between 1927 and 1931, of which *Coriolanus* was the last. The ways in which Poel reshaped *Coriolanus* were influenced, I suggest, by a number of factors that become clear only when we see the play in context. The foremost of these include Poel's theories about the authorship and dramatic construction of non-Shakespearean early modern drama; his desire to dehistoricise and universalise *Coriolanus* and the other plays he produced in this period in order to present a critique of militarism; and his increasing interest in stage space rather than stage furniture and in actors' movements on the stage.

In 1927 Poel re-founded his producing society, the Elizabethan Stage Society, quickly renaming it the Elizabethan Stage Circle. In a letter of 10 December 1926 he told R. N. Green-Armytage that he was reviving the society 'chiefly that it may be a help as propaganda to carry on the agitation for the building of an E[lizabethan]. P[layhouse]' (Anderson 21), but its activities quickly centred on promoting the use of a platform stage for the production of plays by Shakespeare and his contemporaries. On 14 May 1927 Poel wrote to the theatre historian W. J. Lawrence, 'The Platform performance simply means *this*, that I want to show that there was possible movement in the Elizabethan stage not possible on the proscenium stage! [...] For a Shakespearian representation, I am myself content with a balcony, a recess, two doors and the forward platform which must be the same size as that in use in the Fortune theatre!' (Speaight, *William Poel* 85). These statements form an instructive contrast with Poel's *raison d'être* for the Elizabethan Stage Society, which he variously formulated as 'to give practical effect to the principle that Shakspere should be accorded *the build of stage* for which he designed his plays' and 'to illustrate and advance the principle that Shakspere's plays should be accorded *the conditions of playing* for which they were designed'.[3] The projects pursued

---

[1] See especially 8–9, 161–2.
[2] An honourable exception is O'Connor's excellent *William Poel and the Elizabethan Stage Society*, which considers visual evidence for a wide range of Poel's productions.
[3] Programme notes for *Twelfth Night* (Burlington Hall, 21–2 June 1895) and *The Comedy of Errors* (Gray's Inn Hall, 6, 7, and 9 December 1895), Theatre Collection, Victoria and Albert Museum. Quoted in O'Connor, 'Useful' 17–18.

by the Elizabethan Stage Circle aimed to investigate the 'build of stage' for which Shakespeare's plays were designed, but replicating early modern 'conditions of playing' had become less of a priority for Poel.

For one-off performances of Samuel Rowley's *When You See Me You Know Me*, Ben Jonson's *Sejanus his Fall*, John Fletcher's *Bonduca* (re-titled *Britain*), and *Coriolanus,* staged between 1927 and 1932, Poel constructed extended platform stages which seem, at last, to have reached the size of an Elizabethan amphitheatre stage.[4] However, his intention in these late productions seems not to have been to explore in full 'the conditions of playing for which [the plays] were designed' but to explore specific staging and movement not possible on a proscenium stage. In a prospectus for the production of *When You See Me You Know Me*, Poel speculated that the experiment would 'give us some idea as to the way the players of the day moved about on their large stage', and in the programme he wrote, 'It is hoped that this production will shew to some extent, that a performance on a platform stage is different in its effect to one given either upon an apron stage or behind a proscenium' (*When You See Me* Prospectus and Programme). As O'Connor comments, 'As he laid ever greater emphasis upon the importance of a forward platform as the stage for which Shakespeare wrote his plays, Poel's preoccupation with stage pictures became a preoccupation with stage space' ('Useful' 18).

Poel's earliest platform stage may have been that of his 1909 *Macbeth*, performed at Fulham Theatre, which was described as playing 'on a platform stage' in advertising material, but the details are unclear (O'Connor, *William Poel* 90). Far more is known about his next production, a one-off performance of *The Two Gentlemen of Verona* at His Majesty's Theatre as part of Herbert Beerbohm Tree's 1910 Shakespeare Festival. A tiring-house façade, with a balcony, was set up at the back of the proscenium stage, and a platform extension was constructed which reached about 18–20 feet from the proscenium, covering around a third of the stalls. The proscenium stage thus became an inner stage, with a large platform

---

[4] There is some uncertainty about the exact number of platform-stage productions that Poel mounted in this period. In his programmes, Poel describes *Bonduca* as the third platform-stage production and *Coriolanus* as the fifth, but no production is labelled as the fourth. Poel's programme describes the production of *Byron* mounted at the Royalty Theatre on 15 July 1929 as being performed on a 'Tableau platform'; there is nothing in the publicity materials or reviews of *Julius Caesar the Dictator*, performed at the Globe Theatre on 20 July 1930, to indicate the kind of stage used. Allan Gomme in his account of Poel's career described *When You See Me You Know Me* as the first of three platform-stage productions, then crossed out 'three' and interlined 'five' (1066). Poel's widow, Ella C. Pole, wrote that her husband had mounted seven platform-stage productions (Gomme v), but she seems to have included all of his productions of the late 1920s and early 1930s in this count. For Poel's earlier experiments with platform staging, see below.

area extending in front of it, and three levels (platform, inner stage, and balcony) could be employed (see O'Connor, 'Useful' 24). For *Troilus and Cressida*, performed at the King's Hall, Covent Garden, on 10, 15, and 18 December 1912, the set-up appears to have been similar, featuring a two-tier inner stage and a lower level that extended into the auditorium; on one side of the lower stage was a tent, and on the other were curtains representing the entrance to a house (see O'Connor, *William Poel* 99–101).[5]

Poel's platform-stage productions of the late 1920s and early 1930s followed this basic pattern, but an even bigger platform stage was constructed and, at last, the sizes of the theatres used permitted members of the audience to surround the platform on three sides (see O'Connor, *William Poel* 100; Somerset). For *When You See Me You Know Me*, performed on 10 July 1927 at the Holborn Empire, a music-hall, the platform was forty-three feet wide and projected twenty-seven feet over the stalls seats (see Poel, *When You See Me* Prospectus and Programme). Ivor Brown in the *Manchester Guardian* commented that '[a] spectator in the dress circle who had been moved to leap for joy (or the reverse) could have descended without difficulty into the arms of King Henry VIII' ('Mr. Poel' 11). A *Times* review of *Sejanus*, performed in the same venue on 12 February 1928, indicates that a similar set-up was used, Poel having 'constructed for the occasion a large but quite simple platform stage over the auditorium level, beginning at the proscenium edge, and ending at a line ordinarily marked by the fifth or sixth row of stalls in the theatre'; the same reviewer commented on the dark curtains that formed a background, the 'arched entrances within the simple architectural sides of the stage', and 'several short flights of steps to lend a manner of actuality to the platform level' ('Elizabethan Stage Circle [hereafter ESC]: "Sejanus"' 18). Less is known about the precise details of the platform stages constructed for *Coriolanus* and for *Bonduca*, performed at the King's Hall, Covent Garden, on 3 January 1928, but evidence from reviews and the prompt-books suggests that the configurations were similar. *The Times*'s theatre critic comments of *Bonduca*, for instance, that 'Mr. Poel, blessed with plenty of space at the King's Hall, had constructed a large but quite simple platform stage, which gave the players three levels on which to act' ('ESC: "Britain"' 10).

Poel had previously used a portable stage-set, or fit-up, ostensibly designed to represent the Fortune playhouse but with many aspects of

---

[5] The tiers appear not to have been replicated when the production was revived at Stratford-upon-Avon in May 1913.

its design taken from the recently discovered 'De Witt' drawing of the Swan.[6] Although he often added an apron to the front of the proscenium stage, these productions have been characterised as presenting, in Cary M. Mazer's words, 'a verisimilar picture of the theatre in which the plays were originally performed', which demanded that audiences believe 'that they were witnessing an archaeological picture of a past age' (58). This effect is not altogether true of the platform-stage productions, in which the stage, thrusting into the audience, broke down the barriers between actors and spectators far more decisively than earlier Poelian configurations.

The impression of an 'archaeological picture of a past age' was also broken down in other ways, as Poel combined the most 'authentic' stage set-ups of his career with his least authentic production techniques. He made sweeping cuts to the texts, used iconoclastic casting patterns, and on occasion employed costumes in a radically inauthentic manner. Not all of these habits were new. For instance, Poel used an all-male cast for only one production, his 1900 staging of *Hamlet* at Carpenters' Hall (see Lundstrom 93–126; Shaughnessy 39–42), but he frequently used cross-dressing in a less historically supported fashion, casting women as young men in a number of productions. In the 1912 *Troilus and Cressida*, for instance, Thersites was played by Elspeth Keith, while Aeneas was played by Madge Whitman and Paris by May Carey, and in Poel's 1914 *Hamlet*, Rosencrantz was played by Carrie Haase and Guildenstern by Grace Laurence (O'Connor, *William Poel* 96–97; Shirley 11). Poel maintained that women were more suited to certain Shakespearean roles than men, writing in 1916 that

A boy with a sweet, musical voice will give a better rendering of Shakespeare's young heroines than can a girl, and realise the characters more accurately. But on the English stage girls are needed to act the boy lovers; for here young men fail lamentably [...] In the Englishman the necessary quality of voice is wanting to give physical expression to words of love. In real life his love-making is comic and hopelessly unromantic, because unemotional. (*Monthly Letters* 28–9)

With the exception of Paris, none of the roles mentioned above are those of lovers, but Poel may have felt that his general point held true:

It is mere ignorance, on the part of the critics, of the technicalities of the actor's art, which prejudices them from accepting women on the stage in parts which young Englishmen never succeed in making either interesting or convincing.

---

[6] For detailed discussion of the Fortune fit-up and its sources, see O'Connor, *William Poel* 26–31; 'Useful' 19–22.

The differences that arise from differences of figure and sex can to a great extent be overcome by the costumiers and wigmakers. (*Monthly Letters* 29)[7]

Poel used female performers in male roles in *When You See Me You Know Me*, *Coriolanus*, and, notably, *Bonduca*, of which *The Times*'s reviewer commented, 'Perhaps the Hengo, the frank and fearless boy on whom Fletcher spent a good deal of care, was a shade effeminate, but, then, Miss Molly Brown will doubtless plead that she is, after all, a girl' ('ESC: "Britain"' 10).

A frequent charge levelled against Poel is that he was a champion of the uncut text who nonetheless made often-radical cuts in his own perform-ance versions. In a much-quoted passage, he wrote,

To all stage managers who wish to mend or improve Shakespeare I say: 'Hands off! Produce this play as it is written or leave it alone. Don't take liberties with it; the man who does that does not understand his own limitations!' Let us uphold that there is but one rule to be followed when it becomes necessary to shorten one of the poet's plays; and that is to omit lines, but never an entire scene. (*Shakespeare* 180)

As Lundstrom notes, Poel's preoccupation was with textual integrity rather than textual purity; his concern was for producers to pay attention to what could be gleaned of an author's intentions for a text rather than that they should invariably perform a full-length version (7–8). He pro-tested in an unfinished letter drafted in 1931, 'I have consistently through-out my productions made alterations and reconstructions when plays are considered to be unactable or are not being acted, and when it seemed to me that the success of the performance needed some alteration in the play' (Gomme 1151). Many of his critiques of cutting were aimed against specific changes that he thought catered to the whims of over-powerful actor-managers: the excision of Fortinbras in *Hamlet*, for instance, which directly contradicted his own interpretation of *Hamlet* as primarily a play about revenge. Nonetheless, Poel's cuts were often almost as severe as those of commercial actor-managers, and they did, on occasion, extend to the cutting of entire scenes. In the 1912 *Troilus and Cressida*, for example, around a third of the lines were excised; scenes were fused, lines and some scenes were transposed (1.3, for instance, became the first scene after the prologue), and the short scene 4.3 was cut altogether (Shirley 11, 93, 184).

---

[7] O'Connor ('Useful' 28) points out that Poel was also making virtue of necessity, as he seems to have had greater difficulty in recruiting amateur actors than actresses; however, the majority of the actors used in his late 1920s and early 1930s productions were professionals.

Poel's practices in *Coriolanus* thus represent not a betrayal of his principles, but an expression of the ways in which his theories about the stage, and his production practices, had shifted and developed over the years. Nonetheless, his productions of the late 1920s and early 1930s also form a discrete group and therefore merit close comparison. In addition to *When You See Me You Know Me*, *Sejanus*, *Bonduca*, and *Coriolanus*, Poel also produced George Chapman's *The Conspiracy and Tragedy of Byron* (performed at the Royalty Theatre on 15 July 1929 and repeated as a recital on 15 October at the Little Theatre), *Julius Caesar the Dictator*, a custom-made companion play to Shakespeare's *Julius Caesar* (adapted by Poel from material taken from Chapman's *Caesar and Pompey*, Cicero's letters to Atticus, and *Julius Caesar* itself, and performed at the Globe Theatre (now the Gielgud Theatre) on 20 July 1930), and George Peele's *David and Bethsabe* (performed at Mary Ward Settlement, Tavistock Place, on 29 November 1932). All of these plays were rarely performed at this time, even *Coriolanus*, of which one reviewer commented that it followed Poel's 'custom of using a play better known in the study than in the theatre to illustrate his ideas of stage direction' (J.S. 9).[8]

Although *Sejanus* and *Coriolanus* were treated with rather more respect, reviewers of *When You See Me You Know Me* and *Bonduca* were generally uncomplimentary about the plays, seeing them as at best a neutral vehicle for Poel's theories about staging and at worst as a distraction from them. *The Times*'s reviewer of *When You See Me You Know Me* concluded with the hope that 'Mr. Poel's devoted scholarship gives us more and worthier material for judgement' ('ESC: "When You See Me"' 7), while Ivor Brown in his *Manchester Guardian* review of *Bonduca* stated, 'We did not assemble [...] to be stirred or bored by the flourishes and alarums of Fletcher, but to watch Mr. Poel's manoeuvres on a type of stage which the modern theatre denies to its producers' ('Mr. Poel's Platform Stage' 20).

There is nonetheless a logic to Poel's repertory at this time. He commented in the prospectus for *When You See Me You Know Me*, 'It is not intended to act a play of *Shakespeare's* on a replica of the Globe-playhouse platform, since the Shakespeare repertory is too much identified to-day with the proscenium, or picture stage, for playgoers to accept without prejudice the open platform.' Producing obscure and rarely performed plays thus allowed him to bypass the weight of performance history that

[8] Productions of *Coriolanus* in the 1920s included three by men who had previously worked with Poel: Robert Atkins (Old Vic, 1924), William Bridges-Adams (Stratford-upon-Avon, 1926) and Nugent Monck (Maddermarket Theatre, Norwich, 1928). See Ripley 243–58.

dogged his productions of plays such as *Hamlet* and *The Merchant of Venice*.

In addition, Poel identified thematic links between these texts. All are political plays, concerned with questions of rule and, in particular, conspiracy, a subject that preoccupied Poel. A list of 'conspiracy plays' that he compiled in the 1920s, printed in the programme for *Sejanus* and in his *Monthly Letters*, includes *Julius Caesar*, the *Byron* plays, *Coriolanus*, *Bonduca*, and *Caesar and Pompey*. His assertion in this context that '[n]o one realised better than the English people that a complete acknowledgement of the papal authority was incompatible with obedience to the civil power' also suggests the congruence that he may have found between *When You See Me You Know Me* and his other productions of this period (*Monthly Letters* 129).[9] There were also other, more contemporary concerns. Perhaps unsurprisingly, in the context of rising international tension, Poel saw in his 'conspiracy plays' critiques of war and of militarism. He described *Bonduca* as 'a Play illustrating the psychology of War', suggesting that it was a riposte to Shakespeare's *Henry V* and that Fletcher viewed war as 'little better [...] than a game of treachery' (Poel, *Britain* Programme); similarly, he interpreted *Coriolanus* as the tragedy of a young man whose mother has 'taught him to look upon war as the sole aim and end of his existence' (Poel, *Coriolanus* Programme). Before his death in 1934, Poel had intended to stage a platform performance of Coleridge's version of Schiller's *Death of Wallenstein* (perhaps, he thought, with Charles Laughton as Wallenstein), and, as Joyce Crick notes, it is possible to view this plan as a continuation of his productions of the late 1920s and early 1930s: 'True, 1934 was the Coleridge centenary year, but the last projected *Wallenstein* was also part of a Series on War' (44). After Poel's death, Ella Pole, his widow, wrote that he had intended it to be 'on behalf of the Peace Movement – "showing", as he said, "a glimpse of the futile misery of war"' (v).

In his programme note for *Coriolanus*, Poel wrote that the 'apparent aim of the play is to show the ageless spirit of militarism' (*Coriolanus* Programme). The tension between Poel's attention to the historical context of a play's production and his desire to dehistoricise and thereby to universalise it was evident throughout his productions at this time. For instance, *Bonduca* gained some lines from Tennyson's 'Boädicea'

---

[9] Speaight argues that Poel revived the play 'not on account of its dramatic merits, such as they were, but because it seemed to him relevant to the current controversy over the revision of the Prayer Book' (*William Poel* 247).

as a prologue and some lines from Cowper's 'Boadicea: An Ode' as an epilogue; both were apparently 'Spoken by a Victorian Graduate' (Poel, *Britain* Promptbooks 1). *Julius Caesar the Dictator*, similarly, was prefaced by an extract from Keats and concluded with one from Macaulay (Poel, *Julius Caesar* Programme). Even more noticeable in this respect was the use of costume, which at times varied wildly from Poel's earlier practices. *Sejanus* featured costumes that, according to the programme, 'give no historical point to the Roman period. On the contrary, they should be regarded as representing what might have been most conveniently found for use in a contemporary playhouse'; they were described in *The Times* as 'ingeniously unhistorical as regards both the Roman and the Elizabethan periods' ('ESC: "Sejanus"' 18). The majority appear to have been Elizabethan and Roman in style, but Roy Byford's Tiberius was apparently accompanied by men dressed as maharajahs; another factor adding to the simultaneously historicising and dehistoricising effect was the decision to make up Speaight's Arruntius to look like Jonson and Wilfred Walter's Cordus to look like Shakespeare (see Ayres 39; Speaight, *William Poel* 248; Poel, *Sejanus* Programme). A similar approach may have been taken in *Julius Caesar the Dictator*, for which the programme states, 'The costumes are similar to those that would be found in the wardrobe of an Elizabethan theatre' (Poel, *Julius Caesar* Programme).

Notoriously, *Coriolanus* featured an even more chronologically diverse mixture of clothing. Poel originally planned that the costumes should be of the Napoleonic era, but this did not, perhaps, lend itself to the 'ageless spirit' that he sought; as *The Times*'s reviewer pointed out, 'the Napoleonic period is really more definite and particular to us to-day than the Roman'. Instead, therefore, Poel mixed costumes in a dizzying fashion. As J.S. in the *Manchester Guardian* summarised it,

Volumnia stalked upon the scene as an eighteenth-century aristocrat in a Gainsborough picture hat and powdered curls. The tribunes were in the black gowns and white wigs of barristers. The plebeians were attired in costumes which made them look like a cross between decayed members of the French Foreign Legion and English engine-drivers. Aufidius was in the gorgeous robes of an Oriental potentate. One officer was dressed like the Duke of Wellington, with men to match him in period. Another officer was an admiral, and he was attended by bluejackets.

'These', the critic noted, 'were some of the costumes one hurriedly noted down in the darkness, and the list could be lengthened' (9). According to Speaight, Virgilia 'was a pure Pre-Raphaelite. Poel had copied her dress from the photograph of a fashionable beauty at a fancy dress ball, which he had seen in a society journal' (*William Poel* 256).[10]

Coriolanus himself wore a number of different costumes, embodying the production's eclecticism: his first appearance was in a lionskin, carrying a huge, two-handed sword; he later wore 'the full-dress uniform of a Colonel of the Hussars' and after the second interval appeared in the costume of a Roman general (see J.S. 9; Speaight, *William Poel* 255–6; Speaight, *Property Basket* 132–3).[11] Poel commented in a letter to Speaight of 20 April 1931, 'The more I think about your first costume, the more anxious I am to have as a start something that is an emblem more than a personage or portrait of yourself' (Speaight, *William Poel* 255–6). This declaration suggests at least part of Poel's reasoning: despite his interest in the relationship between Coriolanus and Volumnia, he was not aiming to create a psychologically consistent, 'realistic' character, but something between character and emblem. In addition, there must have been a deep irony in Coriolanus's appearance in a Roman general's uniform at the start of the third section of Poel's adaptation, in which he moves against Rome, highlighting the issues of treachery and conspiracy that so intrigued the director.

Another issue that can be viewed with greater clarity when Poel's productions of the late 1920s and early 1930s are considered as a group is that of the text itself. A number of the plays have – or had, for Poel – complicated textual histories that made them amenable to adaptation. The extant text of *Sejanus* appears to have been rewritten by Jonson from a version originally written in collaboration, probably with Chapman (and, Poel thought, possibly with Shakespeare), and Poel's cuts and rearrangements were praised for liberating a theatrical play from a literary artefact. *The Times* remarked, 'We could well believe at the end that the tale of Sejanus had been presented to us very much as it had been presented at the Globe in 1603, before Jonson had decided to revise it' ('ESC: "Sejanus"' 18). The text was cut by around a quarter; Philip J. Ayres notes that, among other changes, 'the Germanicans and Tiberius obviously seemed long-winded to [Poel] – the complaints of the former were heavily pruned, and Tiberius' letter to the Senate cut by half' (40).

---

[10] In a later account, Speaight writes that the production featured 'Volumnia as a Gainsborough *grande dame* in hat and plumes, Sicinius and Brutus as railway porters from the Gare du Nord, and Virgilia as the Blessed Damozel' (*Property Basket* 133).

[11] The promptbooks also direct Coriolanus to appear in a 'consul's robe' (41) and a 'gown of humility' (32, 51); a pencilled note, 'Cor. changes to General's costume' (62), is to be found next to the revised placing of the second interval in copy A.

Similarly, the two-part play *The Conspiracy and Tragedy of Byron* had been censured on its first performance in 1608 and was heavily censored when it was published later in the same year, Chapman referring to it as 'these poore dismembered Poems' (Gabel 277 (line 18)). Poel condensed the two plays into one and freely adapted, as he had done with *Sejanus*. According to *The Times*,

The result is a surprisingly agile Chapman who leaps from scene to scene like the most impetuous of story-tellers. To seek in the text for the pieces that *were* performed is to marvel at – and to applaud – Mr. Poel's selective boldness. He has not preserved the impression of Chapman's own play, of its bulk, of its vast, rich leisureliness; he could not in much less than half-a-day, and we thank heaven he did not try. But he has, almost by a miracle, made of the poem a piece for the theatre – scrappy but alive[.] ('The ESC' 14)

A striking effect was added to the end of the play, which in the 1608 text ends abruptly with Byron's speech on the scaffold. After his speech, the promptbook directs:

The Curtain descends on the upper stage and the fall of the axe is heard. Voices heard below: 'Room for the Masque!' – 'Room lords and ladies for the Masque!'

Curtains open displaying the Court in festive attire, the KING on his throne. Music. Two CHILD DANCERS ENTER with cupid [*sic*] between them and dance to slow and stately melody.

TABLEAU. Curtain of the upper stage opens showing BYRON's body lying on the scaffold with a cloak thrown over it, then front curtain closes. (Poel, *Byron* Promptbooks 63)

Speight, who appeared as Byron, described the scene of trial and execution as 'one of the most exciting in which I have ever appeared' (*Property Basket* 100). In this case, as with *Sejanus*, critics were inclined to praise Poel for his radical treatment of the text, even when (as in the *Times* review of *Byron*) they felt that something had been sacrificed in the process of adaptation.

Poel's treatment of *Coriolanus* was, however, a different proposition, not least because few shared his belief that *Coriolanus* was 'a bad acting play', that there was in 'the composition [...] [of the play] the product of two minds', and that 'the greatest lines' were by Chapman (Poel, *Coriolanus* Programme). In Speight's view, 'It was one thing to take the Biron plays of Chapman and sew them together into an acceptable dramatic shape; but it was quite a different matter to hack about, alter and shamelessly transpose a masterpiece of Shakespeare's maturity' (*William Poel* 258). He misses, however, the crucial fact that for Poel this was *not* 'a masterpiece of Shakespeare's maturity'. Poel's belief that *Coriolanus* was a collaborative play gave him licence to treat it in the same way as he would any other non-Shakespearean work, and, despite his admiration for other aspects of the plays, his opinion of early modern plotting was low. With the exception of Jonson and Ford, Poel believed, 'the art of dramatic construction was [...] but little understood'. 'A unity of design is wanting', he writes, 'as well as continuity of action leading directly to a climax. The interest around one scene is too often lost in the next, and the plays, when judged by modern standards, appear ineffective and unconvincing' (*Lillies That Fester* v–vi). As a result, he felt no compunction about cutting and rearranging even those plays that did not have obvious textual problems, such as *David and Bethsabe*, which was cut down to little more than half its original length, or *When You See Me You Know Me*, from which around 1200 of the original 3200 lines were excised (Speaight, *William Poel* 267; Somerset 118).

Poel's treatment of *Coriolanus* follows this pattern. He cut around 2000 of the play's 3409 lines and much of its most-admired poetry, perhaps because he thought it was by Chapman and perhaps, as Speaight argues, because he thought it was 'a check on the dramatic momentum' (*Property Basket* 134). As John Ripley describes, the action was thereby streamlined into a continuous narrative that fell into three movements: 'Martius's military career, culminating in his nomination for the consulship; his confrontation with the Roman tribunes and citizens leading to a Volscian generalship; and his struggle with his mother terminating in his defeat and death' (262). The general effects were to reduce the role of the Roman populace, whom Poel viewed as 'contemptible' and useful mainly as a device to cause Coriolanus's banishment (*Coriolanus* Programme);[12] to reduce the importance of the relationship between Aufidius and Coriolanus; and to intensify the relationship between Coriolanus and Volumnia. Poel argued that the key to *Coriolanus* lay in the line 'O, mother, mother! What have you done?', commenting, 'Well may he ask this question, for it is his mother who has taught him to look upon war as the sole aim and end of his existence, and now he finds that to save her life he must sacrifice

---

[12] Speaight also suggests that Poel suppressed violence in the play because he was worried about offending the Prime Minister, Ramsay MacDonald, having recently declined a knighthood (*Property Basket* 133). It is difficult to assess the truth of this, but it is worth noting that Poel is at pains in his programme to assert that the presentation of the citizens and patricians 'is no question of the Labour party versus the House of Lords'.

his own! [...] Volumnia is not the tragic queen of the play; she has educated her "boy" to his ruin, and is responsible for his death' (*Coriolanus* Programme). As a result of this refusal to glamorise Volumnia, Poel freely rewrote her final speech to Coriolanus and, strikingly, changed it from verse into prose:

You see, my son, by our attire to what condition your banishment has reduced us. Think with yourself whether we are not the most unhappy of women when fortune has changed the spectacle that should have been the most pleasing in the world, into the most dreadful; when camped in a hostile manner before the walls of his native city. (77)[13]

The final exchange with Aufidius was excised, and the production instead focused on the confrontation between mother and son. Then, according to the promptbook's stage directions, Coriolanus 'walks with the Ladies towards the gate of the City of Rome', the women 'pass through the gates where they are received by the villagers with much cheering', and 'The Mother turns and makes signs to her son to come' (79). Coriolanus replies 'Ay, by and by', the 'curtains of the gate', which presumably separated the proscenium and the platform stage, are closed, and he speaks, 'alone' on the platform:[14]

> O, mother, [my] mother!
> What have you done? Behold, the heavens do ope,
> The gods look down, [and smile in dismal wonder
> As at one forsworn].[15] O my mother, mother! O!
> You have won a happy victory to Rome;
> But for your son – believe it, O, believe it,
> Most dangerously you have with him prevail'd,
> If not most mortal to him, But, let it come. O mother! Wife! (79)

A stage direction then instructs: 'He buries his face in his hands then he walks closely towards the Corioli door, and gives two loud knocks with his fist. The door opens, he enters, and it closes. Singing and dancing heard in the Roman City followed by tumult and killing of CORIOLANUS in the City of Corioli' (79). Coriolanus's final speech appears to have been delivered in a moment of silence following the cheering of the Romans

---

[13] The Theatre Museum Archive has three promptbooks for *Coriolanus*. Copy A has marks for cuts and insertions in Poel's hand, while Copy B, into which the majority of these have been transcribed, is identified as 'Miss Molly Tyson's Copy', Molly Tyson being the stage manager. Unless noted otherwise, quotations are identical in each copy.

[14] Emendations are enclosed in square brackets.

[15] These lines originally read 'and this unnatural scene / They laugh at': they are crossed out and the replacements added in manuscript.

welcoming Volumnia; it was then followed by a dissonant mixture of sounds: singing and dancing on one side of the platform stage, and the sounds of Coriolanus's death on the other. Speaight describes the effect thus: 'That was the end of the play; it may have been magnificent, but it was not Shakespeare' (*William Poel* 261).

Poel was widely criticised for his rescripting of the end of the play, *The Times*'s reviewer complaining that 'Coriolanus's last and most magnificent speech was omitted' ('Chelsea Palace' 14). In an unfinished draft letter of June 1931, Poel excused his omission of the final speech on the grounds that Coriolanus must 'be shown as a sympathetic figure' in order for the play to have a 'satisfactory ending', and that the 'emotions of the audience' could only have 'full play' if he is silent from the point at which he sacrifices his own life for that of his mother. He continues,

The words at the end that are called magnificent have all been heard already on the stage. Twice is Coriolanus called a traitor and twice does he make a spirited rejoinder. Twice does the general publicly call attention to Coriolanus being alone in Corioli. In fact Coriolanus' last speech is harsh and leaves a bad impression. It is not a moment for a man to boast of what he had done. (Gomme 1151)

However, although Coriolanus's speech was excised, it haunted the final moments of the production; Aufidius's provoking speech and his description of Coriolanus as a 'boy of tears', to which Coriolanus's outburst is a direct response, was omitted, but some phrases from the exchange reappeared, according to the promptbook, in the shouts from the offstage populace of Corioli as they killed their erstwhile champion: 'He killed my son, my daughter. How now traitor. Traitor ay traitor Marcius. He killed my father. Hear thou Mars. Name not thy god thou Boy. Insolent villain. Kill. Kill Kill. Hold Hold.'[16]

Poel's striking stage effect at the end of *Coriolanus* is reminiscent of his treatment of Byron's death in his adaptation of Chapman's tragedy, and further connections can be drawn between *Coriolanus* and the productions that preceded it. *Everyman* described Sara Allgood's Volumnia as 'a blatant and bragging Lady Britomartish sort of person', and the *Daily Telegraph* noted her 'hearty Irish bloodthirstiness', while *The Times*'s reviewer praised her 'magnificent force and vitality' in the final scene (Ripley 266; 'Chelsea Palace' 14). The reviewers' reactions to Volumnia, and in particular the recourse in *Everyman* and the *Daily Telegraph* to archaic models of British femininity (Spenserian-Arthurian on one hand, Celtic on the other), recall Poel's earlier platform-stage production of *Bonduca*. Although *Bonduca*

---

[16] Manuscript note on verso of p. 78 (Copy A); the note also appears in copy B.

is rarely read or performed alongside *Coriolanus*, its depiction of a mar-
tial national heroine and her relationship with a compromised military
hero whose loyalty to his native country wavers, fatally, mirrors that of
Shakespeare's play, especially as it was adapted by Poel.

In addition, both adaptations sought to minimise the threat of at least
some of the forces that ranged against hero and heroine. In *Bonduca*, the
Roman soldiers were all played by boys from Fortescue House School,
Twickenham; Speaight describes Margaret Scudamore, who played
Bonduca, as 'a majestic and Amazonian heroine [...] who towered over
her adversaries' (*William Poel* 249), while Ivor Brown in the *Manchester
Guardian* noted the production's 'troops of marching boys' ('Mr. Poel's
Platform Stage' 20).[17] Of *Coriolanus*, *The Times*'s reviewer wrote that the
plebeians were 'admirably done' by the pupils from the same school, a
casting strategy that may have given additional force to Coriolanus's
insistence on branding the plebeians' political ambitions as childish. Poel's
experiments with casting children in adult roles may have been propelled
by his experiences in producing Jonson's *The Poetaster* and Shakespeare's
Comedy of Errors with young people and schoolchildren, but the effects
of the performances of child actors in an otherwise adult cast must have
been very different from those of a wholly juvenile cast.[18]

With regard to the specifics of staging, *Coriolanus* also shows marked
affinities with the productions that preceded it. Reviews and promptbook evidence suggest that for each production the platform was built
around eight inches below the regular stage level and that the inner stage
thus created could be closed off with curtains. For *When You See Me You
Know Me*, Poel followed the set-up used in his 1912 *Troilus and Cressida*
and constructed a 'pavilion' out of curtains on the left- and right-hand
sides of the platform, each with an opening facing into the centre of the
stage; one represented the palace of Henry VIII and the other that of
Cardinal Wolsey and the other bishops (*When You See Me* Promptbooks;

---

[17] A review of *Julius Caesar the Dictator* asks 'what is to be said of a Roman tragedy in which the
armed warriors are so often feminine and almost farcical', but it is not clear whether they are
referring to the casting of women or children, or to effete men ('ESC: "Julius Caesar"' 10). The
crowd in *Sejanus* was probably also composed of children: the programme says that they were
'selected from the students of the Fay Compton Studio of Dramatic Art; also by Miss Euphan
Maclaren'. Euphan Maclaren also supplied a child actor to play Cupid in Poel's production of
Byron and 'Peasant Dancers' in Poel's *Coriolanus*.

[18] On *The Poetaster*, which featured 'a company of young people [...] mostly female', see 'An
Elizabethan Revue' 9. Poel revived the play on his visit to Pittsburgh later in the same year, using
a group of college students as his cast. See Webb 151–3. On *The Comedy of Errors*, performed by a
cast of London County Council schoolchildren, see Poel, *Monthly Letters* 22–4.

Somerset 119). In *Coriolanus* a similar set-up was used, one side entrance representing the gate of Corioli and the other the gate of Rome.

The large platform stage could be used to striking effect: for instance, in the scene in which Coriolanus is obliged to display his wounds publicly, the citizens are directed to 'collect in the upper part of the stage' (*Coriolanus* Promptbooks 33), while Menenius and Coriolanus are left together on the platform. Later, during the build-up to Coriolanus's departure from Rome, 'ALL move into the centre of stage. SICINIUS and BRUTUS come forward from the back of the stage, and speak apart on the right' (53). The effect must have been similar to that described in Brown's account of Poel's *Bonduca*, in which the platform stage 'was used [...] to make conspiratorial groups or rebellious cliques lurk naturally in the shade while a general orated or the Druids performed a sacrifice to hymns of bodeful rhythm' ('Mr. Poel's Platform Stage' 20). Brown seems to have understood more fully than most reviewers Poel's interest in stage space. He writes in his review of *When You See Me You Know Me*, 'There could be much and intricate movement since the platform was bigger than the stage of Drury Lane. There could also be a to-and-fro technique like that used by the cinema' ('Salute' 90), and of *Bonduca* he notes 'how much better the final scenes of scrambling Elizabethan tragedy may be when the armies have some scope for skirmishing and the action moves from plane to plane as well as from wing to wing' ('Mr. Poel's Platform Stage' 20).

Poel's use of the platform stage was also marked by experimentation with simultaneous staging. In a 1925 production of *Arden of Faversham*, staged with what Poel described as 'THE MULTIPLE SCENE', the stage was divided into three sections, each representing a different location (Arden's parlour, the High Road near Rainham Down, and 'A STREET IN LONDON WITH AN ENTRANCE TO FRANKLIN'S HOUSE' (*Arden* Programme)); only one location was used at a time, and the others were curtained off (O'Connor, *William Poel* 73).[19] Two years later, in the production of *When You See Me You Know Me*, Poel had moved on, using different areas of the stage to represent different locations simultaneously, and not enforcing a convention that one part of the stage always represented the same location. J. A. B. Somerset praises in particular the sequence that builds up gradually from a double location, in which King Henry rants on one part of the stage and Prince Edward reads a book on another, to a triple, as soldiers gather to arrest Queen Katherine Parr in the bishops' pavilion.

---

[19] O'Connor notes that a composite stage was also used for a 1905 production of *Everyman* at the Shaftesbury Theatre and for a 1912 production of Kālidāsa's *Śakuntalā* in the Examination Hall of Cambridge University (*William Poel* 73).

'Thus', he comments, 'Poel was able to suggest urgency and build suspense by superimposing parts of four scenes, which led up to the climactic arrest of Katherine for heresy' (120).

Reviewing *When You See Me You Know Me*, Brown suggested that the platform stage 'enables you [...] to realise directly the stage-tactics of the time in which actors were often visible to the audience without being visible to one another' ('Salute' 90). This technique appears to have been used in the opening of *Coriolanus*; in the most heavily annotated of the promptbooks, an extensively reworked opening stage direction reads (pointed brackets indicate manuscript insertions) ~~Five or six~~ <Twelve> PLEBIANS DISCOVERED down stage seated ~~round a table in an Inn~~. <on the steps. Menenius entering from back of stage>' (*Coriolanus* Promptbook 1).[20] This effect was made possible by the radical cuts to the opening lines, noted above, meaning that the citizens voiced their discontent while, presumably unnoticed, Menenius quickly bore down on them.

Concluding her account of Poel's productions of *Hamlet*, Rinda F. Lundstrom notes that the 'perception of Poel as an antiquarian "gone bad" has a double edge. On the one hand, he is damned for quirky historicism, for being out of touch with the times. On the other, he is damned for not following his superannuated methods faithfully enough' (162). As we have seen, critics of Poel's *Coriolanus* often fall into the latter trap, judging it by the standards of productions staged twenty or thirty years earlier and failing to consider it in the context of his other, non-Shakespearean, productions around this time. Lundstrom comments that 'Poel's sense of history was always more lively than these criticisms suggest' (162), and the last productions of his career – when his focus was largely on history plays, be they Roman, French, or biblical – bear out her suggestion. Neither fully historicised, nor fully dehistoricised, they cannot be safely pigeonholed as attempts to recreate an 'authentic' Elizabethan past, but neither, on the other hand, can they be bracketed with the contemporaneous proto-postmodern director's theatre of Terence Gray.

For Ivor Brown, one of the most valuable aspects of Poel's experiments with the platform stage was the light that they threw on those aspects of performance least compatible with the illusionist proscenium-arch stage – such as direct address to the audience – and the simultaneous case that they made for large theatrical spaces. 'We have,' he writes, 'and justly, a cult of the little theatre. Mr. Poel states the case for the large theatre, and

---

[20] This is copy A. Copy B retains the typed stage direction, while copy C adds to it in MS 'from l. to Steps'.

usually manages to prove it' ('Mr. Poel's Platform Stage' 20). Experiments with large-scale intimacy at the Globe and, more recently, in the Royal Shakespeare Company's temporary Courtyard Theatre suggest that it is time for further investigation of Poel's platform stage and its multiple authenticities and inauthenticities.

WORKS CITED

Anderson, Michael. 'William Poel in 1926.' *New Theatre Magazine* 8.1 (Autumn 1968): 20–8.
'An Elizabethan Revue: Ben Jonson's "Poetaster!"'. *The Times* 27 April 1916: 9.
Ayres, Philip J., ed. *Sejanus His Fall*. Manchester: Manchester University Press, 1999.
Brown, Ivor. [Credited as 'I.B.'] 'Mr. Poel and the Platform Stage.' *Manchester Guardian* 11 July 1927: 11.
     'Salute to William Poel.' *The Saturday Review* 16 July 1927: 90–1.
     [Credited as 'I.B.'] 'Mr. Poel's Platform Stage: "Bonduca!"'. *Manchester Guardian* 4 January 1929: 20.
     'Chelsea Palace Theatre: "Coriolanus"'. *The Times* 12 May 1931: 14.
Crick, Joyce. 'William Poel's Wallenstein-Moment'. *Cousins at One Remove: Anglo-German Studies 2*. Ed. Richard Byrn. Leeds: Northern Universities Press, 1998. 42–60.
'Elizabethan Stage Circle: "Britain". By John Fletcher'. *The Times* 4 January 1929: 10.
'Elizabethan Stage Circle: "Julius Caesar the Dictator"'. *The Times* 21 July 1930: 10.
'Elizabethan Stage Circle: "Sejanus His Fall". By Ben Jonson'. *The Times* 13 February 1928: 18.
'Elizabethan Stage Circle: "When You See Me You Know Me." By Samuel Rowley'. *The Times* 11 July 1927: 7.
Gabel, John B., ed. *The Conspiracie and Tragedie of Charles Duke of Byron Marshall of France. The Plays of George Chapman: The Tragedies with Sir Gyles Goosecappe*. Gen. ed. Allan Holaday. Cambridge: D. S. Brewer, 1987: 265–422.
Gomme, Allan. 'William Poel 1852–1934: A Chronological Record of his Published Writings on the Theatre and Theatrical Subjects'. Unpublished TS. Theatre Museum. Z 8699.4.
J. S. ' "Coriolanus": Mr Poel's Production'. *Manchester Guardian* 12 May 1931: 9.
Lundstrom, Rinda F. *William Poel's Hamlets: The Director as Critic*. Ann Arbor: UMI Research Press, 1984.
Mazer, Cary M. *Shakespeare Refashioned: Elizabethan Plays on Edwardian Stages*. Ann Arbor: UMI Research Press, 1981.
O'Connor, Marion. *William Poel and the Elizabethan Stage Society*. Cambridge: Chadwyck Healey, 1987.

'"Useful in the Year 1999": William Poel and Shakespeare's "Build of Stage"'.
    Shakespeare Survey 52 (1999): 17–32.
Poel, William. *Arden of Feversham* [sic] Programme. 1925. Theatre Collection,
    Victoria and Albert Museum, THM/40/1/1.
    Britain [i.e., *Bonduca*] Programme. 1929. Theatre Collection, Victoria and
    Albert Museum, THM/40/1/2.
    Britain [i.e., *Bonduca*] Promptbooks. 1929. Theatre Collection, Victoria and
    Albert Museum, S.1173–1983.
    Byron Programme. 1929. Theatre Collection, Victoria and Albert Museum,
    THM/40/1/2.
    Byron Promptbooks. 1929. Theatre Collection, Victoria and Albert Museum,
    S.1176–1983, S.1177–1983.
    Coriolanus Programme. 1931. Theatre Collection, Victoria and Albert Museum,
    THM/40/1/2.
    Coriolanus Promptbooks. 1931. Theatre Collection, Victoria and Albert
    Museum, S667.1982.
    Julius Caesar the Dictator Programme. 1930. Theatre Collection, Victoria and
    Albert Museum, THM/40/1/7.
    Lilies that Fester and Love's Constancy. New York: Brentano's, 1906.
    Monthly Letters. London: T. W. Laurie, 1929.
    Sejanus his Fall Prospectus and Programme. 1928. Theatre Collection, Victoria
    and Albert Museum, THM/40/1/10.
    Sejanus his Fall Prospectus and Programme. 1928. Theatre Collection, Victoria
    and Albert Museum, S.1214–1983.
    Shakespeare in the Theatre. London and Toronto: Sidgwick and Jackson, 1913.
    When You See Me You Know Me Promptbooks. 1927. Theatre Collection,
    Victoria and Albert Museum, S.1218–1983.
    When You See Me You Know Me Prospectus and Programme. 1927. Theatre
    Collection, Victoria and Albert Museum, THM/40/1/11.
Pole, Ella C. 'Memoir by Ella C. Pole'. Alan Gomme. 'William Poel 1852–
    1934: A Chronological Record of his Published Writings on the Theatre and
    Theatrical Subjects'. Unpublished TS. Theatre Museum. Z 8699.4.
Ripley, John. *Coriolanus on Stage in England and America, 1609–1994*.
    Madison: Fairleigh Dickinson University Press, 1998.
Shaughnessy, Robert. *The Shakespeare Effect: A History of Twentieth-Century
    Performance*. Houndmills: Palgrave Macmillan, 2002.
Shirley, Frances A. *Shakespeare in Production: Troilus and Cressida*.
    Cambridge: Cambridge University Press, 2005.
Somerset, J. A. B. 'William Poel's First Full Platform Stage'. *Theatre Notebook* 20
    (1966): 118–21.
Speaight, Robert. *William Poel and the Elizabethan Revival*. London: William
    Heinemann, 1954.
    The Property Basket: Recollections of a Divided Life. London: Collins, 1970.
Styan, J. L. *The Shakespeare Revolution: Criticism and Performance in the
    Twentieth Century*. Cambridge: Cambridge University Press, 1977.

'The Elizabethan Stage Circle. Chapman's "Duke of Byron"'. *The Times* 16 July
    1929: 14.
Webb, Bernice Larson. *Poetry on the Stage: William Poel, Producer of Verse
    Drama*. Salzburg: Institut für Anglistik und Amerikanistik, 1979.

CHAPTER 4

'A fresh advance in Shakespearean production': Tyrone Guthrie in Canada

Neil Carson

Reviewing the field of Shakespeare studies for the newly established *Shakespeare Survey* in 1948, Allardyce Nicoll pointed out the regrettable lack of adequate spaces in which to experiment with new methods of Shakespearean production. The absence of such facilities, he felt, was a serious hindrance to fuller and further accomplishments in the study of the Elizabethan theatre. Nevertheless, he reluctantly came to the conclusion that, because of the expense involved, the 'dream of a practical stage for the trying-out of theories [...] may never be realized' (16). His pessimism was not misplaced, for the dream of a practicable Elizabethan stage on which more 'authentic' productions of Shakespeare could be mounted had long been cherished by scholars and theatre producers alike. The idea had been championed in the early years of the century by William Poel who saw such a stage as a kind of laboratory in which to recover Elizabethan methods of acting and production. Later it was promoted by various (mostly academic) theatre historians eager to erect a replica of the Globe playhouse. But, in England, the notion of a theatre for Shakespeare's plays became fatally entangled with the idea of a memorial for the playwright himself. The latter, it was argued, should be devoted, not just to the works of the greatest English dramatist, but to the best drama of all countries and all periods: in other words, a true National Theatre. Once that happened, compromise was inevitable. The competing visions of the various boards, administrators, architects, producers, and fundraising bodies, together with two world wars and the growing rivalry between the Old Vic and the Shakespeare Memorial Theatre, effectively brought all progress to a halt.

Among the theatre practitioners discouraged by this apparently endless procrastination, none can have been more frustrated than Tyrone Guthrie, Director and Administrator of the Old Vic from 1936 to 1945 and one of the leading producers of Shakespeare in the country. Guthrie's interest in finding a more satisfactory method of staging the plays of Shakespeare had first been aroused by the work of William Poel. Whereas Poel himself, and some of his disciples such as Harley Granville Barker, seemed primarily concerned with restoring the texts of the plays and ensuring they were spoken clearly and intelligently, Guthrie was more interested in what Prospero called the 'art to enchant'. For him, the heart of the theatrical experience was the actor–audience relationship – the feeling of reciprocity between actor and spectator that produces the kind of wide-eyed engagement of children at a puppet show (*Prospect* 10). This sense of imaginative collaboration between audience and stage is not won by words alone: it is supplemented by spectacle and movement that are often as meaningful as the words themselves (*Acting* 68). He had been confirmed in this belief in 1937 when, in Elsinore with his production of *Hamlet*, he had been forced by a rainstorm to move the actors indoors where they gave an impromptu performance of the play 'in the round'. Feeling the excitement of the spectators packed around three sides of the performers, he became convinced that the actor–audience relationship envisaged by Shakespeare could not be duplicated in a conventional theatre. From that time on, he was determined to find a way to break out of the proscenium arch.

In 1948 at the Edinburgh Festival, Guthrie had directed a production of the medieval morality play, *Ane Satire of the Thrie Estaites*, on an experimental thrust stage built over the Moderator's throne in the Assembly Hall of the Scottish Kirk (*Life* 308). But this had been a temporary stage available only a couple of weeks a year. He had later half jokingly suggested to Anthony Quayle, Artistic Director of the Shakespeare Memorial Theatre, that a reconstruction 'tin Globe' be built on the banks of the Avon. Quayle's rejoinder, that his Board would never support such a project (Quayle 327), was not unexpected and, when Guthrie was asked to return to the Old Vic for a year to sort out a managerial and financial crisis in that organisation, he had to turn his mind to other matters. But the notion of an ideal theatre for Elizabethan plays was not forgotten. In April 1952, speaking to the Shakespeare Stage Society, he explained that such a theatre need not be an exact replica of the Globe. What was essential was to make the contact between players and audience as intimate as possible. The theatre would need to be large enough to pay its way, but small enough for the actors to be heard without speaking too loudly or slowing down their delivery, thereby sacrificing variety in tempo and tone in the verse speaking ('Miss Leighton').

It was amazingly opportune, therefore, that scarcely two weeks later he received a letter from a Canadian acquaintance asking him if he would be interested in going to that country to advise on the possible establishment of a Shakespeare Festival in a small Ontario town called Stratford. The decision was not a difficult one. So weary was he by now of the politics of London theatre and what he had come to regard as the pomposity of its self-conscious torchbearers ('Questors' Theatre') that the prospect of an escape to a naive provincial centre seemed irresistible. Perhaps there, away from the entrenched interests, the bureaucratic interference, the fixed ideas, and inherent conservatism that he had seen block so many innovative schemes in Britain, he might be able to try something new. Replying immediately, he wrote, 'I am most interested in the project if it offers possibilities for a fresh advance in Shakespearean production' (Forsyth 222). The answer he received was astonishingly reassuring: there would be, he was promised, 'no traditions to overcome, no local thespians who have their own ideas', only a completely free hand and a fairly generous budget (Patterson and Gould 59).

Eager to learn more, he visited Canada in July and came away convinced that this opportunity to put his own ideas into practice was not to be missed. Stratford, it turned out, was a small town of some 19,000 set in the rolling countryside of southern Ontario. It shared a remarkable number of similarities with its English namesake. It was situated on a river called the Avon some hundred miles from a larger city called London on a river named the Thames. Its Shakespearean connections were also surprisingly long-standing. Several of its streets and schools were named after Shakespearean characters; after its celebration of Shakespeare's tricentenary in 1864, it received a sundial from its Warwickshire twin and established a Shakespeare Garden in the local park for which it commissioned a (hopelessly romantic) bronze portrait bust of the playwright (Reid and Morrison 20, 26). Nor was the proposed summer festival its first foray into Shakespearean production. In 1905 the Stratford Elks Lodge, in an audacious attempt to raise money, had brought a touring production of *Richard III* to the local Albert Theatre. The enterprise had not been a success and was never repeated, but it had not, apparently, altogether dampened the interest of the city's residents in the presentation of Shakespeare's plays (Reid and Morrison 93).

Another similarity between the two cities was a post-war sense of hopefulness, which in England was manifest in the Festival of Britain. In Canada, this optimism was expressed in submissions presented to the Royal Commission on the National Development in the Arts, Letters and Sciences, known more familiarly as the Massey Commission. One of the most eloquent of these submissions was an assessment of the needs of Canadian theatre written by a former colleague and friend of Guthrie's, Robertson Davies. But a major difference between the two cities was the Canadian Stratford's almost total obscurity in the overall North American context – combined, however, with its access to an international news network linking all parts of the continent. The heavy reliance of most North American newspapers on wire services such as Canadian Press, Associated Press, and Reuters meant that interesting local events could very quickly attract international attention. By July 1952, the proposed Stratford Shakespeare Festival had done just that.

Back in England, having persuaded the Stratford committee that a completely new tent theatre would be required for the Festival, Guthrie was faced with the daunting task of designing it. For help he turned to his friend and colleague, the stage designer Tanya Moiseiwitsch, with whom he had a long working relationship. Moiseiwitsch had already designed a number of brilliant adaptations of Elizabethan stage conditions for productions in Bristol, London, and Stratford (see Edelstein). In these settings, she had succeeded in incorporating the elements of balcony, staircases, and 'discovery space' in various ingenious configurations behind a proscenium arch. What she had never done was design a setting to be seen from three sides. Presenting her with a picture of the Assembly Hall stage (which she had never seen), Guthrie asked her for her suggestions.

As Moiseiwitsch realised, the most efficient way of grouping a large number of spectators unwilling to stand around a stage is to seat them in an amphitheatre encircling it. This arrangement has the double advantage of bringing the back row closer to the performance and making the audience a much more active participant in the action than it would be in a traditional theatre of comparable capacity. Any temptation to mistake the play for reality is curbed by the absence of illusionistic scenery and the palpable presence of the other spectators, which emphasise the play's artificial nature and establish the semi-mythical or ritualistic mode of theatrical performance. Functionally, a major difficulty with theatre 'in the round' is the problem of 'masking': actors from time to time blocking the vision of certain members of the audience. To address this problem, Moiseiwitsch designed a series of concentric stages of increasing diameter and decreasing elevation which allowed subordinate players to descend to a lower level out of the line of sight. This arrangement provided playing areas of various sizes, from the relatively small upper stage, which gave a sense of intimacy to scenes played on this level, to a wider expanse of steps, over which battles and processions could flow.

The design of the rear of the stage presented more complicated problems. Evidence of Elizabethan practice was inconclusive. The only surviving sketch of the interior of a sixteenth-century playhouse – the Van Buchel copy of a drawing by Johannes De Witt of the Swan – showed two large doors in the tiring-house wall with a railed balcony above. Since many of the plays seemed to require a window, an upper level of some kind, and an area that could be concealed, most twentieth-century conjectural reconstructions of an Elizabethan theatre included a curtained 'inner stage' beneath the balcony. By the 1950s, however, the existence of such a feature was being challenged, with some commentators positing the use of a portable 'discovery space' that could have been put into position between the rear doors when needed. It was in this area at the back of the platform that Guthrie and Moiseiwitsch made their most radical innovations. Instead of a flat balcony against or within the back wall, they devised a triangular platform supported on visible pillars and jutting out some eight feet to a point at the very centre of the amphitheatre. Descending from this level (a feature not found in any of the conjectural reconstructions, but part of the Edinburgh Assembly Hall stage) were two matching staircases that led, via landings in front of elevated entrances on each side, to the main level where they converged among the pillars supporting the balcony. Behind the central pillar (and partially obscured by it) was the only rear entrance at stage level. Actors entering beneath the balcony had to veer slightly to left or right before stepping into full view on the main stage. Most revolutionary of all, perhaps, was the total absence of curtains, always hitherto considered indispensable for the concealment or sudden disclosure of furniture or actors so often apparently called for in Shakespeare's plays. Neither on doors nor on windows, above or below the balcony, were to be found these frilly features of virtually all popular reconstructions of Elizabethan theatres. Their elimination was partly for aesthetic reasons (they seemed to jar with the wooden finish of the stage) and partly because of Guthrie's distaste for their use.

Over a period of several weeks, during rehearsals of a revival of their production of *Henry VIII* at the Old Vic, Guthrie and Moiseiwitsch continued their discussions. These led to rough sketches and finally to detailed drawings until, shortly before Christmas 1952, Guthrie was ready to return to Canada with a tiny model of the stage. When he presented it to the now officially constituted Board of Directors of the Stratford Shakespearean Festival Foundation, that body was suitably impressed and seemed remarkably undaunted by the fact that they had just a little over six months to build it.

With plans for the theatre in hand, Guthrie could turn his attention to the question of repertoire. It was early decided that the programme should consist of two plays – one to feature Alec Guinness, who had been hired as the star of the festival, and a second contrasting work in which his co-star, Irene Worth, and the Canadian actors could take prominence. After much discussion, the choice fell on *Richard III* and *All's Well That Ends Well*. The tradition of *Richard III* on the English stage was a long, but far from distinguished, one. It was known to theatre audiences through much of the eighteenth and nineteenth centuries almost exclusively in the horribly mutilated adaptation of Colley Cibber, which reduced Shakespeare's contribution to about 50 per cent of the total, cutting whole scenes and rearranging others to give Richard most of the lines. Clarence, Hastings, Edward, and Margaret were removed; Rivers, Vaughan, and Grey reduced to mutes; and Buckingham presented as an attendant lord rather than a co-conspirator (Hankey 22).

The restoration of Shakespeare's text to the stage was a gradual process, long delayed by theatrical conditions and conventions of taste. Isolated performances of Shakespeare's original text were given by Samuel Phelps in 1845 and Charles Calvert in 1870, but it was not until Irving appeared in a drastically cut text of the play at the Lyceum in 1877 that a slightly more respectable version held the boards. Even this, however, was a distortion. Richard's scenes were highlighted: emotional climaxes or 'points' were emphasised, and striking tableaux devised to encourage admiration or applause. Characters and speeches were eliminated, historic references omitted, and scenes removed or subordinated to heighten the central role. Elaborate full-stage spectacles alternated with scenes played before a curtain or painted drop so that time-consuming set changes might be carried out back stage. The effect was to slow down and break up the action, quite destroying the rhythm of the original and turning Shakespeare's experiment in historical tragedy into Victorian melodrama and the character into a one-dimensional villain.

So powerful was Irving's interpretation, however, that *Richard III* continued to be played as little more than a Grand Guignol melodrama until well into the twentieth century. When Guthrie first produced the play at the Old Vic in 1937, he attempted to restore some of the more interesting psychological dimensions that he felt Shakespeare had added to an 'obviously rewritten play' (Macnamara). In a programme note written by Margaret Macnamara (but undoubtedly reflecting the director's views), these dimensions included Richard's 'obsession with his mother's shame of his deformity and his aching resentment that nobody could ever love him'. Richard's actions were prompted in part by his 'constant terror of his mother which warped his courage to bravado, masking constant fear, and by his secret jealousy of his handsome, petted elder brothers' (Macnamara). In the event, Guthrie's attempt to deepen Richard's character was a failure. Emlyn Williams so emphasised the character's naked villainy that he made Richard's victims seem 'inexcusable simpletons' (*Punch*). Guthrie himself had succumbed to a sometimes fatal addiction to comedy, producing what one reviewer called 'a thoroughly jolly performance', which made 'the most of the fun and the least of the tragedy' (J.G.B.).

In other respects, however, the production marked an early milestone in Guthrie's search for a means of duplicating Elizabethan stage conditions shortly after his visit to Elsinore. He built an apron in front of the stage with steps leading down into the orchestra pit. This arrangement brought the actors so close to the audience that some of Gloucester's terrible deeds were perpetrated within eighteen inches of the front row of the stalls (*Daily Express*). The set consisted of five gothic arches (four windows and one double door), the latter painted with a view of fifteenth-century London and able to be thrown open to show a small interior. The mixture of scenic and non-illusionist conventions was jarring, however, and critics felt that the set became 'unrealistic' during the final battle scene (*Punch*).

The production of the play that caused the most sensation between Guthrie's Old Vic and Stratford Ontario stagings was Laurence Olivier's performance at the Old Vic in 1944. Reviewers were particularly struck by the unconventional physical attractiveness of this Richard: his 'Cavalier grace', as *The Times* termed it ('New Theatre'), combined with the impression of steely intellect, contributed to what the *Observer*'s J. C. Trewin called 'a major Shakespearean performance'. James Agate, on the other hand, while admiring the performance, felt that it was a distortion of Shakespeare's character: for him, Olivier's 'high shimmering tenor' seemed too light to capture the full range of Richard's rage, his physique too slight to convey the power and massiveness of Richard's character. Furthermore, Olivier and his producer, John Burrell, had cut the text, eliminating all but one of Margaret's scenes and thereby continuing the long tradition of actor-manager abridgement (which was carried still further in the film).

The Canadian production, therefore, presented Guthrie with an opportunity to revisit the play in circumstances radically different from those of the Old Vic productions of 1937 and 1944. To begin with, as an actor, Guinness was perhaps better fitted temperamentally to explore the more vulnerable psychological dimensions of the character that had been missed by Williams and ignored by Olivier. Then the non-illusionist stage in Stratford would permit a much more rapid sequence of scenes, which in turn would allow for a more complete text. The unknown factor was the Canadian audience. Since Guthrie could count on neither an extensive familiarity with Shakespeare nor an understanding of medieval English history, he would have to appeal to the Stratford spectators as directly as possible.

When rehearsals began in early June 1953, they had to be conducted on a replica of Moiseiwitsch's stage in a barn in the local fairground, while work on the theatre itself progressed with frustrating slowness. The company that had assembled could hardly have been more diverse: the British actors all had extensive experience in Shakespeare, while the Canadians, by contrast, came from a wide variety of backgrounds and were relatively unfamiliar with classical theatre. Some had returned from drama schools in England where they had gone for training; a few had appeared in summer stock or with the two or three repertory companies existing at the time; many were veterans of radio in Toronto or Montreal; still others were products of the extensive amateur 'Little Theatre' movement. Hardly any were full-time professional performers. The result was a group lacking any uniform style or even a shared methodology. Guthrie had six weeks to forge them into a cohesive acting company.

When the actors moved into the fairground building, it turned out to be hot, disturbingly resonant, and shrill with the twittering of resident bird life. As the actors struggled to be heard over the noise, Guthrie would watch from a discreet distance. At six-foot-three in his sandals and with his closely cropped hair and military bearing, he might easily have been mistaken for an off-duty officer in the guards. From time to time he would interrupt the performers with a loud clap of his hands, striding to the stage to give instructions, illustrate a gesture, or reposition an actor. Then, turning on his heel with a peremptory 'Back!', he would return to his place of observation. His manner seemed brusque, suggesting that his reputation as a martinet might be deserved. But he exercised his undoubted authority with a geniality and wit that quickly won over the cast. Before long the atmosphere was remarkably harmonious.

The first problem was to work out an appropriate style of acting for this new stage. The two major surviving drawings of actors in an Elizabethan theatre – the De Witt sketch of the Swan and the supposed illustration of *Titus Andronicus* – both show the players performing frontally and apparently ignoring the spectators at the sides of the stage. Guthrie had become convinced that the encircling galleries and an audience surrounding the actors would have imposed on them a much more multi-directional orientation. This conviction had been strengthened by his experience in Elsinore and Edinburgh, and now he would be able to put these ideas to the test. At first rehearsals focused on externals. Crowd scenes and processions were carefully choreographed to provide visual variety and focus. Violent episodes and battles were meticulously planned and endlessly rehearsed to minimise the risk of injury to actors (or to members of the audience who would be seated a few feet from the performers). Much attention was paid to the rhythm of the action, eliminating pauses between scenes and emphasising variety and contrast in pace and tone. Gradually, director and performers began to understand and respond to the demands of the open stage.

Meanwhile, the construction of the theatre was alarmingly behind schedule. Following a financial crisis in April, the Chicago manufacturer who was to supply the tent to cover the stage and amphitheatre had temporarily stopped work when payment was delayed. Fortunately the Stratford contractor responsible for the theatre itself, when faced with the same cash shortage, decided to push on with construction although he knew he might never be paid. As opening night drew nearer, it became apparent that the actors would not have the two weeks of rehearsal time in a completed theatre that they had been promised in their contracts. As a compromise, it was agreed that the company would rehearse in the unfinished theatre from ten in the morning until ten at night, while the contractor would be allowed in to work on the building between those times.

The move to the theatre disclosed some hitherto unforeseen problems. Instead of standing nakedly in a large exhibition hall, the permanent stage was nestled in a closely enfolding amphitheatre, which seemed to make the acting area smaller and confine the actors in a more restricted space. The uppermost level of the stage, some ten by twelve feet in area, was ideal for intimate scenes and for establishing a character's dominant presence, but it could seem congested. Another awkwardness was the rather cluttered space behind the main platform. There the traditional balcony had been given a quarter turn so that one corner projected onto the stage, providing a triangular upper level supported by nine slender pillars. This structure provided a strong position above, in the exact centre of the auditorium and on a level with the middle row of the audience. But the pillars and the staircases converging from both sides on the lower level made it difficult to enter quickly from the back. The tunnels beneath the auditorium seating, however, were highly effective, making it possible to fill the stage very quickly for large processions or battle scenes and also providing powerful lines of opposition diagonally across the stage, pulling the action off centre.

As rehearsals progressed in this new space, it became clear to most of the performers that what appeared at first to be constraints could be turned to advantage. The closer proximity of the audience in a semicircular auditorium permitted a greater intimacy, so that even the most formally patterned rhetorical speeches could be made more psychologically convincing. Having to disregard the fact that they could not avoid turning their backs on part of the audience meant that the actors could play much more directly to one another – face to face instead of shoulder to shoulder. The result was both exhilarating, because relationships seemed more natural, but also frightening, since the actors were completely exposed.

For the director, the principal problem was controlling the focus in a space without a common perspective. With no background but the unadorned permanent setting (or, for some members of an audience, a sea of opposing faces), it was impossible to create the sense of a circumscribed environment, such as was possible behind a proscenium arch. Locale had to be established by the disposition of small, portable pieces of furniture or indicative props moved into position by the actors in full view of the audience. This staging placed the responsibility for establishing the scene where it belonged – on Shakespeare's verse and the imaginative engagement of the spectators.

Spectacle was not eschewed, but was provided by elaborate banners, crucifixes, halberds, torches, and especially by sumptuous costumes made to be seen in the round and from a short distance. Still, the most intractable difficulty was preventing the actors from playing predominantly to the 'front' of the house and ignoring those spectators at the sides. Since each segment of the semicircle had its own viewpoint, each would somehow have to be recognised and accommodated. Doing so required imposing a kind of circular movement, not only on crowd scenes, but even on individual actors. Although certain actors' faces would temporarily be hidden from some spectators, the inevitable masking would be minimised in this theatre by the multilevel stage and the steep rake of the amphitheatre, which allowed the audience to observe the movement from a slightly elevated position.

Ultimately, there evolved a style of production adapted to the thrust stage that reflected the highly formal, almost incantatory rhetoric of the play. In some cases, this effect was achieved by capitalising on the

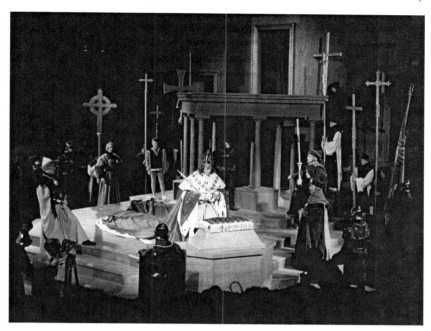

4. Richard III crowned, with, left to right, Robert Christie (Duke of Buckingham), Timothy Findley (Catesby), Jim Colbeck (Page), Alec Guinness (Richard III), George Alexander (Earl of Derby), and Michael Bates (Lord Mayor of London).

necessity for the actors to play to all parts of the house. For her lamentation over the body of Henry VI, for example, Guthrie had Lady Anne circle the bier of her father-in-law as in a formal ritual. Similarly, the three wronged queens – Margaret, Elizabeth, and the Duchess of York – circled one another, 'curling and writhing in an agony of hatred' (Whittaker, *Stratford* xiii). At other times, Guthrie emphasised the ritualistic elements in the action itself. After the coronation, Richard entered from beneath the balcony and crossed to mount a throne on a forward corner of the stage. Behind him, carried by pageboys, trailed an immense crimson robe that literally covered the entire upper level, powerfully suggesting the blood through which Richard had waded to get the crown. The final battle of Bosworth Field began, not with a headlong charge, but with a slow, silent advance of the opposing armies to the beat of a single drum.

Not all of the actors found this new stage equally congenial. Alec Guinness, especially, thought the theatre was awkward to work in. He missed the physical barrier between actor and audience such as is to be found in a proscenium theatre (Kareda). He also deplored the 'unnecessary' movement imposed upon the actor by the need to avoid keeping his back to anyone for very long (Pettigrew and Portman I: 86). Soliloquies appeared to him a special problem since they seemed to require stillness, but it was impossible for the actor to control the whole house while his face was always hidden from half the spectators (Guinness 73). Guthrie, on the other hand, revelled in the greater freedom and scope the stage gave to him as a director and choreographer. The action could be moved swiftly on and off the stage, sometimes even through the audience, with one scene often starting before the actors from the previous one had entirely disappeared. But most importantly, the actor–audience relationship was stronger than in conventional theatres where the performers and spectators were, in effect, in different rooms. Here they shared the same space. The stage spectacle, instead of being remote and two-dimensional like a painting, was present and fully rounded like a sculpture.

The production that finally came together for the opening night on 13 July 1953 was in most respects fairly conventional. There was no attempt to update the work or make it more obviously 'relevant' to recent historical events. Nor was there any mitigation of the traditional horrors: the bleeding corpse of Henry VI, the murder of Clarence, and Hastings's severed head were all vividly presented. Indeed, the inclusion of scenes often omitted, such as the execution of Rivers, Vaughan, and Grey, as well as that of Buckingham, emphasised the villainy of Richard. Nor was there much reduction of the black humour of the play. While not quite so bravura as Olivier in his mockery, Guinness used his talents as a comic actor to underline Richard's thinly veiled contempt for others.

At the same time, there were several ways in which Guthrie did try to show how the play looked forward to *Macbeth* as well as backward to *Tamburlaine*. The inclusion of Clarence's debate about revenge with the two murderers, the reinstatement of all of Margaret's scenes of prophecy, the curses of the three queens, Buckingham's reflections before his execution, and the ghosts' 'blessing' of Richmond on the eve of battle all contributed to an impression of something like a tragic fate informing the play. Guinness, too, attempted to convey more than a smiling, unfeeling demon vulnerable only in his dreams. His pangs of conscience seemed real and continued into his waking hours, unlike the Colley Cibber Richard who becomes 'himself' again upon waking.

Despite these efforts, however, the final production impressed more by its overwhelming spectacle than by its insight into the Shakespearean text. Brooks Atkinson in the *New York Times* called it 'an original show

[created] out of an ingenious setting, stunning costumes and fluid movement', but acknowledged that 'the drama came off second best amid such
powerful externals'. The Toronto critic, Herbert Whittaker, was, perhaps
understandably, more overawed by what he described as 'a production
such as none of us had ever seen in Canada before' (*Globe and Mail*).
But the result was not universally admired. The Shakespearean scholar,
G. Wilson Knight, acknowledged the freedom of movement provided by
the Stratford stage, but felt that 'the rather meaningless background edi-
fice lacked dignity' and that the theatre was inadequate for tragedy (298).
Even Guthrie conceded that the experiment had not been completely successful. 'For some time to come', he conjectured, 'the open stage will still
be in the experimental phase.' The Stratford auditorium embraced too
wide an arc, he felt, and the nearest spectators were too close to the actors
('Shakespeare' 131): 'In our desire to be intimate, we have overdone it. The
stage is a little too small and [...] there are times when this [proximity to
the front row] makes things a little too embarrassing' for actors and audience alike (Pettigrew and Portman 1: 81).

   In retrospect, the production was perhaps less groundbreaking than the
theatre in which it was performed. What was genuinely new was the arrest-
ing immediacy of the theatrical experience made possible by the Guthrie-
Moiseiwitsch stage and auditorium. These latter were a product of English
practice and traditions, but it was the Canadian money, enthusiasm, and cultural environment that had made possible their final realisation. And once
the experiment had been tried, it was rapidly to be duplicated elsewhere.

WORKS CITED

Agate, James. *Sunday Times* 17 September 1944. Cutting. Theatre Museum,
   London.
Atkinson, Brooks. 'At the Theatre: Stratford, Ont., Opens Its Bard Fete With
   Spectacular but Shallow "Richard III"'. *New York Times* 15 July 1953: 22.
Daily Express 3 November 1937. Cutting. Theatre Museum, London.
Edelstein, T. J., ed. *The Stage Is All the World: The Theatrical Designs of Tanya
   Moiseiwitsch*. Chicago: David and Alfred Smart Museum of Art and
   University of Washington Press, 1994.
Forsyth, James. *Tyrone Guthrie*. London: Hamish Hamilton, 1976.
Guinness, Alec. *Blessings in Disguise*. London: Hamish Hamilton, 1985.
Guthrie, Tyrone *A Life in the Theatre*. New York: McGraw-Hill Company Inc.,
   1959.
   'Shakespeare at Stratford, Ontario'. *Shakespeare Survey* 8. Cambridge: Cambridge
   University Press, 1953. 127–31.

Theatre Prospect. London: Wishart & Company, 1932.

Tyrone Guthrie on Acting. London: Studio Vista, 1971.

Hankey, Julie, ed. *Richard III*. Bristol: Junction Books, 1988.

J.G.B. Unidentified newspaper review in V&A Theatre Museum.

Kareda, Urjo. 'Sir Alec Guinness was Stratford's first star'. *Toronto Star* 8 June 1968: 33.

Knight, G. Wilson. *Shakespearian Production*. London: Faber and Faber, 1964.

Macnamara, Margaret. Programme for the Old Vic production of *Richard III*. 2–20 November 1937.

'Miss Leighton as Rosalind'. *The Times* 28 April 1952: 9.

'New Theatre: Richard the Third'. *The Times* 14 September 1944: 6.

Nicoll, Allardyce. 'Studies in the Elizabethan Stage since 1900'. *Shakespeare Survey* 1. Cambridge: Cambridge University Press, 1948. 1–16.

Patterson, Tom, and Alan Gould. *First Stage: The Making of the Stratford Festival*. Toronto: McClelland and Stewart, 1978.

Pettigrew, John, and Jamie Portman. *Stratford: The First Thirty Years*. 2 vols. Toronto: Macmillan of Canada, c. 1985.

Punch 17 November 1937. Cutting. Theatre Museum, London.

Quayle, Anthony. *A Time to Speak*. London: Barrie and Jenkins, 1990.

'Questors' Theatre, Amateur Company's Call for Help'. *The Times* 9 October 1951: 10.

Reid, Barbara, and Thelma Morrison. *A Star Danced*. Stratford: The Beacon Herald, 1994.

Trewin, J. C. *Observer* 17 September 1944. Cutting. Theatre Museum, London.

Whittaker, Herbert. *Globe and Mail* 15 July 1953: 21.

The Stratford Festival 1953–57. Toronto: Clarke, Irwin, 1958.

CHAPTER 5

Authenticity in the twenty-first century: Propeller and Shakespeare's Globe

Abigail Rokison

In 1977 J. L. Styan identified what he described as 'The Shakespeare Revolution', a significant move towards 'authenticity' in the texts and staging of Shakespearean productions that occurred at the beginning of the twentieth century, led by William Poel and Harley Granville Barker. This 'revolution' was both textual and stylistic. Reacting against the elaborate, pictorial realism and the heavily cut and modified texts of the Victorian theatre, these directors sought to restore the Shakespearean text and to explore it in conditions closer to the stage practices of the Renaissance. The work of Poel and Barker left its mark on the British theatre in terms of approaches to textual fidelity and emphasis on the spoken word.[1] However, the 1970s onwards, most notably at the then recently formed RSC, saw an increasing vogue for 'interpretative' productions, characterised by directorial concepts and frequently employing elaborate, mechanical sets (Smallwood 176–8).

In recent years, it has been possible to discern a reaction against this concept-led, technically complex mode of presenting Shakespeare, and a move, once again, towards seeking out methods of production that have a greater affinity to those of Shakespeare's own period. The most obvious instance has been the re-construction of Shakespeare's Globe on London's South Bank. The influence of the Globe's work on methods of staging Shakespeare at other institutions has been noted by a number of practitioners. Tom Piper, resident designer at the Royal Shakespeare Company, identifies 'a move away from large scale, highly visually theatrical versions of Shakespeare's plays [over the past fifteen years] – perhaps in part influenced by the Swan and Globe theatres – towards an emphasis on the power of the language to excite our imagination' and an attempt 'to create a focused, more intimate relationship between the actor and audience' (*Tom Piper* 2).

---

[1] See Peter Hall 195.

Since the completion of the Globe in 1997, others of its kind have emerged throughout the country. Peter Hall has been instrumental in the building of the recently completed Rose Theatre in Kingston, a modern theatre space inspired by the Rose Theatre of 1587. The RSC, partly motivated by the success of productions in its thrust-stage Swan Theatre, is currently transforming the proscenium-arch main house into a space that is designed, according to Artistic Director Michael Boyd, to mirror 'the intimacy of the courtyard theatres Shakespeare wrote for' (RSC).

Directors at the Globe have staged Shakespeare in a range of styles. However, under the artistic directorship of Mark Rylance, productions placed increasing emphasis on 'original practices', and later 'original pronunciation', employed in some performances of *Romeo and Juliet* in 2004 and *Troilus and Cressida* in 2005. The Globe's decision to refer to its productions as 'original practices' rather than 'authentic practices' was made in 1999. Tim Carroll, Associate Director at the Globe from 1999 to 2005, comments that 'authentic practices' is 'a claim that is begging to be shot down. Anybody with an opinion or a bit of knowledge you lack or have chosen to ignore is able to stand up and say, "You're charlatans". We know it would be madness to claim what we do is authentic in detail' (Rawson). However, there was no discernible difference in approach between the 'authentic' and 'original' practices productions. Although the latter may appear to provide practitioners with a licence to be selective about the level of authenticity they seek to attain and the areas in which they wish to introduce more modern practices, this was, to an extent, also the case with the 'authentic practices' productions – for example, in the decision to use African drumming in place of an Elizabethan jig at the end of the 'authentic' practices *Henry V* (Kiernan 9). Carroll's comment suggests that the change of description may have been merely a form of 'get-out' clause for directors fearful of being criticised by academics for their oversights. Some critics have indeed attacked the Globe productions, whether 'authentic' or 'original', for providing audiences with no more than 'an amusement park version of Elizabethan culture' (Bulman, 'Queering' 575, *et al.*). Others have seen in these experiments the development of the theatre as a site for learning about Renaissance theatre practice.[2]

In 1997, the same year as the Globe was completed, Edward Hall established his theatre company Propeller. Hall cites as one of the company's chief aims the performance of 'Shakespeare's plays as they would have been

---

[2] Andrew Gurr describes the theatre as 'a test-tube, the basis for experiments aimed at getting a better idea of how Shakespeare expected his plays to be staged' ('Staging' 159).

done in his time' ('Quartet'). Hall's company provides the most immediate analogue to the theatre companies of Shakespeare's age, having an all-male ensemble, many of whom have been members since the company's first production. However, Propeller's productions differ significantly from the Globe's 'original practices' productions, suggesting an alternative approach to the issue of 'authenticity', through the combination of traditional aspects of Renaissance performance with a contemporary aesthetic.

Where the Globe 'authentic' or 'original' practices productions have provided an audience with insight into the nature of early modern staging, allowing us to envisage how the plays might have looked, and in some cases sounded, when originally performed, it is the 'spirit' of the original staging that Propeller seek to capture. Elements of the work of both companies have been similar in their adherence to aspects of Renaissance theatre practice – the use of 'all-male' casts, the permanent or semi-permanent companies, a simplicity of staging and sparse use of set, the use of live music and sound effects, the centrality of an active actor–audience interaction, and a strong emphasis on the text, which acknowledges its centrality as a tool for the actor given the absence of a director in the Renaissance theatre. However, the ways in which they differ, in terms of style and period setting, are most significant in a consideration of the aims of these productions and the audience's experience of the plays. In some respects, we might see the distinction between the Globe productions and those of Propeller as being somewhat akin to that between the productions of Poel and Barker: the work of the Globe seeks, like Poel, to reconstruct elements of Renaissance theatre, whilst Propeller, like Barker, seeks to 'rediscover' the plays for a modern audience by emphasising the text and stimulating the audience's imagination.

Primarily through a comparison of the Globe and Propeller productions of *Twelfth Night*, I will argue that there are essentially two different forms of 'authenticity' at work in the productions of these companies. I suggest that, whilst the Globe productions provide a fascinating insight into early modern staging, the fact that contemporary audiences do not share the same cultural codes as their early modern counterparts renders aspects of the 'authentic' experience redundant. I argue that Propeller's success resides in their combination of Renaissance-influenced methods of staging with the exploitation of a semiotic code accessible to a contemporary audience. The Globe's new Artistic Director, Dominic Dromgoole, has made the decision to drop the term 'original practices', preferring instead to work 'with Elizabethan costumes, Elizabethan music and some Elizabethan stage practice' but to make the productions more 'jazzy', as he puts it (Calvi). I would argue that the 'original practices' productions were perhaps a necessary learning experience for a theatre in its infancy, proving influential on Shakespearean productions throughout the country, but ultimately one that has proved that meticulous adherence to Elizabethan practice is difficult to justify in a theatre where neither actors, directors, nor audience members are themselves 'authentic'.

The Globe's production of *Twelfth Night* was mounted first at Middle Temple Hall, in February 2002, as a 400th anniversary celebration of its first performance in the same venue in 1602. The production, directed by Tim Carroll, subsequently transferred to Shakespeare's Globe for the 2002 season, which was given the general title of 'Cupid and Psyche', with some changes in cast and necessary alterations to staging for a different shape of venue. Propeller first performed *Twelfth Night* in 1999 at the Watermill Theatre in Newbury, remounting it in 2006–7 at the Watermill and Old Vic theatres with substantial changes in casting. Both the Globe and Propeller productions were notable for their use of an all-male cast in line with Renaissance theatre practice. However, the companies differed in the degree of 'authenticity' with which they pursued this casting choice. The role of Viola in the Globe's Middle Temple Hall production was taken by Eddie Redmayne, a twenty-year-old Cambridge undergraduate. This casting choice was in line with the employment of boy actors on the Renaissance stage and in keeping with the 'original practices' brief for the production. Redmayne may have been older than his early modern counterpart; however, Gurr and Mann both note evidence that, whilst 'boy' players may have joined the Renaissance companies between the ages of 'ten and thirteen' (Gurr, *Shakespearean Stage* 93), some continued to play female roles into their twenties (Mann 47). Redmayne was slight and youthful in appearance and, with his white powdered face, red cheeks and lips, and long wig, one quickly forgot that one was watching a boy. As David Nicol asserts, 'Redmayne's performance demonstrated that boy actors in cross-dressing comedies may be convincing as women.' This chimes with eyewitness accounts of Elizabethan and Jacobean performances, most of which discuss the fictional female characters as if they were real women. Henry Jackson, a member of Corpus Christi College, Oxford, went so far as to seemingly confuse the genders of character and actor. Recalling a production of *Othello* by the King's Men in September of 1610, he reports that 'that famous Desdemona killed before us by her husband, although she always acted her whole part supremely well, yet when she was killed she was even more moving, for when she fell back upon the bed she implored the pity of the spectators by her very face' (qtd in Salgado 30).

However, whilst Redmayne might have been practically unrecognisable as a male, this was certainly not the case with the actors cast in the other female roles of Maria and Olivia: Paul Chahidi and Mark Rylance, both in their forties. Despite the fact that both were, like Redmayne, meticulously dressed in hand-sewn Renaissance clothing complete with authentic fabrics, undergarments and fastenings, heavy make-up and wigs, both were rather more reminiscent of drag artists than actual women. The casting of older female roles on the Renaissance stage is an issue that has generated some debate: were roles such as the Nurse in *Romeo and Juliet* and Cleopatra in *Antony and Cleopatra* played by boy actors or by more mature men on the early modern stage? Juliet Dusinberre suggests that the image of the boy actor in the role of Cleopatra is central to our understanding of the play (46–64). However, Muriel Bradbrook asserts that 'it was customary for men to take the part of older women' (213), and Carol Chillington Rutter, noting the purchase of a woman's gown for the adult player William Bourne (or Bird), concludes that 'it is not difficult to imagine casting men in preference to boys in many female roles: Shakespeare's Volumnia, Juliet's Nurse, Cleopatra, Lady Macbeth, Paulina, and Mistress Overdone' (124–5). Presumably it was on the basis of such academic assertions that Carroll elected to cast Chahidi as the comic, lower-class character Maria. However, the effect of this casting was to turn the character into what Michael Dobson describes as 'more like a nineteenth-century pantomime Dame than either an Elizabethan or a modern Maria' (259). Less immediately justifiable under the remit of 'original practices' was the casting of Mark Rylance, then aged forty-two, as Olivia, a character often perceived as of similar years to Viola. Rylance played Olivia as an Elizabeth I-like figure, an allusion, one imagines, to Leslie Hotson's highly contentious conjecture that the play was written to be performed at court in front of Queen Elizabeth and the role of Olivia conceived as a flattering portrait of the Queen (Hotson 121–3). Whilst Rylance's performance achieved rave reviews at both Middle Temple Hall and the Globe, the audience remained in no doubt throughout that they were watching a man playing this female character.

The Propeller productions, in contrast to those at the Globe, have not made a point of using younger or physically slight actors to play the female roles in their productions or made any attempt to disguise the fact that the women are being played by grown men. An exception to this might be the casting of the small and fine-featured Tam Williams in the role of Viola in the company's production in 2006–7. However, Williams retained his short masculine haircut for the role and did not adopt any

5. The final scene of Propeller's *Twelfth Night*, with Dugald Bruce-Lockhart as Olivia, Joe Flynn as Sebastian, Tam Williams as Viola, and Tony Bell as Feste.

form of make-up to play Viola prior to her disguise as Cesario. Actor Simon Scardifield defends this decision, taken for all of Propeller's productions: 'None of us taking female roles try to look or sound like women. We let the words speak for themselves, as they did in Shakespeare's day' (qtd in Woodcock). Scardifield's assertion points to a form of 'authenticity' at play in Propeller's cross-gendered casting – one that seeks to invoke 'the audience's imagination' in creating a Shakespearean production.

However, Scardifield's comment does not take into account indications that males playing females in the Renaissance theatre made some attempt to sound as well as look like women. Part of the motivation for casting young boys as women must have been the fact that their voices were not yet broken, and whilst we should be wary of treating the rude mechanicals in *A Midsummer Night's Dream* as indicative of Elizabethan stage practice, Quince's instructions to Flute when playing Thisbe to speak 'as small as you will' (1.2.42) suggests that such a vocal delivery was common for the performance of female roles. Similarly, Hamlet in greeting the players addresses the boy player as 'your ladyship', expressing the hope that 'your voice, like a piece of uncurrent gold, be not cracked within the ring' (2.2.410–11).

Edward Hall's explanation of how the company came to be all-male is similar to Scardifield's in emphasising a focus on the text and a desire to liberate the plays through an appeal to the symbolic, representational qualities of the Renaissance stage:

'it started because I directed a production of *Othello* with a mixed cast and I couldn't help them to get to the level of metaphor that a poetic play like that demanded. So when the opportunity came to direct *Henry V*, I was looking around for some new way of really being true to the text, but also giving it our contemporary response. The all-male cast unlocked that for me.' (Qtd in Ravenhill)

According to Hall, with an all-male company 'the audience stops being interested in the sexual chemistry between the actors and starts listening to the words'. However, when Mark Ravenhill asked the rather flippant question 'Surely this is a bit poofy?' in his *Guardian* article on Propeller, he raised a serious point about the homoerotic undertones of cross-gendered casting in Shakespeare. For James C. Bulman, all-male casting, far from distancing the audience from such issues, highlights the themes of sexuality and gender identity ('Bringing'). Hall denies any homoeroticism in his productions, arguing that 'the Elizabethans were not as obsessed as we are with labeling sexuality – they were interested in the emotions of love, and how to express them in poetry' (qtd in Sierz). However, two challenges may be raised to this comment. The first, as posed by critics such as Valerie Traub, is that 'homoeroticism' was a fundamental part of the 'early modern erotic economy', and that plays such as *Twelfth Night* provided their Renaissance audiences with 'spectator pleasure' through a 'transgressive glimpse of multiple erotic possibilities' (135). The second is that, irrespective of how the Elizabethan audience may have viewed sexuality, a 21st-century audience will inevitably bring their own experiences to bear on a production. Whilst the all-male casting of Hall's productions may be part of his desire for an 'authentic' focus on the text and an exploration of the representational quality of the plays, his productions have been viewed as in direct dialogue with current socio-political concerns of same-sex marriage and of equality irrespective of sexual orientation (Finkle).

The Globe's all-male casting has been subject to similar questions about its motivations and its consequences. Whilst Catherine Silverstone sees the all-male productions at the Globe as exhibiting 'anxieties about the representation of homoeroticism' and demonstrating a tendency to 'restrict or limit such representations' (38–9), Bulman dismisses Rylance's 'innocent' assertions that cross-gendered casting permits the recovery of 'layers of meaning that modern practice obscures', asserting that it was in fact 'a tactical ruse by which Rylance coaxes audiences to divest themselves of essentialized notions of gender and sexuality and [...] entertain queer thoughts' ('Queering' 575). Whether this was indeed Rylance's aim – something that I would contest – members of a modern audience, unaccustomed to seeing men taking on Shakespeare's female roles, may indeed find themselves aroused or indeed amused by the relationships enacted on stage. Paul Taylor, writing on the performance of *Twelfth Night* at Middle Temple Hall, asserted that Eddie Redmayne's 'scandalously persuasive' performance as Viola 'would bring out the bisexual in any man' (9), and Edward Hall confirms that school audiences invariably 'make a noise' when two male actors kiss on stage in his productions (Sierz). Irrespective of the 'authenticity' of the action depicted on stage, the gulf between the social and cultural experiences and prejudices of contemporary and Renaissance audiences will undoubtedly affect the former's response to cross-gendered casting.

The two productions of *Twelfth Night* resembled each other in other ways that may be attributed to notions of 'authenticity'. Hall asserts that 'most of the problems of directing Shakespeare on the modern stage are created by the indoor theatre [... :] electric lights, a stage that bears no architectural resemblance to the theatre of Shakespeare's day and a two act tradition with one interval rather than the classic five act structure' ('Propeller'), explaining that he and the Propeller company have aimed 'to create some of the atmosphere that must have been a large part of the experience of watching plays in the outdoor theatre'. This comment sounds like advocacy for a Globe-like production – on an outdoor amphitheatre stage with no lighting. However, Propeller's production of *Twelfth Night* was staged in a series of indoor proscenium-arch theatres, with an atmospheric lighting design. Nevertheless, Hall's production did retain a simplicity in its staging through the removal of 'some of the more naturalistic modern theatre effects' ('Different'). As Hall explains, this was a decision made for his production of *Henry V*, for which the company decided that they would 'deny ourselves some of the modern tools of the indoor theatre. The Chorus, in "creating" the story, would create all the music and sound as well. Everything would be live' ('Theatre'). This has remained a feature of all Propeller's productions: the only recorded sound that the actors can recall having been used was that of the bear roaring in *The Winter's Tale* (Trenchard and Bell). The use of live sound effects and music created by the company was, accordingly, a feature of Propeller's *Twelfth Night*, with a number of the actors playing musical instruments, employing various objects to create percussion, and using their own voices to create the sounds of birds or animals in the garden scenes.

Performing Propeller's *Twelfth Night* in indoor theatres meant that stage lighting was a necessity. Despite Hall's assertion that 'electric lights' are one of the 'problems' inherent in directing Shakespeare in an indoor theatre ('Propeller'), this element was a key part of the creation of the 'ghost-like' (Bell) atmosphere of the production, with side lighting creating shadows in which the masked company could lurk to observe the action. However, elements of Ben Ormerod's lighting design did chime with that of the outdoor playhouses in allowing the actors, in particular Tony Bell, as Feste the fool, to see the audience when talking to them. As Bell explains, Ormerod is a key member of the Propeller team and attends rehearsals in order to ensure that his lighting design serves the company's conception of the play: 'for my fool characters I used to say to him "I like to see the audience", so he would work with me to light me in such a way that I could still clearly see [them]'. Sometimes this means bringing the lights down on the actor, and sometimes bringing them up on the audience.

Hall and his company have used various techniques to emphasise the presence of the actor and the audience in the same space. In most of the productions, the actors have interacted with the audience before, during, and in the interval of the plays. *Twelfth Night* began with Bell walking through the audience whilst the house lights were still up: 'I would acknowledge them and then I would start to play, which was when the house lights came down' (Bell). In the first production of *Twelfth Night* at the Watermill Theatre in 1999, the company assembled in the gardens in the interval, playing musical instruments and singing with audience members. Changes in company personnel in more recent years have led, Bell notes, to a reluctance to all mingle with the audience in the interval; however, this element has been maintained by Bell as the clown/fool. In the 2006–7 *Twelfth Night*, Bell's Feste mingled with the audience in the interval, playing his violin and encouraging the audience to sing along.

Bell sees its benefits as essentially three-fold: 'breaking [...] the barrier between the stage and the audience', 'taking away the formality of the performance and mak[ing] it more spontaneous', and 'whip[ping] them [the audience] up into a entertained frenzy so that when they hit the second half they are ready to continue being entertained'. All these elements, in particular the first two, seem in keeping with the spirit of the Elizabethan amphitheatres. The continuation of this entertainment in the interval can also be seen as a means of preventing the 'two act structure' that Hall bemoans from breaking the atmosphere of the production. Bell, still playing his violin, would wander back to the stage, again with the house lights still up, as if the second half had not yet begun, and there encounter Viola: 'the scene [3.1] would begin, with the house lights still up and I would continue to react to members of the audience during the scene' (Bell). This created a link between the two acts and a continuity from interval entertainment back into the play.

As David Crystal notes, 'one of the most interesting outcomes' of performances at the Globe 'has been to draw attention to the process of dramatic interactivity, demonstrating the creative role of the playgoer' (5). The productions have indicated how within a space such as the Globe, where some audience members are in very close proximity to the actors and where the lighting does not create a boundary between actor and audience, there is room for interplay between stage and auditorium. In a similar manner to Hall and Ormerod's use of the house lights to allow direct contact between actor and audience, the lighting for the Globe's productions has been a central feature of the creation of a sense of shared space. Whilst performances in the Renaissance theatre took place in daylight, beginning at around 2.00 p.m., those at the current Globe occur both in the afternoon and in the evening, necessitating the use of some lighting in order to permit the actors to be seen. However, the stage is not rigged with theatrical lanterns, but rather the whole auditorium is lit with halogen downlighters that simulate, to an extent, the conditions of a day-time performance.

Similarly to Propeller's use of live music in the interval of their productions, the Globe's production of *Twelfth Night* at Middle Temple Hall began with a pre-show entertainment, clearly designed to draw the audience into the world of the play. Audience members were invited to partake of mulled wine and Elizabethan sweetmeats and other delicacies, whilst Renaissance music was played from the hall's balcony. However, before audiences were permitted to enter the hall, they were led through the actors' dressing room, where the performers were applying make-up and getting into costume. This seemed a rather clumsy attempt at audience–actor interaction and cannot have been perceived as 'authentic'. Far from drawing the audience into the Renaissance atmosphere, this moment of rather awkward voyeurism felt like a museum exhibit. The moment was made increasingly strange by the fact that the actors seemed unsure as to what they were doing: were they pretending to be Jacobean actors, or were they simply themselves? Should they ignore the audience members in modern clothes traipsing through their dressing room, or should they interact with them, and if so, how? Taylor's account of his interaction with Rylance in this dressing-room space epitomises these difficulties. Dressed in his female undergarments, Rylance approached and asked 'Are you coming to see – to *hear* the show tonight?' Taylor comments on the significance of Rylance's self-correction: 'Shakespeare's original audience (in a way that is still vibrant in the word) would have said – as Theseus does, anticipating the mechanicals' interlude in *A Midsummer Night's Dream* – "I will hear that play".' Irrespective of whether this comment is accurate (Gabriel Egan's research would suggest otherwise),[3] the anachronism is captured in Rylance's informal parlance and use of the word 'show' alongside his correction of his use of the word 'see', as if attempting to personate a Renaissance actor.

As Nicol comments, this pre-play entertainment raised another significant issue in terms of the production's 'original practices' brief: 'an implicit assumption that producing *Twelfth Night* in accordance with its Elizabethan origins requires only that the actors wear the correct clothing, and that the audience is supplied with aniseed cracknels beforehand. Other, equally Elizabethan qualities – such as the words, ideas, characters and situation in the play – were assumed to be instantly translatable to a modern audience.' This feature of the Globe's productions requires interrogation and merits comparison with the work of Propeller in considering the question of whether, as Dennis Kennedy has argued, the attempt to emulate aspects of Elizabethan staging has 'the virtue of highlighting Shakespeare's otherness' (187) rather than drawing a modern-day audience closer to his plays. Despite the observed similarities in aspects of staging that might be described as broadly 'authentic', the Globe and Propeller productions of *Twelfth Night* differed significantly in terms of aesthetic and atmosphere. Whilst the Globe production adhered to an Elizabethan or Jacobean setting in its use of music, clothing, make-up, and properties,

---

[3] Gabriel Egan, undertaking an analysis of early modern theatrical terminology as contained within the plays of the Literature Online database, concludes that 'plays were much more commonly thought of as visual rather than aural experiences in the literary and dramatic writing of the period' (332).

the Propeller production was essentially modern in style: set in a dust-sheet covered, decrepit country estate, the company, clad in evening wear, were suspended in a party which 'had never begun and never finished' (Bell).

The Globe's production of *Twelfth Night* was meticulously researched, with the music adapted from contemporary sources, the actors costumed down to their undergarments according to Renaissance fashions and the strict sumptuary laws of the early modern period, properties fashioned in accordance with Renaissance techniques, and bowing, fighting, use of hats and weapons performed with strict adherence to early modern etiquette. In the early stages of rehearsal for the revival of the production at the Globe, the company worked closely with The Tudor Group, who live for sustained periods of time re-enacting Tudor and Elizabethan life. The company were instructed in, amongst other things, the social rules governing bowing and the etiquette of hats: 'for social equals it would have been acceptable to converse with their hats off. If you were talking to someone of a higher status it would have been polite to keep their [*sic*] hat off until told or indicated to "recover". A person with the advantage of higher status would keep their hat on' (Ryan 8). Jessica Ryan comments that, having learnt the societal norms, certain actors found ways in which their characters might depart, or seek to depart, from these: 'for example, a character such as TW [Timothy Walker, who played Malvolio at the Globe] was clearly hesitant about bowing to another character such as MB [Michael Brown, who took over from Eddie Redmayne as Viola]' (10). Once again, we are faced with the problem of Elizabethan theatre practice intersecting with a 21st-century audience. Whilst adherence to, or more significantly departure from, conventional etiquette in these matters might have revealed something about characters and their relationships with others to a Renaissance audience, these elements of 'authenticity' are liable to be lost on a 21st-century audience. Equally, whilst Jenny Tiramani and her team at the Globe may have gone out of their way to adhere to Elizabethan sumptuary laws in clothing the actors, the significance of a character appearing in a particular colour to signify her or his social status, although readily accessible to a Renaissance audience, is unlikely to be so to a modern audience member.

With Propeller's modern-dress *Twelfth Night*, the audience were, by contrast, able to make judgements about the nature, status, or occupation of a character due to a shared understanding of contemporary codes of dress. The black of Olivia's dress signified not her social status, but her emotional state – in mourning for her brother and father. In the 2006–7 production, Jason Baughan's Sir Toby, wearing a red military jacket whilst the other characters wore black suits, was immediately recognisable as an ex-military man, whilst the excessive blue eye-shadow and accentuated black eye make-up worn by Chris Myles's Maria signified the character's overt sexuality. Enabling the modern audience to recognise the social status, emotions, or intentions of a character from their clothing mirrors the use of costume as a signifier on the Renaissance stage. However, the broadly contemporary setting of this production did not prevent the characters from drawing foils when the occasion demanded, resisting the urge to transform references to swords into guns or other modern weaponry. This eclectic aspect of the production's design may be seen to approximate the experience of the Renaissance audience. The Peachum drawing of *Titus Andronicus* – apparently depicting the play in performance in the Elizabethan period – shows, despite the play's setting in ancient Rome, the characters dressed predominantly in Elizabethan clothing with some concessions towards Roman costume. Similarly, Cleopatra's demand in *Antony and Cleopatra* that Charmian 'cut [her] lace' indicates the original costuming of the character in a Renaissance bodice in an ancient Egyptian setting (1.3.71).

The use of music in the Propeller *Twelfth Night* was similarly eclectic. For the 1999 production, the music was based on a combination of folk songs from different eras, simply arranged by Bell to be played on his violin, whilst the music for the 2006–7 production under the influence of Jon Trenchard made use of a capella songs, adapted from traditional Elizabethan folk tunes into 'four to six part harmony in a 20th century Vaughan Williams style' (Trenchard). Trenchard's arrangements were also influenced by Hall's assertion that 'he saw all the characters in Illyria being trapped in repetitive cycles until the twins begin to change their perceptions', using repeated chords and phrases and keeping all the music in the key of C minor, gradually morphing into the relative major and reaching this in the final verse of the final song: the intention was to give 'the audience the unconscious feeling of liberation and relief at the very end of the play – again to use the music to enhance the story-telling' (Trenchard). As can be seen from this comment, Propeller's work emphasises clarity in story-telling for its modern audiences.

Attempts to create an 'authentic' experience of the Renaissance theatre through an adherence to elements of Elizabethan theatre practice are subject to challenges inherent not only in the expectations and reactions of a modern audience, but also in the nature of the 21st-century theatre and its actors. The Globe's production of *Twelfth Night*, for example, came in for criticism about its lack of consistency in 'original practices' casting. As Michael Dobson wryly observed, 'apparently sexual discrimination can be permitted in the name of historical authenticity, but not racial' (258). Dobson refers to the casting of the black actor Terence Maynard as Orsino at Middle Temple Hall, a move undoubtedly influenced by modern regulations relating to racial equality in the work-place and one which director Tim Carroll defends on the basis that '"it's a pure accident of history" that there were no black actors then' (Rawson). However, Carroll's comment clearly indicates the confusion within the theatre as to the balance between authenticity and modernity in 'original practices'. Is it not also an 'accident of history' that the original Globe did not have electrical lighting, sound equipment, and the finances to employ a cast of hundreds? And, if so, might the theatre not just as well employ all these elements in its productions?

Another concession to the modern theatre made by the Globe 'original practices' productions is, of course, the presence of a director and the inclusion of a standard four-to-five-week rehearsal period for each production. This practice stands at odds with Renaissance theatre practice, in which there was no such directorial figure and a period between productions of no more than two weeks, leaving minimal time for rehearsal. One might question why, if the company is keen to explore elements of Elizabethan staging through its productions, it is not keen to experiment with the use of individual cue parts, limited group rehearsal, and the absence of a directorial figure. The answer is surely that this practice stands at too great odds to the customary experience of 21st-century actors and audiences and the sort of preparatory work with which they are familiar. The preparation process for *Twelfth Night* demonstrated the inevitable influence of modern conceptions of character building. One of the exercises carried out in the first week of rehearsals involved the actor playing Viola speaking his lines referring to each of the other characters, and the other actors speaking their characters' lines about Viola, in order that the company might gain an overall impression of the character (Ryan 12–13). For Renaissance actors, working from individual parts containing only their own lines and a brief cue, such character information would not have been available when preparing for a role. Nevertheless, as Yolanda Vasquez explains, the role of the director or 'Master of Play', as he was known under Rylance's artistic directorship, has tended, in the 'original practices' productions, to be more 'organic': 'mostly it is up to us to find the movement and the rhythm ourselves, and the director is there to make sure that it does look okay and to make sure that the story is being told'.

Edward Hall is, by contrast, a more noticeable presence as a director. Propeller's productions, whilst simple in terms of staging and technical aspects, have, as Bell notes, been 'very conceptually based', with the concepts 'worked out way before we start rehearsals' by director Hall and designer Michael Pavelka. The concept for the company's production of *Twelfth Night* was based primarily on the French film *Last Year at Marienbad*, 'a black and white film' in which 'perspectives change [...] nothing really happens – everyone is in evening dress performing actions that never really begin and never really end. It is a mysterious and rather decadent setting' (Bell). It was also influenced by sources as diverse as the ballroom scene in Stanley Kubrick's *The Shining* and the commedia dell'arte (Bell). The play began with Feste entering the stage, which was ridden with dust-sheets, and revealing the characters hidden beneath them. Meanwhile, the company, when not required by the action, would lurk in or near the large onstage wardrobes as masked observers, in a manner that clearly draws some influence from the work of Brecht. Hall's production did not attempt to drag Shakespeare up to date by giving the production a recognisable and specific 21st-century setting. Rather, it drew on imagery with which contemporary audience members might be familiar, whilst retaining a symbolic quality. The set was simple and versatile and the use of props minimal, allowing one scene to move swiftly into another, a feature of Elizabethan staging that Hall sees as essential to the successful performance of Shakespeare.

Both the Globe 'original practices' and Propeller productions, then, have employed elements of Renaissance-inspired staging – minimal set and properties that permit a continuity of action, the encouragement of interaction between actor and audience, and live music and sound effects – which I would argue are extremely successful in providing the plays with the pace, simplicity, and imaginative appeal that must have been a feature of their presentation on the Renaissance stage. However, whilst the Globe productions have been concerned with adhering to an Elizabethan aesthetic and its practice, Propeller's work has combined these elements with the use of modern dress, properties, and music, creating a different form of authenticity through a closer replication of audience experience rather than a greater accuracy of reproduction. I would argue that this type of 'authenticity', which appeals to a shared cultural code between stage and audience, is more successful in engaging spectators and providing them with visual and aural signifiers as to the social and emotional status of the characters.

As this discussion has illustrated, it is impossible to recreate the experience of seeing (or hearing) or performing Shakespeare's plays on the Renaissance stage. Attempts to mirror precisely Elizabethan theatre practice inevitably fall foul of 21st-century employment regulations, institutional methods, actor training, and customary theatrical practice. As a result, the Globe 'original practices' productions seem inconsistent in their relationship to Renaissance theatre practice: not employing women but employing black actors, clothing the actors in authentic Renaissance clothing in order to inform their movement and characterisation, but providing them with a rehearsal process that makes use of modern theatre techniques and post-Stanislavskian methods of characterisation. Equally, no matter how 'authentic' a production might be in its adherence to early modern theatre practice (much of which is, in any case, unrecoverable), since a modern audience cannot be rendered 'authentic' in their cultural and social experiences and sensibilities, their experience of such a production is likely to be quite different from that of the original audiences. The recreation of the subtleties of Renaissance clothing and etiquette does not contain the meaning for 21st-century audiences that it did for sixteenth-century ones. Similarly, for a modern audience, whose primary encounter with male cross-dressing in the theatre is the pantomime dame or drag-queen figures such as Dame Edna Everage and Lily Savage, the experience of watching a man play the role of a woman differs significantly from that of a Renaissance audience, for whom this was customary practice.

The reviews of these two productions give an indication of the way in which they engaged with a modern audience. Whilst both were extremely well received, the focus of the reviews of each was quite different. Those for the Globe production stressed the stylistic elements of the production: the 'authentic Elizabethan experience' to which the audiences were treated, with its 'fabulous', 'beautiful' costumes (respectively, Cavendish, 'Review'; Brown; Coveney). Brian Logan's *Time Out* review hailed the production as 'Shakespeare as it should be',[4] epitomising the sensibility that maintains that Shakespeare performed in a Renaissance setting is somehow closer to the 'intentions' of the author. By contrast, the Propeller reviews seemed more concerned with the mood of the piece:[5] its ability to mix broad humour with melancholy and the 'ingenuity and imagination' behind the production (Spencer). It is interesting to note that Mark Shenton's comment about the 'novelty of the youthful, vigorous reinvention' (46) of the play seems partly

---

[4] Maddy Costa in the *Guardian* cited the production as 'The Globe's most historically authentic to date', John Peter in the *Sunday Times* as 'a true Elizabethan performance' (697), and John Gross in the *Sunday Telegraph* as fulfilling 'what surely must be one of the theatre's principal aims – giving audiences some idea of what performance at the original Globe would have been like'.

[5] Michael Billington (*Guardian*) commented on the production's ability to capture 'the play's opal-like shifts of mood: the sadness within the comedy, and the absurdity within the love story', Spencer (*Daily Telegraph*) on the 'atmosphere of something rich and strange', and Sarah Hemming (*Financial Times*) on its 'dreamy strangeness', whilst Patrick Marmion (*Mail*) found, in the mixture of 'grotesque comedy' and 'dark undercurrents', 'Fun that makes you think' (46).

inspired by the all-male casting, a feature that in the Globe production was interpreted by critics as traditional. That the same feature of two productions can be interpreted so differently is indicative of the contrasting styles of the two and the atmosphere conjured by each: the Globe's of 'authenticity' and Propeller's of 'comic and theatrical invention' (Shenton 47).

It seems that, with the departure of Mark Rylance from the Globe, 'original practices' productions have had their day. Under the artistic directorship of Dominic Dromgoole, we can see a move towards a style of staging Shakespeare that, whilst drawing on the influences of the space and the practices of the Elizabethan theatre, has abandoned the rhetoric of 'original practices' and instead opened itself to a more liberal approach: 'It's impossible to pursue authenticity without a degree of anachronism. We'll go with what seems right for each piece' (Cavendish, 'Get ready'). Dromgoole's approach seems more akin to that of Hall and his company. For Dromgoole, like Hall, the power of the Renaissance theatre is based on a 'fierce relationship between the stage and the audience' (Dromgoole), and this feature continues to predominate successfully at the Globe, now that the more dogmatic fidelities to Elizabethan stage practice have ebbed away. At the same time, the work of Propeller continues to engage audiences across the world. With each production exploring new settings and influences, the work constantly adapts to suit the changing tastes of audiences and to incorporate contemporary cultural references that keep the productions fresh and relevant. Meanwhile, approaches to staging Shakespeare that draw on those elements of Renaissance staging practices that effect a connection between actor and audience, encourage the imaginative engagement of the spectator, and allow the plays fluidity and momentum are becoming increasingly common. However, those that prove most successful show an appreciation of the fact that practitioners and audiences are operating within a quite different social, cultural, and technical environment.[6]

---

[6] Michael Boyd's recent productions of the history plays at the RSC were staged in the temporary Courtyard Theatre, a space modelled on Renaissance stages and one 'in which both audience and actors are in continual dialogue' (Piper, 'Histories'). The set was inspired by 'what we know of Shakespeare's own playhouse' and its capacity for 'suggestive possibilities for locations without requiring new scenery for each one' (Piper, 'Histories'). However, whilst the setting of seven of the eight plays was broadly medieval, it drew both on 'images of medieval battlefields, castles and the paintings of Bosch' and 'contemporary artists such as Bacon and Bourgeois' (Piper, 'Histories'). The 'medieval' costumes incorporated anachronistic elements such as 'contemporary army boots' and elements of 'First World War uniforms' (Piper, *Exploring*), and *Richard III*, whilst performed on the same set as the other plays, was designed with a modern setting. Equally, whilst the notion of an ensemble is influenced partly by the largely permanent companies for which Shakespeare wrote, the company has employed women and actors from various ethnic groups, including casting a black Henry VI, in line with modern working practices.

WORKS CITED

Bate, Jonathan, and Eric Rasmussen, eds. *The RSC Shakespeare: The Complete Works*. London: Palgrave Macmillan, 2007.

Bell, Tony. Personal interview. 21 March 2008.

Billington, Michael. Review of *Twelfth Night*, dir. Edward Hall. *Guardian*. *Theatre Record* 27 (2007): 44.

Bradbrook, Muriel. *Shakespeare: The Poet and His World*. London: Methuen, 1980.

Brown, Georgina. Review of *Twelfth Night*, dir. Tim Carroll. *Mail on Sunday*. *Theatre Record* 22 (2002): 695.

Bulman, James C. 'Bringing Cheek by Jowl's *As You Like It* out of the closet: The politics of gay theatre'. *Shakespeare Bulletin* 22.3 (2004): 31–46.

'Queering the Audience: All-male Casts in Recent Productions of Shakespeare'. *A Companion to Shakespeare and Performance*. Ed. Barbara Hodgdon and William B. Worthen. Oxford: Blackwell, 2005. 564–87.

Calvi, Nuala. 'Shakespeare's Globe to be heart of original writing again – Dromgoole'. *The Stage* 17 January 2006. www.thestage.co.uk/newsstory. php/11267/shakespeares-globe-to-be-heart-of-original, accessed 18 April 2008.

Cavendish, Dominic. 'Get ready for some fireworks'. *Telegraph* 1 May 2006. www.telegraph.co.uk/arts/main.jhtml?xml=/arts/2006/05/01/btdromo1. xml&page=2, accessed 25 April 2008.

Review of *Twelfth Night*, dir. Tim Carroll. *Daily Telegraph*. *Theatre Record* 22 (2002): 696.

Costa, Maddy. Review of *Twelfth Night*, dir. Tim Carroll. *Guardian*. *Theatre Record* 22 (2002): 696.

Coveney, Michael. Review of *Twelfth Night*, dir. Tim Carroll. *Daily Mail*. *Theatre Record* 22 (2002): 695.

Crystal, David. *Pronouncing Shakespeare*. Cambridge: Cambridge University Press, 2005.

Dobson, Michael. 'Shakespeare Performances in England, 2002'. *Shakespeare Survey* 56 (2003): 256–86.

Dromgoole, Dominic. 'Dominic Dromgoole of The Globe: Theatre forgets what it's there for'. *Sunday Times* 2 March 2008. http://entertainment.timesonline.co.uk/tol/arts_and_entertainment/stage/theatre/article3448325.ece, accessed 25 April 2008.

Dusinberre, Juliet. 'Squeaking Cleopatras: Gender and Performance in *Antony and Cleopatra*'. *Shakespeare, Theory, and Performance*. Ed. James C. Bulman. London: Routledge, 1996. 46–67.

Egan, Gabriel. 'Hearing or Seeing a Play?: Evidence of Early Modern Theatrical Terminology'. *Ben Jonson Journal* 8 (2001): 327–47.

Finkle, David, 'A Midsummer Night's Dream'. *Theatre Mania* 18 March 2004. www.theatermania.com/content/news.cfm/story/4507, accessed 18 April 2008.

Gross, John. Review of *Twelfth Night*, dir. Tim Carroll. *Sunday Telegraph*. *Theatre Record* 22 (2002): 698.

Gurr, Andrew. 'Staging at the Globe'. *Shakespeare's Globe Rebuilt*. Cambridge: Cambridge University Press, 1997. 159–68.

The Shakespearean Stage. London: Cambridge University Press, 1970.

Hall, Edward. 'A Different Kind of Resonance'. Touring Programme for *The Taming of the Shrew* and *Twelfth Night*, 2007.

'A Midsummer Quartet'. *Theatre Communications Group*. 2006. www.tcg.org/publications/at/Mar04/midsummer.cfm, accessed 26 March 2008.

'Propeller and The Watermill Theatre'. Touring Programme for *A Midsummer Night's Dream*, 2003.

Propeller: In the Company of Men. www.propeller.org.uk, accessed 26 March 2008.

'Theatre: Where There's a Will'. *Sunday Times* 9 January 2005. http://entertainment.timesonline.co.uk/tol/arts_and_Entertainment/article408642.ece, accessed 26 March 2008.

Hall, Peter. *Shakespeare's Advice to the Players*. London: Oberon, 2003.

Hemming, Sarah. Review of *Twelfth Night*, dir. Edward Hall. *Financial Times*. *Theatre Record* 27 (2007): 46.

Hotson, Leslie. *The First Night of Twelfth Night*. London: Rupert Hart-Davis, 1954.

Kennedy, Dennis. 'Shakespeare and Cultural Tourism'. *Theatre Journal* 50.2 (1998): 175–188.

Kiernan, Pauline. *Research Bulletin 2: Henry V*. March 1998. www.globelink.org/docs/Henry_V_1997.pdf, accessed 26 March 2008.

Logan, Brian. Review of *Twelfth Night*, dir. Tim Carroll. *Time Out*. *Theatre Record* 22 (2002): 696.

Mann, David. *Shakespeare's Women: Performance and Conception*. Cambridge: Cambridge University Press, 2008.

Marmion, Patrick. Review of *Twelfth Night*, dir. Edward Hall. *Daily Mail*. *Theatre Record* 27 (2007): 45–6.

Nicol, David. 'Review of *Twelfth Night*', dir. Tim Carroll. *Early Modern Literary Studies* 8.1 (2002): 10.1–23. http://extra.shu.ac.uk/emls/08–1/nicolrev.htm, accessed 18 April 2008.

Peter, John. Review of *Twelfth Night*, dir. Tim Carroll. *Sunday Times*. *Theatre Record* 22 (2002): 696–7.

Piper, Tom. 'Designing the Histories'. *The Histories*. RSC publication, 2008: 42–3.

Exploring Shakespeare: Richard III. www.rsc.org.uk/explore/workspace/2626_2719.htm, accessed 25 April 2008.

Tom Piper on His Role as Associate Designer. 2004. www.rsc.org.uk/rscfiles/tom_piper_designer.pdf, accessed 26 March 2008.

Ravenhill, Mark. 'Surely this is a bit poofy?' *Guardian* 24 January 2005. http://arts.guardian.co.uk/features/story/0,,1397113,00.html, accessed 26 March 2008.

Rawson, Christopher. 'Stage Preview: Shakespearean company brings an original "Twelfth Night" to Pittsburgh'. *Post-Gazette* 2 November 2003. www.postgazette.com/ae/20031102globe1102fnp2.asp, accessed 26 March 2008.

RSC. *Transforming Our Theatres: The Courtyard Theatre.* 2006. www.rsc.org.uk/transformation/courtyard/default.asp, accessed 26 March 2008.

Rutter, Carol Chillington. *Documents of the Rose Playhouse.* Manchester: Manchester University Press, 1984.

Ryan, Jessica. *Research Bulletin 26: Twelfth Night.* July 2002. www.globelink.org/docs/Twelfth_Night.pdf, accessed 26 March 2008.

Salgado, Gamini. *Eyewitnesses of Shakespeare.* London: Chatto and Windus, 1975.

Shenton, Mark. Review of *Twelfth Night*, dir. Edward Hall. *Sunday Express. Theatre Record* 27 (2007): 46–7.

Sierz, Aleks. 'Edward Hall: Like father, like son'. *Independent on Sunday.* 14 August 2003. www.independent.co.uk/arts-entertainment/theatre/features/edward-hall-like-father-like-son-535864.html, accessed 18 April 2008.

Silverstone, Catherine. 'Shakespeare Live: Reproducing Shakespeare at the "New" Globe Theatre'. *Textual Practice* 19 (2005): 31–50.

Smallwood, Robert. 'Director's Shakespeare'. *The Oxford Illustrated History of Shakespeare on Stage.* Ed. Jonathan Bate and Russell Jackson. Oxford: Oxford University Press, 1996. 176–96.

Spencer, Charles. Review of *Twelfth Night*, dir. Edward Hall. *Daily Telegraph. Theatre* 27 (2007): 45.

Styan, J. L. *The Shakespeare Revolution.* Cambridge: Cambridge University Press, 1977.

Taylor, Paul. 'A Night to remember'. *Independent* 2 February 2002, Weekend Review: 9.

Traub, Valerie. 'The Homoerotics of Shakespearean Comedy'. *Shakespeare, Feminism and Gender.* Ed. Kate Chedgzoy. Houndmills: Palgrave, 2001. 135–60.

Trenchard, Jon. Email interview. 28 October 2007.

Vasquez, Yolanda. Personal interview. 19 December 2005.

Woodcock, Peggy. 'Pregnant pause for swell role'. *Chester Chronicle* 30 April 2005. http://shakespearemag.blogspot.com/2005_04_01_archive.html, accessed26 March 2008.

PART II

Attitudes towards sex and gender

CHAPTER 6

Performing beauty on the Renaissance stage

Farah Karim-Cooper

Judith Butler's *Gender Trouble* asks the reader to think of gender as 'a *corporeal style*, an "act" as it were, which is both intentional and performative, where *"performative"* suggests a dramatic and contingent construction of meaning' (177). Butler's early work has been interpreted to suggest the radical freedom with which bodies can transgress socially prescriptive norms, though in subsequent publications she revises this view slightly. She argues, in an interview with Peter Osbourne and Lynne Segal in *Radical Philosophy*, 'that this voluntarist interpretation, this desire for a kind of radical theatrical remaking of the body, is obviously out there in the public sphere. There's a desire for a fully phantasmatic transfiguration of the body. But [...] I don't think that drag is a paradigm for the subversion of gender' (36). Butler insinuates that her purpose in *Gender Trouble* was not to create restrictive parameters by suggesting that being in 'drag', for example, constitutes the total disruption of gender categories, but that cross-dressing is one transgressive instance of gender identity subversion. But she does suggest that gender can be enacted through a 'stylisation' of the body, and I have argued elsewhere that such stylisations are constructed by clothing and adornment. Literary critics of the Renaissance such as Marjorie Garber reinforce the idea of gender performativity by arguing that cross-dressing on the early modern stage brought to light the fact that gender roles are socially constructed. For most new historicist and materialist critics, cross-dressing in early modern England, either for the stage or in the street, 'signaled subversion, resistance, and transgression and that the sex-gender system of early modern England was in a state of flux' (Cressy 439). Although much has been made of the enactment of gender, boy actors, and the Renaissance stage, discussions about representations of female beauty have not really held a place in early modern theatre histories or mainstream Shakespearean criticism. Any investigation into the performance of beauty should sit within the critical discourse on gender performativity, focusing on the relationship between early modern theories of beauty and the materiality of the parts that constructed the boy actor's body and its performance. This chapter is primarily interested in the performance of idealised notions of female beauty on the English Renaissance stage. Did the use of boy actors disrupt or problematise the very notion of 'female' beauty? How did early modern boy actors enact beautiful women in a material, physical sense? And how might these artificial enactments of beauty have shaped or affected audience responses to particular female characters whose beauty seems quite central to their identities?

'PRETTY DIMPLED BOYS' AND THE PROBLEM OF FEMALE BEAUTY

According to early modern biology, 'sexual difference was increasingly viewed as a fact of nature'; however, although 'biological sexual features were certainly considered to be "natural" or essential', they were not 'imagined to be fixed or immutable' (Fisher 2, 6). The mutability of gender identity enables its performance culturally and theatrically. While there have been many studies of performing gender on the English Renaissance stage, very little attention has been paid to the question of staging beauty, as I have said. Stephen Orgel's analysis of the performance of gender does ask an important question: 'What did audiences see when they went to theatre, the female character or the boy beneath the dress?' (31). Orgel's argument, however, manages to evade the issue of beauty, focusing instead on women's apparel as a 'cover for the homoerotic body' (34). Acknowledging that '[t]he boy player was apparently as much an object of erotic attraction for women as for men' (71), Orgel lays down the foundations for uncovering female beauty on the early modern professional stage, but he argues ultimately for the desirability of the boy actor, without questioning what constituted this desirability or how it might have been figured in feminine terms other than through clothing.

Contemporary receptions of female enactments on the professional stage tell us very little about the performance of beauty. The Oxford scholar Henry Jackson contemplates the pity evoked by the King's Men's performance of *Othello* in Oxford in 1610. Focusing on the character of Desdemona, Jackson seemingly erases the identity of the boy by privileging the tragic woman the boy impersonated, demonstrable in Jackson's use of the pronoun 'she': 'although she always acted her whole part supremely well, yet when [...] she fell back upon the bed she implored the pity of the spectators by her very face' (qtd in Orgel 32). Jackson does not acknowledge what Orgel calls the 'double-gendered' figure on the bed. Instead, Desdemona is, for all intents and purposes, a woman able to move the spectators with her face or countenance. Aristotelian and Renaissance physiognomy designated the face as the outward codifier for mental or internal character. The boy actor performing the part of Desdemona in this performance was clearly skilled at registering his character's pain and grief, so much that it moved the spectators to pity. Another equally valid interpretation, however, is that the facial beauty of the boy actor was able to evoke the same response from the audience. Neo-Platonic philosophies of beauty accounted for its ability to move one to tears because outward beauty reflected inward grace. The question that seems unanswerable, however, is whether this 1610 audience responded emotionally to the acting skills of the boy or to his pity-evoking beauty.

Orgel cites Chapman's *May Day* as another example of the double-gendering of the boy actor, without making anything of particular verbal cues as to his physical beauty. Leonoro's boy is hired out as an actor, and Quintiliano says:

Afore heaven, 'tis a sweet-faced child, methinks he should show well in woman's attire … I'll help thee to three crowns a week for him, and she can act well. Hast ever practised, my pretty Ganymede? (3.3.228–33, qtd in Orgel 32)

The use of the terms 'sweet-faced' and 'pretty' is meant to gesture towards the good looks of the prospective boy actor. But Orgel's analysis does not concern itself with what passages like this tell us about the physical beauty of boy actors: whether it was a necessary prerequisite or a determining factor in the provocation of desire. What these verbal cues indicate is that often the performance of female identity is implicitly linked to the performance of beauty and that female beauty was often characterised in the same way as the beauty of young children. The love poetry of the Italian Renaissance drew upon ideals of beauty that had been established in ancient Greece and Rome. Elizabethan poets were heavily influenced by both traditions, but mainly by painting poetic portraits of women with golden hair, high foreheads, pale complexions, and vermilion cheeks. It has been argued that by the Renaissance period the ideal of beauty was related in explicitly feminine terms. Charting the evolution of beauty theory, Anthony Synnott notes that 'the paradigms of heavenly love, and perfect beauty, were male, for the Greeks (*Symposium* 180–81); indeed it was not until the Renaissance that the female became the paradigm of beauty' (613). I would complicate this argument, however, by suggesting that the motif of the beautiful boy in Renaissance literature demonstrates the high value placed upon the beauty of young children, specifically boys. As Rictor Norton's study of homosexual desire in pastoral poetry argues, the beautiful boy was dominantly personified by Cupid or Adonis, and in examining the latter as the archetype of masculine beauty Norton suggests that Venus's passion for him is actually her desire to claim his beauty as hers. Indeed, Adonis's features resemble those of the mistresses of sixteenth-century love poetry, with lily, rose, and ivory tints.

Significantly, the figure of Adonis is described by Venus as 'more lovely than a man', designating his liminal position between boy and manhood. The description of his beauty represents a conflation of the classical and Italian traditions. He is described, seemingly, in feminine terms:

> 'Thrice fairer than myself,' thus she began,
> 'The field's chief flower, sweet above compare,
> Stain to all nymphs, more lovely than a man,
> More white and red than doves or roses are,
>   Nature, that made thee with herself at strife,
>   Saith that the world hath ending with thy life.
>   (*Venus and Adonis* lines 7–12)

'Chief flower', 'more white and red than doves or roses': while typifying the Renaissance archetype of male beauty, Adonis simultaneously represents the archetype of female beauty. What is tantalising is that the descriptions of youthful male and female beauty in the Renaissance were the same, suggesting that the fair complexion and the rosy cheeks were signifiers of innocence and virtue. In neo-Platonic terms, these were the key components of external beauty because they were physical manifestations of goodness. But when we consider the beauty of children, particularly young boy actors, the figure of Cupid emerges as a multifaceted symbol, which generated a variety of complex meanings. Norton's argument about Cupid in Renaissance poetry is that *he* represents a kind of sexual intermediary between the poet and his mistress:

Cupid is not merely an allegorical five-letter word, but a beautiful, young, naked boy. Exclusively heterosexual relationships between one man and one woman are rare in Renaissance love-lyrics: the relationship is nearly always a *menage a trois* [*sic*] between a man, a woman, and this beautiful, young, naked boy. It is a mistake to regard Cupid's every appearance as simply an indicator that the hero has fallen in (heterosexual) love.

The boy actor can be perceived in similar terms. Anti-theatricalists warned against the homoerotically charged pageant of young boys dressing and gesturing like women on the professional stages of early modern London. On the surface, they appeared to be women, but underneath lay the bare bodies of, as Norton describes Cupid, 'beautiful, young' boys. The bodies of the boy actors, through their performances of femininity, mediated heterosexual desire even while they triggered anxieties about its convergence with homoerotic provocation. In this way, the beauty of the boy actor is linked to the psychosexual desire it may have provoked from an audience.

Michael Shapiro's inquiry into cross-dressing and cross-casting in the public playhouses raises the question of how boy actors or 'play-boys' would have performed female gender identity, but dismisses such a question owing to the lack of evidence about performance practices. Lucy Munro's study of the Children of the Queen's Revels highlights episodes in the company's repertory when the female body, for example Sophonisba's, 'is to be admired, desired and objectified' (144). Munro's thoroughgoing research into the repertory of one company of boys demonstrates that it was a well-established tradition for boy actors to perform not only beauty, but virtue as well, each of which, as we have seen, was synonymous with the other according to neo-Platonic theory. Although Munro's purpose does not include discussion of the company's potential materialisations of female beauty, her work provides many examples in the repertory of the Children of the Queen's Revels where the portrayal of beauty, desirability, and virtuous heroine-ism was necessary. These qualities are particular to youth and to femininity, but the *type* of beauty enacted on the part of young boy actors, whether regarded so or not, was *intended* to at least gesture toward female. However, given that the features of male, pre-adolescent beauty had a strong identification with those of female beauty, perhaps it did not register explicitly as one or the other.

Nevertheless, the beauty of women was a common preoccupation of early modern playwrights. Before delving any further into the question of how female beauty might have been enacted or understood to have been enacted on the early modern stage, it is important to remind ourselves what general conceptions of beauty shaped the Renaissance ideal. The standard of beauty established by early Greek and Roman philosophers was enlarged upon by the architects of aesthetic philosophy during the Italian and English Renaissance. Plato's philosophy of beauty set out in his *Symposium* hinged upon the idea that beauty was an outward sign of goodness, which in turn led to wisdom and happiness – an internal attribute manifested outwardly. Aristotle's departure from Platonic theory lay mostly in the shift in focus from the interior to the exterior. For him and many others, the properties of true beauty were proportion, symmetry, and chromatic harmony: 'the chief forms of beauty are order and symmetry and definiteness' (*Metaphysics*, qtd in Synnott 614). Synnott points out that '[f]aces, rather than beauty, were what fascinated Aristotle', but that he saw the face as a pertinent register for the 'mental character' of the subject (614). Both Classical and Renaissance commentators defined female beauty not as a construct, but rather as an external sign of internal goodness. Władysław Tatarkiewicz points out that the Sophists of Athens 'defined beauty as "that which is pleasant to sight or hearing"' (165). This definition broadened the idea of what might be beautiful, as beauty became attributed not only to art but to music as well. By the fifteenth century, neo-Platonic philosophers had already developed the relationship between outward and inward beauty to incorporate the doctrines of Christian virtue and divine inhabitance. Marsilio Ficino talks about beauty as a reflection of God's countenance: 'the source of all beauty and love is God', he writes (230).

Formulations of beauty in early modern England tended to incorporate most of the varying Classical, medieval, and continental theories. Generally, beauty was aesthetic; it was physical and metaphysical, and, whether masculine or feminine, it reflected virtue – 'the comeliest outsides are naturally [...] more virtuous within' – and was defined by its ability to please (Feltham 324). What was equally dominant and related to the neo-Platonic formulations was the idea that to be beautiful or 'fair' was to be white, but with a 'lustre', a radiant shine that indicated the pious virtue of the subject, as Thomas Campion muses: 'Follow those pure beames whose beautie burneth, / That have so scorched thee' (lines 9–10). Focusing specifically on female beauty, Agnolo Firenzuola's fifteenth-century treatise on the beauty of women insists that the skin of the woman must be white *and* glistening to create that 'certain luster, as ivory does' (15), and this chromatic ideal endured throughout the early modern period. The use of artificial means, however, to construct this formula of beauty was deemed philosophically (but not necessarily culturally) to be unacceptable because beauty was defined by its relationship to nature, and, for Renaissance Protestants, nature was synonymous with God. If indeed beauty is constructed cosmetically, then it is not true beauty, which, according to neo-Platonic theory, is luminous, divine, and rooted in spiritual piety. Returning, then, to the question of boy actors, given these definitions, female beauty on stage in a material sense must be artificially constructed; therefore, because it is an *enactment* of beauty, it is not true beauty. The beauty attributed to music is true, because it is linked, as

Thomas Browne outlines, to 'harmony, order, or proportion: and thus far we may maintain the music of the spheres'; in other words it is celestial and divine (347). Equally, as Tatarkiewicz reminds us, 'the words *harmonia* and *symmetria* were closely connected with the theory's application to the domains of hearing and sight respectively' (167). Thus, visual art and architecture also relied upon symmetry and proportion and therefore could aspire to true beauty. But how did early modern theorists define theatrical beauty? Thomas Heywood offers the most famous defence of acting, suggesting that the art deserved to be classed into the same aesthetic category as painting:

> Oratory is a kind of a speaking picture [...] Painting likewise, is a dumbe oratory, therefore may we not as well by some curious *Pigmalion*, drawe their conquests to worke the like loue in Princes towards these Worthyes by shewing them their pictures drawne to the life, as it wrought on the poore painter to bee inamored of his owne shadow [?] (*Sig.* B3v)

Heywood's argument is that, like painters, theatrical orators have the ability to create images that evoke powerful responses. Thus, the cognitive reception of performance is linked to its beauty; the audience determines the aesthetic value of the theatrical product.

Although the precise effect of the performance of beauty cannot be known with any certainty or exactness, it seems clear that, whether or not audiences responded to the beauty of the young boys or to their female enactments, during the Renaissance they were both defined in the same terms: pale complexions, rosy cheeks, glowing skin, and curly golden tresses comprised the feminine ideal as well as the prepubescent masculine one. Shakespeare acknowledges this double-gendered ideal when he writes in praise of the beauty of his young male subject in Sonnet 20: 'A woman's face with natures own hand painted, / Hast thou the Master Mistris of my passion' (lines 1–2). Perhaps, then, the employment of boy actors is evidence enough that ideal female beauty was not entirely un-representable on the early modern stage. Yet the question remains of whether or not boy actors could perform a radiant, luminous beauty without the help of white lead and egg glaze, or ground hog's jawbone with poppy oil, or a sprinkling of crushed pearl. In my view, boy actors would have used make-up, which raises a paradox: cosmetic beauty was designated false and corrupt, but on stage cosmetics constructed a kind of theatrical beauty.

Dramatic attempts to represent beauty are also cued by stage directions and by the many descriptions of beauty located in early modern play texts.

Such cues may gesture toward a set of understood conventions, what Alan Dessen calls 'theatrical vocabulary' developed between the playwrights, the actors, and the audience. In fact, detailed descriptions of beauty in plays may point to the recognition that true beauty is absent on stage. Meanwhile, the lack of description may *also* point to the absence or un-representability of true beauty, such as Marlowe's apostrophe to Helen of Troy in *Dr Faustus*. When Faustus asks 'Was this the face that launched a thousand ships, /And burnt the topless towers of Ilium?' (5.1.108–9), he emphasises the power of her legendary beauty and designates the face as the primary location and manifestation of human beauty, but he does not describe it. Helen's beauty is un-representable because, fundamentally, beauty exists in its subjective reception. Shakespeare demonstrates this point in *The Two Gentlemen of Verona*, when Julia examines the portrait of Sylvia and compares their features:

> Here is her picture: let me see; I think
> If I had such a tire, this face of mine
> Were full as lovely as is this of hers;
> And yet the painter flatter'd her a little,
> Unless I flatter with myself too much.
> Her hair is auburn, mine is perfect yellow:
> If that be all the difference in his love,
> I'll get me such a color'd periwig.
> Her eyes are grey as glass, and so are mine;
> Ay, but her forehead's low, and mine's as high.
> What should it be that he respects in her,
> But I can make respective in myself,
> If this fond Love were not a blinded god? (4.4.184–96)

Julia points out that her hair is 'yellow' – the desired colour according to poetic tradition – and that her eyes are the same colour as, and her forehead no lower than, her rival's. In other words, she is at least if not more attractive than Sylvia, but, strangely, Proteus, like Demetrius in *A Midsummer Night's Dream*, destabilises the traditional ideal of beauty by manifesting a preference for an alternative female aesthetic. The passage would seem to suggest, however, that it is quite simple to perform various modes of beauty: 'I'll get me such a color'd periwig' indicates that the prosthetic attachment of false hair makes it easy to imitate the preferred woman in the portrait, even if it means that established ideals of beauty must be subverted through cosmetic alteration. What this passage plainly suggests is that beauty is complexly subjective. It would seem, then, that when one is called beautiful on stage, it is up to the audience to imagine what exactly that beauty is; particularly in Shakespearean drama, beauty is presented as multifaceted, suggesting that its performance was equally varied. In the meantime, while the passage suggests that beauty is subjective, it also asks the audience to believe Julia *is* a beautiful woman even as she is impersonated by a young male actor who may or may not be a beautiful boy. This passage requires the audience to enable the performance of beauty by imagining it, perhaps suggesting that a 'realistic' portrayal would have worried the actors very little. While the interrogation of normative beauty in this scene may stem from its un-representability on stage, true beauty can nevertheless be enacted, encoded through the bodies of the actors, through their cosmeticised impersonations, and through their gestures and movements. As it only exists in the 'eye of the beholder', it is also registered and perceived by the audience.[1]

While one theory of beauty emphasises the abstract notions of piety, virtue, and goodness, another theory focuses on the concrete features of beauty, such as hair colour, eyes, facial complexion, lips, neck, hands, the sound of the voice, height, deportment, and gesture. The possibility of cosmetic embellishment has further problematised aesthetic theories of beauty in Renaissance discourse: because the physical embodiment of the ideal of beauty is accessible, easily imitated through the acquisition and consumption of material ingredients, beauty is also a commodity. Professional acting companies would have had access to this commodity because it was essential to their theatrical imaginings. Cosmetics, costumes, wigs, and jewellery all enable the performance of gender and, more specifically, are the tools for constructing a stylised version of female beauty or theatrical beauty. Performances of femininity by boys in the early modern period highlighted the fact that female physical beauty was composed of symmetrical and chromatic interrelationships between detachable parts.

MATERIALISING BEAUTY: THE ACTOR'S 'PARTS'

On stage, beauty is conveyed by outward signs, such as the ones I have just listed; therefore, beauty is semiotic. Female beauty is also constructed from detachable parts; therefore, beauty can be characterised as prosthetic as well. In his analysis of the materialisation of the gendered body, Will Fisher discusses the various theories of prosthesis, settling upon the notion that, 'although prostheses are in a sense objects that can be removed from

---

[1] I am grateful to Tom Cornford for this idea of beauty being encoded through the bodies of actors.

the body, they also shape or materialize the body and self in important ways' (31). Fisher sees cultural artefacts as well as detachable parts of the body, such as hair and beards, as identity-forming objects that constitute prosthesis. His focus is on how cultural artefacts 'work to "fashion" the sexed body and produce masculinity and femininity' (19). In my own study of cosmetics in the Renaissance period, I identify the contemporary perception of cosmetic beauty as fundamentally prosthetic (Karim-Cooper), demonstrating how this fact of beauty was satirised notoriously in Jacobean city comedy, specifically by Ben Jonson. In *Epicoene, or the Silent Woman* (1609), Mistress Otter's husband reveals the secrets of his wife's dressing chamber and reduces her to nothing but cosmetic parts, suggesting the absence of beauty on the surface or beneath the layers of objects:

A most vile face! and yet she spends me forty pound a year in mercury and hog's-bones. All her teeth were made i' the Blackfriars, both her eyebrows i' the Strand, and her hair in Silver-street. Every part o' the town owns a piece of her [...] She takes herself asunder still when she goes to bed, into some twenty boxes; and about next day noon is put together again for an hour, but for her quarters [...] (4.1.255–62)

While this satirical blazon is designed to mock contemporary female adornment rituals, it also self-reflexively gestures to the medium of theatre itself and highlights the figure of the boy actor, whose eyebrows might indeed have been purchased in the Strand and wig in Silver Street, and who very likely was constructed of parts that may have been found in boxes in the tiring house. Ironically, however, all of these parts put together, according to Otter, create a kind of grotesque figure, a monster of sorts – the very opposite of beauty. Mary Shelley's Dr Frankenstein was misled by the theory of prosthetic beauty that suggested that the compilation of separate, perfect parts should result in a perfect, harmonious whole. But the opposite was true for many Renaissance writers and satirists like Jonson. Jonson, who spent years writing for boy companies and was perhaps well versed in their adornment practices back stage, seems to suggest that beauty cannot be constructed through artificial means; does this mean then that it cannot be performed within these theatrical conditions?

Anti-theatricality was another strand of audience reception in early modern England, and the portraits these writers painted of boy actors in women's clothing were often grotesque, monstrous, androgynous, or hermaphroditic. The horror for a Puritan like William Prynne, who published his anti-theatrical polemic *Histrio-Mastix* in 1633, is the mutability of the actor's body, that it can transform itself into something other (particularly the female 'other') than what God has designed, and by definition this would constitute ugliness. Thomas Beard in *The Theatre of God's Ivdgements* (1597) writes that men who dressed in women's clothing and 'ornaments' became 'lascivious and effeminate' and 'monstrous' (419–20). What these examples show is the importance placed upon the outward parts in determining not only gender identity but also aesthetic quality. For these writers and other anti-cross-dressing polemicists, the articles of clothing and adornments that say 'woman', once placed on the body of a boy or young man, corrupt and deform his body; in other words, these prosthetic accoutrements do not allow for the performance of beauty, but rather the performance of a cross-gendered deformity.

Will Fisher deliberately broadens definitions of the body and prosthesis accordingly to include items like hair, beards, handkerchiefs, and codpieces, seeing them 'as things that are unproblematically assimilated into the body and self' and finding 'continuity between interior and exterior, as between nature and culture, sex and gender' (32, 33). There is a similar relationship between an actor and the prosthetic parts that help to construct the character he is portraying, the prosthetic parts thus enabling continuity between actor and character. The parts of beauty that would have been available to Elizabethan and Jacobean actors included periwigs, facial paint (white and black), lip colours, vermilion for cheeks, and cork and kohl for eye enhancement. Boy actors would very likely have used make-up to create their 'beautiful women'; Olivia in *Twelfth Night* provides a crucial example, because her beauty is a subject for consideration in the play: she protests that her beauty is natural (as would any self-respecting aristocratic lady who paints her face), although Viola (as Cesario), being female and acquainted with the secrets of a lady's chamber, boldly insinuates that the opposite may be true. Whether or not Olivia is a painted lady, this scene clearly marks a self-reflexive moment in the theatre, as the boy actor playing her emphatically denies his character is painted, even as he is painted up to signify his female role. The facial paint in this instance thus enables continuity between the actor and the character he embodies. The scene also interrogates contemporary definitions of female beauty, by demonstrating that the impersonation of it is so viable, and also by not giving away the precise detail of Olivia's beauty.

In attempting to answer the question of how beauty might have been performed on the early modern stage, I have suggested that, first, one must examine the theories of beauty shaping the Elizabethan and

Jacobean ideal; second, it is important to incorporate into the theory of gender performativity the constitutive properties of female beauty. I have suggested two possibilities for the performance of female beauty on the early modern stage: one, that it is possible through the mediating body of the beautiful boy actor and a range of material prosthetics that could construct a kind of theatrical beauty, and, two, that the performance of beauty regardless of its precise definition would be enabled by the audience's cognitive engagement. A third possibility depends upon whether or not painted or prosthetically enhanced femininity was perceived as actual beauty, or a mere representation of it, or a theatrical *interpretation* of it. In some of Shakespeare's plays, characters looking upon painted beauty can experience the same feelings of awe, wonder, and pleasure that we feel when looking upon a perfectly symmetrical sculpture or piece of art or when listening to a mathematically precise musical score. In *The Merchant of Venice*, for example, Bassanio's triumph in the casket scene is followed by a brief apostrophe to Portia's counterfeit:

> Here are sever'd lips,
> Parted with sugar breath; so sweet a bar
> Should sunder such sweet friends. Here in her hairs
> The painter plays the spider, and hath woven
> A golden mesh t'entrap the hearts of men
> Faster than gnats in cobwebs. But her eyes –
> How could he see to do them? Having made one,
> Methinks it should have power to steal both his
> And leave itself unfurnish'd. Yet look how far
> The substance of my praise doth wrong this shadow
> In underprizing it, so far this shadow
> Doth limp behind the substance. (3.2.118–29)

For a moment, Bassanio is enraptured by the beautiful portrait of his mistress. He looks into the painted eyes, admires the golden tresses of her hair, and imagines the sugary breath that might emit from the carefully 'sever'd lips'. It is an absolute portrait of beauty – but he suddenly realises that he dwells on the 'shadow' when the 'substance' is standing right next to him. This is a perplexing moment on stage. What do we see? It is unlikely that the audience can see the painting, so it relies upon the detailed description; although the boy actor painted with cosmetics and wearing a blond periwig might indeed reflect the description, we have already determined that we can never know how realistically beautiful the enactment of femininity was. But Sophistic aesthetic theory suggests that beauty lies in its effect upon the observer. For Shakespeare the point of this stage-picture – an apostrophe to painted beauty, next to a painted boy actor – is to suggest that the enactment of beauty relies upon two things: the reaction or response of the character to an embodied object of beauty, and the audience's collaborative and collective reinforcement of such responses. The boy actor performing the beautiful heiress performs an ideal of beauty that can be expressed through either pre-adolescent male or female features, but Portia's true beauty is, finally, entirely enacted or constructed through the detailed description of the painted representation, thus leaving it to the audience to imagine and to determine its essential nature.

WORKS CITED

Beard, Thomas. *The Theatre of God's Ivdgements: reuised, and augmented.* London, 1631.

Browne, Thomas. *Religio Medici. Seventeenth Century Prose and Poetry.* Ed. Alexander M. Witherspoon and Frank J. Warnke. 2nd edn. New York and London: Harcourt Brace Jovanovich, 1982. 334–49.

Butler, Judith. *Gender Trouble: Feminism and the Subversion of Identity.* New York and London: Routledge, 1990.

Campion, Thomas. 'Follow thy faire sunne unhappy shadowe'. *The Penguin Book of Renaissance Verse.* Ed. David Norbrook and H. R. Woudhuysen. Harmondsworth: Penguin, 1993. 329–30.

Cressy, David. 'Gender Trouble and Cross-Dressing in Early Modern England'. *Journal of British Studies* 35.4 (1996): 438–65.

Dessen, Alan C. *Recovering Shakespeare's Theatrical Vocabulary.* Cambridge: Cambridge University Press, 1995.

Feltham, Owen. 'Of Women'. *Resolves, Divine, Moral and Political. Seventeenth Century Prose and Poetry.* Ed. Alexander M. Witherspoon and Frank J. Warnke. 2nd edn. New York and London: Harcourt Brace Jovanovich, 1982. 323–4.

Ficino, Marsilio. *Commentary on Plato's Symposium. Philosophies of Art and Beauty: Selected Readings in Aesthetics from Plato to Heidegger.* Ed. Albert Hofstadter and Richard Kuhns. Chicago: Chicago University Press, 1964.

Firenzuola, Agnolo. *On the Beauty of Women.* Trans. Konrad Eisenbichler and Jacqueline Murray. Philadelphia: University of Pennsylvania Press, 1992.

Fisher, Will. *Materializing Gender in Early Modern English Literature and Culture.* Cambridge: Cambridge University Press, 2005.

Garber, Marjorie. *Vested Interests: Cross-Dressing and Cultural Anxiety.* London: Routledge, 1991.

Heywood, Thomas. *An Apology for Actors.* London, 1612.

Jonson, Ben. *Epicoene; or the Silent Woman.* 1609. *Drama of the English Renaissance, Vol. 2: The Stuart Period.* Ed. Russell A. Fraser and Norman Rabkin. New York: Macmillan, 1976. 101–41.

Karim-Cooper, Farah. *Cosmetics in Shakespearean and Renaissance Drama.* Edinburgh: Edinburgh University Press, 2006.

Marlowe, Christopher. *Dr Faustus.* 1592. *Drama of the English Renaissance, Vol. 1: The Tudor Period.* Ed. Russell A. Fraser and Norman Rabkin. New York: Macmillan, 1976. 297–321.

Munro, Lucy. *The Children of the Queen's Revels.* Cambridge: Cambridge University Press, 2005.

Norton, Rictor. *The Homosexual Literary Tradition: An Interpretation.* New York: Revisionist Press, 1974. Also online as 'Lovely Lad and Shame-Faced Catamite'. *The Homosexual Pastoral Tradition.* http://rictornorton.co.uk/pastor05.htm, accessed February 2008.

Orgel, Stephen. *Impersonations: The Performance of Gender in Shakespeare's England.* Cambridge: Cambridge University Press, 1996.

Osbourne, Peter, and Lynne Segal. 'An Interview with Judith Butler'. *Radical Philosophy* 67 (1994): 32–9.

Prynne, William. *Histrio-Mastix: The Players Scourge.* London, 1633.

Shakespeare, William. *The Riverside Shakespeare.* Ed. G. Blakemore Evans. Boston, Mass.: Houghton Mifflin, 1974.

Shapiro, Michael. *Gender in Play on the Shakespearean Stage: Boy Heroines and Female Pages.* Ann Arbor: University of Michigan Press, 1994.

Synnott, Anthony. 'Truth and Goodness: Mirrors and Masks – Part 1: A Sociology of Beauty and the Face'. *British Journal of Sociology* 40.4 (1990): 607–36.

Tatarkiewicz, Władysław. 'The Great Theory of Beauty and its Decline'. *Journal of Aesthetics and Art Criticism* 31.2 (1972): 165–80.

CHAPTER 7

The artistic, cultural, and economic power of the actress in the age of Garrick

Fiona Ritchie

The fame of the eighteenth-century actress Hannah Pritchard has now faded from theatre history, eclipsed by that of David Garrick, the leading theatrical figure of the day. But Pritchard was of great significance to the playgoing public of her era. On 5 November 1772 an announcement appeared in the *London Evening Post*:

The following is the inscription upon the monument of Mrs. Pritchard, which was put up last Wednesday at the East end of Westminster-abbey, next to Shakespeare, and opposite to Handel's monument:

'This tablet is here placed by a voluntary subscription of those who admired and esteemed her. She retired from the stage, of which she had long been the ornament, in the month of April 1768, and died at Bath in the month of August following, in the 57th year of her age.

> Her comic vein had ev'ry charm to please,
> 'Twas nature's dictates breath'd with nature's ease.
> E'en when her powers sustain'd the tragic load,
> Full, clear, and just, th'harmonious accents flow'd;
> And the big passions of her feeling heart
> Burst freely forth, and sham'd the mimic art.
> Oft, on the scene, with colours not her own,
> She painted vice, and taught us what to shun;
> One virtuous track her real life pursu'd.
> That nobler part was uniformly good.
> Each duty there to such perfection wrought,
> That, if the precepts fail'd, the example taught.
> W. WHITEHEAD, P.L.'

Pritchard was so greatly admired by the theatre audience that a subscription fund was raised in order to memorialise her in Westminster Abbey, one of the nation's most sacred spots, next to the statue of Shakespeare, placed there by a similar subscription in 1741 as eighteenth-century bardolatry heightened. The monument included an expression of her public's admiration and esteem for the actress, as well as lines composed by the Poet Laureate, praising Pritchard's virtuous life and paying tribute to her natural and passionate acting style.[1]

This little-known detail of theatre history is an important one, since Pritchard's memorialisation alongside Shakespeare occurred several years before Garrick was buried in the same spot in 1779. Indeed, it was not until 1797 that a memorial to Garrick was erected in Poets' Corner. Garrick's interment in Westminster Abbey has long been considered proof of his star status as an actor, and the placing of his monument close to Shakespeare's considered evidence of how much he contributed to bardolatry. In fact, the history of English theatre in the eighteenth century is often narrated through the figure of Garrick. His life story is so well known that he seems to stand in synecdochically for the major changes in the theatre world at this time, including the championing of Shakespeare and the drive to increase the respectability of the acting profession. If Garrick's burial next to Shakespeare in Poets' Corner is considered symbolic of the era, why is Pritchard's commemoration not taken as indicative of eighteenth-century theatre history? The answer seems to lie in the fact that the details of Garrick's career are amply documented in more mainstream and accessible sources such as biography and dramatic criticism, whereas evidence of the actress's impact on theatre and society needs to be sought out by those who care to look.[2] In addition to performance records and dramatic criticism, this chapter examines other sources under-explored by theatre criticism and theatre history. By widening the range of material considered to include lesser-known biographical information, such as particulars of the actress's salary, her wealth at death, and the property she owned, as well as the commemoration of the female performer in painting and print culture, a more detailed understanding of the eighteenth-century Shakespearean actress emerges. Focusing on the careers of Hannah Pritchard and her contemporary Catherine Clive, this analysis of the Shakespearean actress will explore what artistic, cultural, and economic power she was able to exercise in an era in which

---

[1] The Chapter Act Book of Westminster Abbey states that Pritchard's monument was accepted 'on Account of her distinguished Abilities and her unexceptionable moral character'. The Funeral Fee book notes that the monument was paid for by Lord Nuneham. Pritchard's monument was subsequently moved to the triforium (an area of the Abbey currently not accessible to the public) to make way for a memorial to Samuel Johnson, unveiled in 1939.

[2] Recent feminist approaches to theatre history have emphasised the need to consider alternative sources in order to uncover the full details of the onstage and offstage life of the actress. See for example Bratton and Gale and Gardner.

one man seemingly dominated the London stage. How was her performance of Shakespearean roles evaluated? Was she considered respectable
and desirable company in polite society? How much economic autonomy
did she have? The chapter seeks to redress the bias towards Garrick as
Shakespeare's sole champion, taking a fresh look at theatre history and
its sources in order to detail the social and economic standing of female
performers in the mid eighteenth century and their contribution to the
popularisation of Shakespeare.

THE STATUS OF SHAKESPEARE ON THE EIGHTEENTH-CENTURY STAGE AND THE 1740–1 REVIVAL

Garrick's efforts to promote Shakespeare are well known. James Granger's
Biographical History of England claims that 'Mr. Garrick, who thoroughly
understands Shakespeare, has exhibited a thousand of his beauties, which
had before escaped the mob of actors and of readers; and has carried his
fame much higher, than it was ever carried in any former period. It is
hard to say whether Shakespeare owes more to Garrick, or Garrick to
Shakespeare' (1: 288 note). Written in 1769, when Garrick's Shakespeare
Jubilee frenzy was at its height, Granger's evaluation is perhaps exaggerated. Neither does Granger recognise that Garrick deliberately linked
himself with Shakespeare in the public imagination in order to bolster his
own fame. Indeed, as Heather McPherson has noted, Garrick's 'greatest
stroke of genius in the arena of self-fashioning was undoubtedly the conflation of his image with Shakespeare's'.[3]

McPherson is right to point out that, although Garrick 'played a seminal role in reclaiming Shakespeare for the stage', he 'did not actually ini-
tiate the Shakespeare revival', as has sometimes been claimed. This was
in fact demonstrated by Arthur H. Scouten as early as 1945, although the
significance of his argument has long been overlooked. Scouten outlines
the boom in performances of Shakespeare in the period before Garrick
took to the stage, a phenomenon to which he would have been exposed,
and concludes that Garrick deliberately took advantage of a 'fashion
[that] had already set in', riding 'the wave of the rapidly increasing popularity of William Shakespeare' ('Shakespeare's Plays' 268). In fact 1740–1,

---

[3] Garrick was so successful at associating himself with Shakespeare in the public imagination that
commentators quickly took up and propagated the idea, as is evident from Granger's comment.
This continued after his death and the inscription on the monument erected to his memory in
1797 explicitly linked Garrick with Shakespeare: 'Shakespeare and Garrick like twin stars shall
shine / And Earth irradiate with a beam divine' (qtd in Stone and Kahrl 644).

the season preceding Garrick's official London acting debut, saw a successful and significant Shakespeare revival. At this time, female performers proved to be instrumental in the restoration of three long-neglected Shakespearean comedies to the Drury Lane stage: *As You Like It*, *Twelfth Night*, and *The Merchant of Venice* all centre on powerful heroines and as such were dependent for much of their success on the actresses who performed these parts. Each of these three revivals featured Hannah Pritchard and Catherine Clive, two of the most talented actresses of their era who both performed in numerous Shakespeare plays.[4]

As You Like It was performed on 20 December 1740, advertised as 'Not Acted these Forty Years' and 'Written by Shakespear'.[5] Phoebe was played by Elizabeth Bennet, Audrey by Mrs Egerton, Celia by Catherine Clive and Rosalind by Hannah Pritchard.[6] This was followed by *Twelfth Night*, staged at Drury Lane on 15 January 1741 with Maria Macklin as Maria, Pritchard as Viola, and Clive as Olivia, billed as 'Never Acted there before' and 'Written by Shakespear'. The third revival was *The Merchant of Venice*, staged at Drury Lane on 14 February 1741 with Clive as Portia and Pritchard as Nerissa. All three productions represented major revivals: *Twelfth Night* had been performed briefly in the Restoration but there is no record of a performance of either *As You Like It* or *The Merchant of Venice* since before the closure of the theatres in 1642.[7] Contemporary commentary on these revivals is scarce, since dramatic criticism was still in its infancy at this time. But, despite the absence of substantial narrative evaluation of the performances of Pritchard and Clive in the 1740–1 season, the performance records clearly demonstrate the success of this

---

[4] The other great Shakespearean actress of the Garrick era was Susannah Cibber. However, since she did not participate in the 1740–1 Shakespeare revival, she is omitted from consideration in this chapter. For another reading of this season which argues that the revival of these three plays, which all prominently feature cross-dressing heroines, was motivated by the success of Margaret Woffington in breeches and travesty roles at Covent Garden earlier in the season, see Ritchie, 'Shakespeare and the Eighteenth-Century Actress'.

[5] All performance information, such as dates, cast lists and quotations from playbills, is taken from Scouten, *The London Stage Part 3*.

[6] Mrs Egerton's first name is not recorded in Highfill, Burnim, and Langhans.

[7] For details of the performance history of Shakespeare's plays after 1660, see Odell. When the impetus for the mid-eighteenth-century Shakespeare revival is not attributed to Garrick, it is often credited to Charles Macklin, who was responsible for the revival of *The Merchant of Venice* (a play that had only been staged in drastically adapted comic form as Granville's *The Jew of Venice* since 1701). Macklin's decision to restore this play to the stage proved enormously popular as the audience felt he used a new, more naturalistic acting style to portray Shylock. But it should be acknowledged that the success of Macklin's revival owed a great deal to Clive and Pritchard, the principal actresses in his company. The trend for reviving Shakespeare plays that featured strong comic roles for women meant that *The Merchant of Venice* was bound to meet with enthusiasm.

revival: *As You Like It* was enormously popular, being performed an incredible twenty-eight times that season, *Twelfth Night* was performed nine times, and *The Merchant of Venice* had an impressive total of twenty performances, running until the end of the season.[8] *As You Like It, Twelfth Night*, and *The Merchant of Venice* became stock plays after their revivals in this season and were still in the repertory at Drury Lane in 1776, when Garrick ceased to be manager.[9] In fact, *The Merchant of Venice* was the most frequently performed Shakespearean comedy in the mid eighteenth century, with *As You Like It* in second place (Lynch 97). Garrick not only took advantage of a pre-existing trend for Shakespeare, he also capitalised on the success of female performers in popularising Shakespeare in performance when he began his own efforts to promote the Bard through his acting career. Clive and Pritchard paved the way for Garrick's arrival on the London theatre scene.

THE ARTISTIC ACHIEVEMENT OF THE SHAKESPEAREAN ACTRESS

Garrick's first official London performance has become the stuff of legend. Thomas Davies describes the event:

On the 19th of October, 1741, David Garrick acted Richard the Third, for the first time, at the playhouse in Goodman's Fields [...] Mr. Garrick's easy and familiar, yet forcible style in speaking and acting, at first threw the critics into some hesitation concerning the novelty as well as propriety of his manner [...] But after he had gone through a variety of scenes in which he gave evident proofs of consummate art, and perfect knowledge of character, their doubts were turned into surprize and astonishment; from which they relieved themselves by loud and reiterated applause. (*Memoirs* 1: 39–40)

Garrick's choice of a Shakespearean role for his debut was probably a calculated one. A few months earlier, on 29 January 1741, the monument to Shakespeare had been unveiled in Poets' Corner, inspired by

---

[8] In addition to the successful reinstatement of these three neglected Shakespeare plays to the stage, the season saw an unprecedented number of performances of Shakespearean drama. Scouten notes that, by the end of the season, Drury Lane had produced fourteen Shakespeare plays for a total of eighty-five performances in 192 acting nights ('Increase' 199). Although seen as Shakespeare's champion, Garrick never made Shakespeare's works such a strong focus of the theatrical repertory during the period in which he managed Drury Lane. Shakespeare plays were also revived at the other theatres, presumably in a bid to compete with Drury Lane: Scouten notes that from mid-December to the end of March there were only six acting nights without a production of Shakespeare at one of the three houses ('Increase' 199).

[9] See Scouten's Table B of repertory plays and revivals ('Increase' 193–4).

the recent revival of his plays on the London stage. This was almost certainly the beginning of Garrick's deliberate strategy to enhance his own reputation by allying himself with Shakespeare's burgeoning fame. The Shakespearean roles performed by Garrick offered him an important means by which to prove his professional worth, providing him with 'classic' parts in which he could demonstrate his acting talent.

Davies's account appears in his biography of Garrick, published in 1780, shortly after Garrick's death, and as such perhaps paints an embellished picture of the actor's debut in a bid to suitably commemorate his achievement. Although neither Clive nor Pritchard was the subject of a major biography in the period, analyses of their acting did appear in the dramatic criticism published later in the century and such accounts supplement the performance data contained in *The London Stage*, providing further evidence of the achievement of the eighteenth-century Shakespearean actress. Just as Shakespeare's works provided Garrick with a means of establishing his histrionic talent, Shakespearean drama also offered actresses a way to prove their acting skill. What is more, an analysis of commentary on Clive and Pritchard further demonstrates their success in popularising Shakespeare on the stage.

Catherine (Kitty) Clive, a key performer in the 1740–1 Shakespeare revival, was praised by Davies as 'the superior comic actress of the theatre' (*Dramatic Micellanies* II: 408) and widely celebrated for her natural and easy manner of acting: 'Original in spirit and in ease, / She pleas'd by hiding all attempts to please' (Churchill lines 413–14). Indeed, she was described in Samuel Derrick's *A General View of the Stage* as a female Garrick:

I believe that of all actresses who have appeared in the comic vein, Mrs. Clive's superior talents have always been pre-eminent [...] Mrs. Clive is not only the most useful, but the most entertaining actress on the Stage: nay, if we consider her variety of powers, and her exertion of them, I fancy we may safely allow her to be the Garrick of the ladies. (287–8)

Clive was also a talented singer and many of her roles (she was a notable Polly in *The Beggar's Opera*) showcased her vocal talents. Indeed, her singing skills were one of the ways in which she popularised Shakespeare: the revival of *As You Like It* was advertised as having 'The Songs new Set by Mr. Arne', and 'When daisies pied' (the 'Cuckoo Song') from *Love's Labour's Lost* was also inserted into the play in order to provide an opportunity for Clive to sing (Lynch 96). The fact that this song remained part of *As You Like It* for many years to come demonstrates that Clive played an important part in the play's success (Brissenden 52).

Clive's representation of Portia in *The Merchant of Venice* was not a critical success: Davies described it as mere 'buffoonery' (*Memoirs* II: 190), and Francis Gentleman thought it 'a ludicrous burlesque on the character, every feature and limb contrasted the idea Shakespeare gave us of Portia' (I: 297). It was, however, a popular triumph: Gentleman conceded that she 'obtained no small share of applause' for the role (I: 297) and the first production had a remarkable run. In this case, the audience apparently disagreed with the critics and Clive continued to play Portia regularly, often making her first appearance of the season in this part: the *Biographical Dictionary* notes that she performed the role for her benefit at Covent Garden in 1744 (at the command of the Prince and Princess of Wales) and then opened the next three seasons at Drury Lane as Portia (Highfill, Burnim, and Langhans III: 350). Presumably Clive continued to act the part because it was popular with the theatre audience, even if her performance was not critically acclaimed. Critical commentary can only tell us part of the story and should not be considered in isolation from performance records.

Pritchard's popularity with theatregoers is demonstrated by her Westminster Abbey memorial, and it was Shakespeare that first brought her to the public's attention and allowed her to build her reputation as an actress. According to Davies, her performance as Rosalind in the 1740 revival of *As You Like It* 'at once established her theatrical character' and created a buzz around her subsequent performances: 'her fame was now enlarging every day by the eagerness which the town expressed to see her in various attitudes' (*Memoirs* II: 177–8). John Hill confirms that Pritchard's appearance as Rosalind marked a turning point in her career:

The first speech that ever obtained Mrs. Pritchard a loud applause was in her Rosalind,

Take the cork out of thy mouth, that I may drink thy tidings.

The praise she received for her spirited manner of speaking this, gave a new spirit to all the rest; she was applauded throughout, and for ever after. (195)

He further describes her as 'the best actress of the British stage' (195). Perhaps more strikingly, there is also visual evidence of Pritchard's (and Clive's) success in this play: Francis Hayman painted the wrestling match from *As You Like It* in the early 1740s.[10] Since Hayman was a scene painter at Drury Lane in this period, and given the popularity of the production, he may well have chosen to depict how this scene was represented on the

---

[10] The painting is in the Tate collection and is reproduced in Vaughan's biography of Pritchard.

stage. This painting is a rare early image of two important eighteenth-century actresses and as such deserves to be paid greater attention as an important source for theatre history.

Pritchard frequently performed opposite Garrick and contemporary critical commentary makes clear that they were considered equally skilled. This approach is evident from the response to their performances in *Much Ado About Nothing*, in which they first appeared together on 14 November 1748. Davies claimed that 'the excellent action of Mrs. Pritchard in Beatrice, was not inferior to that of Benedick. Every scene between them was a continual struggle for superiority; nor could the audience determine which was the victor' (*Memoirs* II: 164). Arthur Murphy, however, seems to suggest that the success of the play was mostly due to Pritchard: 'Mrs. Pritchard was Garrick's rival in every scene; which of them deserved the laurel most was never decided: but their united merit was such, that *Much ado about Nothing* continued to be a favourite comedy, as long as that excellent actress chose to perform the part' (I: 155–6). The theatrical records demonstrate the success of their pairing: the play had fourteen per-formances that season and remained popular in the following years.

As well as being an accomplished comic actress, Pritchard was also skilled in tragic roles. The ability to act in both comic and tragic drama was relatively unusual; at this time, most performers stuck to one 'walk', either comedy or tragedy.[11] Pritchard, however, was 'not confined to any one walk in acting, she ranged through them all; and, what is singular, she discovered a large degree of merit in every distinct class of it' (Davies, *Memoirs* II: 178). This versatility was a skill also attributed to Garrick; furthermore, it was a talent ascribed to Shakespeare, seen as equally pro-ficient in writing in either genre, as Edmund Burke's epitaph for Garrick makes apparent: 'Shakespeare was the chosen object of his study: in his action, and in his declamation he expressed all the fire, the enthusiasm, the energy, the facility, the endless variety of that great poet. Like him he was equally happy in the tragic and comic style' (qtd in Stone and Kahrl 648). Pritchard's ability to perform both comic and tragic parts is another way in which she matched Garrick's acting skill and shows her to be an equally worthy interpreter of Shakespeare.

Pritchard also rivalled Garrick in the sheer diversity of the parts she played, in many cases creating roles in revivals of long-neglected plays,

---

[11] Samuel Foote described Clive as 'the best Actress in her Walk, that I, or perhaps any Man living, has seen' but claimed that she 'has been a little unhappy in her Choice of some Parts', implying that she was skilled as a comic actress but not as a tragedienne (41–2).

with no previous performances in living memory on which to model her interpretations. The list of Shakespearean parts that she performed makes the full range of her acting ability apparent: her most popular roles included Lady Macbeth, Beatrice in *Much Ado About Nothing*, Gertrude in *Hamlet*, Viola in *Twelfth Night*, Queen Katharine in *Henry VIII*, Hermione in *The Winter's Tale*, Mrs Ford in *The Merry Wives of Windsor*, Rosalind in *As You Like It*, and Queen Elizabeth in *Richard III*. Garrick performed a total of sixteen Shakespearean roles over the course of his career but Pritchard had an even greater mastery of the canon, performing twenty-eight different parts.[12]

By considering contemporary dramatic criticism not in a vacuum but in conjunction with performance records and details of the repertory, as well as lesser-known sources such as theatrical painting, it becomes clear that, even when he arrived on the London theatre scene, Garrick was not solely responsible for the status of Shakespeare on the eighteenth-century stage. Female performers also influenced the theatrical presentation of his works and brought Shakespeare to the forefront of the public imagination. Garrick himself recognised the part played by actresses in staging and promoting Shakespeare, and Clive and Pritchard became central members of his company when he took over the management of Drury Lane in 1747.[13] These actresses remained instrumental in the presentation and popularisation of Shakespeare in the Garrick era.

THE CULTURAL AUTHORITY OF THE FEMALE PERFORMER

In addition to his promotion of Shakespeare, Garrick is also famous for his attempts to improve the status and respectability of the acting profession. McPherson has explored the way in which Garrick used portraiture in order to construct a respectable public persona which went beyond previous representations of the actor: 'The numerous non-theatrical portraits of Garrick consolidated his image as a cultivated man of taste. Focusing on the private man rather than the actor, they highlight his social status as

---

[12] This information is taken from the lists of parts given in Appendix B in Stone and Kahrl and Appendix 1 in Vaughan.

[13] Thomson notes that Garrick was careful in choosing his performers and always did so 'with an eye to establishing a stable company and a high standard of performance'. Garrick made Drury Lane the country's leading theatre company, 'but it was not [...] a one-man show' (Thomson); although considered the star performer of the eighteenth-century stage, Garrick could not successfully perform Shakespeare alone.

a gentleman and his literary vocation.' As part of this endeavour, in 1754 Garrick purchased a country house at Hampton-on-Thames, furnished by Chippendale, remodelled according to the latest fashion by Robert Adam and with grounds landscaped by Capability Brown. Adam also designed the octagonal temple to Shakespeare installed in the grounds by the river in 1755, in which a statue of Shakespeare sculpted by Roubiliac was placed. Johan Zoffany's picture of Garrick and his wife on the lawn outside the temple, with the life-size Shakespeare statue just visible, is a calculated depiction of Garrick as country gentleman and admirer of Shakespeare.

Clive and Pritchard also strengthened the social standing of theatre performers by making efforts to present themselves as respectable members of elite society. Both actresses apparently aspired to and actively sought out the same genteel country estate lifestyle as Garrick, the three performers moving to the Twickenham area within months of each other.[14] Clive's close friend Horace Walpole offered her rent-free lodging at Little Strawberry Hill around 1754, she having written to him some years earlier that, 'Tho' I am now representing women of qualitty and cobblers wives, etc. etc. to crowded houses; the charecture I am most desierous to act well is; a good sort of countrey gentlewoman at Twickenham' (qtd in Highfill, Burnim, and Langhans III: 354). Pritchard purchased a nearby house known as Ragman's Castle in 1755. Further evidence of the impact eighteenth-century actresses had on society can be found in an unexpected source. On 22 May 1775, a notice appeared in the *Morning Chronicle and London Advertiser* advertising the publication of a new work ('Elegantly Printed on fine writing paper, and covered with marble'):

A PEEP into the PRINCIPAL SEATS and GARDENS in and about TWICKENHAM, (the residence of the GRACES) containing, among others, a delightful description of the beauty and situation of Mr. Pope's, Mr. Cambridge's, My Lord Radnor's, Horace Walpole's, Mr. Garrick's, Mr. Hudson's, the Duke of St. Alban's, the Countess of Suffolk's, Mrs. Pritchard's, Mrs. Clive's, and several others.

The residences of Clive and Pritchard are here considered on a par with those of high society. Indeed, in this list of 'Graces', actresses

---

[14] Biographical information on Clive is taken from Crouch's entry in the *Oxford Dictionary of National Biography* and the *Biographical Dictionary* by Highfill, Burnim, and Langhans. Details of Pritchard's life and career are taken from the *Biographical Dictionary* entries on Pritchard and her husband William, and from Vaughan's biography. A biography of Clive by Berta Joncus entitled *Kitty Clive, Goddess of Mirth: Creating a Star through Song (1728–1765)* is forthcoming from Boydell & Brewer.

outnumber actors (Garrick is the only male performer listed) and ladies of the 'quality'.[15] The inclusion of Clive and Pritchard in this work provides another example of how broadening our parameters to consider sources often overlooked by theatre historians can help us to build up a fuller picture of the cultural significance of the eighteenth-century actress.

Pritchard's influence reached beyond the auditorium of Drury Lane not only to the country world of Twickenham but even as far as the court. She was appointed dresser to the future Queen Charlotte for her wedding to George III and for their coronation, held in September 1761. In fact, Pritchard seems to have had a second career as a designer and dressmaker. She and her husband owned Pritchard's Warehouse in Covent Garden, which provided theatrical costumes and fashionable clothes for society events. Although the business was largely run by the Pritchards' daughter, Judith, and her husband James Spilsbury, Anthony Vaughan, Pritchard's biographer, claims that her stage appearances constituted 'the perfect vehicle for advertising' (65). As a leading actress, Pritchard would have been given a generous dress allowance and expected to provide her own clothing for performances. Doubtless most of her attire came from Pritchard's Warehouse and, when customers were directed there to purchase tickets for the actress's benefit nights, they would also have been able to acquire the latest fashions displayed by Pritchard on the stage. Vaughan, whose work constitutes the most substantial research so far on this aspect of Pritchard's life, further claims that her role in the marriage and coronation of Queen Charlotte went beyond fashion and included lessons to the Princess and her entourage on bearing and deportment (87).

Kimberly Crouch points to a shift that occurred in the eighteenth century with regard to the relationship between actresses and the upper-class women in their audience and suggests that it is demonstrative of the actress's ability to transcend the hierarchy of class through her portrayal of aristocratic women on the stage:

---

[15] That actresses were readily accepted in elite social circles is demonstrated by Clive's inclusion by Walpole's friends Etheldreda, Viscountess Townshend, Isabella Seymour-Conway, Countess of Hertford, and Lady Anne Connolly on an excursion to see George III's coronation. The *Biographical Dictionary* asserts that Clive was as successful as Garrick in creating a place for herself in country society: 'by the time she retired she had become a figure as well-known in the fashionable countryside near Twickenham as David Garrick was' (Highfill, Burnim, and Langhans III: 355). At her death in 1785, Clive was buried in Twickenham churchyard, at the heart of the genteel community of which she had become an important part. Pritchard was also buried in Twickenham when she died in 1768, but in 1772 the memorial tablet sponsored by her loyal fans was placed next to the statue of Shakespeare in Westminster Abbey, making Pritchard the first performer to be accorded such an honour.

The change that took place during the century, from actresses accepting cast-off gowns from their patrons to patrons asking actresses' advice for dress, initially from caprice and then more seriously, suggests that actresses were so successful at taking on the characteristics of their wealthiest and most socially secure patrons that they became worthy of imitation. Fashionable dress and the effective use of it by actresses establishes another point at which the relationship between aristocratic women and actresses became more than the simple one between patron and patronized. ('Public Life' 73)

Pritchard's offstage role in the world of dressmaking and fashion has long been overlooked but demonstrates that she was at the forefront of this movement which placed actresses as cultural icons emulated by members of the 'quality' and even by royalty. This prominence was a direct result of the audience's acknowledgement of her artistic power as an actress, known primarily for her Shakespearean roles. To my knowledge, not even in the case of Garrick does comparable evidence exist of a male performer exerting a similar influence over the upper-class members of his audience. Garrick's life outside the theatre has received considerable attention; more note must be taken of the public life of his female contemporaries in order to fully appreciate the important place actresses occupied in society.

THE ACTRESS'S ECONOMIC POWER

Garrick's wealth at death has been estimated at around £100,000 (Stone and Kahrl 677; Thomson). A large portion of this of course came from his position as theatre manager: when he retired, Garrick was able to sell his share of the Drury Lane patent for £35,000.[16] Garrick was careful to leave generous legacies to his wife and other family members, as well as arranging for the eventual bequest of his substantial play collection and the Roubiliac statue of Shakespeare to the British Museum. Garrick's meticulous will, with its liberal provisions for family members and careful arrangements for the disposal of property and personal effects, is a reflection of the gentlemanly status that he had achieved in eighteenth-century society.[17]

Although Clive and Pritchard were not involved in theatre management and therefore could not amass the kind of wealth that Garrick

---

[16] According to Lawrence H. Officer's website *Measuring Worth*, Garrick's £100,000 in 1779 had the purchasing power of over £10,000,000 in 2007. The sale of his share of the patent is equivalent to about £3,500,000 today. All subsequent details of the monetary value in today's terms of amounts quoted here are derived using the calculators on this website.

[17] For details of Garrick's two known wills, see Appendix G in Stone and Kahrl.

was able to accrue, both women made a considerable amount of money from their acting careers. At the time of her death, the *London Chronicle* claimed that Clive had 'retired with a small fortune, and contentedly enjoyed what she had acquired by her own labour', and later in the month the newspaper reported that 'Mrs. Clive's property, to the amount of near 800l. is divided between her brother and sister'.[18] Clive was apparently paid around £300 per season (her best-paid season was 1766–7, when she made £315) and received the fourth highest salary in the company, presumably after Garrick, Cibber, and Pritchard (Kinservik 17).[19]

Like Clive, Pritchard died a wealthy woman. She was able to leave handsome legacies to the three daughters who survived her, bequeathing them Ragman's Castle, her property in Twickenham, as well as the lease (with thirty years remaining) on Pritchard's Warehouse on Tavistock Street, in addition to money, jewellery, and personal effects.[20] Indeed, she seems to have been the breadwinner of the family: when her husband, William, passed away in 1763, his will declared that he owed most of his estate to 'the industry of my dear and loving wife Hannah Pritchard' and he appointed her his sole executrix (qtd in Highfill, Burnim, and Langhans XII: 186). William Pritchard had attempted a career as an actor, performing minor roles in small companies, but unlike his wife he was not ultimately successful as a performer. In the early 1740s, shortly after her enormous success in the Shakespeare breeches revival of the beginning of the decade, Pritchard was apparently supporting the family financially: the *Biographical Dictionary* claims that William 'lived off his wife's career' at this time (Highfill, Burnim, and Langhans XII: 172). William later turned to administrative roles in the theatre but was never able to match his wife's earning power. In the 1746–7 season, he was employed as treasurer at Covent Garden for a salary of £2 per week. His wife, however,

---

[18] See the *London Chronicle*, 6 and 29 December 1785. This figure is equivalent to over £800,000 today.

[19] £315 per season is equivalent to earnings of almost £430,000 today. For a broader view of actresses' salaries and economic status in the period, see Nussbaum. Clive's high earning power was perhaps bolstered by her willingness to defend her financial rights in public and in print. In 1744, she published a pamphlet, *The Case of Mrs. Clive Submitted to the Publick,* in which she accused Fleetwood and Rich, the managers of Drury Lane and Covent Garden, of collaborating in order to drive down actors' salaries (8). Clive used the pamphlet to publicise the financial injustices done to her by the theatre managers – she claimed that Fleetwood owed her 'a Hundred and Sixty Pounds, twelve Shillings [around £25,000 in modern terms], which he has acknowledged to be justly due' (18) – and begged for the public's 'Favour and Protection' since she lacked 'a Fortune to support me, independent of my Profession' (21). Clive's pamphlet makes clear that the theatre provided her professional identity and sole form of income and that she was prepared to defend her right to decent remuneration for her acting talent.

[20] Pritchard's will is housed at the National Archives as PROB 11/942.

was earning considerably more, with wages of £5 per week.[21] In 1747 they were both engaged by Garrick and Lacy at Drury Lane: Pritchard as the leading actress and William as the treasurer. William continued working as the Drury Lane company treasurer until his death in 1763 but, as his will makes clear, he was never as financially successful as his wife.

Like most of her fellow actresses, Pritchard did not come from a wealthy family and her high economic status was obviously a result of her hard work and talent as a performer. Because not as spectacular as the wealth amassed by Garrick, the financial situations of Clive and Pritchard have not attracted critical comment. However, details of their wealth at death and information on their salaries confirm that female performers were suitably remunerated for their artistic achievement. This data constitutes important evidence that allows us to appreciate the comfortable economic position that the eighteenth-century actress was able to attain. By linking itself with the increasingly culturally significant Shakespeare and making concerted efforts to increase its respectability in the eyes of the public, the acting profession was no longer necessarily a financially unstable venture and instead could offer an attractive and steady income to its practitioners. Although Garrick is usually identified as the main proponent and beneficiary of these changes, the evidence amassed here demonstrates that Clive and Pritchard also contributed to and profited from the changes in the economic status of the theatre world taking place at this time.

CONCLUSION

Garrick's position as the manager of Drury Lane theatre presumably gave him more power in choosing his own roles and in influencing the theatre repertory in favour of Shakespeare, as well as an increased social standing and a significant fortune. But a new reading of theatre history shows that he was not alone in enjoying a large degree of artistic, cultural, and economic authority as a result of his involvement in the acting profession. The appearance of Clive and Pritchard in a tourist guide to the elite houses of Twickenham and Pritchard's role as a leader of fashion and polite conduct demonstrate that both actresses were not only considered respectable and desirable company but were deemed worthy of imitation by the public. Both were able to achieve financial independence and even

---

[21] In modern terms, William Pritchard was earning just under £2,900 per week while his wife received over £7,000, two and a half times her husband's salary.

comfortable wealth from their stage careers. Furthermore, as an analysis of the Shakespeare revival of 1740–1 and contemporary commentary on these two female performers makes plain, they contributed significantly to the presentation and popularisation of Shakespeare in the mid eighteenth century. Ample evidence of the eighteenth-century actress's life and career exists in material that has yet to be fully explored. Once we begin to consider a greater range of sources, details of her influential performances of Shakespeare, as well as the cultural status and economic success that acting enabled the female performer to achieve, can finally be uncovered.

I am grateful to Erin Hurley and Diana Solomon for their comments on this essay.

WORKS CITED

Bratton, Jacky. *New Readings in Theatre History*. Theatre and Performance Theory. Cambridge: Cambridge University Press, 2003.

Brissenden, Alan. Introduction. *As You Like It*. By William Shakespeare. Oxford World's Classics. Oxford: Oxford University Press, 1993. 1–86.

Churchill, C[harles]. *The Rosciad*. Dublin, 1761.

[Clive, Catherine.] *The Case of Mrs. Clive Submitted to the Publick*. London, 1744.

Crouch, Kimberly. 'Clive, Catherine (1711–1785)'. *Oxford Dictionary of National Biography*. www.oxforddnb.com/view/article/5694, accessed 3 June 2008.

'The Public Life of Actresses: Prostitutes or Ladies?' *Gender in Eighteenth-Century England*. Ed. Hannah Barker and Elaine Chalus. London: Longman, 1997. 58–78.

Davies, Thomas. *Memoirs of the Life of David Garrick, Esq. Interspersed with Characters and Anecdotes of his Theatrical Contemporaries. The Whole Forming a History of the Stage, which Includes a Period of Thirty-Six Years*. 2 vols. London, 1780.

Dramatic Micellanies [sic]: Consisting of Critical Observations of the Several Plays of Shakespeare: With a Review of his Principal Characters, and those of Various Eminent Writers, as Represented by Mr. Garrick, and Other Celebrated Comedians. With Anecdotes of Dramatic Poets, Actors, &c. 3 vols. London, 1784.

[Derrick, Samuel.] *A General View of the Stage*. London, 1759.

Foote, Samuel. *The Roman and English Comedy Consider'd and Compar'd. With Remarks on The Suspicious Husband. And an Examen into the Merit of the Present Comic Actors*. London, 1747.

Gale, Maggie B., and Viv Gardner, eds. *Women, Theatre and Performance: New Histories, New Historiographies*. Women, Theatre and Performance. Manchester: Manchester University Press, 2000.

[Gentleman, Francis.] *The Dramatic Censor; or, Critical Companion*. 2 vols. London, 1770.

Granger, James. *A Biographical History of England*. 2 vols. London, 1769.

Hayman, Francis. *The Wrestling Scene from 'As You Like It'*. Tate, London.

Highfill, Philip H., Jr, Kalman A. Burnim, and Edward A. Langhans, eds. *A Biographical Dictionary of Actors, Actresses, Musicians, Dancers, Managers & Other Stage Personnel in London, 1660–1800*. 16 vols. Carbondale: Southern Illinois University Press, 1973–93.

[Hill, John.] *The Actor: Or, a Treatise on the Art of Playing*. London, 1755.

Kinservik, Matthew J. 'Benefit Play Selection at Drury Lane 1729–1769: The Cases of Mrs. Cibber, Mrs. Clive, and Mrs. Pritchard.' *Theatre Notebook* 50 (1996): 15–28.

London Chronicle. 6 December 1785.

London Chronicle. 29 December 1785.

London Evening Post. 5 November 1772.

Lynch, James. *Box, Pit, and Gallery: Stage and Society in Johnson's London*. Berkeley: University of California Press, 1953.

McPherson, Heather. 'Garrickomania: Art, Celebrity and the Imaging of Garrick.' www.folger.edu/template.cfm?cid=1465, accessed 3 June 2008.

Morning Chronicle and London Advertiser. 22 May 1775.

Murphy, Arthur. *The Life of David Garrick, Esq*. 2 vols. London: Wright, 1801.

Nussbaum, Felicity. 'Actresses and the Economics of Celebrity, 1700–1800'. *Theatre and Celebrity in Britain, 1660–2000*. Ed. Mary Luckhurst and Jane Moody. Basingstoke: Palgrave Macmillan, 2005. 148–68.

Odell, George C. D. *Shakespeare from Betterton to Irving*. 2 vols. New York: Dover, 1966.

Officer, Lawrence H. *Measuring Worth: Purchasing Power of British Pounds from 1264 to 2007*. www.measuringworth.com/ppoweruk/?redirurl=calculators/ppoweruk, accessed 19 August 2008.

Pritchard, Hannah. Will. National Archives, London. PROB 11/942.

Ritchie, Fiona. 'Shakespeare and the Eighteenth-Century Actress.' *Borrowers and Lenders: The Journal of Shakespeare and Appropriation* 2.2 (Fall/Winter 2006): lachesis.english.uga.edu/cocoon/borrowers/request?id=590887, accessed 3 June 2008.

Scouten, Arthur H. 'Shakespeare's Plays in the Theatrical Repertory when Garrick Came to London.' *Studies in English*. Austin, University of Texas Press, 1945. 257–68.

   'The Increase in Popularity of Shakespeare's Plays in the Eighteenth Century: A Caveat for Interpreters of Stage History.' *Shakespeare Quarterly* 7 (1956): 189–202.

Scouten, Arthur H., ed. and introd. *The London Stage, 1660–1800: A Calendar of Plays, Entertainments and Afterpieces Together With Casts, Box-Receipts and Contemporary Comment, Compiled from the Playbills, Newspapers and Theatrical Diaries of the Period. Part 3: 1729–1747*. 2 vols. Carbondale: Southern Illinois University Press, 1961.

Stone, George Winchester, Jr, and George M. Kahrl. *David Garrick: A Critical Biography*. Carbondale: Southern Illinois University Press, 1979.

Thomson, Peter. 'Garrick, David (1717–1779).' *Oxford Dictionary of National Biography*. www.oxforddnb.com/view/article/10408, accessed 3 June 2008.

Vaughan, Antony. *Born to Please: Hannah Pritchard, Actress, 1711–68. A Critical Biography*. London: Society for Theatre Research, 1979.

Westminster Abbey Acts of Chapter, 16 June 1772.

Westminster Abbey Funeral Fee Book 1760–83.

Zoffany, Johan. *The Shakespeare Temple at Hampton House, with Mr and Mrs David Garrick*. Tate, London.

CHAPTER 8

Women writing Shakespeare's women in the nineteenth century: The Winter's Tale

Jan McDonald

Shakespeare has no heroes; – he has only heroines. (Ruskin 100)

To introduce a chapter on nineteenth-century women writing about Shakespeare's heroines with a quotation from a pillar of the male literary establishment might seem perverse. However, the choice highlights one of the paradoxes encountered in investigating the topic. The women were writing in a context that was largely male-dominated. By their very act of writing (and especially of performing), they contravened the masculine construct of 'ideal womanhood', yet their work indicates that for the most part they did not challenge the male hegemony: the 'ideal woman' was a concept to which they broadly subscribed. Prevailing social, scholarly, and theatrical orthodoxies conditioned the content and the methodology of their work.

Significant among these was 'bardolatry', the worship of Shakespeare as a national icon: '[W]heresoever [...] English men and women are, they will say to one another: "Yes, this Shakespeare is ours; we produced him, we speak and think by him; we are of one blood and kind with him"' (Carlyle 114). Shakespeare's rediscovered genius was harnessed throughout the nineteenth century to provide a moral touchstone for British citizens; to inspire a revival of national painting and sculpture; to endorse national achievements in science, engineering, and technology in the Great Exhibition of 1851; to promote tourism, particularly in Stratford; and to generate a plethora of souvenirs for popular consumption.

The fashion for bardolatry influenced, and was encouraged by, changes in the theatrical repertoire. The ending of the monopoly of Covent Garden and Drury Lane in the production of serious drama in 1843 enabled the former 'minor' houses to mount the plays of the national Bard. Shakespearean production in the latter part of the century flourished as the actor-managers, Charles Kean at the Princess's, Samuel Phelps at Sadler's Wells, and Henry Irving at the Lyceum, followed the fashion for pictorial realisation, archaeological and historical reconstruction, and spectacular crowd scenes. Queen Victoria's and Prince Albert's passion for theatrical entertainment encouraged an increase in middle-class audiences, who brought with them their preconceptions of 'correct' social conduct, respectability, gentility, and a commitment to the principle of male hegemony in public and family life.

The role of women within this societal structure was as restricted as it was idealised. The pursuit of the feminine ideal is exemplified in the sale of a quarter-million copies of Coventry Patmore's *The Angel in the House* (1854–6). Affectionate, although not passionate, the 'perfect' Victorian woman was constructed as being quiet, modest, subservient, domestic, and of unimpeachable integrity and fortitude; her prime duty was to ensure the welfare of her husband and children, by providing them, both by precept and example, with a sound moral education. The 'womanly woman' was the appointed guardian of the ethical standards not only of the home but of the nation.

The appropriation of Shakespeare as a 'national treasure' and the popularity of his dramas extended to an interest in his female characters. In Shakespeare, as Julie Hankey points out, 'women [were] provided with a patron saint. [The] virtual canonization of Shakespeare in the nineteenth century was closely paralleled by the promotion of women, or rather Woman, within the Victorian system of values' (50). Was it not logical to conclude that England's greatest dramatist, understanding women as well as he did, had bequeathed a future model for England's ideal woman? As Carol J. Carlisle notes, 'The feminine ideal discerned in Shakespeare's characters by many critics of the nineteenth century was much the same as the ideal held up to women in everyday life' ('The Critics' 68). Unsurprisingly, both in its criticism and in its theatre, as well as in daily life, the nineteenth century reconstructed Shakespeare's female characters according to its own conception of womanhood.

Paradoxically, the marriage between bardolatry and the 'Angel in the House' was brokered in part by the women of the stage, who by the very nature of their profession did not fit the feminine ideal. Sarah Siddons had demonstrated that Shakespeare provided excellent opportunities for the female actor. Subsequent stars, including Fanny Kemble, Helen Faucit, and Ellen Terry, made their reputations largely in Shakespearean roles. Since much of their repertoire was increasingly drawn from a source above reproach, the anti-theatrical prejudice that had degraded women of the acting profession diminished, and the women's stage roles had a positive effect on their reputations in private life. The publication by some of their interpretations of Shakespeare's female characters bestowed an additional quasi-scholarly respectability on what had hitherto been regarded as a questionable business for a woman.

WOMEN 'WRITING' SHAKESPEARE'S WOMEN

From a growing number of women writing about Shakespeare's heroines in the Victorian period, I have selected three non-performers, Anna Jameson, Mary Cowden Clarke, and M. Leigh-Noel, and two actors, Helen Faucit and Ellen Terry. In the case of the performers, I also consider as 'writings' their stage representations, particularly of characters in *The Winter's Tale*, a detailed case study of which concludes the chapter. None of these women conformed to the Victorian ideal of the 'womanly woman', in that all were active and successful in the public sphere in occupations traditionally practised and dominated by men and were, by choice or necessity, financially independent of a male 'protector'. Indeed, by marketing their talents, they were often the providers for their dependants as well as for themselves. Yet, despite their status as independent women in the public gaze, the declared objective of their writing was to improve the lives of their female readers by providing a series of ideal role models validated by the Shakespearean stamp of excellence. All state this purpose unambiguously.

The introduction to Anna Jameson's *Characteristics of Women, Moral, Poetical and Historical* (1832)[1] takes the form of a quasi-Socratic dialogue in the scholarly setting of a library, between Alda (Anna Jameson) and Medon, a male friend. Alda states that she wrote the book 'for her own pleasure', denying that she seeks to promote the rights of women or 'to maintain the superiority of [her] sex' (*Shakespeare's Heroines* 3). She does, however, aspire to improve the quality of women's lives: 'It appears to me that the condition of women in society, as at present constituted, is false

---

[1] Anna Jameson (1794–1860) earned her living as a governess from the age of sixteen until her marriage in 1825. Her virtual desertion by her husband meant that she was once more thrown on her own resources. She turned to writing and produced popular lightweight books on a variety of subjects, all with an underlying moral and educational purpose, many designed for women readers. Her only book on a Shakespearean topic, *Characteristics of Women, Moral, Poetical and Historical* (1832), was inspired by her association with the Kembles, the leading theatrical family of the period. *Characteristics* was highly successful, running to seven editions by the end of the century. The title was changed to *Shakespeare's Heroines* in 1896. Anna Jameson's literary output is in itself undistinguished, but in overcoming the social and financial consequences of her husband's desertion and carving an independent career, she was an exceptional woman.

in itself, and injurious to them, that the education of women, as at present conducted, is founded on mistaken principles, and tends to increase fearfully the sum of misery and error in both sexes' (4). She seeks to make her point by providing examples from Shakespeare's plays because his characters 'combine history and real life; they are complete individuals [...] real human beings' (10). Moral and educational purposes harness bardolatry to render them more effective.

In her article in *The Girl's Own Paper* (1887), 'Shakespeare as the Girl's Friend', Mary Cowden Clarke[2] also held up Shakespeare's female characters as exemplars to promote contemporary women's moral education:

From his youthful women [a girl] can gain lessons in artlessness, guilelessness, modesty, sweetness, ingenuousness and the most winning candour: from his wives and matrons she can derive instructions in moral courage, meekness, magnanimity, firmness, devoted tenderness, high principle, noble conduct, loftiest speech and sentiment. (562, qtd in Altick 232)

The same sentiments are evident in *The Girlhood of Shakespeare's Heroines* (1850–1), a series of novellas tracing the lives of the heroines from their early childhood until the opening of the drama. Nina Auerbach describes them as 'falling somewhere between the bildungsroman and pre-Freudian case history' (*Woman* 212). Although the stories may be dismissed as sentimental fairytales, a moral message is not lacking: Victorian parents could learn from their Shakespearean predecessors the deleterious effects of lax discipline or neglect on their offspring (Katharina 'the Shrew' and Lady Macbeth, 'The Thane's Daughter', being two examples) and the contrasting benefits of a sound moral upbringing, evident in the dutiful and wise Portia.

M. Leigh-Noel's *Shakespeare's Garden of Girls*[3] took its title from Tennyson's 'Queen-rose of the rose-bud garden of girls' (*New Shakespere* 107*). Leigh-Noel praises Shakespeare for having been 'the first to create *real* women in poetry' and expounds her aim 'to distil their fragrance for the benefit of others [...] to point out beauties that had hitherto escaped

---

[2] Mary Cowden Clarke (1809–98) was the first woman to make a profession of writing about Shakespeare, 'an anomalous "sister" within the brotherhood of Victorian Shakespearean scholarship' (Thompson and Roberts, 'Mary Cowden Clarke' 175). She published the highly praised *Complete Concordance to Shakespeare* (1844–5) and edited *Shakespeare's Works, with a Scrupulous Revision of the Text* (1859–60), regarded as the first scholarly edition by a woman. She collaborated with her husband, Charles, on two further editions in 1864 and 1866. Dedicated bardolators, the Cowden Clarkes were much respected in nineteenth-century literary circles. George Eliot, however, found it 'amusing to see how these small celebrities [...] make their living out of Shakespeare' (Haight 329–30).

[3] Of M. Leigh-Noel, later Mrs M. L. Elliott, little is known. She published *Lady Macbeth: A Study* in 1884 and was one of only three women to give papers at The New Shakespere [*sic*] Society between 1880 and 1886. These lectures constituted the basis for *Shakespeare's Garden of Girls* (1885).

notice' and thus 'to gladden her readers' (ii, iv). On the title page and
in the preface, she quotes from Charles Cowden Clarke's *Shakespeare-
Characters: Chiefly Those Subordinate* (1863) to clarify her purpose, the
celebration of Shakespeare's influence on the social liberation of women
in England: 'Shakespeare is the writer of all others whom the women of
England should take to their hearts, for I believe it to be mainly through
his intellectual influence that their claims in the scale of society were
acknowledged in England' (Leigh-Noel i). Cowden Clarke's bardolatrous
claim might be justified in terms of his wife's scholarly career but is somewhat overstated with regard to women less privileged.

Helen Faucit,[4] regarded as the epitome of the Victorian ideal woman
both on stage and in her domestic life, defined her volume, *On Some of
Shakespeare's Female Characters*, as 'The endeavour to present a living picture of womanhood as divined by Shakespeare and held up by him as an
ideal for women to aspire to, and men to revere' (qtd in Martin 405). Her
fellow actor Ellen Terry,[5] however, was a rather more robust bardolator, in
apostrophising these

Wonderful women! have you ever thought how much we all, and women especially, owe to Shakespeare for his vindication of women in these fearless, high-
spirited, resolute and intelligent heroines? Don't believe the anti-feminists if they
tell you, as I was once told, that Shakespeare had to endow his women with vir-
ile qualities because in his theatre they were always impersonated by men. (*Four
Lectures* 81)

In her later years, Terry was an ardent supporter of women's suffrage and
a founder member of the Actresses' Franchise League; when she can,
she chooses to celebrate the more feisty qualities of the characters she
discusses.

---

[4] Both Helen Faucit (1817–98) and Ellen Terry (1848–1928) came from theatrical backgrounds,
where the expectation was that children would be employed in the 'family business' from an
early age; they were already icons of the Victorian stage by the time they turned to print. Faucit
began writing about the Shakespearean characters she had performed in two letters to her friend,
Geraldine Jewsbury. Her husband, Sir Theodore Martin, encouraged her to extend the number
of heroines and to publish the letters in *Blackwood's Edinburgh Magazine*. The collected letters
appeared as *On Some of Shakespeare's Female Characters: By One Who Has Personated Them* in
1885, by which time Faucit had retired from the stage. Although she stresses that the volume
began as a private project, it consolidated and, to an extent, preserved her iconic status.

[5] Terry's lectures on Shakespeare – she preferred to call them 'discourses' – were delivered over a
period of ten years from 1911–22, after she ceased performing in the professional theatre. They
included long extracts from her favourite stage roles and those, such as Rosalind, which she
had never had the chance to perform. Her daughter's partner, Christopher St. John (Christabel
Marshal), encouraged their publication, taking upon herself the role of editor and ghost writer.
Four Lectures on Shakespeare, which included 'The Triumphant Women' and 'The Pathetic
Women', appeared in 1932.

While all these authors seek to be enabling, to raise woman's self-esteem, and to contribute to her moral education, there is, with the partial exception of Terry, no serious challenge to the patriarchal hierarchy implicit both in Shakespeare's authorship and in nineteenth-century society. The writers' dedications are revealing in this context. Although Jameson and Leigh-Noel chose women performers, Fanny Kemble and Mary Anderson respectively, established male writers and artists predominate in Cowden Clarke's *Girlhood*. Her story of 'Imogen the Peerless' is dedicated 'To the [predominantly male] Shakespeare Society in honor [*sic*] of the principle of its institution'. Faucit's book is dedicated to Queen Victoria, but her choice of recipients for her public 'letters' includes Robert Browning, John Ruskin, and Lord Tennyson. In works by women, ostensibly written for women's instruction and pleasure, with female fictional characters as their subject matter, the majority of the dedications implicitly make a bid for validation by seeking association with the literary giants of the male canon.

Paradoxically, the women's aim appears to be to guide their readers to become the kind of women they themselves were not. The pursuit of this purpose determines their selection of Shakespearean characters, namely those that most obviously display the qualities desirable in the nineteenth-century 'ideal woman': tragic heroines Ophelia, Juliet, Desdemona, and Cordelia; comic heroines Beatrice, Rosalind, and Portia; and historical figures Queen Katharine and Constance. Imogen was a favourite; Hermione and Perdita feature regularly. The selection is, of course, also conditioned by which plays were popular in the contemporary repertoire, a choice primarily determined by patriarchal actor-managers: Jameson focuses on the most celebrated roles of the Kembles, while Faucit and Terry for the most part discuss their own stage successes.

Jameson, Leigh-Noel, and Terry group the characters according to their predominant characteristics and/or the circumstances of their upbringing and environment. As Linda Rozmovits points out, such classification is rarely 'innocent': 'Typologies classified and described characters from Shakespeare according to their moral and behavioural type and by this means sought to derive [...] an orderly, comprehensive, and morally authoritative account of human, but especially female, nature' (35). The categories selected are in part interpretative but they are also prescriptive, in the sense that they are dictated by the attributes the authors seek to recommend. Thus they limit the woman reader's choice of role model rather than providing a paradigm for liberation. Jameson's groups comprise 'Characters of Intellect', rather 'too bold and frank in expression'

(18) for nineteenth-century taste; 'Characters of Passion and Imagination', who are less admirable than 'Characters of the Affections'; and 'Historical Characters', the last being something of a catch-all. Leigh-Noel's lectures to the New Shakespere Society expand on the horticultural imagery of her title, with divisions into 'Hothouse Flowers', women whose characters have been conditioned by their upbringing in warm climates or in the stifling environment of a royal court; 'Hardy Blossoms', whose distinctive characteristic was their ability to survive; and 'Wild Flowers', beautiful and good women, unspoilt by sophisticated society (*New Shakespere* 107*). Ellen Terry's categories, 'Triumphant Women' and 'Pathetic [in the sense of 'feeling'] Women', are dictated by imagined physical as well as psychological characteristics: ' "[T]riumphant" [...] women were *tall* – strong physically as well as mentally. I cannot produce any evidence that the women I am going to talk about in this lecture [on pathetic women] were small and slim, of rather frail physique, but that is how I see them with my mind's eye' (*Four Lectures* 125). Such a distinction demonstrates Terry's personal focus on physicality and pictorialism as a performer.

Although there is no category for 'wicked' women – no Regans, Gonerils, or Cressidas appear – all the writers tackle the thorny issue of Lady Macbeth following the reading in Sarah Siddons's 'Remarks on the Character of Lady Macbeth', published in Thomas Campbell's biography (1834), an interpretation very different from her 'fiend-like' performance. Siddons describes Lady Macbeth as 'fair, feminine, nay, perhaps, even fragile' (II: 10), her wicked actions the result of wifely devotion, and her subsequent mental anguish evidence of the remorse of a noble conscience. Evil is explained, even partly excused, by uxoriousness, a recognised Victorian virtue.

In terms of their critical approach, all the women write in the tradition of 'character' or psychological criticism of Shakespeare's plays that dominated the period from Maurice Morgann's *Essay on the Character of Sir John Falstaff* (1777) to A. C. Bradley's *Shakespearean Tragedy* (1905). Character criticism was a product of the rise of the novel and a manifestation of the Romantic privileging of individual psychology over the neoclassical concern with rationality and social order. This approach focused on the *dramatis personae*, rather than on textual analysis. The characters were investigated as if they were 'real' people, and their early history examined (or created) to explain their psychological motivation. William Richardson's 'On Shakespeare's Imitation of Female Characters' (1788), 'a turning point in critical attitudes to Shakespeare's women' (Carlisle, 'The Critics' 59), was written in this vein. Richardson treats individual heroines as actual women who, both in Shakespeare's time and in the late eighteenth century, had few opportunities to 'display their talents and dispositions' (342). In his casting of Shakespeare as a supporter of women's education and development, and in his choice of exemplary heroines to whom he attributes many of the qualities desirable in the 'angels' of the next century, he set a pattern for later female writers.

In the theatre, a growing regard for psychological realism in performance was evident in the revolutionary approach to acting heralded by Macklin and Garrick in the 1740s. The actor was becoming increasingly concerned with the creation of a truthful, consistent, and lifelike representation of a dramatic character. In practice, many nineteenth-century performers used the same methods in preparing their roles as were codified by Constantin Stanislavsky in *An Actor Prepares* (1937). His 'System' or 'Grammar of Dramatic Art' demonstrates the synergy between character criticism and naturalistic acting with its focus on the actor's need for emotional and physical truth in building a role, which was assisted by creating a life for the character outside the scripted action. Cowden Clarke, Leigh-Noel, and Faucit provide past histories for the stage heroines, the last giving them a future as well. Kathleen McLuskie observes that '[o]ne of the most common strategies of liberal mimetic interpretation is to imagine a past life, a set of alternatives and motivation for the characters' (96), echoing Nina Auerbach's view of the nineteenth-century tradition 'in which women extract Shakespeare's heroines from the text of their plays and exalt them as womanhood's inspiration' (*Woman* 210). Freeing female characters from a male-authored text could be seen as a metaphor for freeing living women from a male-authored society, but, although the writers do concern themselves with women's societal role, none is sufficiently radical to justify such a reading. While the writers' novelistic approach might be seen as detaching the heroines from the dramas, the performers, irrevocably circumscribed by the conditions of theatrical production, in which the performance text, setting, and actors' interpretations were determined by actor-managers, considered the characters in context: Faucit makes clear that a study of the whole play and not solely of her own dramatic character was an essential part of her preparation for playing a role (Martin 403), while Terry's practice of including lengthy readings of extracts from the drama in her Lectures contextualised her discussion of the female characters. Unlike Sarah Siddons in her essay on Lady Macbeth, Faucit's and Terry's interpretations in print do not differ radically from their stage performances. Terry, however, describes how her playing of Beatrice was affected by the adherence to traditional stage business at the Lyceum, and particularly by Henry Irving's playing of Benedick: 'I have played Beatrice hundreds of times, but not as I know she ought to be played. I was never swift enough at the Lyceum where I had a too deliberate, though polished and thoughtful, Benedick in Henry Irving' (*Four Lectures* 97).

Nevertheless, as a result of the prevailing vogue for character criticism, the writings of the actors and the non-performers do have certain similarities. Georgianna Ziegler observes of Jameson's work that 'her consideration of a character's background and motives, her evocation of settings [...] and her close attention to the subtlety of feelings expressed by a character in a certain scene [...] all point to a way of thinking about character that is similar to what we have seen with the actresses' ('Actress' 103). Frances Anne (Fanny) Kemble, however, was clear about the essential difference between the 'critical' and the 'theatrical' intelligence:

[T]here is no reason whatever to expect that fine actors shall be necessarily profound commentators on the parts that they sustain most successfully, but rather the contrary [...] The dramatic faculty [...] lies in a power of apprehension quicker than the disintegrating process of critical analysis, and [...] perception rather than reflection reaches the aim proposed. (11–12)

Kemble's distinction illuminates the principal difference between the writings of the actors and the non-performers: namely, that the actors are at pains to point out that their true commentary is to be found in their performances rather than on the page. Faucit claims to 'have no gift for painting in words what I thought of Shakespeare's women. I tried to entirely in action [...] How impossible to put into words their intense emotions' (Letter to Ellen Drew Braysher, 20 March 1861). While making a serious attempt in her writing to show how she realised a part in performance, she acknowledges the impossibility of achieving this. 'No one who does me the honour to read these studies will gather from them what I did upon the stage, or how I did it, for this is more than I myself could tell' (Martin 404). Ellen Terry, declaring that 'an ounce of practice is worth a pound of theory', asserts: 'An actress does not study a character with a view to proving something about the dramatist who created it' (*Four Lectures* 80). Christopher St. John's Introduction underlines Terry's insistence that the lectures were written to be 'heard, not to be read':

[W]ithout the improvisations she made when she was lecturing, without the illumination of her views and ideas provided by her acting of the interpolated scenes, her lectures would be only half themselves. Readers who had not heard them might wonder why scholarly critics had welcomed them as an important contribution to the study of Shakespeare. (8)

The realisation of the dramatic character on stage, despite the exigencies of contemporary theatrical conventions and idiosyncratic actor-managers, best demonstrates the results of their research and textual analysis. Their commentaries they see as mere shadows of the performances.

Endowing dramatic characters with a literal reality together with the increasing quest for psychological realism in performance led to a close identification of the actor with the role. Both Terry and Faucit see the task of the actor as being, in Terry's words, 'to translate the character into herself, how to make its thoughts her thoughts, its words, her words' (*Four Lectures* 80). Faucit asserts that she enjoyed 'the great advantage of throwing my own nature into [the characters'], of becoming moved by their emotions: I have, as it were, thought their thoughts and spoken their words straight from my own living heart and mind' (*Characters* viii). Indeed, audiences came to assume that the virtues of the dramatic character were replicated in the character of the actor. Terry was adored by the highly respectable Lyceum audience for her charming stage persona, despite her somewhat irregular private life. Faucit, in her domestic role as Lady Martin, was the epitome of 'The Angel in the House', because she interpreted the parts she played in terms of the Victorian ideal of womanhood.

The character of Lady Macbeth presented her with a problem, however. It was a role that she found difficult to write about and distasteful to perform. She notes in the Appendix to *Shakespeare's Female Characters* that, despite being pressed by 'many friends' to include it, she declined, because 'it would not be prompted by the love for my subject which has made the writing about my favourite heroines comparatively easy' (401). In performing this role, her usual technique of 'throwing her own nature' into a character was impossible for her. As Julie Hankey points out, 'The part marked the limits for her of autobiographical Shakespeare' (64).

The tendency to subsume the actor in the character (and vice versa) was strengthened by the popularity of theatrical prints, portraits, and postcards, frequently depicting her in a Shakespearean role. Many editions of the plays were illustrated with pictures of actors, so that readers formed their image of the character from its stage interpreter. The reprint of Jameson's *Characteristics/Shakespeare's Heroines* in 1900 replaced original etchings by the author with 'twenty-six portraits of famous players in character'. The publisher's note justifies the change: 'Idealized conceptions [...] are apt to be removed from actuality, while with portraits of women of genius, accustomed to impersonate the characters, we see them, not as abstract conceptions, but with all the incidents of a human personality intervening' (v). Whose 'human personality' intervened, one might ask: that of the actor herself, the actor 'going as' the character, or the Shakespearean 'original'? Helen Faucit's volume was illustrated by portraits of herself. To the reader's eyes, Juliet *is* Faucit, and Faucit *is* Juliet. The same dual identity is evident throughout.

THE WINTER'S TALE

The Winter's Tale provides useful exemplars for a detailed study of the critical approach to Shakespeare's heroines adopted by women writers and performers in the nineteenth century. Helen Faucit concluded her essay on Hermione with the words, 'I have had to write of three exquisite types of womanhood – the mother, the maiden and the friend' (*Characters* 392). Faucit names three '*types* of womanhood', each type being in effect a sub-category of the 'exquisite' ideal, and each having a recognised code of social and moral behaviour. The women commentators do not as a rule interrogate this code, but rather provide interpretations of the three female characters that demonstrate their conformity to it. Focusing on Hermione's supreme maternal qualities, Perdita's youthful purity and modesty, and Paulina's spirited loyalty to her friend, they excuse, or explain, or pass over any possible deviations from the ideal.

The *Winter's Tale* was not performed after the Restoration until David Garrick's *Florizel and Perdita, a Dramatic Pastoral* (in effect Acts 4 and 5), which appeared in 1756 and lasted throughout the eighteenth century. John Philip Kemble restored much of Acts 1–3 at Drury Lane in March 1802 and in his subsequent Covent Garden productions, with Sarah Siddons as Hermione (Shattuck i–iv, [1–5] 6–80). This adaptation was the basis of most nineteenth-century stage versions, including that used by William Charles Macready, with Helen Faucit as Hermione. In line with theatrical practice of the time, however, the integrity of even the 'restored' version was compromised by Victorian notions of propriety (for example, the omission of overt references to Hermione's pregnancy) and by a desire to accommodate elaborate scenic effects. Charles Kean (1856), whose re-introduction of the Time Chorus was largely motivated by the opportunities it offered for spectacle, was intent on producing a series of historically accurate pictures of ancient Greece on stage and sacrificed more of Shakespeare's text than Kemble, cutting all references that did not fit with his chosen period. Beerbohm Tree took scenic splendour even further in his three-act version in 1906, which featured Ellen Terry as Hermione as part of her jubilee celebrations. Little was left of the play's original structure, a new 'unity' being created by the focus on Apollo and his attendant singing priests.

The effect that these textual changes by male producers had on the women's performances and/or the audiences' reception of *The Winter's Tale* is difficult to determine. They were symptomatic of the fashion for spectacle, and Faucit and Terry would have known no other way of presenting Shakespeare on stage. Terry, a pictorial actor *par excellence*, avowed that elaborate settings assisted rather than hindered her playing (*Story of My Life* 10). The stage versions in which the women performed were conditioned by the social context in which they performed, as were their interpretations of individual characters.

Hermione: 'the mother'

The New Shakespere Society's Transactions (1880–6) reveal a general anxiety over the absence of 'good mothers' in Shakespeare's plays and expound on the detrimental effect the lack of maternal guidance had on the daughters. Hermione, therefore, was especially attractive to nineteenth-century audiences and commentators as a rare embodiment in Shakespeare of the maternal ideal. Both Jameson and Faucit attribute Hermione's sixteen years of voluntary exile from public life and her withdrawal from her repentant husband to a deeply felt duty to wait for the return of her lost child as predicted by the oracle. To her noble qualities of patience, dignity, honour, and fidelity is added the supreme virtue of motherly devotion.

Sarah Siddons, celebrated for her portrayal of 'distressed' and self-sacrificing mothers in both Shakespearean and contemporary dramas, set the pattern for stage interpretations of the character throughout the century and influenced the women who wrote about it. 'Whatever Hermione is, Mrs Siddons has made her her creation' (*Morning Chronicle* 12 November 1807, qtd in Bartholomeusz 53). Both of Hermione's principal appearances, namely the trial scene (3.2) and the statue scene (5.3), provide opportunities for the display of maternal feelings. In the first, she is eloquent in her own defence; in the second, her silence is broken only by her blessing on her daughter. One might ask whether the Queen's lengthy speeches in her trial contravened the feminine ideal of modest reticence, but any potential criticism in this vein was minimised in Kemble's standard stage version (Shattuck 34–8), first, by cutting the second of her three long speeches, that relating to the accusation of her alleged infidelity with Polixenes and of her 'treacherous' conspiracy with Camillo, and, second, by introducing business to underline her weakened state after childbirth. Throughout she remains very still, a possible prefiguring of her later appearance as the 'statue'. She begins to speak while seated, rises at key points in her testimony, only to subside again into her chair, as physical exhaustion overcomes her effort to plead her innocence. At the announcement of Mamillius's death, the Kemble text interpolated the line, 'Oh, Oh, Oh, my son' (38).

Actors too tailored their readings to justify Hermione's untypical volubility and to avoid any suggestion of excess of passion. Helen Faucit's letter on Hermione describes how she imagined Hermione's progress from the palace through the streets to the courthouse and how she was moved by the sympathetic silence and the tears of her loving subjects, which prepared her emotionally for her powerful delivery of Hermione's plea of innocence (*Characters* 360). Hermione's defence was presented not as meretricious rhetoric, but as a supreme effort of will by a sick woman, supported by her loyal subjects, to defend her honour and her children. In a nineteenth-century theatrical context that privileged the melodramatic mode, a breach of the stereotypical passivity of the heroine was licensed when her children were under threat.

The high point of Siddons's performance, the scene in which the Queen's statue is brought to life, became the focus of the later commentaries, unsurprising in a period when *tableaux vivants* were popular at court and in middle-class drawing rooms. Illustrations of the play frequently depict the actor playing Hermione as the statue, including Siddons, Mrs Kean, Mary Anderson, Faucit, and Terry. The fashion for producing *The Winter's Tale* as a 'Greek' play meant that the statue appeared resplendent in classical draperies (although Mrs Kean's modesty demanded an anachronistic crinoline). As Gail Marshall observes, 'the time-defying Classical mode absorbs the contradictions between eternal ideals and temporal female forms' (3). In other words, Hermione, as a living woman who has demonstrated the qualities of fidelity, endurance, and maternal love, is a supreme example of the nineteenth-century ideal of womanhood, but her appearance as a stone statue gives permanence to this ideal: the fact that she/the statue is presented in classical attire, and is thus uncircumscribed by contemporaneity, further valorises both the character and the ideal she represents.

Jameson lists Hermione as one of the 'Characters of the Affections', 'in which [...] the moral qualities predominate over fancy and all that bears the name of passion [... they] are best studied in repose' (157). It is fitting then that Hermione becomes a statue, 'with perfect command over her own feelings [...] complete self-possession' (167). Her silence reveals her 'sacred and awful charm', her 'strength and virtue' (169). Significantly, she breaks that silence only to bless Perdita, her child restored. Mary Cowden Clarke's story of Hermione's early life cites the same qualities as being present in the young girl as those Jameson praises in the adult. Leontes, on making the acquaintance of his future queen, finds her 'more nearly allied to sculptured marble than to living womanhood' (259). According to Cowden Clarke's interpretation, Hermione is 'statue-like' in her stillness and silence long before Paulina effects her reincarnation, leading one to the conclusion that the closer she came to being a living sculpture the closer the Victorian woman came to the ideal. In Faucit's discussion of the statue scene, in which her aim was to be in a 'natural posture' rather than 'rigidly statuesque', she focused her attention 'by picturing what Hermione's feelings would be when she heard Leontes' voice, silent to her for so many years' (*Characters* 386). The triumph of Faucit's 'statue' seems to have been her ability to maintain a delicate balance between the 'real' woman and the marble, arguably mirroring the duality of Faucit's 'womanly' performances in private life and on stage.

In *Four Lectures*, Ellen Terry includes only a brief reference to Hermione, applauding her dignity, loyalty, and pity, her comments on the play being focused on her role as Mamillius in 1856. Fifty years later she played Hermione, her last major Shakespearean part, in Beerbohm Tree's production at His Majesty's, one noted for overpowering, if beautifully executed, scenery and a corresponding massacre of Shakespeare's text. Terry, who by this time was having great difficulty in learning lines, often substituted her own language, 'which sounded just as good as Shakespeare's' (Pearson 132). In the statue scene, where Faucit created a miraculous living saint and 'felt awed by the soul of Hermione entering into hers' (392), Ellen Terry laughed:

A dreadful thing – I laughed last night!! as the statue! & I'm laughing now! Who could help it! With Leontes shouting & Paulina shouting they just roared so I cd not help it!. ... You see (as a statue) I don't look at 'em – I only hear them – & it's excruciatingly funny (Letter to Graham Robertson, 6 September 1906, qtd in Auerbach, *Ellen Terry* 283)

Was her mirth simply occasioned by the disembodied ranting of her fellow actors, or did Terry at the end of her career appreciate the irony of playing a stage icon of feminine virtue and maternal devotion?[6]

---

[6] In *Ellen Terry and Her Secret Self* (London: S. Low, Marston & Co. (1931)), Terry's son Edward Gordon Craig discusses her lack of maternal qualities at length.

Perdita: 'the daughter'

Perdita, to a modern reader or spectator, is not a realistic character. She is Proserpina, the mythical harbinger of Spring, the symbol of rebirth and renewal, effecting resurrection and redemption. But to the Victorian age she was a perfect candidate for idealisation, the perfect daughter to her adopted, and to her real, family, the perfect hostess of the pastoral feast, the perfect partner for a royal prince. That such a small part – she has only 127 lines – should receive such critical attention underlines the critical bias of the period. To Jameson she is 'the union of the pastoral and the romantic with the classical and poetical' (121), described in such glowing terms as 'delicate', 'elegant', 'sweet', 'artless', 'noble', 'graceful', possessed of 'strength and moral elevation' and 'a sense of truth and rectitude' (125). Leigh-Noel sees Perdita as 'another of Shakespeare's girl flowers that are wild by association and surroundings but cultivated and refined in origin and extraction' (277): her 'simple country life, instead of deteriorating her life[,] has refined it' (278). Like Jameson, Leigh-Noel flirts with the nature/nurture binary, contrasting pastoral Bohemia with the sophisticated court of Sicily, thus endorsing the popular nineteenth-century notion that simple goodness is associated with rural life, while the sophisticated metropolis harbours criminality and evildoing. Faucit, in common with the other commentators, idealises Perdita's pastoral childhood with the shepherd's wife as her mother figure, but her royal birth should be evident: 'This is left to the impersonator of Perdita to suggest. The audience must be made to feel as well as to see the princess' (*Characters* 373). Victorian Perditas were generally played by the company *ingénue*, and none seems to have achieved the duality of simplicity and nobility that Faucit seeks or the perfection Jameson and Cowden Clarke depict, being variously described as simpering, arch, or 'merely pretty' (Bartholemeusz 75).

Paulina: the 'friend'

The character of the passionate, articulate, and feisty Paulina presented a challenge to those intent on mapping Shakespeare's women onto conventional icons. Irene Dash recounts that the part had been regarded as problematic for some time:

As early as 1733 [...] Lewis Theobald [...] suggested emending a line of Paulina's because it seemed out of character for a woman. Theobald challenged the propriety of Paulina's calling the King a fool (III.ii.186) [...] Samuel Johnson interpreted Paulina's apology to Leontes after her strong condemnation of his actions as illustrative of 'the sudden changes incident to vehement and ungovernable minds' [...]. (134–5)

Anna Jameson, noting that 'The character of Paulina [...] has obtained but little notice, and no critical remark (that I have seen)' (170), accuses her of being 'too violent, too hard on Leontes' (172), yet admits that Shakespeare's drawing of her character is 'yet one of the most striking beauties of the play; and it has its moral too' (170):

> [Paulina] is [...] a clever, generous, strong-minded, warm-hearted woman, fearless in asserting the truth, firm in her sense of right, enthusiastic in all her affections; quick in thought, resolute in word, and energetic in action; but heedless, hot-tempered, impatient, loud, bold, voluble and turbulent of tongue; regardless of the feelings of those for whom she would sacrifice her life, and injuring from excess zeal those whom she most wishes to serve. [...] But Paulina, though a very termagant, is yet a poetical termagant in her way. (171)

The message for Jameson's target readers, seeking models of womanly behaviour, is that however righteous and principled a woman might be, however loyal a friend, her means of expression and her actions must be circumscribed by propriety.

Managers, actors, and commentators in the nineteenth century engage with various strategies to mitigate the effect of the deviant behaviour of the character. John Philip Kemble's restored text omits significant numbers of Paulina's lines, notably her refusal to be silenced (2.2.51–3), her resistance to male domination when it conflicts with her personal honour (2.3.47–50), and her merciless catalogue of Leontes' crimes against his wife, his children, and his friends (3.2.181–96). Excising these passages softens what were perceived to be unfeminine characteristics: volubility, boldness, independence of mind, and lack of compassion. Paulina is being reclaimed for perfection. The cuts, however, did not prevent Mrs Charles Kemble being criticised for being 'too coarse' in Kemble's production of 1807: 'What must we think of this noble lady's dignity with the courtiers [... when she] wanted nothing but an oil-skin gypsy bonnet and a basket under her arm to be as energetic a fish-woman, as ever was clamourous [*sic*] in the praise of eels' (*News* 15 November 1807, qtd in Bartholemeusz 53). The reviewer's inability to reconcile Paulina's vociferous speech with her noble appearance reveals how steeped he was in the received ideology of his time.

Helen Faucit played the part of Paulina at Drury Lane in 1835. She does not discuss her own performance, but in *Shakespeare's Female Characters* she likens Paulina's function in the drama to that of a Greek chorus. On her announcement of the 'death' of Hermione, 'Into her lips Shakespeare seems as if he wished to put, as the Greek tragedians did those of the

Chorus, the concentrated judgement of every man and woman in his kingdom' (366). As Mrs Charles Kemble appears to have done in performance, Faucit identifies Paulina's virtues with 'the common people' to whose honest, if unsophisticated, sentiments she gives a voice. Anna Jameson also describes Paulina as 'a character strongly drawn from *real and common life*' (171, my italics). Mary Cowden Clarke focuses on Paulina's challenge to patriarchal hierarchy, applauding her 'for boldly confronting her royal master himself with plain-spoken remonstrance and rebuke' (*Girlhood* 360–1). In her backstory recounted in *Girlhood*, Clarke praises her qualities of 'earnestness and conviction' in her defence of her father, unjustly exiled by the Emperor of Russia himself (202): the young Paulina is represented as a vociferous defender of innocence against regal authority, thus giving her a function as the popular voice of virtue confronting injustice and wrong-headed power. Implicitly the commentators explain (or excuse) Paulina's deviation from one feminine ideal, that of silent acquiescence, by attributing her passionate volubility to another feminine ideal, that of moral rectitude.

Another strategy to mitigate the perceived unwomanliness of the character was employed by Maud Tree, Paulina in her husband's 1906 production: she took full advantage of his inclusion of the newborn Perdita in the prison scene. *The Era* (8 September 1906) records that

Paulina is holding forth in an indignant tirade against the jealous tyrant, Leontes, her eyes flash, she stamps with her foot, when Emilia [...] approaches with the infant princess in her arms. At the sight of the babe Paulina's anger evaporates at a breath, the strident note leaves her voice as if by magic, as she coos as softly over it as a dove with a nestling. (Bartholemeusz 129)

A demonstration of maternal feelings, the supreme expression of true womanliness, is engaged to save the scold from censure.

The prevailing trend in performances and commentaries throughout the century was to smooth over, or to find reasons for, Paulina's assertiveness. Nevertheless, although Faucit believed that 'Paulina should be played by an actress of the first order' (*Characters* 354), in the nineteenth century the part was usually assigned to reputable, rather than star, performers. Whatever her acknowledged strengths of character and the strategies employed to bring her within the iconic pale, Paulina still fell below the expected standard of womanly excellence and was therefore less attractive to an actor at a time when performer and role were so closely identified.

CONCLUSION

A study of the writings by nineteenth-century women, both actors and commentators, on Shakespeare's heroines reveals more about received assumptions regarding the contemporary ideal woman than it does about Shakespeare. While individual authors wrote for financial gain or personal promotion, overall their work reveals a desire to educate, to support, and to entertain their 'sister women'. There is general consensus among commentators and performers regarding the *interpretation* of the characters. The only difference, and because of the prevailing fashion for character criticism that is minimal, lies in the approach taken to the subject by those who have 'personated' the characters on stage and the 'closet' critics, the former giving commentary on how their performance choices were made. All the women assume that their readers are committed to self-improvement and seek to facilitate that process by offering models of good behaviour and warnings of potential pitfalls, culled from an unimpeachable source. While they are committed to improving woman's lot, they do so, with the possible exception of Terry, by assisting her to become closer to 'what she should be' according to contemporary ideology. The validity of the ideal, the 'womanly woman' which had as much to do with politics as with gender, is not seriously questioned.

WORKS CITED

Altick, Richard D. *The Cowden Clarkes*. London: Oxford University Press, 1948.
Auerbach, Nina. *Ellen Terry: Player in Her Time*. London: J. M. Dent, 1987.
    Woman and the Demon: The Life of a Victorian Myth. Cambridge, Mass: Harvard University Press, 1982.
Bartholemeusz, Denis. *The Winter's Tale in Performance in England and America, 1611–1976*. Cambridge: Cambridge University Press, 1982.
Campbell, Thomas. *Life of Mrs Siddons*. 2 vols. London: Effingham Wilson, 1834.
Carlisle, Carol J. *Helen Faucit: Fire and Ice on the Victorian Stage*. London: Society for Theatre Research, 2000.
    'Helen Faucit's Acting Style'. *Theatre Survey* 17 (1976): 38–56.
    'The Critics Discover Shakespeare's Women'. *Renaissance Papers* (1979): 59–73.
Carlyle, Thomas. *On Heroes, Hero-Worship, and the Heroic in History*. London: Chapman and Hall, 1890.
Cowden Clarke, Mary. *The Girlhood of Shakespeare's Heroines*. 3 vols. London: W. H. Smith, Simpkin, Marshall & Co., 1850–1.
    'Shakespeare as the Girl's Friend'. *The Girl's Own Paper* June 1887: 562–4.
Dash, Irene. *Wooing, Wedding and Power: Women in Shakespeare's Plays*. New York: Columbia University Press, 1981.

Faucit, Helena [Lady Martin] *On Some of Shakespeare's Female Characters*. New and Enlarged Edition. Edinburgh and London: William Blackwood, 1891.

Unpublished correspondence to Ellen Braysher and Amelia Edwards, 1860–90, in Somerville College, Oxford. (I am grateful to Dr Brenda Moon for drawing my attention to these letters.)

Haight, Gordon S., ed. *George Eliot Letters*. Vol.1. London: Oxford University Press; New Haven: Yale University Press, 1954.

Hankey, Julie. 'Helen Faucit and Shakespeare: Womanly Theater'. *Cross-Cultural Performances: Differences in Women's Re-Visions of Shakespeare*. Ed. M. Novy. Urbana and Chicago: University of Michigan Press, 1993. 50–69.

Jameson, Anna. *Shakespeare's Heroines*. 2nd edn, 1833. Rpt. London: George Bell & Sons, 1900.

Johnston, Judith. *Anna Jameson: Victorian Feminist*. Aldershot: Scolar, 1997.

Kemble, Frances Anne. *Notes upon some of Shakespeare's Plays*. London: Richard Bentley and Son, 1882.

Leigh-Noel, M. *Shakespeare's Garden of Girls*. London: Remington & Co., 1885.

McLuskie, Kathleen. 'Patriarchal Shakespeare; Feminist Criticism and Shakespeare'. *Political Shakespeare: New Essays in Cultural Materialism*. Ed. Jonathan Dollimore and Alan Sinfield. Manchester: Manchester University Press, 1985. 88–108.

Marshall, Gail. *Actresses on the Victorian Stage: Feminine Performance and the Galatea Myth*. Cambridge: Cambridge University Press, 1998.

Martin, Sir Theodore. *Helena Faucit (Lady Martin)*. Edinburgh and London: William Blackwood & Sons, 1900.

Murray, Christopher. 'Macready, Helen Faucit and Acting Style'. *Theatre Notebook* 23 (1968): 21–5.

The New Shakespere Society's Transactions 1880–6. London: For the Society by Trubner & Co., 1886.

Pearson, Hesketh. *Beerbohm Tree*. Westport, Conn.: Greenwood Press, 1956.

Richardson, William. *Essays on some of Shakespeare's Dramatic Characters*. 5th edn. London: J. Murray and S. Highley, 1797.

Rozmovits, Linda. *Shakespeare and the Politics of Culture in Late Victorian England*. Baltimore and London: Johns Hopkins University Press, 1998.

Ruskin, John. 'Of Queens Gardens'. *Sesame and Lilies*. London and Glasgow: Collins, [c. 1918].

Shakespeare, William. *The Winter's Tale*. Ed. Susan Snyder and Deborah T. Curren-Aquino. The New Cambridge Shakespeare. Cambridge: Cambridge University Press, 2007.

Shattuck, Charles H., ed. *The John Philip Kemble Promptbooks*. Vol. IX. Charlottesville: For the Folger Shakespeare Library by the University Press of Virginia, 1974.

Terry, Ellen. *Four Lectures on Shakespeare*. Edited with an introduction by Christopher St. John. London: Martin Hopkinson Ltd., 1932.

The Story of My Life. London: Hutchinson & Co., 1908.

Thomas, Clara. *Life and Work Enough: The Life of Anna Jameson*. London: Macdonald, 1967.

Thompson, Ann, and Sasha Roberts. 'Mary Cowden Clarke: Marriage, Gender and the Victorian Woman Critic of Shakespeare'. *Literature and Culture*. Vol. II of *Victorian Shakespeare*. Ed. Gail Marshall and Adrian Poole. Basingstoke: Palgrave Macmillan, 2003. 170–89.

Ziegler, Georgianna. 'The Actress as Shakespearean Critic: Three Nineteenth-Century Portias'. *Theatre Survey* 30 (1989): 93–109.

CHAPTER 9

'Not our Olivia': Lydia Lopokova and Twelfth Night

Elizabeth Schafer

In 1933 Lydia Lopokova (1892–1981), the forty-one-year-old Russian prima ballerina, played Olivia for the Old Vic and Sadler's Wells theatre company. This *Twelfth Night* was Tyrone Guthrie's opening production in his very first season at the Vic-Wells and, while reviews were generally mixed, nearly all took the view that casting Lopokova as Olivia was a disaster. In a famous essay for the *New Statesman and Nation*, Virginia Woolf was, by comparison with most reviewers, very restrained, but she did pronounce that Lopokova's performance was 'not our Olivia' ('"Twelfth Night"' 385), thereby raising questions about what might constitute 'our Olivia' in 1933 and who 'we' might be. The witness provided by Woolf and other reviewers is particularly crucial in relation to this *Twelfth Night*, because the Vic-Wells archive was damaged during bombing in 1941 and no promptbooks remain. As a consequence, apart from some stagily posed promotional photographs, the major extant source of information on this performance has to be the reviews.[1] Given that online resources are currently making historical reviews more and more easily accessible, and it is becoming increasingly tempting to rely on reviews, even though their limitations – such as time and space restrictions, the politics of the newspaper in which they appeared, and occasionally personal vendettas by reviewers – are apparent, it seems appropriate to propose three readings of Lopokova's failure to perform 'our Olivia' that complicate the reviewers' consensus. Firstly, expanding on Jacky Bratton's discussion in her *New Readings in Theatre History* of 'Genealogy as women's history' (178–80) and following her suggestion that genealogy can be used 'to unpick some of the previous academic narratives of power' within theatre (196), I will situate Lopokova's performance within a lesbian genealogy for *Twelfth Night*. Secondly, because the major 'narrative of power' in relation to this

---

[1] These photographs are held in the Vic-Wells Association archive, V&A Theatre Collection, but are also much reproduced in the reviews: see *Twelfth Night* reviews collection (1933) 71–85, Birmingham Central Library.

production is the reviewers' testimony that it was a failure, I will also 'unpick' their narrative by exploring how Lopokova herself was read at that time by the audience base for her performance, the Vic-Wells community. Thirdly, I will suggest that acknowledgement of the theatre management practices that produced this performance might enable a very different, dance-centred reading of Lopokova's Olivia. In this exploration, I am not necessarily attempting to question the reviewers' aesthetic and critical judgement, and I am certainly not trying to reconstruct Lopokova's performance as a success, whatever that might mean, but to open up further the question of who 'our Olivia' might be.

LOPOKOVA'S OLIVIA

In playing Olivia, Lopokova was attempting to make a crossover from ballet into dramatic acting, but it would have been difficult for her to suppress thirty years of strenuous training in her first discipline, and many reviews attest to the balletic aspect of her Olivia and the fact that her 'speaking' body performed much around the articulation of Shakespeare's lines. At this stage in her career, Lopokova was past her best in terms of energy (she first danced with the Ballets Russes in 1910), but her dancing had always been famous for its vitality, energy, and exuberance: casting her as Olivia was definitely a decision to cast not the dying swan but the dancing soubrette.[2] It was not only putting on stage a performer mostly accustomed to communicating with her body, through the medium of dance, but a performer who was specifically known for character dancing. And it is important to remember that, whatever the reviewers made of this Olivia, the physicality of Lopokova's performance would have been deliberate, with little left to chance: as a dancer Lopokova was accustomed to precision choreography, to technically assured use of space.

The reviews usefully mark out very clear expectations in 1933 about how Olivia should and should not be performed, and for the vast majority of the reviewers Lopokova's performance was unacceptable for two reasons: her Russian accent mangled Shakespeare's words, and her physicality, what her body performed silently around the lines, subverted the dignity of 'our Olivia'.[3] Lopokova's pronunciation, which *The Times* suggested might be 'Illyrian', was, however, far less of an issue than her

---

[2] See Mackrell, who comments that during Lopokova's career she had 'never been compared to a swan – only to a sparrow, a canary, or at best a humming-bird' (xix).

[3] On the subject of Lopokova's articulation, in a letter to Ethel Smyth (31 July 1933), Woolf characterises Lopokova as speaking 'English like a parrokeet' (*Sickle* 209).

physicality and, in particular, her Olivia's lively, vivacious, and enthusiastic pursuit of Cesario, which was felt to be inappropriate for a character
the *Daily Telegraph* pronounced 'the most humourless female in literature'.
Lopokova's Olivia according to this reviewer was 'divested of dignity'.[4]
The *Sketch*, which stated that Olivia was the 'most gracious and aristocratic of all [Shakespeare's heroines]', was confident that Lopokova's 'giggles and pouts' were not right. The *Evening Standard* missed the decorum
of a 'Junoesque Countess Olivia', and the *Sunday Referee* described Olivia
as 'a Moscow minx' who made lots of running exits, exits which would
have been very much a characteristic of Lopokova's usual medium of
dance. The *Sunday Pictorial* argued that Lopokova was miscast because
she 'is no grand lady. Also her accent makes her scenes sound like [the
Russian revue group] Chauve-Souris. And imagine Olivia scampering
from Malvolio like a rabbit in a fright as she utters her dignified, "Let not
this fellow ..." etc.' The point hammered home by the reviewers is that
they expected and wanted to see *dignity* in performances of Olivia.

There were two dissenters to the condemnation of Lopokova: the *Daily
Express*, under the fighting headline 'Lopokova's Superb Olivia', claimed:

All preconceived ideas of Olivia, the haughty beauty, she brushed aside at the
outset by the magic expressiveness of her hands. They acted for her. The audience were fascinated.

The immortal words twisted her tongue but Mme. Lopokova only regarded
them as guide-posts for her sensitive, full-blooded acting.

The reviewer concluded (erroneously) that everyone would be 'bewitched
by the fairy grace of this actress-dancer'. Only one other review offered
any praise for Lopokova: the *New Age* found her performance 'delicious'
but offered no details about what this deliciousness entailed. The *Daily
Express* review, however, works from an appreciative focus on the physical, the 'magic expressiveness' of Lopokova's hands, at the expense of the
traditional centre of critical attention, Shakespeare's words. The review
also, in using the description 'full-blooded', suggests an alternative to the
traditional acting from the neck upwards associated with some classical
English acting of the period. This is balletomane reviewing, which saw
Lopokova as a major star and Shakespeare as assistant to the choreographer, but Lopokova's fellow ballet dancer, Robert Helpmann, was also
more positive than most reviewers in recalling that when Lopokova 'drew

---

[4] In some cases, the reviewer's desire for dignity may be due to the idea that Olivia's 'historical
original is Queen Elizabeth herself' (*Christian Science Monitor* 9 October 1933).

down her veil and said *is't not well done* with adorable artless pleasure' she 'brought down the house' (qtd in Mackrell 336).

It was certainly the physicality of Lopokova's performance and the enthusiasm with which she set about pursuing her Cesario, the twenty-seven-year-old Ursula Jeans, that produced the most suggestive commentary from reviewers. The *News Chronicle*, which thought Lopokova's performance 'quite out of character' for Olivia, particularly regretted that this Olivia 'made violent love to Viola'. The *Star* also disapproved of 'this doll-like figure' who 'bounced up and down the whirling steps, made perfect gestures and threw herself into a frenzy of passionate love-making'. The *Sunday Referee* similarly records that Olivia 'makes violent advances to Viola'. While the phrase 'making love' in 1933 did not necessarily denote full sexual congress, it certainly indicates something, as the *Daily Express* put it, 'full-blooded'. In addition, Lopokova brought to Olivia something of her offstage celebrity status: for decades she had been gossip-column fodder as she pursued her dancing career in Europe, the USA, and London and associated with brilliant artists and alternative lifestyles. Lopokova's friendships with figures like Stravinsky, Diaghilev, Massine, Nijinsky, and Picasso gave her an aura of non-normative exoticism and raciness without the precise details of her affairs necessarily being known. Even Lopokova's association with the Bloomsbury set – a group that on the whole despised her intellectually and resented her capture of, and marriage to, John Maynard Keynes – would, for some, have coloured her Olivia with non-normative associations and a questioning of compulsory heterosexuality and sexual exclusivity.[5]

Virginia Woolf's essay on the Old Vic *Twelfth Night* was published ten days after most other reviews, so she had plenty of time to ponder the general critical rejection of Lopokova's Olivia. Woolf, like many other reviewers, was acutely aware of the expressiveness of Lopokova's body, and her essay is a consummate, and oft-quoted, piece of writing on performance.[6] However, the essay was written through gritted teeth. Lopokova asked Woolf to review the production, and Woolf very reluctantly agreed: on 10 September 1933 Woolf wrote to Ethel Smyth that 'Lydia makes me write about 12th Night. Must go to London to Old Vic' (*Sickle* 223). Her diary for the same day notes, 'I must read 12th night for Lydia's extortion (an article on her appearance)' (*Diary* 179). Then on 19 September she wrote to Quentin Bell:

---

[5] Until Lopokova married Keynes, Bloomsbury had perceived him to be indubitably homosexual.
[6] Briggs comments on the fact that the essay is the 'closest' Woolf came to writing a formal essay on Shakespeare (125), although in some ways 'she never stopped writing about him' (128).

well, have you read the mornings paper on Lydia? The D.T. is scathing. My god; what shall I say? I think the only possible line to take is how very exciting it is to see Shakespr mauled; of course one might make play with the idea that the Elizabethans were just as unintelligible; and throw in a hint about opposites being the same thing as equalities – if you take my meaning. Either the worst, or the best – that sort of remark. Well. Pity me. (*Sickle* 227)

Woolf then saw Guthrie's *Twelfth Night* on the night of 20 September, having already digested the overall critical reaction and, writing to Lady Ottoline Morrell on 7 October 1933, she admitted:

Oh how I hated writing that tough little article! Poor Lydia asked me to do it – she attached great value to her acting – she wants to be an actress – and the whole thing was a dismal farce, and she is out of the Cherry Orchard in conse-quence.[7] But never will I write about a friend again. They may wear the stones out on their knees before I go through that agony. (*Sickle* 229–30)

The fact that Woolf's review also appeared in a newspaper that had evolved out of a recent merger between the *Nation*, run by Lopokova's husband, John Maynard Keynes, and the *New Statesman* is, of course, significant, and, in writing to Quentin Bell on 14 October 1933, Woolf notes that Keynes and Lopokova 'liked my article on her' (*Sickle* 235).[8]

Woolf, as she suggests she might in her letter to Quentin Bell, spends most of the review meditating on the disjunction between page and stage and how real, live actors may compare and challenge a reader's preconceptions. Having put off the moment of pronouncing judgement on the production as long as she reasonably could, Woolf eventually concedes that it was a disappointment and that, although the challenge the production posed to her preconceptions of *Twelfth Night* may be valuable, she disliked most of what she saw. However, Woolf does pro-vide a vivid evocation of Lopokova in action, which is worth quoting at length:

Madame Lopokova has by nature that rare quality which is neither to be had for the asking nor to be subdued by the will – the genius of personality. She has only to float on to the stage and everything round her suffers, not a sea change, but a change into light, into gaiety; the birds sing, the sheep are garlanded, the air rings with melody and human beings dance towards each other on the tips of their toes possessed of an exquisite friendliness, sympathy and delight. But our Olivia was a stately lady; of sombre complexion, slow moving, and of few sym-pathies. She could not love the Duke nor change her feeling. Madame Lopokova

---

[7] *The Cherry Orchard* was the next play in the Vic-Wells season.
[8] Briggs comments that Woolf's 'review is so carefully worded that, at first glance, one might mis-take it for praise' (125).

loves everybody. She is always changing. Her hands, her face, her feet, the whole of her body, are always quivering in sympathy with the moment. She could make the moment, as she proved when she walked down the stairs with Sebastian, one of intense and moving beauty; but she was not our Olivia. ('"Twelfth Night"' 385)

Woolf particularly evokes the physicality of this Olivia, and Lopokova's biographer, Judith Mackrell, comments, 'Ironically, this description, fantastical and obligated as it was, ranks as one of the most vivid snapshots ever published of Lydia in performance' (337).

A LESBIAN GENEALOGY

One way of contextualising Lopokova's physically disconcerting Olivia is by means of a lesbian genealogy for *Twelfth Night* in performance, although no reviewer of Lopokova's Olivia who wanted to keep their job in 1933 was going to discuss her performance explicitly in terms of lesbian desire, and there is no evidence that Lopokova intended to perform such a desire: Lopokova privately recorded that she wanted to play Olivia as 'haughty and princess like [and] beautiful if possible in clothes, speech, ankles and wrists'.[9] This description does not quite coincide with the reviewers' vision of running exits, giggles, pouts, scampering and balletic physicality, and 'beautiful [...] ankles' would have been partly obscured by the Caroline costumes of the production. However, it is important to acknowledge that when Lopokova's Olivia was seen to be 'making love' so enthusiastically to Cesario it *could* have been read as lesbian – whatever Lopokova's views on the subject – in 1933. It was sometimes possible to stage gay and lesbian characters in mainstream theatre in the UK before the legal milestone of 1968 when censorship of such performances was technically relaxed, especially when using canonical texts:[10] for example, the role of the Tailor in Tyrone Guthrie's 1939 production of *The Taming of the Shrew* was performed in a very camp way by dancer Robert Helpmann – then beginning *his* crossover from ballet into an acting career at the Vic-Wells – and this character was then presumably read as gay by many. What is more, the trial of Radclyffe Hall's lesbian novel *The Well of Loneliness* in November 1928 had alerted everyone who read newspapers to the existence of lesbian culture in England,

---

[9] Letter from Lydia Lopokova to John Maynard Keynes 20 April 1933, qtd in Mackrell 335.
[10] The first time *Twelfth Night* went officially gay in the UK was in Jonathan Miller's 1969 production for the Oxford & Cambridge Shakespeare Company, a production that toured the UK and the USA.

and Lopokova was performing for a theatre company that, for some, had the reputation of being a 'lesbian stronghold' (Findlater 240). Although the description 'lesbian stronghold' is sensationalist, the Vic-Wells manager Lilian Baylis certainly employed and networked with high-profile lesbians such as Lady Rhondda, promoted the work of lesbian artists such as Ethel Smyth and Gertrude Stein, and had many extremely close professional, single, and feminist women friends such as actor-dramatist Cicely Hamilton and stockbroker (Beatrice) Gordon Holmes.[11] Ironically enough, in spite of Virginia Woolf's categorical statement that this was 'not our Olivia', the potentially lesbian dynamic in the physicality of Lopokova's performance was in some ways very close to home for Woolf, whose relationship with Vita Sackville-West had been marked in 1928 with the publication of *Orlando*.

While this essay is not an essentialist argument for collapsing the artists' professional and personal lives, I am suggesting that interpretation of Olivia (and Viola) could be broadened by acknowledging readings and performances produced by women living an experience of difference; the lesbian genealogy I am proposing for *Twelfth Night* offers a master narrative that helps locate Lopokova's physicality in her Olivia's pursuit of Cesario in a historical context. My genealogy begins with the lesbian actress Margaret Webster (1905–72), who later became an extremely successful director in the USA. Webster's work is still rather undervalued, and her later directing career became blighted by her blacklisting by HUAC during the 1950s – she was a left-leaning supporter of Equity unionism, as well as being, for the time, relatively out as a lesbian within her own social circle.[12] Webster is likely to have seen Lopokova's performance as she was working at the Vic-Wells at the end of the 1932–3 season, playing Lady Macbeth, and she was based in London until relocating to the USA in 1937. Webster's own personal engagement with *Twelfth Night* was complex and various. She first played Viola for the indefatigable if occasionally rough and ready Philip Ben Greet in 1928 (Webster, *The Same* 321). Later Webster directed *Twelfth Night* for the Theatre Guild on Broadway in 1940, in a production starring Maurice Evans and Helen Hayes, which ran for 128 performances and was a great commercial success. Webster records that Helen Hayes was wary of being directed by a woman (*Don't Put* 96), and that, in Webster's view, 'the best performance' was not that of the stars, Hayes and Evans, but that of the 'the least known of its principal players, Sophie Stewart', who as Olivia 'managed to hold all [the

[11] See Schafer, *Lilian Baylis*.　[12] See Barranger.

play's] elements together and in focus' (94). Olivia is not usually seen as the linchpin of the play in this way. Webster felt disappointed with the production overall but believed this was 'because I loved *Twelfth Night* very much and the gap between my vision and the concrete result was wider than it had ever been before' (98).

Webster directed *Twelfth Night* in a period during which she 'gravitated towards a lesbian subculture of theatre artists that included Mady Christians and Eva Le Gallienne' (Barranger 121). Webster's friendship with the actor-director Le Gallienne dated back to 1913 when Webster (then aged eight) first encountered the fourteen-year-old Le Gallienne on holiday. In adult life the two women became friends and worked on many productions together. Around the summer of 1941 they became lovers (Barranger 121). Le Gallienne had herself directed *Twelfth Night* in New York in 1926, when she herself played Viola and her then-lover, Gladys Calthrop, designed the show.[13] In this production all the major characters of the play, with the sole exception of Olivia, were costumed as puppet-like creations. Production photographs held in the New York Public Library indicate that the visuals signalled very clearly that the only 'real' major character being represented on stage was the Olivia of Beatrice Terry: certainly the *New York Times* (21 December 1926) thought that among the puppet-like characters 'Olivia alone remains literal'. Le Gallienne's and Calthrop's construction of Olivia as a real woman in a land of puppets suggests a sympathetic focus on the character and her predicament.

Twelfth Night also provides a connection forwards to Webster's fourteen-year relationship with the novelist Pamela Frankau, which dated from 1953 (Barranger 260). Frankau's 1949 novel *The Willow Cabin* draws on, and quotes extensively from, *Twelfth Night*, and the central character, an actress named Caroline Seward, actually performs the role of Viola when she comes on as understudy, a performance described in detail through the eyes of a man who is in love with her (Frankau 40–4).[14] Frankau was bisexual, and *The Willow Cabin* depicts her relationship with the poet Humbert Wolfe in the guise of the reckless, career- and reputation-destroying love-affair on which Caroline embarks with a married man, Michael Knowles. Caroline eventually achieves career success after Michael's death and

---

[13] This was Le Gallienne's first foray into Shakespeare: Sheehy notes that up until then Le Gallienne's attitude had been 'God save me from Shakespeare [[…]] I can't help being bored to death with him!' (156).

[14] The production was characterised by its black and white costumes, which suggests some debt to the famous 1932 'black and white' production of *Twelfth Night*, directed by Robert Atkins (see below).

H.ANELAY

MISS CUSHMAN AS " VIOLA," AND MISS SUSAN CUSHMAN AS   OLIVIA," IN "TWELFTH NIGHT," AT THE HAYMARKET THEATRE

HAYMARKET THEATRE.

THE annexed Illustration is taken from the 5th Scene of the 1st Act of
" Twelfth Night;" the characters being *Viola* (Miss Cushman). and
Olivia (Miss Susan Cushman) ; as lately performed at the Haymarket.
The following lines relate to the sketch :—

> *Olivia.*   Get you to your Lord;
> I cannot love him ; let him send no more ;
> Unless, perchance, you come to me again,
> To tell me how he takes it. Fare you well :
> I thank you for your pains : spend this for me.
>   *Viola.* I am no fee'd post, Lady : keep your purse
> My master, not myself, lacks recompense.
> Love make his heart of flint, that you shall love ;
> And let your fervour, like my master's, be
> Plac'd in contempt ! Farewell, fair cruelty !   [*Exit.*

6. Anelay's illustration of Charlotte Cushman (Cesario/Viola) and Susan Cushman
(Olivia) in Act 1, Scene 5, lines 234a–43.

establishes a complex and loving relationship with his widow, Mercedes.
The interplay between these three characters is frequently haunted by
Twelfth Night and the relationships between Olivia, Orsino, and Viola.

This web of *Twelfth Night* connections can be expanded further, by
means of Margaret Webster's theatre history writing, back to 1846, when
the celebrated (lesbian) actress Charlotte Cushman performed Viola/

Cesario for Webster's illustrious forbear, Benjamin Webster (1798–1882), the manager of the Haymarket Theatre.[15] Cushman was actually reluctant to play *Twelfth Night* in London and wrote so to Benjamin Webster (who played Feste in this production): 'Take my word for it, all old parts are bad for me in consequence of *comparison*. I cannot stand this test well. I know myself perfectly ... As I look on Viola now – it is *weak* for me, and my sister does not wish to do Olivia in London' (qtd in Webster, *The Same* 66). On the evidence of the illustration published in the *Illustrated London News* (11 July 1846: 29), non-normative dynamics were in play in this performance. Cushman avoided the femininity that was seen at the time to be *de rigueur* in the role of Cesario and epitomised in the performances of Ellen Tree/Kean as Viola. Predictably, reviewers focused on Cushman's Viola at the expense of her sister Susan's Olivia, although the light and shading in the *ILN* illustration encourages the viewer to focus on Susan rather than Charlotte Cushman. *The Times* (26 June 1846: 5) records Charlotte Cushman's performance as 'intelligent', if unconventional, avoiding 'gaiety' and instead emphasising 'earnestness throughout'. Cushman delivered the line when Viola realises Olivia is in love with her – 'I am the man!' (2.2.22) – 'as the expression of a serious conviction' instead of, as was more usual, a joke. Cushman also played 'She never told her love' (2.4)

according to a very clever conception. Instead of adopting the obvious mode of rendering the sentiment prominent, and dropping for a while the character which Viola has feigned, she makes visible the intention to shield her feelings, by assuming the tone of an indifferent narrator, so that the pathos of the situation is more than usually suppressed. (*The Times* 26 June 1846: 5)

However, this reading also plays down one of the most memorable expressions of heterosexual desire in the play. Meanwhile, Susan Cushman's Olivia was applauded because, 'in those delicate situations where the lady has to be the love-maker', she 'expressed the sentiment alike with earnestness and delicacy', displaying 'quietness of manner' and 'an earnestness of purpose'. What is most striking about *The Times*'s review is the thrice-repeated use of 'earnestness' to characterise the Cushmans' *Twelfth Night* and its testimony as to the lack of traditional comedy. The implication is

---

[15] Laurie Osborne (96–8) has explored some of the potential for lesbian readings of Olivia in the nineteenth century, in particular in reference to John Lucas Tupper's poem 'Viola and Olivia', published alongside an etching by Walter Deverell; see also Melchiori on this engraving. Osborne, however, does not engage with the possible impact of Cushman's performance. The Cushman sisters, of course, had great success playing Romeo and Juliet opposite each other.

that the Cushmans knew, and performed the knowledge, that the social consequences of same-sex love were deadly serious.

Such knowledge also connects, in the broad-brush lesbian genealogy I am proposing, forward from Cushman and Webster. Contemporary theatre, drawing on feminism and the gay and lesbian liberation movements, has often expanded the theatrical horizons for Olivia, especially in the work of theatre artists associated with these political movements. For example, Ariane Mnouchkine's 1982 *Twelfth Night* focused on love as a madness that drives people wild and featured an extraordinary Olivia.[16] When Olivia was struck by love for Cesario, Odile Cointepas's Olivia expressed it in an extraordinary, wild, and completely frenzied dance around the stage, an extra-textual whirling dervish performance accompanied by insistent, frantic percussion. While subsequently other characters performed similar dances – Antonio for love of Sebastian, Malvolio at the end of 2.5 for love of what he thinks is his future – the fact that Olivia's was the very first of these dances, as well as being a quite startling burst of energy suddenly exploding into a generally enervated theatrical world, meant that it was this dance that had the most impact. In particular, because Olivia's energy contrasted so starkly with the drooping, wailing caricature Orsino (who appeared so ridiculous that the audience laughed loudly at him every time he appeared), part of the impact of Olivia's dance was to make Olivia a real centre for this production, an effect enhanced by the fact that Joséphine Derenne's Viola became infected by Orsino's weeping and wailing, particularly in 3.1, and was therefore not a go-getting Viola/Cesario who might detract much dramatic interest from Olivia. Meanwhile Toby – played by Philippe Hottier – and his cronies were clearly signalled, both by virtuoso clowning routines and by their 'theme music', as broad clown characters, not to be taken seriously. John Arnold's Malvolio was unusually ridiculous by late twentieth-century standards and, again, provided little competition in terms of sympathetic engagement for the remarkable, and physicalised, frenzy of Olivia.

Theatre practitioners such as Cushman and Mnouchkine are not, of course, alone in taking the performance of Olivia's predicament seriously, and it is not, nowadays, that unusual to suggest that Olivia may be disappointed to find she is married to Sebastian instead of Cesario.[17]

---

[16] Mnouchkine originally planned this production, which opened on 10 July 1982, to be an all-female one, but in the end only Andrew and Curio were cross-cast and played by women. For images of this production, see www.lebacausoleil.com/SPIP/article.php3?id_article=95.

[17] Recent productions that have clearly attempted to consider that Olivia might prefer Viola to Sebastian at the end of *Twelfth Night* include, for example, those directed by Stephen Beresford in London in 2004 and Neil Bartlett at the RSC in 2007; see Hamburger for some German

The challenge of Olivia's sexuality can also be placed by Irene Dash's discussion of how 'Olivia suffers both in criticism and staging' because she 'forthrightly expresses her desire' (212). However, a lesbian genealogy of *Twelfth Night* and Olivia in performance establishes the longevity of a lesbian presence in productions of this play. It is unlikely that the original performances of *Twelfth Night*, in which Shakespeare himself appeared, explored this dimension of Olivia, as, no matter how skilled the boy actors were, this aspect would be extremely difficult for them to perform.[18] However, it is also important to note that the practitioners considered here – Cushman, Le Gallienne, Webster, Mnouchkine – were/are all extremely successful, accomplished, and experienced theatre workers. Not anarchic, alternative, fringe practitioners setting out to shock everyone (not to denigrate the great value such work can have) but theatrical heavyweights, in their practice these woman have consistently exhibited acute, if not necessarily conventional, theatrical intelligence. Mapping out something of their engagement with *Twelfth Night* renders the unacceptable Olivia of Lopokova less extraordinary and suggests that Lopokova's dramatically unruly, balletic body, performing far more than most reviewers wanted to see, actually helps to highlight how entrenched reviewers had become on the subject of 'their Olivia' and of how Olivia ought to be performed: as Woolf put it in her essay, at least Guthrie's production 'has made us compare our Malvolio with Mr. Quartermaine's; our Olivia with Madame Lopokova's; our reading of the whole play with Mr. Guthrie's; and since they all differ, back we must go to Shakespeare. We must read *Twelfth Night* again' ('"Twelfth Night"' 386).

THE VIC-WELLS COMMUNITY

Another approach to Lopokova's Olivia that diverges radically from that of the reviewers is to read the performance via the *Old Vic and Sadler's Wells Magazine* (henceforward *OVM*), the community newsletter of the Old Vic and Sadler's Wells audiences. This magazine positions Lopokova's

---

examples. There are, of course, other examples of clearly lesbian Olivias in action, including the tiresome soft porn film of the play directed by Ron Wertheim, funded by Playboy, which plays very much to all the clichés of the *Playboy* gaze.

[18] For a consideration of the desires that may have been available in the original performances of *Twelfth Night* and in other plays of the period featuring women characters wooing other women, see Michael Shapiro, especially Chapter 7, 'Anxieties of Intimacy: *Twelfth Night*'. Shapiro's discussion includes the desires that may have been performed in Richard Brome's *A Mad Couple Well Matched*, a play that very clearly looks back to the Viola narrative in *Twelfth Night* and which was adapted by Aphra Behn as *The Debauchee*.

Olivia indubitably as 'ours', in the sense of belonging to and being appreciated by the Vic-Wells community. While the *OVM* never reviewed work at the Vic or the Wells, its coverage of items relating to Lopokova and *Twelfth Night* suggests a different master narrative from that appearing in the newspaper reviews.

The Vic-Wells audiences knew Lopokova as a star dancer who generously supported the new Vic-Wells ballet company, support that included dancing for them for free. So the *OVM* for March 1933, in reporting on preparations for the ballet company's first production of *Coppelia*, signals indebtedness to Lopokova very clearly:

> At the instigation of Madame Lopokova, M. Sergeyeff, at one time ballet-master of the Imperial School at Moscow, has arrived from Paris to produce the ballet. As he speaks very little French and less English, the company will no doubt have some exciting rehearsals; but Madame Lopokova has been endlessly kind in translating the various letters which have passed arranging the matter. (1)

Lopokova was to dance the title role, which she had declared 'her farewell appearance in ballet'; the writer in the *OVM* hopes Lopokova will change her mind and stresses how 'generously [Lopokova] has led the Vic-Wells ballet' and what 'memorable occasions' these performances have been. The *OVM* for April 1933 reports that Lopokova was 'not only her enchanting self on the stage, but a tower of strength during rehearsals', and is delighted to report that Lopokova has agreed to 'her third and extra performance of "Coppelia"' (1). The reviewers were also enthusiastic: the *Observer* (26 March 1933) enjoyed Lopokova's 'every step, smile, and gesture', her 'gaiety, sense of character, and style', and concluded, 'Her protean doll dances in Act II. were inimitable, and made this old ballet seem as fresh and delightful as ever.'

The *OVM* for September 1933, when *Twelfth Night* opened, contains mini-biographies of cast members for the following year. Lopokova's 550-word biography concentrates on her dance career, but does attempt to establish that she has serious acting credentials: she appeared

> as a child-actor on the Imperial stage, [...] in speaking parts in many operas and plays, including Shakespeare's 'A Winter's Tale' and 'A Midsummer Night's Dream' with Chaliapin, Komisarjevska, Savina and other great Russian actors of the pre-war tradition [...] She has also appeared since 1927 in speaking parts in Calderon's 'Life's a Dream', Shakespeare's 'Lover's Complaint', Milton's 'Comus' and a sketch by Molnar.

The *OVM* returned to chronicling Lopokova's activities in January 1934. The Vic-Wells ballet was then embarking on preparation for the first-ever performance of *The Nutcracker* in England, and Lopokova was again translating for Sergeyeff in rehearsal, although, 'Until we see the finished work, it is difficult to tell whether we shall like the real thing better than Madame Lopokova's playing of all the parts – an old gentleman taking snuff, a naughty girl refusing to greet the guests, and a little girl with her doll – at once' (2). All this coverage suggests that the famously partisan Vic-Wells community would be responding to Lopokova's Olivia generously, no matter how much she mangled Shakespeare's metre. It also suggests that they could have been reading, and appreciating, her Olivia through the filter of her Swanilde/Coppelia, a reading that would look for and enjoy energy and liveliness, rather than the reviewers' desideratum in Olivia of dull dignity.

MANAGING WOMEN

One person who indubitably benefited from Lopokova's Olivia was the manager of the Vic-Wells, Lilian Baylis: her theatres received a lot of attention (that is, free publicity) in the brouhaha following the opening night but, more importantly, by means of the casting of Olivia, the Vic-Wells dance company was continuing to build up a relationship with the influential and generous Lopokova and her extremely wealthy husband. Awareness of the management practice behind Lopokova's performance produces a salutary master narrative that marginalises Shakespeare in terms of this *Twelfth Night*.

It is important to remember that at this stage English ballet was not the significant cultural force it is today and that the Vic-Wells ballet still had a very long way to go before it was to evolve into its current form of the English Royal Ballet. In 1933 the creation, the nurturing, and the development of a serious English dance company were projects very dear to the heart of Baylis, a former dance teacher, as well as to the director of the ballet company, Ninette de Valois. As a manager Baylis was famous for – by normative standards – eccentric management: for doing the unexpected, for trying to save money, and for being a forceful presence, a larger-than-life personality. She famously took no notice of reviewers – for a long time she refused to give them free seats – and it is likely Baylis would have been happy to field a few critical brickbats on *Twelfth Night* for the long-term net gains her ballet company derived in the form of the backing of the Camargo Society, a society founded in 1930 to encourage, nurture, and produce British ballet and dominated by Lopokova and Keynes.

That these gains were significant is demonstrated in the *OVM* for January 1934, which reports that the Camargo Society was substantially increasing its support for the Vic-Wells ballet (2). By February 1934 the *OVM* was reporting proposals to fuse the Camargo Society and the Vic-Wells ballet company (2); what happened eventually was that the Camargo Society's rights to ballets and all its existing resources, including scenery and costumes, were divided up between the Vic-Wells ballet company and Marie Rambert's dance company.

Awareness of this narrative might help shed light on the question posed by the *Daily Telegraph* reviewer when he demanded 'What possessed anybody to give the part of Olivia to Lydia Lopokova?' The casting decision, of course, would have ultimately rested with the director of the production, Tyrone Guthrie. As a director, Guthrie was always willing to take risks, and it is certainly possible he decided that his vision of *Twelfth Night* had to include Lopokova as Olivia. However, Guthrie's own writings offer no comment on the startling idea of casting Lopokova in that role.[19] Indeed, Guthrie's account of his arrival at the Vic-Wells stresses that for him the crucial move was hiring Flora Robson for the company. It was his 'duty to propose a programme and a cast for the season' (Guthrie 105), and Guthrie's priorities in terms of the company can be deduced, from his own account, as securing the services of Charles Laughton, Athene Seyler, Ursula Jeans, Leon Quartermaine, Roger Livesey, Morland Graham, Marius Goring, and James Mason. In fact, Guthrie mentions almost every major player in his company except for Lopokova. And all Guthrie has to say in retrospect about this *Twelfth Night* is that, although he personally liked the set (which was modernist), it was probably a mistake.

It may be that Guthrie blanked his memories of Lopokova's performance. However, Guthrie had no previous history in relation to Lopokova, and his previous career had involved him mostly working away from London, and Lopokova's and Keynes's spheres of influence, in northern Ireland (in radio) and in Scotland. Guthrie could have discovered his Olivia in March 1933 when Lopokova publicly declared in an interview that, 'When I have finally said farewell to dancing [...] I should like to act. I should like to be a comedy actress. I wish I could find a manager to give me the small part of a soubrette' (*Observer* 26 March 1933: 21). Lopokova suggested she might play 'that girl in "The Master Builder"' and ruminated, 'Could I do tragedy? How could one do tragedy with a nose like

---

[19] James Forsyth's biography of Guthrie also contains no information on Lopokova.

this? But I think I could do dramatic parts. I should like to do a dramatic ingénue, if such a thing exists.' Lopokova's biographer, Judith Mackrell, states that Guthrie approached Lopokova very soon after the publication of this interview in April 1933 and suggested she play Olivia.[20] Mackrell also relates that 'a campaign was launched to dissuade [Lopokova] from accepting' and that Dadie Rylands attempted to persuade her that the role of Maria – which was played by one of Guthrie's chosen actresses, Athene Seyler – was better suited to her talents. Lopokova herself was nervous about playing Olivia and had coaching from Keynes over the summer preceding the rehearsal period.[21]

The fact that Lopokova was in search of 'a *manager* to give me the small part of a soubrette' (my italics) makes it seem possible, however, that the idea of casting her as Olivia came from the Vic-Wells community rather than from Guthrie.[22] Certainly, the fact that Lopokova was so speedily dropped from *The Cherry Orchard*, Guthrie's next production after *Twelfth Night*, suggests that he was not completely committed to Lopokova's cause.[23] However, the casting, or miscasting, of Lopokova also helped create an implicit debate, via the negative reviews, on what behaviour is proper for a woman in a position of power and authority. Olivia is unusual in the plays of Shakespeare simply in being a woman who rules her own household. Sebastian's testimony in 4.2 indicates that, at least in his view, she rules well, even though she has not always been portrayed this way in the theatre.[24] But it is also noteworthy that for his first two plays at the Vic-Wells, an institution famously ruled by a strong-minded woman, Guthrie chose two 'big house' plays, *Twelfth Night* and *The Cherry Orchard*, where the houses in question are ruled, with varying degrees of responsibility, by a woman. That programming in itself is suggestive of a meditation on the subject of managing women.

Finally, it is also important to note that the stage history of Olivia actually indicates that Lopokova's Olivia was not as aberrant as the reviewers

---

[20] Mackrell falls for the contemporary reviewers' line on Olivia and characterises her as 'this most stately and solemn of Shakespeare's women' (335), as well as the 'slow, fastidious and literal-minded heroine of Shakespeare's vision' (336).

[21] Mackrell states Lopokova was 'obviously crushed' by her failure as Olivia (338).

[22] Lopokova also downplayed the role of directors – then called producers – in her *Observer* interview, commenting that at the time 'Producers seem to me on the whole to be lacking' and praising a production of *The Green Bay Tree* that she had seen recently, adding the rider 'And who produced it? Mr. Milton Rosmer – an actor!' (*Observer* 26 March 1933: 21).

[23] See above: Virginia Woolf, letter to Lady Ottoline Morrell, 7 October 1933 (*Sickle* 230).

[24] The stage history analysis in this chapter is based on my volume on *Twelfth Night* for Cambridge University Press's Shakespeare in Production series.

suggested. Olivias have not always been, as the 1933 reviewers wanted, mature and full of dignity. During the eighteenth century, for example, Olivia was a singing role, often played by beautiful young actresses who were musically accomplished, such as Kitty Clive and Elizabeth Farren. These attractive, singing Olivias often feature in playbills advertising *Twelfth Night*, and the fact that they will sing is clearly a major selling point. While these singing Olivias would not have fitted comfortably with Virginia Woolf's vision of 'our Olivia' – 'stately', 'sombre', and 'slow moving' – they seem quite in sympathy with Lopokova's half-dancing Olivia. Indeed, it is worth noting that Olivia continued to sing in the twentieth century and actually did so in a very successful production nearly contemporary with Lopokova's performance: in 1932, Robert Atkins directed a *Twelfth Night* in which Phyllis Neilson-Terry's Olivia sang, and this production, which became known as the 'black and white' *Twelfth Night*, was so successful it was not only revived many years running but also inaugurated the tradition of playing Shakespeare in Regent's Park.

Lopokova's physically enthusiastic Olivia also has many descendants today. Indeed, it has become unremarkable to play Olivia as physically exuberant, sometimes even a man-eater, with Sebastian often emerging for 4.3 in a dishevelled state, indicating he and Olivia have had sex and suggesting that Olivia has half-ravished him. However, modern productions that make Olivia lurch from mourning sister to sexual predator can invoke a really misogynist dynamic, especially when Toby and his cronies are played as vile, with the punishment they mete out to Malvolio bordering on torture: the more Olivia fails to restrain those who clearly should be restrained, the more implied blame attaches to her, and the more her suitability for government is questioned. This line of interpretation has gained impetus from the increasing interest, post-Irving, in presenting Malvolio as a tragic hero: the worse Malvolio's suffering becomes, the more Olivia's household is seen to be out of control, and the more her governance is implicitly condemned.

If nothing else, Lydia Lopokova's Olivia, simply by running foul of the reviewers, helps to mark out vividly what was and what was not acceptable to reviewers in an Olivia in 1933. Just how entrenched reviewers could be on this subject is particularly clearly illustrated by reference to one area where Lopokova did *not* upset them: age. In 1933 reviewers were adamant that Olivia should not be young, despite the fact that there is nothing in the play to pin down her age and despite the fact that the theatre had been casting Olivia as young and frisky for years. Indeed some reviewers – presumably unconsciously – were almost attempting to write young Olivias out of theatre history: so reviews of production after production claim, when confronted by a young Olivia, that this performance is breaking the mould and flouting tradition, even when the very same reviewer had said precisely the same thing about the last youthful Olivia he had reviewed. Three examples, from among many, make this clear: of Gwynne Whitby playing Olivia in Andrew Leigh's Old Vic production of 1927, the *Observer* (9 January 1927) opined: 'Gwynne Whitby has youth and charm, but hardly experience enough to queen it over the state given her by Shakespeare'; in 1931, Joan Harben's Olivia, in an Old Vic production directed by Harcourt Williams, was 'little more than a child, not a creature of almost Royal dignity' (*The Times* 7 January 1931); and yet in 1939 the Olivia in Irene Hentschel's production at Stratford was for *Daily Telegraph* critic W. A. Darlington, who had seen both Whitby's and Harben's performances, 'not the stately and mature lady we are used to but a charming little wilful heiress hardly out of the school room' (14 April). The reviewers' refusal to concede that their norm of a mature, dignified Olivia did not reflect actual theatre practice really highlights how set their views were on the subject of this particular character.

At a time when ever easier online access to historical reviews risks making them the dominant voice in the history of Shakespeare in performance, unpicking some of the disturbances created by Lopokova's physicality as Olivia is particularly salutary. Other ways of reading this performance will inevitably produce other master narratives, but a genealogy of Olivia and lesbian theatre workers, the contribution Shakespeare made (via Lopokova's Olivia) to the creation of what was to become the English Royal Ballet, and the unpredictable impact on the stage history of Shakespeare of eccentric theatre management practices all expand and complicate the discussion of what *Twelfth Night* can mean in performance, and of what is acceptable behaviour in 'our Olivia'.

I would like to thank Jacky Bratton, Richard Cave, Vincent Jones, Eleanor Lowe, Lesley Reidel, Peta Tait, and Libby Worth, who commented on earlier versions of this chapter.

WORKS CITED

Barranger, Milly S. *Margaret Webster: A Life in the Theater*. Ann Arbor: University of Michigan Press, 2004.

Briggs, Julia. 'Virginia Woolf Reads Shakespeare: Or, her Silence on Master William'. *Shakespeare Survey* 58 (2005): 118–29.

Bratton, Jacky. *New Readings in Theatre History*. Cambridge: Cambridge University Press, 2003.

Darlington, W. A. Review of *Twelfth Night*, dir. Irene Hentschel, Memorial Theatre, Stratford-upon-Avon, 13 April 1939. *Daily Telegraph* 14 April 1939.

Dash, Irene. *Women's Worlds in Shakespeare's Plays*. London: Associated University Presses, 1997.

Findlater, Richard. *Lilian Baylis: The Lady of the Old Vic*. London: Allen Lane, 1975.

Frankau, Pamela. *The Willow Cabin*. London: Heinemann, 1949.

Guthrie, Tyrone. *A Life in the Theatre*, London: Hamish Hamilton, 1960; Columbus Books, 1987.

Habicht, Werner, D. J. Palmer, and Roger Pringle, eds. *Images of Shakespeare: Proceedings of the Third Congress of the International Shakespeare Association, 1986*. Newark, Del.: University of Delaware Press, 1988.

Hamburger, Maik. 'A Spate of *Twelfth Night*s: Illyria Rediscovered?' Habicht, Palmer, and Pringle. 236–44.

Mackrell, Judith. *Bloomsbury Ballerina: Lydia Lopokova, Imperial Dancer and Mrs John Maynard Keynes*. London: Weidenfeld and Nicolson, 2008.

Melchiori, Barbara Arnett. 'Undercurrents in Victorian Illustrations of Shakespeare'. Habicht, Palmer, and Pringle. 120–8.

Mnouchkine, Ariane, dir. *La Nuit des Rois*. 10 July 1982, Avignon Festival; 6 October 1982, Cartoucherie, Paris. Video record of performance, Drama Department, University of Kent at Canterbury.

The Old Vic and Sadler's Wells Magazine, University of Bristol Theatre Collection.

Osborne, Laurie E. *The Trick of Singularity: Twelfth Night and the Performance Editions*. Iowa City: University of Iowa Press, 1996.

Review of *Twelfth Night*, dir. Andrew Leigh, Old Vic, 3 January 1927. *Observer* 9 January 1927.

Review of *Twelfth Night*, dir. Harcourt Williams, Old Vic, 6 January 1931. *The Times* 7 January 1931.

Reviews of *Twelfth Night*, dir. Tyrone Guthrie. *Twelfth Night* reviews collection (1933) 71–85, Birmingham Central Library: *Christian Science Monitor* 9 October 1933, *Daily Express* 19 September 1933, *Daily Telegraph* 19 September 1933, *Evening Standard* 19 September 1933, *New Age* 12 October 1933, *New Statesman and Nation* 30 September 1933, *News Chronicle* 19 September 1933, *Sketch* 19 September 1933, *Star* 19 September 1933, *Sunday Pictorial* 24 September 1933, *Sunday Referee* 24 September 1933, *The Times* 19 September 1933.

Schafer, Elizabeth. *Lilian Baylis: A Biography*. Hatfield: University of Hertfordshire Press, 2006.

Twelfth Night. Shakespeare in Production. Cambridge: Cambridge University Press, 2009.

Shakespeare, William. *Twelfth Night*. Ed. Elizabeth Story Donno. The New Cambridge Shakespeare. Updated edn. Cambridge: Cambridge University Press, 2003.

Shapiro, Michael. *Gender in Play on the Shakespearean Stage: Boy Heroines and Female Pages*. 1994. Ann Arbor: University of Michigan Press, 1996.

Sheehy, Helen. *Eva Le Gallienne: A Biography*. New York: Alfred A. Knopf, 1996.

Twelfth Night, dir. Eva Le Gallienne, 1926. Production photographs. New York Public Library.

Webster, Margaret. *Don't Put Your Daughter on the Stage*. New York: Alfred A. Knopf, 1972.

The Same Only Different: Five Generations of a Great Theatre Family. London: Victor Gollancz, 1969.

Woolf, Virginia. *The Diary of Virginia Woolf, Volume IV: 1931–1935*. Ed. Anne Olivier Bell, assisted by Andrew McNeillie. London: Hogarth Press, 1982.

The Sickle Side of the Moon: The Letters of Virginia Woolf 1932–34. Ed. Nigel Nicolson and Joanne Trautman. London: Hogarth Press, 1970.

'"Twelfth Night" at the Old Vic'. *New Statesman and Nation* 30 September 1933: 385–6.

CHAPTER 10

Measure for Measure: *Shakespeare's twentieth-century play*

Christine Dymkowski

As the only play always to have been included in the category of Shakespeare's 'problem plays', which F. S. Boas first identified in 1896, *Measure for Measure* has received considerable critical attention during the last hundred-odd years. However, Shakespeare's text has not received the same measure of theatrical attention or respect: the Folio version of *Measure for Measure* has no substantial stage history until the second half of the twentieth century, and particularly until 1970 onwards. From the Restoration until 1720 it was performed only in heavily adapted versions: William Davenant's, which amalgamated it with characters from *Twelfth Night* and *Much Ado about Nothing*, and Charles Gildon's, which virtually cut the Duke and Lucio from the play and omitted the comic characters altogether. The eighteenth century saw Shakespeare's text performed fairly regularly, albeit in James Quin's and J. P. Kemble's heavily cut versions, while the nineteenth century saw far fewer productions, again in severely cut versions that catered to popular distaste for the sexual matters integral to the plot. Even that champion of authenticity, William Poel, bowdlerised the play when he produced it in 1893 and 1908, a move that did not prevent the vicar and residents of Stratford from protesting at the play's being performed at all. Such attitudes prevailed well into the twentieth century, with protests against productions of the play occurring throughout the 1930s.[1] However, while there were only 6 productions of the play at Stratford in the 65 years between 1884 and 1949, there have been 14 in the 56 years between 1950 and 2006, 11 of them since 1970.[2]

---

[1] For a succinct stage history of the play up to 1974, to which I am indebted for my account here, see Miles, Appendix D, 298–318.

[2] The *World Shakespeare Bibliography Online* (www.worldshakesbib.org) confirms the play's late twentieth-century theatrical renaissance: as of 24 April 2008, the *Bibliography* recorded 299 productions of the play in English since 1962, almost half as many as *Hamlet* received (704). In comparison, the other problem plays, *All's Well that Ends Well* and *Troilus and Cressida*, had 129 and 82 respectively.

A greater openness to the sexual matters addressed by the play is partly responsible for its changing reputation and popularity in the theatre, but does not go very far to account for the complex and multiple interpretations of *Measure for Measure* that have been seen on English stages during the past forty years or so. Such interpretations have reflected, or been seen to reflect, very different attitudes to gender, sexuality, and the relationship between the individual and the state. However, the relationship between different theatrical interpretations of the play and varying social, sexual, and political ideologies and realities is hardly a straightforward one. For instance, whether Isabella is presented (or seen) either as a cold-hearted prude or as a distraught woman faced with sexual violation, whether she accepts the Duke's proposal at the end or is free to reject him, whether – if she does comply – she does so because she has discovered her own sexuality or because the Duke has successfully replaced Angelo as a sexual predator tells us little about prevailing cultural attitudes, or even about the intention behind the production. Depending on overall treatment of the play, an Isabella who ultimately rejects the convent can, for example, very well represent a more self-realising, and therefore more feminist, vision of the character than one who makes clear she intends to return to it – and vice versa. As Sheila Rowbotham comments in regard to the seemingly unlikely congruence of right-wing campaigners against sexual permissiveness and radical feminist ones against pornography in the 1980s, '[i]t was no longer just authoritarian patriarchal control versus sexual freedom: the lines had blurred' (506).

In other words, just as very different routes can lead to the same destination and different motivations to the same demands, different directorial intentions can lead to physically similar stagings.[3] In addition, intention is no guarantor of reception. Graham Nicholls, discussing John Barton's seminal 1970 RSC production, 'often described as "the one in which Isabella rejected the Duke"', notes that 'Barton has always denied that he intended any simple interpretation. "What I actually intended", he has said, "was that Isabella's response should be open-ended. ... The last thing that I presented on stage ... was Isabella wondering, puzzling about what she should do"' (77). Given the upsurge of feminist consciousness in the late 1960s, as well as legislation reforming divorce and matrimonial property law (Rowbotham 341–2), it is unsurprising that others read the staging differently: *The Times*'s Irving Wardle thought she looked 'dismayed'

---

[3] Information from promptbooks and even reviews is sometimes limited to mention of physical action, with no description of accompanying emotion – for instance, 'they look at one another' – making it difficult if not impossible to reconstruct the tenor of a scene.

(2 April), while the *Listener*'s D. A. N. Jones saw this Isabella, in what he called 'a feminist production', more dramatically 'glaring out at the audience, silent rage written all over her high forehead and stubborn chin. She is to be a chattel after all' (9 April).[4] Consequently, in trying to disentangle the ways in which English stagings of *Measure for Measure* since 1970 have intersected with and reflected the cultural moments of their production, I will focus on their critical reception, exploring the underlying assumptions and competing discourses that the reviews reveal. The elements of the play that particularly resonated with contemporary reviewers vary from production to production but relate, in the main, to the characterisation of Isabella, the Duke, and the minor characters and to the presentation of the state apparatus that surrounds them.

THE 1970S

The question of contemporary relevance informs reviewer opinion during the 1970s: whether or not they thought the play had it, the underlying assumption of many critical responses is that productions of it should. In this regard, in an era of sexual 'freedom' that assumed female willingness to adopt traditionally male attitudes towards sex, Isabella's attitude often proved problematic to reviewers' acceptance of the play's premise. In discussing Barton's production, for instance, the *Sunday Times*'s Harold Hobson commented, in the light of contemporary mores, on the Shakespearean character's 'wholly selfish determination to preserve her chastity' (5 April), and the *Evening Standard*'s Milton Shulman similarly dismissed her as 'an impossible prig suffering from some sort of frigidity complex' (2 April). However, presented with the 'honest intensity' of Estelle Kohler's Isabella, Shulman was surprised to find this 'impossible female both tolerable and touching' – nevertheless, despite his response, he suspected that, given the character's attitude, 'these days [the play] has to be played strictly for laughs'. Hobson, on the other hand, found Kohler's interpretation appropriate, but he saw her rather as 'a [melodramatic] exhibitionist', 'the only possible way of presenting the play today – if it is to be presented at all, for which [he saw] no urgent necessity'. This perception of the play's lack of relevance underlies John Barber's *Daily Telegraph* complaint about Barton's misguided attempt to

---

[4] Unless otherwise noted, pre-1983 reviews of RSC productions come from the relevant *Theatre Records* of the Shakespeare Centre Library (hereafter SCL *TR*); Barton's are from (Series A) 78 (10 January – 11 April 1970): 132–46. For readers' convenience, dates of original publication are given where possible.

inject psychological realism into characters who should be 'extravagantly monstrous' (Angelo), 'spectacularly fanatical' (Isabella), and 'urbane and even godlike' (the Duke) and into a play that must end with Isabella as a 'happy duchess' (6 April).[5]

Although in this case Isabella's concern for her chastity failed to resonate with critics, the play's framework, in which private morality, public law, and the application of justice intersect in highly unsatisfactory ways, made it an increasingly relevant vehicle for the expression of social and political anxieties throughout the rest of the decade. As Michael Billington recounts, the

image of Britain on the verge of disintegration was one that had great potency in the early Seventies, and it's not hard to understand why. On the one hand, the post-war consensus had broken down as governments strove to become ever more authoritarian: the immediate reaction to the crisis in Northern Ireland, for instance, was the imposition of direct rule from Westminster and the policy of internment without trial [...] Terrorism had also become a European phenomenon. Alongside the IRA and the Angry Brigade in Britain, the Red Brigade in Italy and the Red Army faction in Germany assassinated political and judicial figures [...] Increased terrorism, of course, meant increased government security; which, in turn, fuelled left-wing fears of declining individual liberty. Wherever you looked there was a sense of incipient chaos in the Seventies which was keenly reflected in the drama of the time. (222–3)

Very often the attempt to make *Measure for Measure* reflect such times resulted in radical adaptations that were accepted on their own terms, such as those by Howard Brenton (Northcott Theatre, Exeter 1972) and Charles Marowitz (Open Space, London 1975), and radical productions that were not, such as Keith Hack's in 1974 for the RSC.[6] But whereas Hack's attempt to present the play, via very heavy cutting, interpolated speeches, and caricatured characters, as a 'fable of social oppression' (Gibbons 70) was critically derided as a betrayal of Shakespeare's text, Sue Dunderdale's equally radical 1978 production for Avon Touring Theatre was hailed as a 'triumph' (Carleton and Foot), making the play speak persuasively for both feminist and socialist values.

The company's leaflet/programme describes *Measure for Measure* as 'a play about power and the abuse of power in a state that is showing

---

[5] Useful descriptions of Barton's production can be found in Williamson 167–9; Scott 61–3, 68, 70–1; Nicholls; Gay 129–31.

[6] For Brenton's adaptation, see Bull's introduction in Brenton 12–14; for Marowitz's, see Scott 65–7, 69–70, 74; Nicholls 57–8, 64ff.; Almansi 99–100. Gibbons's edition of *Measure for Measure* contains useful descriptions of Marowitz and Hack (69–70), the latter drawn from Peter Thomson's account in *Shakespeare Survey* 28 (1975): 137–49.

every visible sign of weakness [... The production is set] firmly in a modern context – Italy today, a state marked by deep crisis and corruption, where terrorism is frequent and women struggle against an overtly "macho" society.' As the production featured seven actors, four of them women, Claudio became Isabella's sister Claudia, Pompey Poppaea, and Barnardine Belladonna, all living in Turin rather than Vienna.[7] However, as both many reviews and the promptbook[8] itself make clear, there was 'manifest respect for the text' (Carleton), with very few cuts and minimal changes.[9] For instance, the exchange in 1.2 explaining why the pregnant Claudia is being sent to prison needed very little more than a change in pronouns and the deletion of 'by him':

POPPAEA: Yonder woman is carried to prison.
MISTRESS OVERDONE: Well, what has she done?
POPPAEA: A man.
MISTRESS OVERDONE: But what's her offence?
POPPAEA: Groping for trouts in a peculiar river.
MISTRESS OVERDONE: What? Is there a maid with a child?
POPPAEA: No, but there's a woman with a maid. You have not heard of the proclamation, have you? (71–8)

In reviewer Don Carleton's opinion,

The change from Claudio to Claudia seems to have strengthened the role – in many conventional productions Claudio can seem more than a little spineless when he begs his sister to sacrifice her honour for his life. Claudia (here a woman who herself saw no dishonour in premarital sexual encounters) was asking a 'sister' inhibited by religion to do something reasonable, or at least arguable, in the face of rank injustice. Claudia is altogether more sympathetic than Claudio and the dramatic situation is intensified.

The Times's Ned Chaillet similarly felt that the company '[made] the most of the feminist possibilities of Claudio's transformation into a woman',

---

[7] Carleton's review of the Bristol performance notes the cast: Frank McDermott (Duke and Elbow), David Yip (Escalus, Lucio), Clive Flowers (Angelo, Abhorson), Cordelia Ditton (Poppaea), Claire Grove (Belladonna, Provost, Marina), Cotchie D'Arcy (Claudia), Maureen O'Donnell (Isabella); Marriott's admiring review of the London performance indicates that John Matshikiza replaced David Yip. The promptbook makes clear that the other characters remained in the play, with David Foot's appreciative review in the *Guardian* noting that the cast 'treble[d] up, [...] always in an intelligently practical way'.

[8] I am very grateful to Sue Dunderdale for lending me her copy of the original promptbook, as well as for providing copies of reviews. Besides these sources, I have been able to draw on my own still vivid memory of the production, which I saw on 28 September 1978, at the Roundhouse, London. The leaflet/programme can be found in the company's file at the Theatre Museum, London.

[9] Foot expressed his surprise that the text had not been 'savaged', and D.F.B. noted that 'the text has been revised slightly'.

calling her 'a free-loving realist who cannot understand for a moment how her sister's maidenhead can be worth more than her life'. Carleton likewise found Poppaea 'more sympathetic' than Pompey, 'her profession as bawd here more forced by female and social circumstance than by choice'.

The *Daily Telegraph*'s reviewer, D.F.B., noted the 'company's intention [...] to emphasise the theme of repression by the State and, incidentally, the oppression of women', judging that '[i]n both respects it succeed[ed] admirably'; adding that the changes 'compel[led] one to listen to the play as though for the first time', he found the interpretation 'a valid way of presenting the play'. Chaillet similarly commented on the company's creation of 'a powerful, didactically clear picture of the oppression of women without sacrificing their picture of a class-ridden society'. Carleton makes clear that the approach was evident even before the play began: 'patriotic Verdi choruses [...] welcomed the audience to the theatre', and designer Sarah Paulley had the stage 'painted as the Italian flag' and 'overlaid with a red banner'; programmes were 'distributed like radical propaganda', and one of the women actors spray-painted a wall with '"I belong to myself"' in Italian. The introduction of 'an unwritten sub-text which deals with state secrecy, police brutality and, pre-eminently, woman's oppressed role in society' was, in Carleton's view, 'rarely made explicit; it emerged in the acting, in visual rather than verbal references. On two occasions only, in wickedly amusing (and vigorously presented) songs, [did] the cast allow themselves clear statements.'[10]

Dunderdale's 'ingenious reworking' of the play was 'finally effective beyond expectation in the scene of the Duke's return' (Chaillet). The 'vicious, calculating Duke' and his deputy 'continue[d] to share one thing throughout the women's complaints: a brotherly exercise of power. Like two mafioso [*sic*] they embrace[d], snap[ped] their fingers and [bade] the women to do as they [were] told' (respectively, D.F.B. and Chaillet). Even more chillingly, the Duke's 'final command that Isabella marry him [took] on the same vile connotations as Angelo's intended rape' (Chaillet). The audience's shocked realisation that the Duke had 'rescued' Isabella only to use her himself was palpable the night I saw the production.

The production's major alteration occurred at the end of the play, when the Duke failed to speak the lines commuting Lucio's death sentence: as Chaillet noted, 'the Duke's real rage [was saved] for Lucio, the common

---

[10] The promptbook indicates a 'not getting caught song', accompanied by two guitars, at Poppaea's entrance. Dunderdale notes there was also 'a song in the prison in place of Pompey's long speech', written by Cordelia Ditton, who played Poppaea (email, 28 May 2008).

man who dared to insult his betters'.[11] The promptbook makes clear that Claudia and the condemned Lucio, left alone on stage, exchanged a version of their earlier lines:

CLAUDIA: Why, how now, Lucio? Whence comes this restraint?
LUCIO: From too much liberty ... (1.2.106–7)

Carleton describes how Claudia '[did] not offer him her love or the comfort of her body; instead she offer[ed] him the hope of the triumph of the people and conclude[d] the evening with a spirited rendering (in which he gradually join[ed]) of [...] the "Bandiera Rossa"'. It was 'passionately well done', working 'as a moment of pure theatre', a view with which other critics concurred: 'the play end[ed] in a crescendo of impassioned political statement', the company '[making] their position clear [...] with a rousing rendition of the Italian communist anthem without seeming for a moment out of place' (respectively, Foot and Chaillet).[12]

Although so firmly set in contemporary Italy, Dunderdale's production allowed its foreign setting to function in the same way Shakespeare's own historical settings and non-English locations do: to reflect the present place and time in a way that allows a distanced scrutiny. Political violence, as Billington reminds us, was not confined to Italy: 'after seven IRA bombs exploded in London in January 1977, violence on the mainland became a regular feature of British life' (242). At the same time, more and more official attention was being paid to women's legal rights and needs, with the passage of the Sex Discrimination Act in 1975 and the Domestic Violence and Matrimonial Proceedings Act in 1976 (Billington 243) and, in the same year, the opening of the first Rape Crisis Centre in London, even though there were still 'instances of blatant male bias in the legal system' (Rowbotham 407, 431).[13] The production's implied alliance

---

[11] Although reviews do not comment on the fact, it was perhaps significant that, in an otherwise white cast, Lucio was played first by the Anglo-Chinese actor David Yip and then by the black South African actor John Matshikiza: despite 'its protests against the Tories' 1971 Immigration Act [...w]hen Labour won the 1974 election it moved very quickly to tighten the rules even further [...When] right wing Tory MPs tabled motions demanding urgent discussion on the "changing demographic character of Great Britain" (meaning of course the colour of people's skin) [, ...] Labour's home secretary [...] responded by assuring them that Labour would maintain "strict immigration control" and would "root out" illegal immigrants and overstayers. By 1978 Labour had buried its conscience for good, a fact demonstrated by Merlin Rees's famous television admission that all immigration controls were aimed at stopping "coloured" immigration' (Brown).

[12] Thirty years later, the exhilaration of that moment still remains vivid in my own memory.

[13] Rowbotham gives the example of a judge releasing a man 'who had violently raped a seventeen-year-old on the grounds that the rapist "allowed his enthusiasm for sex" to get the better of him [...]' (431).

between socialism and feminism was similarly reflected in actual events, with the TUC in 1978 organising 'a march of 100,000 for abortion rights', its 'first ever demonstration on a non-workplace issue' (Rowbotham 416). In addition, 'Labour introduced welfare cuts and wage restraint' after the 1976 sterling crisis and IMF loan, an 'onslaught on working-class living standards [that was] combined with an ideological recasting of those who are dependent on welfare' (Rowbotham 406). Unsurprisingly, Dunderdale's and Hack's were not the only productions of *Measure for Measure* to pay attention to class issues; Barry Kyle's for the RSC, also in 1978, recognised such economic disadvantage, refusing to draw a moral distinction between the play's 'high' and 'low' characters.[14]

An understanding of Isabella's position – if not downright sympathy for it – crept into reviews as the 1970s wore on and feminist attitudes became more current. Jonathan Miller directed the play in 1974 for the National Theatre's touring production, reviving it the following year with a different cast at Greenwich Theatre. Whereas a few years earlier the hesitation of Barton's Isabella in response to the Duke's proposal aroused much critical consternation, reviewers now seemed ready to accept her outright rejection of him: reviewing the NT production, J. W. Lambert thought Gillian Barge 'chillingly brought off her introduction [...] of a discordant note' at the end of the play (*Sunday Times* 24 February 1974).[15] Miller's setting of the play in Freud's Vienna allowed a psychological realism, so that 'virtually every character from the brothel keeper to the Duke's deputy can exemplify the same repressions' (Irving Wardle, *The Times* 14 August 1975). Within such a context, Isabella's attitude towards sex became not only credible but no longer idiosyncratic; Felix Barker, for example, was convinced that Penelope Wilton's Isabella would sacrifice her brother rather than her virginity (*Evening News* 14 August 1975). By the end of the decade, reviews of Peter Gill's 1979 Riverside Theatre

---

[14] Reviewing Kyle's production, Benedict Nightingale in the *New Statesman* (7 July 1978) noted its use of 'a trio of whores, patently pox-ridden beneath their come-on wigs and glad rags, and all desperately afraid that the clean-up campaigners will destroy their precarious livelihood, to suggest that the woes of Vienna have as much to do with poverty as passion. It transforms Barnadine from the usual dissolute ruin into a sort of Aryan Caliban, the stark naked but not undignified victim of other people's oppression, in order to make a similar point' (SCL *TR* 101: 48). Reviewing the London transfer, the *Yorkshire Post's* Anthony Seymour commented that the production made one 'understand why goodness hides grossness, and why bawds and murderers have qualities of nobility' (20 November 1980, SCL *TR* 105: 5). Accounts of Kyle's production can be found in Rutter 26–40, Gay 134–6, Scott 64 ff. passim, and Nicholls.

[15] Reviews of Miller's and of Gill's productions come from clippings in the relevant production files at the Theatre Museum, London (hereafter TM).

production showed a noticeable shift in language in regard to Isabella's position. Milton Shulman, for instance, though still contending that it was easy nowadays to 'dismiss [the character] as a frigid prig', warmed to Helen Mirren's portrayal of 'a woman battling for her dignity rather than her soul' and 'admired her [...] for [the] haughty imperiousness with which she rejected the male arguments that she was being intolerably fussy about her body' (*Evening Standard* 24 May 1979).[16] Shulman was not alone in recognising the gendered nature of judgements about Isabella's dilemma: Michael Coveney, in commenting that Mirren's Isabella 'really believes that *rape* is more horrible than death' (*Financial Times* 24 May 1979, my italics) accepts the violation inherent in Angelo's proposal rather than belittling Isabella as being simply frightened of sex.[17]

THE 1980S

In May 1979, the election of Margaret Thatcher ushered in eighteen years of Conservative Party rule; it was also followed by a spate of productions of *Measure for Measure* that seemed to offer direct commentary on the state of the nation under the Tories, specifically in terms of its increasing authoritarianism, its rampant free market ideology, and its ultimately hypocritical moral posturing. Reviewers of the first of David Thacker's three productions, which he mounted at the Young Vic in quick succession in May 1985, May 1987, and April 1989, were quick to spot its relevance to all of these issues. As Ros Franey commented in *City Limits* (24 May, *LTR* 5 (1985): 451),[18] this modern-dress production began 'with an awesome PA/Secretary vetting visitors. Plenty of overtones of an authoritarian state encroaching upon a liberal-minded populace' alluded to the contemporary political situation, wherein, following the successful establishment of the Greenham Common peace camp in 1981, 'The Thatcherite right responded by extending the definition of subversion in an effort to

[16] Interestingly, Shulman, also admiring 'the flow and precision of her spoken words, which enabled her to sound quite natural, accusing Angelo of "concupiscible intemperate lust"', concluded, 'A girl who can say that will never be raped!', a comment that serves both to minimise the threat to Isabella and to maximise her non-existent power.

[17] Chaillet had used the same word in reviewing Dunderdale's production the year before; see above. In reading through reviews of the past thirty-odd years, I have been struck by how often reviewers expect a mutual sexual tension in the scenes between Angelo and Isabella and are disappointed when it is not evident.

[18] Unless otherwise indicated, all reviews of post-1980 productions are quoted from the relevant issue of *London Theatre Record* (hereafter *LTR*), which from 1981 to 1990 collated reviews of all London productions; after 1990, when it became *Theatre Record* (hereafter *TR*), it included reviews of regional productions as well.

control the media and the legal system and redefining the meaning of national security to include protest groups like CND', as well as organisations like the National Council for Civil Liberties and trade unions (Rowbotham 481). Two NCCL officers that MI5 had under surveillance, Patricia Hewitt and Harriet Harman, were subsequently to serve on the Labour government's front bench (Rowbotham 482).[19]

The *Daily Telegraph*'s Keith Nurse agreed that *Measure for Measure* was 'very much a play for today. Human values are being measured in the cold, calculating terms of the market place', leading to anarchy, while *Time Out*'s Helen Rose found it 'pertinent', given 'the government's blatant double standards and Thatcher's moralistic return to Victorian values' (respectively, 15 and 23 May, both *LTR* 5: 451). Rose and Franey, who also understood why '[t]his interesting play about corruption in high places and sexual duplicity is enjoying a well-deserved flurry of revivals', certainly had in mind Cecil Parkinson's resignation from the government in October 1983, the first in a string of sex scandals involving married politicians that dogged the Conservative Party throughout the 1980s and 1990s ('Sex and scandal'). Consequently, reviewing Thacker's 1987 revival, the *Independent*'s Alex Renton found its 'relevance for today [...] abundantly clear; the conflict of public virtue and private vice could hardly be more apposite as new revelations about the Profumo affair appear in the Sundays, and Cecil Parkinson's return to grace is again mooted' (20 May, *LTR* 7 (1987): 609). Nick St. George also noticed 'powerful parallels with the New Puritanism of the present day' (*BBC Radio London*, 16 May, *LTR* 7: 609), while the *Guardian*'s John Vidal was struck by the production's

> overwhelming sense of the court as a banker's boardroom, of government reduced to a chamber of commerce, where economics are valued above humanity, corruption is fundamental and flawed men promote dogma and repression in the name of sound and sensible husbandry. It stinks *and* it is unashamedly relevant. (15 May, *LTR* 7: 609)

It is clear from responses such as these that Isabella's resistance to Angelo's proposition no longer surfaced as an anachronistic problem for reviewers: the focus was instead on the corrupt political system that could engender the deputy's behaviour.

B. A. Young thought that '[t]he relevance to our own times depends more on our newly-critical attitude towards the sexual freedom of the 1960s, paralleled by Angelo's sudden restrictions' (*Financial Times* 15

[19] The BBC publishes a useful 'Secret State: Timeline' at http://news.bbc.co.uk/1/hi/programmes/ true_spies/2336987.stm, which provides more detail than I am able to give here.

May, *LTR* 7: 608), which provides further insight into why Isabella was no longer a target for critics' displeasure: AIDS and HIV, first identified in 1981 and 1983 respectively, began to spread throughout the 1980s ('Timeline'), encouraging a backlash against the sexual permissiveness that had earlier been current.[20] Nicholas Hytner's 1987 RSC production vividly evoked a world in which two cultures collide *and* collude and where sexual licence has both an attractive energy and a commodifying emptiness: as Billington describes it, Mark Thompson's set had

> twin industrial towers resting on massive bases of beaten gold. The impression [...] is of hollow pomp; and it is reinforced by the arrival of the Viennese bureaucracy in cutaway coats and knee-breeches as if they had all been suited by Black Rod. But the first of many shocks comes when the towers swivel round to usher us into a contemporary Hell's Kitchen where smoke issues from holes in the ground and the bawds and tapsters sport satiny knickerbockers suggesting an updated version of the Hitlerjugend. (*Guardian* 13 November, *LTR* 7: 1498)

Billington read the set as visually representing 'the need for some kind of sane balance in society between unchecked licence and repressive order', while Helen Rose saw it rather as underlining 'the dual nature of each character involved in the drama' (*Time Out* 18 November, *LTR* 7: 1495).

Innumerable reviewers allude to the *West Side Story*-like eruption of the scene Hytner interpolated after 1.1, set amongst the huge pipework they found reminiscent of the Pompidou Centre: as Hytner's promptbook describes it, a wino, Abhorson, a gentleman, police constables, and a female prostitute congregate outside a 'loo entrance'; Lucio, other gentlemen, and Pompey 'throw cocaine and keys to each other'; a man comes out of the underground loo, goes to Abhorson, and they 'talk money', eventually 'go[ing] down loo' together and re-emerging some time later; a policeman enters and takes money from Pompey, presumably bribed, before exiting; Froth buys drugs from Pompey, and eventually the arrested Claudio is dragged on. As the scene occurred so early in the play, Abhorson was here an anonymous figure, but when he later met Pompey in prison and the latter alluded to his 'hanging look', Abhorson rather defensively or fearfully picked his briefcase up and held it in front of his crotch (archive video, 1987). Although none of the reviewers noted Abhorson's duality as breaker of and upholder of the law, the interpolated scene clearly showed a society where corruption was rampant and where sexual activity was mostly a fiscal commodity. Reviewers did, however, comment on the

---

[20] Rowbotham notes that 'By the mid-1980s the panic generated because of AIDS had contributed to a mood of sexual conservatism which stressed the connection between sex and danger' (510).

production's timeliness[21] and 'topicality' (Billington 1499 and Jim Hiley, *Listener* 20 October, *LTR* 8 (1988): 1416), 'present[ing] a vision of society where both moral authoritarianism and the cult of laissez-faire are shown up' (Nicholas de Jongh, *Guardian* 12 October, *LTR* 8: 1415).

Roger Allam's Duke was one of the most satisfying and illuminating aspects of Hytner's production, a self-questioning and anguished ruler who could not be more different from the moral certainties and unwavering righteousness of Prime Minister Thatcher, who in 1980 had famously declared she was 'not for turning' (*BBC*, '10 October'). In the opening scene, Allam was visibly full of angst and self-doubt, seeming to measure himself against his vision of Angelo, questioning whether his own difficulties were the result of his character or of his position: there was a palpable sense of wonder – rather than of disbelief – when he spoke about Angelo's qualities. When he visited Claudio in prison, his 'Be absolute for death' speech became introspective at 'happy art thou not' (3.1.21), shifting again to focus on Claudio at 'If thou art rich' (25) and becoming internal once more at 'Thou hast neither heat' (37), until he finally shouted in agony, 'What's yet in this / That bears the name of life?' (38–9): instead of the insensitive and impersonal disquisition the speech can often seem, in Allam's hands it became an acute piece of self-analysis.[22] Similarly, in his discussion with Isabella later in the scene, the Duke spoke 'A remedy presents itself' (192) as if he had only just thought about Angelo's broken engagement to Mariana: Allam's delivery, emphasising 'well-seeming' (212), 'pretending in her' (215), and 'unjust unkindness' (227) in describing Angelo's actions, clearly indicated his sudden realisation of Angelo's hitherto unsuspected libellous deceit (archive video, 1987). Later, in 4.3, when Isabella returned to the prison expecting to hear that Angelo had sent her brother's reprieve, her sudden appearance while the Duke and the Provost were still completing their plans – Hytner's Provost did not exit here – agitated the Duke, triggering his impromptu decision not to tell her of Claudio's rescue (archive video, 1988). Allam's interpretation made the Duke a credible and sympathetic human being, rather than a

---

[21] Jim Hiley (*Listener* 19 November, *LTR* 7: 1496) called the Stratford production 'timely', 'opening [...] on the very day of the Synod's Great Sex Debate', as did Jack Tinker when it transferred to the Barbican (*Daily Mail* 11 October, *LTR* 8: 1418), noting Thatcher's 'eagerly-predicted thoughts on the New Morality' and 'the hazards of putting such mighty matters into the hands of fallible instruments of government'. See also Tinker, *Daily Mail* 12 November, *LTR* 7: 1496; Michael Coveney, *Financial Times* 13 November, *LTR* 7: 1497; Billington 1498; and Patrick Marmion, *What's On* 19 October, *LTR* 8: 1417.

[22] The line readings were slightly different at the Barbican, according to the archive video, 1988: at 'Thou art not thyself' (19), Allam paused after 'not', heavily emphasised 'thyself', and beat his

manipulative or God-like figure testing Angelo and Isabella and abdicating his own responsibility.[23]

Many reviewers could not quite get the measure of Josette Simon's Isabella, not because of any inadequacy in her acting but because, as the reviews reveal, she did not fit into any of their preconceived notions about the character. For instance, Billington complained that 'she never suggests that Isabella is shocked into an awareness of her own moral rigidity or the sexuality she has carefully suppressed' (*LTR* 7: 1498), Peter Kemp was disappointed that she 'gets nowhere near the character's clenched purity, insecurely clamped down emotions and hard adolescent absolutism' (*Independent* 12 October, *LTR* 8: 1414), and Tony Dunn was surprised that 'in her first appearance [...] she caresses [Lucio's] coat, looks flirtatiously over her shoulder, and establishes a girlishness at the centre of her role which she never abandons' (*Tribune* 4 November, *LTR* 8: 1415). As Milton Shulman put it, 'Religious fanaticism or sexual frigidity are the only two valid excuses' for Isabella's rejection of Angelo, 'and Josette Simon conveys neither of these traits' (*Evening Standard* 11 November, *LTR* 8: 1418). It did not occur to these reviewers that, in this world of corrupted and venal sexuality, a devout woman might be fully aware both of her own sexual nature and of the lack of opportunity to explore it in ways she might find fulfilling. Indeed, other critics indicated Simon's success in presenting just such an Isabella: 'an uncomplicated, sensible sort of girl, too straightforward for tragedy' (Andrew Rissik, *Independent* 13 November, *LTR* 7: 1497), she was 'at once appealing and tough' (Francis King, *Sunday Telegraph* 15 November, *LTR* 7: 1498), 'dignified and touching' (Martin Hoyle, *Financial Times* 11 October *LTR* 8: 1416), 'evinc[ing] a tangible faith unspoilt by priggishness' (Michael Coveney, *Financial Times* 13 November, *LTR* 7: 1497). In Jim Hiley's view, 'The production [was] firmly on her side' (*Listener* 19 November, *LTR* 7: 1496).[24]

Given her portrayal, the production left open Isabella's decision at the end of the play. Throughout his closing speeches, Allam's Duke kept looking at Isabella but then addressing other characters, giving the sense of his wanting to speak to her, losing his nerve, and putting it off. At 'if you'll a willing ear incline' (5.1.528), Allam emphasised the first word;

---

breast. The speech became internal at 'dust' (21), and the final word of 'Thou art not certain' (23) was emphatic.

[23] My understanding of Allam's interpretation of the Duke is drawn from my viewing of the archive videos; his own valuable account of playing the role, which illuminates many aspects of Hytner's production, shows how well his performance conveyed his intentions.

[24] See also Jack Tinker, *Daily Mail* 12 November, *LTR* 7: 1496.

Simon either shook her head or simply looked at him, before walking up stage and seemingly away. However, she then turned around, and the play ended with the Duke and Isabella looking intently at each other (archive video, 1987).[25] Coveney saw her response as 'disdainful resistance' (*Financial Times* 13 November, *LTR* 7: 1497), but for King 'the indecisiveness of the ending [...] carrie[d] rare conviction' (*Sunday Telegraph* 15 November, *LTR* 7: 1498).[26]

THE 1990S

Measure for Measure continued to serve as a political weathervane throughout the next decade. In March 1990, the imposition of the highly unpopular 'poll tax' led to the worst riots London had seen for a hundred years (*BBC*, '31 March') and to massive civil disobedience, with 20 per cent of people in England and Wales refusing to pay the tax (*BBC*, '14 August'). In November 1990, Thatcher's intransigence over Europe and the single currency, as well as the poll tax, forced her out of office (*BBC*, '22 November'), although the Conservatives remained in power.[27] In 1993, her successor, John Major, announced that it was 'time to get back to basics: to self-discipline and respect for the law, to consideration for others, to accepting responsibility for yourself and your family, and not shuffling it off on the state' (*John Major*, 'Quotations'). His statement, widely interpreted as a call for a moral crusade (*John Major*, 'Policies'), made the phrase 'back to basics' an oft-quoted reference point both in political and cultural spheres: it also became a very uncomfortable one for the Tories,

---

[25] In the archive video of the 1988 Barbican transfer, Isabella did not look at the Duke as he spoke his proposal (529); she then turned to look at him and did not respond, prompting his 'So' (530). She then went up stage and stood, turning to look down stage at the Duke as the lights faded.

[26] Allam writes, 'We thought probably they did [marry], but only after a very long conversation' (40). It is worth noting that, in Adrian Noble's 1983 RSC production, which I saw both on stage and in the archive video, Juliet Stevenson and Daniel Massey convincingly showed Isabella and the Duke developing a mutual love as the play progressed, so that her acceptance of his proposal at the end was a positive means of self-fulfilment for both characters.

[27] Between June and September 1992, London Bubble Theatre, founded in 1972 with a mission to create theatre to involve the capital's citizens (*London Bubble*), toured London's outer districts with its production of *Measure for Measure*, a 'fascinating and extremely topical exploration of political and sexual hypocrisy', with Angelo seeming 'a kind of Jacobean Cecil Parkinson' (Pemberton). According to one reviewer, the play was treated as forum theatre (Stanfield), and the polemical programme certainly suggests that the play was used to stimulate discussion about law and its enforcers, about the implied contract between citizens and governments: 'unpopular laws can arise when those who make the laws and those who are supposed to follow them have a different vision of the kind of society they would like [...] (the Poll Tax leaps to mind) [...] We look to our politicians [...] to observe the standards of behaviour which they foist on us. So it shocks us (or maybe it only "used" to shock us) when upright male politicians have affairs with

who went on to suffer from a string of sexual and financial scandals under Major's leadership (see *BBC News*).

Given the failure of those in power to live up to their prescriptions for everyone else, the phrase echoes throughout reviews of Declan Donnellan's Cheek by Jowl production of *Measure for Measure*, which started its tour in February 1994 and arrived at the Lyric Hammersmith in June.[28] Unsurprisingly, Stephen Boxer's Duke was 'cut down to size as a meddler who toys with people's lives. The final scene [...] finds the assembled company grim-faced with resentment. The Duke has played God and we live in a secular age [...] if you accept the Duke, not Angelo, as the (unwitting) villain of the piece, it paints a desolate picture of a society with no point of moral reference' (Hoyle). Paul Taylor went further in his negative appraisal of the Duke, seeing him and Angelo as 'doppelgängers, both control freaks, both, in their different ways, angling to get their hands on Isabella' (*Independent* 21 June, *TR* 14: 757).

Steven Pimlott's RSC production, which opened later the same year, prompted similar allusions.[29] The programme, which showed a pregnant naked woman with her head bandaged, only her eyes uncovered, pointed to the feminist emphasis of this production: it contained excerpts from the academic Marilyn French's *Shakespeare's Division of Experience* and from the journalist Nick Davies's recently published series of *Guardian* articles about prostitution in Britain. Davies's investigation had discovered that

All through the 1980s, as the poorest 10% of the population became more poor, the prostitution industry boomed: the number of women prosecuted quadrupled between 1981 and 1991. In the late 1980s, these adults were joined by adolescents, aged 16 to 18, who had been pushed out of their homes by the poll tax and then stripped of their benefits. Prostitution was far more lucrative than begging, far

their female secretaries or are found in strange circumstances in cars on Hampstead Heath' (programme, Theatre Museum, London). In 1993, John Major replaced the poll tax with the community charge (*BBC*, '14 August').
[28] The following reviews of Donnellan's production in *TR* 14 (1994) allude to Major's phrase and/or to current politics/politicians: Neil Smith, *What's On* 22 June: 756; Nicholas de Jongh, *Evening Standard* 20 June: 756; Martin Hoyle, *Financial Times* 21 June: 757; David Nathan, *Jewish Chronicle* 24 June: 757–8; Michael Billington, *Guardian* 20 June: 758; Irving Wardle, *Independent on Sunday* 19 June: 758; Michael Coveney, *Observer* 13 March: 758; Bill Hagerty, *Today* 24 June: 758; John Peter, *Sunday Times* 26 June: 758, 761.
[29] The following reviews of Pimlott's production in *TR* 14 (1994) allude to Major's phrase and/or to current politics/politicians: Jack Tinker, *Daily Mail* 21 October: 1291; Maureen Paton, *Daily Express* 21 October: 1291; Charles Spencer, *Daily Telegraph* 24 October: 1292; Nicholas de Jongh, *Evening Standard* 21 October: 1292; David Nathan, *Jewish Chronicle* 28 October: 1292–3; Benedict Nightingale, *The Times* 22 October: 1294; James Christopher, *Time Out* 26 October: 1294; Bill Hagerty, *Today* 21 October: 1295.

less trouble with the law than thieving. Once that age group was established on the pavements, their younger brothers and sisters followed. The price of children on the streets is falling, a sure sign in any market that the supply has increased. (Qtd in Pimlott, programme)

Accordingly, in 1.2, while Pompey was talking to Mistress Overdone, a little girl entered and Pompey took her hand (archive video), welcoming this 'latest recruit' to the brothel (Hagerty). Ashley Martin-Davies's unitary set emphasised the connections between legal and illegal establishments: 'a grim, balconied institutional room' (Spencer), semicircular in shape, it served at once as 'prison-chamber, courtroom and assembly-hall' (de Jongh), thus showing how 'the effect of decisions made at the top is instantly registered lower down the social scale' (Irving Wardle, *Independent on Sunday* 23 October, *TR* 14: 1292). Paul Taylor observed how Pimlott positioned, '[on] the upper balcony [...] and under brutal guard, [...] the neglected, victimised characters whose fate is being so hazardously decided below' (*Independent* 22 October, TR 14: 293).

Louise Doughty noted the production's 'general tone [...] of darkness and oppression – of women pitting their bravery and cunning against the system' (*Mail on Sunday* 30 October, *TR* 14: 1291). The system was shown both as rotten – Elbow very blatantly planted a picklock on Pompey (archive video) – and as patriarchal: in the final scene, the onstage onlookers laughed heartily when Isabella confessed she had yielded to Angelo, but there was just a murmured 'oh' in reaction to Angelo's demand, and no reaction at all to the revelation that he had failed to keep his side of the bargain (archive video). The connection to British society was literalised on stage, with fifty or sixty 'citizens of Stratford' representing the 'Citizens of Vienna' (programme): as Nightingale commented, 'There they sit, a great wall of clerics, professors, magistrates, barristers and nobs in their dog collars, wigs and black gowns', their 'long chortle of clubby male glee' entirely 'predictable'. However, although Juliet was present on the 'upper gallery, still gagged and handcuffed' (Wardle), she was not passive, bouncing happily in her seat when the Duke, wearing the traditional black cap, repeated the sentence of death against Angelo (archive video). Similarly, Mariana was presented as an abstract painter, busy on a huge new work in 4.1, far removed from Tennyson's passive victim longing for death (archive video). Understandably, when Michael Feast's Duke proposed to Stella Gonet's Isabella, she 'first slap[ped] him, then embrace[d] him before finally bursting into baffled tears' (Spencer). The ending was very tentative, Isabella and the Duke standing looking at each other, hands clasped in front of them (archive video). As Taylor commented, Pimlott's ending brought out 'the grim farce of the drama's wilfully cobbled-together happy ending by allowing the lights to fade very slowly on a state of ludicrous wavering'.

The RSC next staged the play in 1998, Michael Boyd's production opening on the eve of the first anniversary of Labour's overwhelming 1997 election victory. Boyd seemingly set the play in pre- and post-revolutionary Russia: costumes included Cossack-type shirts and boots, grey-belted army uniforms (which the promptbook described as KGB), Tsar-like white jacket with sash for the Duke, and the dress of Orthodox priests (archive video). The play began with the Duke 'clearly going through some form of nervous crisis [...] slumped in his chair with an empty gin bottle by his side' (Billington, *Guardian* 2 May, *TR* 18 (1998): 576); he then fled the stage before his attendants broke down the door and listened to the 'scratchy recording of his opening speech [...] played over an ancient phonograph' (archive video and Charles Spencer, *Daily Telegraph* 4 May, *TR* 18: 577). Once in power, Angelo 'install[ed] spies everywhere and surrounded himself with gun-toting guards' (Billington, *Guardian* 27 January, *TR* 19 (1999): 16),[30] so that, in the final scene, the Duke was able to regain power only with the help of armed partisans (archive video).

As critics remarked, Boyd's 'emphasis [gave] the play a more overtly political tilt than usual' (Nightingale 17). Kate Stratton found that, 'instead of a morality play about mercy and justice, it's a deeply political study of tyranny: its myopia, its concern with image, even its contradictoriness' (*Time Out* 13 May, *TR* 18: 577). Billington commented on Boyd's 'highly persuasive metaphor for the modern world. Moral crusades, he suggests, often disguise a political authoritarianism and power is a mask for hypocrisy [...] the production works because it expresses a central truth: that you cannot divorce morality from politics' (576).[31]

---

[30] Also reviewing the 1999 Barbican transfer, Benedict Nightingale noted that Angelo '[a]t first [...] wears the sort of Russian peasant costume that Bolshevik intellectuals affected in the early days, later a grey uniform that, were you to add a swastika or a skull emblem, would suggest the SS' (*The Times* 22 January, *TR* 19: 17). At Stratford, Billington commented on his move 'from Gandhiesque white suit to military uniform' (576).

[31] Reviewing the Barbican transfer, Billington admired the way the production 'unearths the enduring link between religious and rightwing extremism' (16). Carol Woddis, writing in the run-up to President Clinton's impeachment (*Clinton*), saw 'contemporary parallels' in this 'morality play about power, manipulation, private desire and public office[:] suddenly women's voices – Isabella and Mariana and their attempts to gain justice for abuse suffered at the hands of the chief law-maker, Angelo – make one think of Clinton and the difficulties his female accusers have in being believed' (*Herald* 5 May, *TR* 18 (1998): 577).

Jane Edwardes, in noting how the production explored 'a country's shift from Babylonian excess, through puritanism, to a full-scale military state with a spy on every corner' (*Time Out* 27 January, *TR* 19: 17), pinpoints how it may have resonated in a Britain that had overwhelmingly rejected Conservative policies on 1 May 1997, only to find 'New' Labour hesitant in implementing the radical change that had been mandated:[32] although there were no direct parallels between the Duke's coup d'état and Labour's election victory, the question of how political change is negotiated was highly relevant to both.

SINCE 2000

Measure for Measure has continued to be regularly revived throughout the new millennium, with productions at Manchester's Library Theatre (2000), Bristol's Tobacco Factory (2001), the National Theatre's schools tour (2002), and London's Arcola Theatre (2003).[33] Its resonance with contemporary life continues, sometimes because of and sometimes despite staging decisions: watching Sean Holmes's 2003 RSC production, for instance, Paul Taylor was 'thrillingly convince[d]' of Isabella's 'religious faith. The survival of the body is of far less importance to her than the condition of the immortal soul' (*Independent* 6 May, *TR* 23: 580), while Jeremy Kingston was struck by the fact that '[n]owadays the major problem' with the play is not Isabella – rather, 'the focus of unease' is the Duke (*The Times* 5 May, *TR* 23: 579). Both comments seem rooted in actual experience – of a world of suicide bombers and of messianic leaders who take their countries into 'just' wars against the will of the people – rather than in details of the production itself. Similarly, reviewing Jonathan Dove's 2004 production at Shakespeare's Globe, Fiona Mountford noted 'the startling echo of the current international political situation, [Mark Rylance's] Duke [...] an essentially good though increasingly desperate man who uses highly dubious means to justify what he sees as a beneficent end' (*Evening Standard* 1 July, *TR* 24 (2004): 846). In the same year, however, Simon McBurney's production for the National Theatre and Complicité took every opportunity

---

[32] See, for instance, Billington, *State* 362, and Rowbotham 550–3. For the scale of the 1997 Labour victory, see http://news.bbc.co.uk/onthisday/hi/dates/stories/may/2/newsid_2480000/2480505. stm.

[33] Perhaps reflecting the increasing corporatisation of British public life, in Jack Shepherd's modern-dress production at the Arcola Vienna was 'run like a company by a chief executive [...] with murky motives' (John Peter, *Sunday Times* 8 June, *TR* 23 (2003): 706).

to link the play visually to the current political situation: prisoners wore 'orange overalls like those in Guantanamo Bay', 'an image of George Bush flashe[d] up on mention of a "sanctimonious pirate"', and 'modern-style surveillance [...] from secret servicemen to television monitors' was everywhere present (respectively, Georgia Brown, *Mail on Sunday* 30 May; Billington, *Guardian* 28 May; John Gross, *Sunday Telegraph* 30 May; all *TR* 24: 703). Charles Spencer thought that Paul Rhys's Angelo initially reminded him 'of our own Rev Tony Blair' and that 'Naomi Frederick's Isabella superbly capture[d] the frightening certainty of the Christian fundamentalist' (*Daily Telegraph* 28 May, *TR* 24: 703), while John Nathan saw the production as 'an attack on American neo-conservatism, and that country's love affair with state execution' (*Jewish Chronicle* 4 June, *TR* 24: 703). But even Peter Hall's 2006 production for his own Bath company, with 'Jacobean costumes [that] anticipate[d] the 17th century's intensifying conflicts between those of puritanical and of more cavalier morals', seemed 'strikingly contemporary, too, with state clamp-downs leading to the arrest of citizens who've done little wrong; with heated judicial disagreements about liberal tolerance and the spread of amorality; with revelations of top-level corruption and, oh yes, a sexually dodgy deputy leader' (Kate Bassett, *Independent on Sunday* 16 July, *TR* 26 (2006): 825).[34]

As Roger Allam observed in his own account of playing the Duke, 'Peter Brook has likened Shakespeare's plays to planets. At certain points in history particular plays orbit closer or further away from the earth. *Measure for Measure* seems close to us now because it examines questions of the unresolved tensions between public and private worlds, and it looks at these tensions through the prism of sexuality' (40). In other words, it is not at all surprising that – whether or not Isabella does so to the Duke – recent audiences so readily 'a willing ear incline' to a play that, by serving 'as the glasses where they view themselves', can so 'Fully unfold' to them 'The nature of our people, / Our city's institutions', and 'the properties [Of government]' (5.1.528; 2.4.126; 1.1.29, 9–10, 1).

I am grateful to the Society for Theatre Research, whose 2006–7 John Ramsden Research Award helped to fund my investigations in Stratford and London during my one-term study leave in 2008.

---

[34] John Prescott, deputy leader of the Labour Party, had recently admitted having an affair with an aide; see http://news.bbc.co.uk/1/hi/uk_politics/4945170.stm.

WORKS CITED

Allam, Roger. 'The Duke in *Measure for Measure*'. *Players of Shakespeare 3*. Ed. Russell Jackson and Robert Smallwood. Cambridge: Cambridge University Press, 1993. 21–41.

Almansi, Guido. 'The Thumb-screwers and the Tongue-Twisters: On Shakespearian Avatars'. *Poetics Today* 3.3 (1982): 87–100.

BBC. 'On this day: 10 October 1980'. http://news.bbc.co.uk/onthisday/hi/dates/stories/october/10/newsid_2541000/2541071.stm, accessed 2 June 2008.

'On this day: 31 March 1990'. http://news.bbc.co.uk/onthisday/hi/dates/stories/march/31/newsid_2530000/2530763.stm, accessed 11 August 2008.

'On this day: 14 August 1990'. http://news.bbc.co.uk/onthisday/hi/dates/stories/august/14/newsid_2495000/2495911.stm, accessed 11 August 2008.

'On this day: 22 November 1990'. http://news.bbc.co.uk/onthisday/hi/dates/stories/november/22/newsid_2549000/2549189.stm, accessed 11 August 2008.

BBC News. 'UK Politics: The Major Scandal Sheet'. 27 October 1998. http://news.bbc.co.uk/1/hi/uk_politics/202525.stm, accessed 7 August 2008.

Billington, Michael. *State of the Nation: British Theatre since 1945*. London: Faber & Faber, 2007.

Boas, Frederick S. *Shakspere [sic] and his Predecessors*. London: Murray, 1896.

Boyd, Michael, dir. Archive video. *Measure for Measure* RST 1998. RSC/TS/2/2/1998/MEA1. Shakespeare Centre Library, Stratford.

Measure for Measure. Promptbook. *Measure for Measure* RSC/SM1/1998/MEA1 Shakespeare Centre Library, Stratford.

Brenton, Howard. *Three Plays*. Ed. John Bull. Sheffield: Sheffield Academic Press, 1989.

Brown, Ruth. 'Racism and Immigration in Britain'. *International Socialism Journal* 68 (1995). http://pubs.socialistreviewindex.org.uk/isj68/brown.htm, accessed 21 May 2008.

Carleton, Don. 'Measure for Measure'. *Plays and Players* September 1978: 22.

Chaillet, Ned. 'Ingenious reworking: Measure for Measure'. *The Times* 20 September 1978. Cutting.

Clinton Impeachment, A Basic Chronology. http://academic.brooklyn.cuny.edu/history/johnson/clintontimeline.htm, accessed 12 August 2008.

D.F.B. 'Roundhouse Downstairs: "Measure for Measure"'. *Daily Telegraph* 21 September 1978. Cutting.

Foot, David. 'Bristol: Measure for Measure'. *Guardian* 3 July 1978. Cutting.

Gay, Penny. *As She Likes It: Shakespeare's Unruly Women*. London and New York: Routledge, 1994. 134–42.

Gibbons, Brian, ed. *Measure for Measure*. By William Shakespeare. The New Cambridge Shakespeare. Cambridge: Cambridge University Press, 1991.

Hytner, Nicholas, dir. Archive video. *Measure for Measure* RST 1987. RSC/TS/2/2/1987/MEA1. Shakespeare Centre Library, Stratford.

Archive video. *Measure for Measure* Barbican 1988. RSC/TS/2/2/1988/MEA1. Shakespeare Centre Library, Stratford.

Promptbook. *Measure for Measure* RSC/SM/1/1987/MEA2. S5049 Vol. 1. Shakespeare Centre Library, Stratford.

John Major. 'Policies: Back to Basics'. http://www.johnmajor.co.uk/policies.html, accessed 7 August 2008.

'Quotations'. http://www.johnmajor.co.uk/quotations.html, accessed 1 August 2008.

London Bubble Theatre Company. 'Mission Statement'. 2007. http://www.london bubble.org.uk/mission, accessed 11 August 2008.

Marriot, R. B. 'Measure for Measure'. *The Stage.* 28 September 1978. Cutting.

Miles, Rosalind. *The Problem of 'Measure for Measure': A historical investigation.* London: Vision Press, 1976.

Nicholls, Graham. *'Measure for Measure': Text and Performance.* Houndmills: Macmillan Education, 1986.

Noble, Adrian, dir. Archive video, recorded 6 January 1984. *Measure for Measure.* RSC/TS/2/2/1983/MEA1. Shakespeare Centre Library, Stratford.

Pemberton, Mark. *Good Times.* 11 June 1992. Company File. Cutting. Theatre Museum, London.

Pimlott, Steven, dir. Archive video. *Measure for Measure* RST 1994. RSC/TS/2/2/1994/MEA1. Shakespeare Centre Library, Stratford.

Measure for Measure. Programme. Shakespeare Centre Library, Stratford.

Promptbook. *Measure for Measure* RSC/SM/1/1994/MEA2. Shakespeare Centre Library, Stratford.

Rowbotham, Sheila. *A Century of Women: The History of Women in Britain and the United States.* Harmondsworth: Penguin, 1999.

Rutter, Carol. *Clamorous Voices: Shakespeare's Women Today.* London: Women's Press, 1988.

Scott, Michael. *Renaissance Drama and a Modern Audience.* Houndmills: Macmillan, 1982.

'Sex and scandal in the corridors of power'. *Mail Online.* 26 April 2006. http://www.dailymail.co.uk/news/article-384312/Sex-scandal-corridors-power.html, accessed 2 June 2008.

Stanfield, Keith. *City Limits.* 10 June 1992. Company File. Cutting. Theatre Museum, London.

Theatre Records. Shakespeare Centre Library, Stratford.

'Timeline of AIDS History'. *AIDS Newspaper Archive.* http://www.aidsarchive.com/Timeline.aspx, accessed 3 June 2008.

Williamson, Jane. 'The Duke and Isabella on the Modern Stage'. *The Triple Bond.* Ed. Joseph G. Price. University Park and London: Pennsylvania State University Press, 1975. 149–69.

PART III

Questions of identity

CHAPTER 11

Shakespeare and the rhetoric of scenography
1770–1825

Christopher Baugh

In 1776 when David Garrick retired from Drury Lane, Tom Paine, living in Philadelphia in revolutionary America, published *Common Sense*, in which he wrote that

A French bastard landing with an armed banditti and establishing himself King of England, against the consent of the natives, is, in plain terms, a very paltry, rascally original. It certainly hath no divinity in it [...] The plain truth is that the antiquity of English monarchy will not bear looking into. (16–17)

Observations such as these, and of course the American war of independence of that year, accelerated the increasingly contentious debate to identify the true extent and nature of the English constitution. The contest centred upon the idea of a constitution predicated upon the authority of ancient custom. In reality, 'ancient custom' was the canon of defining landmarks of English (Whig) history that culminated with the ultimate Whig triumph in the parliamentary settlement of 1688. This understanding was pitted against the popular and populist thrust of Tom Paine, and especially his *Rights of Man* (1792), which rejected the genealogy of 'ancient custom' and proposed a constitution based upon empirical observation and the rationality of 'common sense'. In a similar vein, and at the same time, Edmond Malone (1741–1812) initiated a rational, factually based approach to the study of Shakespeare and rejected a history and study of Shakespeare based upon anecdote and myth – Thomas Postlewait credits Malone with 'establishing the documentary foundation for Shakespearean scholarship' that led to E. K. Chambers and Samuel Schoenbaum (55).

Shakespeare, firmly established as the national poet and, through Garrick's Shakespeare Festival and the subsequent Jubilee (1769), as the 'Bard of Avon', provided the establishment with a powerful, popular, and increasingly populist theatrical spectacle whose patriotic, scenographic rhetoric could be set against that of the French Revolution and of sixpenny popular editions of Paine's work. But, as Ralph G. Allen noted, 'It is one of the curious ironies of British Theatre history that major improvements in staging nearly always are associated with non-literary popular entertainments rather than with the classic plays of the English repertory' (7). Accordingly, this chapter considers the way in which attitudes and approaches towards scenography and tropes of spectacle and especially of antiquarianism became crucial both to the staging of Shakespeare and to the development of national identity and the birth of a national theatre.

During the period 1775 to 1830, approximately one play out of every six that was acted in London was written by Shakespeare.[1] At the same time, critical commentaries by Charles Lamb (1775–1834), William Hazlitt (1778–1830), James Leigh Hunt (1784–1859) and Samuel Taylor Coleridge (1772–1834) were establishing a new tradition of academic Shakespeare scholarship. Malone produced his own edition of the plays in 1790; he created a documentary chronology for the plays and was the first to use the records at Stratford-upon-Avon to try to generate a documentary biography of Shakespeare. The first scholar to examine Henslowe's papers, he wrote 'A Historical Account of the English Stage' in 1790 and served as literary adviser to John Philip Kemble (1757–1823) at both Drury Lane and Covent Garden theatres.

But at the same time, Shakespeare's plays were cut, adapted, and remade to suit the rapidly expanding circuit of minor 'illegitimate' theatres that sprang up within the urban environment. The Theatrical Representations Act of 1788, allowing local authorities to grant licences to performing companies, created a rapid expansion of theatre in the provinces and generated a popular awareness of the plays at all levels of presentation. In addition, popular galleries devoted to the display of paintings of scenes from Shakespeare's plays were considered the source of important subject matter for a new British school of history painting. Alongside this heightened Shakespearean sensibility, it is important to place the revolution in scenography and to identify some of its effects upon staging Shakespeare that took place during these years. The attitudes and ambitions of theatre artists of the time formulated an approach to, and bestowed values upon, Shakespearean staging that were significant and lasted until well into the twentieth century.

By the middle of the nineteenth century, artists had developed a genealogy of historical tropes to which painters returned time and again: Alfred

---

[1] *The London Stage 1776–1800*, ed. Charles Beecher Hogan (Carbondale and Edwardsville: Southern Illinois University Press, 1968) makes this judgement quite secure up until 1800. However, the great expansion of provincial theatre following the 1788 Theatrical Representations Act makes this figure much more approximate.

rejecting invasion by the Danes; King John with the barons signing the Magna Carta; Richard III and the confinement of the young princes in the Tower of London; Queen Elizabeth I and the Earl of Essex; Charles I demanding the surrender of the impeached members of Parliament; the martyrdom of Charles I; and Oliver Cromwell contemplating the body of the dead king.[2] Unsurprisingly, these headline events closely paralleled those used to articulate the 'ancient custom' of pro-establishment, anti-Paine constitutionalists.[3] This visual Whig historiography provided contemporary governments with a powerful sense of ancestral and cultural legitimacy to support the ruling establishment, threatened by revolutionary French ideas and the republican ideals of Paine, whose *Rights of Man* simultaneously legitimised the constituting of the United States of America and encouraged Jacobin and anti-establishment sympathy in Britain during the war with France. The theatre developed scenographic parallels, drawn especially from Shakespeare's plays, to these headlines of history which, in their own way, became iconic tableaux expected and demanded by audiences: an expensively staged procession in *Henry VIII* through the streets of London as it might have been 'in olden times'; the emblem of the tyrannical monarch Richard crying 'Off with his head, so much for Buckingham' in Colley Cibber's 1699 version of *Richard III*, which was still the standard acting edition of the London theatre; Richard III awakening from his ghostly nightmare; King Lear standing with the dead Cordelia in his arms; Hamlet knocking over his stool as he rises at the appearance of the ghost in Gertrude's chamber; Romeo breaking open the tomb of Juliet; Prospero as a stage magician presenting the masque of wedding in *The Tempest*; Macbeth and the witches – all of these, and, of course, the countless images of English resolve and determination and the opportunities for spectacular pageant in the history plays, developed as icons of scenic rhetoric that served to generate a reassuring sense of history, cultural continuity, and moral ascendancy and, naturally, lent support to the legitimacy of the British establishment.[4]

---

[2] These historical 'headlines' are illustrated and considered by Roy Strong in *And When Did You Last See Your Father: The Victorian Painter and British History* (London: Thames & Hudson, 1978).

[3] 'When Henry Yorke, the Sheffield reformer, was on trial in 1795, his defence turned upon this point: "In almost every speech I took essential pains in controverting the doctrines of Thomas Paine, who denied the existence of our Constitution […] I constantly asserted on the contrary, that we had a good constitution, that magnanimous government which we derived from our Saxon fathers, and from the prodigious mind of the immortal Alfred".' See E. P. Thompson, *The Making of the English Working Class* (Harmondsworth: Penguin, 1968) 95.

[4] Of continuing importance are the illustrations and the discussion of the iconography of Shakespeare performance in W. Moelwyn Merchant, *Shakespeare and the Artist* (London: Oxford University Press, 1959), especially 77–94.

New scenographic practices and attitudes rapidly found fertile soil in the febrile atmosphere of metropolitan theatre, spectacle, and show during the 1790s whilst Britain contemplated the events taking place in France. In particular, and in a range of formats – theatrical, painted, engraved, and printed – the *idea* of Shakespeare became a powerful catalyst for both generating and contemplating national identity. For example, his characters and themes might be understood both to support a firm, established monarchy through their insistence upon degree, just laws, and statutory order and to approve, in justified cases, the legitimate overthrow of establishment tyranny, particularly given Shakespeare's sympathy for and understanding of common people. The role of Shakespeare within contemporary political debate has been well argued by Jonathan Bate in his work on politics, theatre, and criticism.[5]

Scenographic revolution was taking place during a time of immense cultural and societal change in the period roughly spanning 1775 and 1815. For example, the demography, reputation, and ownership of London theatre by the end of the period were greatly different to what they had been during the late working years of Garrick. At the beginning of the period, the Covent Garden district, located midway between the political power of the Westminster Parliament and Court and the mercantile power of the City of London, had been the artistic and cultural epicentre of the country. It was a centre of ostentatious and conspicuous consumption, as Joseph Roach notes: 'Standing between City and Court, reflecting and provoking them both as in Janus-faced hyperbolic mirrors, magnifying the aspirations and opportunities of their patrons to consume and to be seen consuming, were the professional theaters and commercial exchanges – public gathering places rivalled in capacity only by churches' (123). Within a few hundred metres of the theatres of Covent Garden and Drury Lane, there lived and worked the artists and thinkers who created and commanded national taste and consumption: Garrick, Johnson, Sheridan, Goldsmith, Reynolds, Loutherbourg, Blake, Chippendale, Sheraton, Arne (and on occasions Haydn, Mozart, and C. P. E. Bach). Covent Garden, with its theatres, clubs, coffee houses, and arcades and promenades for strolling, posing, and display, dominated fashion and style. But within little over a generation this area became squashed and congested between the expansion of the City to the east and the demand for living space from Westminster and Soho to the west. The large houses around the piazza of

---

[5] Jonathan Bate, *Shakespearean Constitutions: Politics, Theatre, Criticism 1730–1830* (Oxford: Clarendon Press, 1989).

Covent Garden, built in the seventeenth and early eighteenth centuries as the elegant London homes of the aristocracy, were rapidly commercialised into apartments and increasingly overcrowded tenement dwellings. The theatre district, once set at the heart of London's principal 'ludic' space, became a potentially dangerous and certainly a much less fashionable place to live or visit. By the close of the period, with just a few exceptions, the nation looked elsewhere for its artistic and cultural values – to the Lake District, Derbyshire, Somerset, Hampshire, Sussex, and Suffolk; the artist rejected metropolitan values and sought inspiration in the country, whilst London rapidly took on its over-powering and Dickensian identity as the 'infernal Wen'.[6]

As the upper and literary classes relinquished their dominance of Covent Garden during the 1790s, the theatres acquired (or had thrust upon them) some of the reputation for urban violence of revolutionary France. Sheridan's tub-thumping adaptation of Kotzebue's play of resistance and revolution, *Pizarro* (Drury Lane, 1799) filled the enlarged theatre with populist rhetoric, spectacle, and bravura. The OP (Old Price) riots that erupted at Covent Garden Theatre in September 1809 during a performance of *Macbeth* lasted for sixty-six nights and turned the auditorium into a place of political and social contest. Although initiated by the increase in seat prices and changing practice in the auditorium, it is significant that the riots made the performance of Shakespeare, the public playhouse, and their threatened 'ancient' traditions sites of contested ownership and national identity.[7] David Worrall says:

During the Covent Garden 1809 OP riots [...] the 1790s Jacobin Henry Redhead Yorke in the *Political Review* (16 September 1809) fulminated against 'that unfeeling Jewess, [the singer] Angelica Catalani' (alleged to have been hired at £4,000 per year), declaring, 'I am for rebellion; and, let me tell King John [Kemble, manager], that if he will not give us the English spirit of Garrick, we will give him and his Frenchified crew, the spirit of Marat'. (48)

At the same time, the public demand for performances outstripped licensed theatre provision at Covent Garden and Drury Lane and the 'Summer' Patent to present plays at the Haymarket Theatre, and a new 'illegitimate' Shakespeare began to flourish in the increasing number of

---

[6] William Cobbett (*Weekly Political Register*, 5 January 1822) says, 'But what is to be the fate of the great wen of all? The monster called, by the silly coxcombs of the press, "the metropolis of the empire".' Francis Sheppard considers the range of this metaphor in his *The History of London. London 1808–1870: The Infernal Wen* (London: Secker & Warburg, 1971).

[7] See the detailed account of the social and political significance of the OP riots in Marc Baer, *Theatre and Disorder in Late Georgian London* (Oxford: Clarendon Press, 1992).

minor, unlicensed theatres of the period. *Macbeth* appeared as a burletta with songs and dances for the witches, enabling it to be performed in a minor theatre where legitimate plays were forbidden. *Richard III* was frequently performed on horseback or even by an infant prodigy such as the thirteen-year-old 'Young Roscius', Master William Henry West Betty, during the seasons of 1804–5. Such 'illegitimacy' gave the performance of Shakespeare increased political significance at a time when England cast a fearful eye at the populism of revolutionary France. The perceived decline in dramatic standards, exemplified by the minor theatres, was regarded by many as a denigration of the British spirit, a threat to the 'Constitution', and a sure sign of impending revolution and republicanism. Shakespeare and his respectful presentation in the licensed Royal theatres were considered to be crucial emblems of a national tradition under threat from popularising 'illegitimate' and unlicensed performance, such as pantomime, equestrian drama, and melodrama.[8] Illegitimate performance, with its mixture of content and styles, represented a dangerous hybridity, a break with order, degree, and proper governance in what were, after all, Royal theatres. Nevertheless, with greatly enlarged auditoriums and in a period of declining aristocratic patronage, the patent theatres were obliged to compete in the market economy. Spectacle and scenic tableaux, infant phenomena, performing dogs, and equestrian Shakespeare appeared at Drury Lane, and the stage at Covent Garden was strengthened to take the additional weight of horses and elephants.

By the second decade of the nineteenth century, it is symptomatic that the 'beaux' and 'belles' of eighteenth-century Covent Garden, with painted faces, extravagant wigs, and punishing corsetry; with high-heeled shoes and clothes derived from formal courtly dress; and with dramas located in metropolitan, fashionable drawing rooms should become the 'bucks' of the Regency period. The 'buck' abandoned the powder, the wig, and knee breeches in favour of trousers, and riding boots were preferred. The intricate lace of the eighteenth-century *jabot* at the neck became the tousled and casually wrapped neck-wear of the new age, and women rejected corsets, adopting the softer flowing 'classical' dress of the Empire style and simpler, more natural hair-styles; meanwhile, their dramas (whether in the plays of Joanna Baillie or Elizabeth Inchbald or the novels of Ann Radcliffe or Jane Austen) became located in the manor houses, castles, and ruins of the countryside. Within a

---

[8] For a detailed account of performance in the minor theatres, see Jane Moody, *Illegitimate Theatre in London, 1770–1840* (Cambridge: Cambridge University Press, 2000). For an account of the politicisation of Romantic theatrical cultures, see Worrall.

couple of decades, the imagery of David Garrick, Angelica Kauffman, and George Washington is replaced with the wild and tousled images of Beethoven, Robbie Burns, and Jane Austen. As is frequently the case (cf. 'designer' punk), a ruling class under cultural and political threat colonised and made fashionable the clothing of its opponents – in this case, the *sans-culottes* styles of the citizenry. The late classicism and control of Mozart gave way to the turmoil and emotional demands of Beethoven. Within a late symphony of Haydn, for example, the two worlds – that of the 'beau' and of the 'buck' – frequently collide in adjacent movements. The urgency and speed of these cultural transitions, of course, was not a phenomenon unique to Great Britain; European *Stürm und Drang* and political revolution rapidly overturned the fashions and iconography of the *ancien régime*. Its effects within Britain, however, created a significant context for the staging of Shakespeare and the scenographic changes that had initially developed to serve the needs of pantomime and popular spectacle.

Macadamised[9] highways facilitated the beginning of timetabled public stage-coach travel, and a sharp increase in popular tourism heightened an awareness of location and the distinctiveness of place. Landscape may be, as Elinor Fuchs suggests, 'a primary lens through which to comprehend human culture' (39). Perhaps in that way the mountain landscapes of the English Lakes, Derbyshire, and Snowdonia became expressions of national culture and identity as well as the object of the artist's brush. The journey, the turnpike highway, the rural ramble, the change of scene, and the transition of place and climate achieved enhanced aesthetic and cultural significance during the late eighteenth and early nineteenth centuries.[10] During his last ten years at Drury Lane, David Garrick's 'Entertainments' featured topographically specific, detailed, and topical scenes. The most significant contribution of Philippe de Loutherbourg (1741–1812) to the development of scenography was to suggest that topography, location, and site may take on the role of a performer within the theatre; that the stage setting should no longer be considered as a generic or formal background location – the tragic palaces, the comic houses, and

---

[9] This process, invented by the Scottish civil engineer John Loudon McAdam (1756–1836), used a product of the distillation of coal to bind stone aggregate together to create a firm and weather-proof road surface. McAdam published a series of articles between 1810 and 1820 that outlined his scientific methods for creating roads and high-speed turnpike highways.

[10] The aesthetic concerns of early pictorial theatre are the subject of my 'Philippe James de Loutherbourg and the early pictorial theatre: Some aspects of its cultural context', *Themes in Drama: The Theatrical Space,* ed. James Redmond (Cambridge: Cambridge University Press, 1987) 99–128.

the pastoral scenes of the stock scenic tradition.[11] Loutherbourg implied that the stage scene, as in his Drury Lane settings for *A Christmas Tale* (1773) and *The Wonders of Derbyshire* (1779), should try, in its suggested location and imagery, to establish a harmony and synergy between the scenic representation and the characters of the dramatic situation. Scenic location might no longer simply present a generic emblem of mountains and rocks as a painted background to the dramatic action, but, through the use of ground-rows, cut pieces, and stage lighting, could serve to bring together and integrate dramatic character and scenic representation. The 'Peak's Hole' scene from *The Wonders of Derbyshire* presented a moodily illusionist representation of the vast cave located beneath Peveril Castle at Castleton in Derbyshire. Significantly, for his painting of *The Tempest*, Joseph Wright of Derby chose this popular emblem of stage mystery (remarkably similar in composition to Loutherbourg's setting) in which to locate Prospero, posed as a stage magician, revealing the masque of Iris, Ceres, and Juno to Miranda and Ferdinand whilst the drunken pantomime clowns Stephano and Trinculo cavort with Caliban.[12]

There is no evidence that Loutherbourg ever made a scenography for a Shakespeare play, although his name is associated with three drawings for *Richard III* presented to Henry Irving in the late nineteenth century.[13] Nevertheless, he initiated new technologies of scenic representation and re-defined the working practice of the scenographer;[14] most importantly, his practice defined the attitudes and the opportunities of stage location. The ideas and practice were initially used to create pantomime spectacle and *divertissements* but later became central to the staging of Shakespeare. Loutherbourg proposes that, in taking on the function of dramatic participant, the location and its stage representation might achieve something of the power of diction of the actor. Not only could the scene reflect the character and, through new lighting technologies, the atmosphere of the dramatic action, but it could also acquire the ability to serve as emblem and icon of the moment of stage action: a visual comparator with the actor's 'points' of performance. But this emblematic status was not limited to scenic statement: it extended to the *entire* stage performance. It augmented

[11] See my account of stock scenery in 'Scenography and Technology', *The Cambridge Companion to British Theatre 1730–1830*, ed. Jane Moody and Daniel O'Quinn (Cambridge: Cambridge University Press, 2007) 43–56.

[12] The painting survives only in Robert Thew's coloured engraving of 1792.

[13] The status and provenance of these designs attributed to Loutherbourg are considered in my 'Three Loutherbourg Designs', *Theatre Notebook* 47.2 (1993): 96–103.

[14] See my account of Loutherbourg's ideas concerning the role of the scenographer in *Garrick and Loutherbourg* (Cambridge: Chadwyck-Healey, 1990) 29–31.

the actor's 'points' to require the representation of the actor *within* the visual environment – a bringing together of hitherto disparate theatrical elements into the completeness of scenographic performance. For example, the engraved frontispieces of collected editions of plays such as *The British Theatre* (1808) illustrate clear connections between actors' points and their dependence upon scenic emblem. *Richard III* is illustrated by the image of

7A Frontispiece for *Richard III* from *British Theatre*, ed. Elizabeth Inchbald, 25 vols., London, 1808.

7B. Frontispiece for *Hamlet* from *British Theatre*, ed. Elizabeth Inchbald, 25 vols., London, 1808.

7C. Frontispiece for *King Lear* from *British Theatre*, ed. Elizabeth Inchbald, 25 vols., London, 1808.

7D. Frontispiece for *Henry IV Part 1* from *British Theatre*, ed. Elizabeth Inchbald, 25 vols., London, 1808.

7E. Frontispiece for *Romeo and Juliet* from *British Theatre*, ed. Elizabeth Inchbald, 25 vols., London, 1808.

Richard asleep in his tent – an image made memorable by Garrick on the stage and on the easel by William Hogarth in his painting of Garrick in the role in 1745 – and the Ghost of Henry crying 'Awake, Richard, awake'. *Romeo and Juliet* is typified by the balcony as Romeo climbs up to Juliet, and *Hamlet* by the horror of Hamlet as the Ghost appears in Gertrude's closet – an iconic emblem of the play ever since Nicholas Rowe's 1709 edition of the play used it to show Thomas Betterton playing the role.[15]

Such scenographic rhetoric developed and extended Loutherbourg's practice where, for example, a scenic spectacle at Drury Lane of the topical Portsmouth Naval Review extended language and patriotically concluded David Mallet's and James Thomson's *Alfred* (1773):

> Yet ere you go
> One moment, Alfred, backward cast your eyes
> On this unfolding scene; where pictur'd true
> As in a mirror, rises fair to sight,
> Our England's genius, strength and future fame.

Here is seen the ocean in prospect, and ships sailing along. Two boats land their crews. (3, ix)

'Rule Britannia', the unofficial national anthem of Great Britain, was written by Thomas Arne in 1740 when *Alfred* was first staged. It now served as scene-change music to accompany Loutherbourg's scenographic emblem. *Omai; or, a trip round the world* (Covent Garden, 1785) concluded with a scenography that spoke eloquently and assertively of colonial attitudes that would become a distinctive feature of production values in nineteenth-century theatre:

The Boats of all the Islands are seen entring [*sic*] the Bay, and – when arriv'd, the Ambassadors from the different powers enter in procession with presents to Omai – preceded by the English Captain & Sailors – who salute him as the Ally of Britain & compliment him with an English Sword, which he tells him has more virtue than all the Talismans in the Universe [...] [16]

Meanwhile the Captain sings in recitative:

> Accept from mighty George our Sovereign Lord,
> In sign of British Love, this British Sword,
> OBEREA: Oh, Joy! away my useless Spells & magic Charms,
> A British Sword is proof agst [*sic*] the World in Arms. [17]

---

[15] *The British Theatre* with biographical and critical remarks by Mrs Inchbald, 25 vols., London, 1808.

[16] *Harlequin Omai a Pantomime design'd by Mr Loutherberg* (sic), 1785, MS with notes on recitations & songs, V&A Theatre Museum, London. MS 1198–1986.

[17] *Omai, Songs, &c., in Pantomime*, John O'Keeffe. MS 713, Catalogue of the Larpent Plays in the Huntington Library, San Marino, California.

It is significant for our survey that the fulsome review of *Omai* in *The Times*, 26 December 1785, includes this rhetorical question:

To the rational mind, what can be more entertaining than to contemplate prospects of countries in their natural colouring and tints. To bring into living action, the customs and manners of different nations! To see exact representations of their buildings, marine vessels, arms, manufactures, sacrifices and dresses?

The heightened concern for history and, in the light of the French Revolution, for the legitimacy of national heritage quickly transferred the substance of this question to a theatrical consideration of the customs, manners, and buildings of Britain: a consideration especially appropriate and evident in the treatment of the plays of Shakespeare.

Four years after *Omai* at Covent Garden, the Boydell Shakespeare Gallery opened at 52 Pall Mall on 4 May 1789. This huge undertaking by Alderman John Boydell (1719–1804) created a gallery of paintings illustrating and inspired by the plays of Shakespeare. Subscribers to the project eventually received engravings of the exhibited paintings, and John and his son Josiah Boydell published a nine-volume illustrated edition of the plays edited by George Steevens between 1791 and 1802. The Gallery exhibited 34 pictures at its opening in 1789, and 22 more were added in the following year; thenceforth, year by year, the number was increased. In 1805, the last time the collection was seen together before being dispersed, the catalogue listed 167 paintings.[18] Boydell's preface to *A Catalogue of the Pictures in the Shakespeare Gallery* (1789) declared that, 'To advance the art towards maturity, and establish an *English School of Historical Painting*, was the great object of the present design' (iii, qtd in Friedman 64). Boydell had significant theoretical support for his ambition. In his Fourth Discourse, Sir Joshua Reynolds had advocated topics of history as subject matter for the easel artist, furthermore stating that an appropriate subject 'ought to be either some eminent instance of heroick action, or heroick suffering. There must be something either in the action or in the object, in which men are universally concerned, and which strikes upon the publick sympathy' (*Discourses* 57). Reynolds was an important supporter of Boydell's project and, writing to the Duke of Rutland on 13 February 1787, he said: 'But the greatest news relating to *virtù*, is Alderman Boydell's scheme of having pictures and prints taken from those pictures of the most interesting scenes of Shakespeare, by which all the painters and engravers find engagements for eight or ten years' (*Letters* 174).

---

[18] The fullest account of the Gallery is in Winifred H. Friedman, *Boydell's Shakespeare Gallery* (New York and London: Garland, 1976).

8. Harlow's painting of Sarah Siddons as Lady Macbeth in Act 1 of the play, c. 1805.

Additional factors helped to focus the attention of the easel painter upon the emblematic scenography of Shakespeare. As the intense images of Henry Fuseli (1741–1825) and William Blake (1757–1827) indicate, Shakespeare's characters, narratives, and themes were well able to supply the situations and locations of the 'other' worlds of the romantic and millennial gothic imagination. His foreboding castles and menacing supernatural worlds could be conjured by the haunted and charged performances of Kemble and Sarah Siddons (1755–1831), and iconography of their performance is reflected in a number of paintings for the Gallery. James Northcote made a painting (1799) of Richard III contemplating the young princes in which Richard bears a striking resemblance to Kemble: heavy brows, corners of the mouth turned down, and cleft chin. Kemble had appeared in the role at Drury Lane as early as 1783, and by 1788 he played the role regularly. John Downman made a painting of *As You Like It* (1797) for Boydell in which his Rosalind bears a close resemblance to Sarah Siddons and the location has much of the scenic quality and atmosphere of Loutherbourg's 'Kensington Garden' setting for *Omai*. Henry Harlow's portrait of Siddons as Lady Macbeth established an enduring emblem of Shakespeare's character that illustrates Boaden's description of Siddons's performance, which showed 'the daring steadiness of her mind, which could be disturbed by no scruple, intimidated by no danger' (307). Loutherbourg's own painting in his miniature theatre – The Eidophusikon[19] – established a tradition of scenic spectacle that rapidly fed into the Shakespearean canon of stage iconography. The playbill for Edmund Kean's *King Lear* at Drury Lane Theatre in 1820 advertised 'A Land Storm After the manner of *Loutherbourg's Eidophusikon*. Designed and executed by Marinari and Assistants'.

The scenographic contribution of William Capon (1757–1827) expanded the approach of Loutherbourg and initiated a concern that the stage should present accurate scenic representations of past architectures and styles of clothing. The desire by artists and actor-managers to achieve an 'archaeological' and reconstructive status in theatrical presentation lay at the heart of the achievement of nineteenth-century managers who sought to 'illustrate' Shakespeare, such as William Charles Macready (1793–1873)[20] and Charles Kean (1811–68). Their concerns for a carefully studied, educational, and, above all, socially respectable and responsible theatre were built upon this foundation of 'authentic' scenographic archaeology. Whilst Loutherbourg offered mountain scenes, waterfalls, crumbling rocks, and emblems of British naval pride and colonial ambition, Capon contributed meticulously detailed and researched

[19] See my account of the Eidophusikon in *Garrick and Loutherbourg* 78–83.
[20] Macready said, in his farewell to the stage on 26 February 1851, that it had been his 'ambition to establish a theatre, in regard of decorum and taste, worthy of our country, and to have in it the plays of our divine Shakespeare fitly illustrated' (293).

architectural scenes, designed for his principal employer, John Kemble, at Drury Lane and later at Covent Garden. Capon's work corresponded closely with both the Shakespeare 'history' painters of the 1790s and, by the second decade of the nineteenth century, with the intense popularity of the historical novels of Sir Walter Scott[21] and the general romantic and political enthusiasm for England's medieval and Tudor past. This enthusiasm was reflected in an influential series of scholarly books and folios devoted to recording and tabulating the ancient castles, manor houses, armour and weapons, and clothing styles of the nation.[22] It is equally significant that the period of Capon's work coincided with the historical and editorial work of Malone, to whom Kemble dedicated *Macbeth Reconsidered* (1786), his essay of detailed textual analysis of the nature and historicity of Shakespeare's plays. The designer's attitude paralleled this growing desire to conceive of the plays of Shakespeare as being firmly located within a precise historical context that inevitably reflected contemporary visual and architectural styles – in other words, the site specificity of Shakespeare's plays.

Critical response to the gothic detail and seemingly authoritative historicism of Capon's stage paintings suggests the timely significance of his innovations. However, it was still rare that a play would be 'through designed' by a single artist, and Capon customarily worked alongside other painters who were chosen to design individual scenes in plays according to their scenic speciality. Responsible with Thomas Malton for the 'Gothic Apartment at Dunsinane', he worked within a team of six scenic artists preparing the twelve scenes listed by *The World* (22 April 1794) for Kemble's production of *Macbeth* at Drury Lane (21 April 1794).[23] It is perhaps of some significance that the earliest reference to Capon should be the listing of his name in 1783 with that of Thomas Greenwood (scene painter at Drury Lane, 1781–94, who also worked on *Macbeth*) as responsible for the interior refurbishment of the theatre: getting rid of the bright, glittery, and glazed Adams auditorium

[21] Sir Walter Scott's *Waverley* was published in 1814.

[22] Of especial significance to the staging of Shakespeare were Joseph Strutt's *The Regal and Ecclesiastical Antiquities of England* (1773) and *Complete View of the Dress and Habits of the People of England* (1796–9), Francis Grose's *Treatise on Ancient Armour and Weapons* (1786), Charles Alfred Stothard's *The Monumental Effigies of Great Britain* (1811–33), the antiquarian and theatre costume designer James Robertson Planché's *History of British Costumes* (1834), Henry Shaw's *Specimens of Ancient Furniture Drawn from Existing Authorities* (1836), and Joseph Nash's *The Mansions of England in the Olden Time* (1839–49). See especially Strong, *And When Did You Last See Your Father?* 47–71.

[23] For a detailed analysis of the scenes in this production and the six painters responsible for them, see Donohue.

of 1775, they replaced it with the darker, more sombre appearance that focused attention away from the audience and towards the scenic space. Capon worked with Greenwood and Gaetano Marinari, another Drury Lane painter, on scenes for *Jack of Newbury* (1795), *Richard III* (1796), and William Ireland's forged Shakespearean fantasy, *Vortigern*. The re-building of the patent houses in the 1790s, and again when Covent Garden and Drury Lane theatres were destroyed by fire in 1808 and 1809, necessitated the urgent re-stocking of the scenic stores, and Capon provided scenes of Gothic streets, chambers, and Tudor halls, which in the case of Covent Garden were still regularly in the scenic stock for several decades.

But these enlarged stages also required and encouraged a new stagecraft, which indicates that Capon's innovations had an important scenographic and technical element, as well as the purely aesthetic response to audience taste. The size, variety, and sheer quantity of scenery became important, as did the fact that Capon was beginning to break away from the regularity of the purely two-dimensional painted wing shutters and back-scenes and to introduce significant quantities of large three-dimensional constructed scenery. There were, however, serious drawbacks to this aspect of Capon's work, which quickly became both a remarked upon and a regrettable feature of stage practice. For example, the twelve scenes prepared for Kemble's *Macbeth* (1794) required the use of a drop curtain, painted by Thomas Malton and representing the inner court of a palace with dome and rotunda, so as to hide the lengthy scene changes; the irritated critic of *The Oracle, and Public Advertiser* (22 April 1794) referred to this device as the 'perpetual *curtain*'. George Colman complained of the scenography in the preface to his play, *The Iron Chest* (1796):

> my consent was, abruptly, requested to a transposition of two of the most material scenes in the second act: and the reason given for this curious proposal, that the present stage of Drury […] was so bunglingly constructed, that there was not time for the carpenters to place the lumbering framework, on which an abbey was painted, behind the representations of a Library, without having a chasm of ten minutes in the action of the Play; and that in the middle of an act. (ix)

Drury Lane was barely two years old at this time, which indicates the rapidity of new scenographic ambition. But unlike the plays of Shakespeare, this play, along with Joanna Baillie's *De Monfort* (1800), again with Capon's scenes, might be termed 'modern' in the sense that they are all really rather trivial works, made stage-worthy on account of the opportunities they offered for spectacle and scenic effect. The

European Magazine reported on Baillie's play, 'The audience, however, though they rapturously applauded the Composer and the Scene Painter, hissed the dialogue almost from beginning to end' (May 1801, 359), *The Gentleman's Magazine* adding that 'The Artist, at great pains and labour, followed the style of building of the fifteenth century [...] whereby, the spectator, for a short space, might indulge his imagination to believe he was in some religious pile' (May 1801, 409). In a similar way, the tension between the claims of literary coherence and faithfulness to Shakespeare and of powerful scenography would continue throughout the century.

Capon's surviving designs and sketchbooks show intricately drawn 'caprices' of Tudor chambers and street scenes that may have served as stock scenes for many of Shakespeare's history plays. But it is important to note that, in spite of his knowledge of antiquarian architecture, his visual image of the past was undoubtedly as 'constructed' as that portrayed, for example, in Scott's novels. Nevertheless, his place within the development of the scenic language of theatre and the staging of Shakespeare is significant, and Capon contributed an aura of authority and scholarly research to the role of scenographer. His direct influence in this respect upon later scenic artists such as Alexander Nasmyth (1758–1840), John Henderson Grieve (1770–1845), Clarkson Stanfield (1793–1867), Grieve's sons Thomas (1799–1882) and William (1800–44), Frederick Lloyds (1818–94) and William Telbin (1813–73) was considerable.[24] From within our contemporary eclectic, post-modern scenographic approach to the performance and staging of Shakespeare, it may be hard not to smile at the earnest, antiquarian concern to carefully locate his plays within detailed and studiously researched scenic locations. A short series of contributions by the anonymous 'An Artist and an Antiquary' to *The Gentleman's Magazine* in 1800–1 passionately articulated a desire and rationale for scenographic change, and the need to bestow upon Shakespeare production a similar degree of scenic and costume attention to that traditionally given to pantomime and other theatre spectacles. Perhaps in response to what was seen as corrupted and bowdlerised Shakespeare in the minor theatres, the patent theatres needed to be made aware of their responsibility both to Shakespeare and, importantly, to the nation's heritage. All the contributions are entitled 'Of the Impropriety of Theatrical Representations, so far as they relate to

---

[24] Hilary Norris, 'A Directory of Victorian Scene-Painters', *Theatrephile* 1.2 (1984): 38–52 is a useful source of biographical and production information and, inevitably, describes significant developments in the staging of Shakespeare.

the Scenery, Dresses, and Decorations, when brought forward as illustrations of the Antient [*sic*] History of this Country' (Vol. 70, April 1800, 318). The recurring plea of the articles is that the care and attention consistently paid to the design and development of music theatre and spectacle should equally be provided in the presentation of Shakespeare: 'why do we see them [Shakespeare's plays] exhibited without the smallest attention to our antient [*sic*] costume, or a decent expenditure to render them respectable to audiences familiarized to a continual display of rich and magnificent spectacles, ballet dances, and pantomimes?' (318). The writer provides the rationale for doing this which was to underpin the scenography of Shakespeare for the next 100 years:

Shakespeare's historic plays would become a captivating source of information and instruction to the patriot, the historian, and the artist. Here, as in a mirror, should we see the shades of our great forefathers pass before our wondering sight, awfully grand, and pathetically interesting. (319)

And in an issue a year later the 'artist and antiquary' asserts 'how absolutely necessary it is, that the stage should become the faithful mirror of past times, to instruct, not mislead' (Vol. 71, May 1801, 408). The persistence of a stock tradition with respect to costume was a significant concern, and the writer complains about the production of *Cymbeline* (Covent Garden, 1800):

The dress of Ballarius has served [...] many years either for the old shepherd in the *Winter's Tale*, or old Norval in *Douglas*, the old rustick in *Damon and Phyllida*, or for a long *et cetera* of other pastoral characters which fill theatric scenes. (Vol. 70, supplement for the year 1800, 1267)

Perhaps indicating the extent and importance of contemporary antiquarian scholarship, the articles concluded in May 1801 that

From these remarks it will be seen to what a low ebb the costume attention of managers is reduced. Surely the historic tide, from the course of public reprehension, must soon turn, and bring before them the experience and advice of those men, who, from Antiquity's distant shores, have brought some of her brightest gems, to tell a present age the majesty of former times. (Vol. 71, May 1801, 410)

Whilst the ambition and spirit of scenographic change emerged during the 1790s and early 1800s, the stock tradition appears to have continued – especially for costume. It may well be that change in the attitude towards costume was slower since actors, in addition to their reputedly conservative attitudes, were traditionally responsible for providing their own stage clothes. Shortly before his retirement from the stage in March 1851, Macready noted with tired relief that, as he shed the roles that he had acted for over thirty years, he could now sell his costumes: 'Webster came and offered £5 for every dress; there were twenty-five, but I withdrew the armour [...] I am glad to be rid of the clothes, etc., and glad to have the £100 in my pocket' (290). Similarly, personal and costume props such as crowns, helmets, and swords were the personal responsibility of the actor. Hence there developed what is, to the 21st-century theatre artist, a somewhat alien sense of ownership and belonging between the actor and, for example, the sword that might be used in *Richard III* throughout an entire stage career. Accounts exist from throughout the nineteenth century, describing the burden placed upon the actors and the extent of their ownership of the physical appearance of the characters that they played and of their personal props. However, notwithstanding the persistence of stock costume – especially for the travelling and provincial actor – significant moves were undertaken early in the century that reflected the growing concern for antiquarian history and national heritage. Kemble, for example, had paid particular attention to costume in his *Macbeth* (1794) and, as Joseph Donohue says, citing Walter Scott,

Kemble introduced extensive reform in stage costume, collecting ideas 'with indefatigable diligence from illuminated manuscripts, ancient pictures, and other satisfactory authorities ...'. But Kemble did not follow his sources with slavish pedantry, Scott continues. Like Shakespeare himself, he carried his scene back into remote times while still retaining 'the manners and sentiments of his own period,' so blending the modern with the antique as 'to give an air of truth to the scene.' (71)

James Robinson Planché (1796–1880) designed the costumes for Charles Kemble's production of *King John*, which opened at Covent Garden on 24 November 1823. Planché began his career in the theatre as a writer working initially for minor theatres such as the Lyceum, the Adelphi, and Sadler's Wells. Exploiting the huge popularity of Scott's historical novels, he wrote *Kenilworth Castle, or, the Days of Queen Bess*, produced at the Adelphi on 8 February 1821, and in 1822 he became resident writer at Covent Garden. In *Recollections and Reflections* (London, 1872) and in terms that closely echo the concerns expressed by *The Gentleman's Magazine* over twenty years earlier, Planché accounts for his costume work on Kemble's production of *King John*: 'I complained to Mr Kemble that a thousand pounds were frequently lavished on a Christmas pantomime or an Easter spectacle, while the plays of Shakespeare were put upon the stage with make-shift scenery, and, at the best, a new dress or two for the principal characters' (qtd in Jackson 163). Kemble gave his designer full authority to supervise the costumes, but Planché complained that, 'In the theatre, however, my innovations were regarded with distrust and jealousy' (qtd in Jackson 164). The stage manager (John Fawcett 1769–1837) considered his dignity offended by the directorial authority given to Planché, and the traditional director of stage spectacle at Covent Garden (Charles Farley 1772–1859) was concerned that he would be put out of business if Shakespeare's plays were to be given such attention to staging. Planché recorded:

Never shall I forget the dismay of some of the performers when they looked upon the flat-topped *chapeaux de fer* [...] of the twelfth century, which they irreverently stigmatised as *stewpans*! Nothing but the fact that the classical features of a Kemble were to be surmounted by a precisely similar abomination would, I think, have induced one of the rebellious barons to have appeared in it [...] When the curtain rose, and discovered King John dressed as his effigy appears in Worcester Cathedral, surrounded by his barons sheathed in chain mail, with cylindrical helmets and correct armorial shields, and his courtiers in the long tunics and mantles of the thirteenth century, there was a roar of approbation, accompanied by four distinct rounds of applause, so general and so hearty, that the actors were astonished. (Qtd in Jackson 164–5)

The production was an important artistic and financial success, and Planché claimed (from his vantage point of 1872) that 'a complete reformation of dramatic costume became from that moment inevitable upon the English stage' (qtd in Jackson 165). A significant contribution to that 'reformation' was Planché's publication in 1834 of the first serious and properly sourced history of costume that still holds its place in the scenographer's library.[25]

Nonetheless, Planché was somewhat disingenuous in his assessment of the overall effect of the 1823 *King John* on scenography. The theatre and the repertoire system of the nineteenth century relied upon a company's ability to maintain a considerable range of Shakespeare plays in its stock; it was further predicated upon the independently employed status of the travelling actor who continued to have a financial responsibility for a significant part of his/her wardrobe. Furthermore, the considerable expense of a fully designed Shakespeare revival, such as those undertaken by Charles Kean at the Princess's Theatre during the 1850s, meant that many individual scenographic units – properties, thrones, banners, arms, and weaponry – continually entered the generic playhouse stock to be used, repainted, and re-furbished until discarded. Notwithstanding such cautions, however, by the time of Planché's *King John*, very important changes of attitude and production value had taken place with regard to the staging of Shakespeare.

---

[25] J. R. Planché, *A History of British Costume, from Ancient Times to the Eighteenth Century* (London: Charles Knight, 1834; Teddington: Senate, 2001).

Whilst Garrick, through his own productions and his Jubilee festival at Stratford-upon-Avon in 1769, had effectively 'constructed' Shakespeare as the national Bard, it was in the decades that straddled the millennium, during the French Revolution and the wars with France, that staging Shakespeare became intimately implicated within the making of an increasingly dominant national historiography. The plays could be seen to support both pro- and anti-establishment values: to befriend both monarch and republican; to belong to, and to support, for example, both the self-improving Lancashire weaver and the local landowner enclosing the landscape and creating industrialised agriculture. And if Shakespeare was indeed central to national identity and history, then the theatre had a duty, as *The Gentleman's Magazine* was quick to assert, to hold a respectful and carefully researched mirror to historical society so that we might 'see the shades of our great forefathers pass before our wondering sight, awfully grand, and pathetically interesting' (Vol. 70, April 1800, 319). As such, significant moments of the plays, sometimes but not always comparable with the actors' great soliloquies and 'points', achieved the status of scenographic emblem whose visual rhetoric paralleled the importance and contemporary popularity of easel paintings of Shakespeare scenes. New technologies of the Industrial Revolution, and especially those deriving from the mining and chemical industries,[26] enabled and supported a revolution in the lighting and painting of the stage. The 1788 Theatrical Representations Act provided the legislation that facilitated the rapid growth of a theatre industry throughout the country, and the plays of Shakespeare, with their defining emblems and tropes of scenographic performance, became central to the construction of the nation's culture.

WORKS CITED

Allen, Ralph G. 'Capon's Scenes for Melodrama'. *Theatre Research* 8.1 (1966): 7–17.
Boaden, James. *Memoirs of Mrs. Siddons*. 1827. London: Gibbings and Co., 1896.
Colman, George. *The Iron Chest*. Dublin: P. Wogan, J. Rice, and G. Folingsby, 1796.
Donohue Jr, Joseph W. 'Kemble's Production of Macbeth (1794): Some Notes on Scene Painters, Scenery, Special Effects, and Costumes'. *Theatre Notebook* 21.2 (1996): 63–74.

---

[26] There is some account of the effects of new industrial technologies in my 'Scenography and Technology'.

Friedman, Winifred H. *Boydell's Shakespeare Gallery*. New York and London: Garland, 1976.

Fuchs, Elinor. 'Reading for Landscape: The Case of American Drama'. *Land/Scape/Theater*. Ed. Elinor Fuchs and Una Chaudhuri. Ann Arbor: University of Michigan Press, 2002. 30–50.

Jackson, Russell. *Victorian Theatre*. London: A. & C. Black, 1989.

Macready, William Charles. *The Journal of William Charles Macready*. Ed. J. C. Trewin. London: Longmans, 1967.

Paine, Tom. *Common Sense*. 1776. *Thomas Paine, Rights of Man, Common Sense and Other Political Writings*. Ed. Mark Philp. Oxford: Oxford University Press, 1995. 5–59.

Postlewait, Thomas. 'The Criteria for Evidence: Anecdotes in Shakespearean Biography 1709–2000'. *Theorizing Practice: Redefining Theatre History*. Ed. W. B. Worthen with Peter Holland. Basingstoke: Palgrave Macmillan, 2003. 47–70.

Reynolds, Sir Joshua. *Discourses on Art*. 1771. Ed. Robert R. Wark. San Marino, Calif.: Huntington Library; Oxford: Oxford University Press, 1959.

The Letters of Sir Joshua Reynolds. Ed. Frederick Whiley Hilles. Cambridge: Cambridge University Press, 1929.

Roach, Joseph. 'Vicarious: Theater and Synthetic Experience'. *Theorizing Practice: Redefining Theatre History*. Ed. W. B. Worthen with Peter Holland. Basingstoke: Palgrave Macmillan, 2003. 120–35.

The Gentleman's Magazine. Vol. 70, April 1800; Vol. 70 (supplement for the year) 1800; Vol. 71, May 1801.

Worrall, David. *Theatric Revolution: Drama, Censorship and Romantic Period Subcultures 1773–1832*. Oxford: Oxford University Press, 2006.

CHAPTER 12

The presence of Shakespeare

Susan Bennett

GLOBAL SHAKESPEARE, LOCAL SHAKESPEARE

Within the field of Shakespeare studies, a long-burgeoning scholarly interest in performance has tended to follow two particular trajectories. The first has turned, not surprisingly, on the axis of heritage and authenticity so as to foster an especial focus on those performances that might be thought to carry particular and significant cultural/historical weight. It has sometimes appeared as if Shakespeare's own imprimatur is attached to the Royal Shakespeare Company's productions – that the Stratford season 'is' Shakespeare – and, more recently, performances at London's Shakespeare's Globe have been credited as another privileged site for this kind of scrutiny. In the case of the Globe, while the actual performances have often been negatively reviewed, its location and materiality are exhibited as all-important in understanding a historical through-line that cannot be ignored. National tourism has applied both energy and agility in marketing the town of Stratford-upon-Avon and the replica of the Globe as, among other things, cultural bait for the heritage industry, which has assured a particular viability for the production of Shakespeare's plays in the contemporary moment, part, Michael Bristol would suggest, of the playwright's transformation into a 'reservoir of cultural capital' (51).

The second, more recent but equally vital, focus for the study of the performances of Shakespeare's plays is the first's diametrical opposite. Here there has been an impulse to a kind of global sampling so that performances are analysed and interrogated precisely at their points of cultural dissonance and difference from those foundational English performances as the inevitable aesthetic and, more broadly, cultural touchstone. This node of enquiry has engaged a broader post-colonial interest in global reproduction as significant ground on which to parse many of the key questions about flows of capital, people, and products. Specifically in this instance, as Yong Li Lan puts it, '[t]he production of a Shakespeare play outside Europe and North America seems invariably an act of producing not only, or even mainly, the play, but rather, a cultural relationship to what Shakespeare represents: the heritage of the Western literary classic, the English language, and Shakespeare's global cultural status' (251). Such a focus has unquestionably produced an engaging and important body of work on 'Shakespeare in [name your non-English-speaking country or continent]'. Indeed, this approach has added much not only to Shakespeare studies, but also to scholarly comprehension of cross- and intercultural performance, as well as globalisation studies more generally. Yet, it is still worth observing that this development has a great deal to do with a new mobility, access to travel and tourism for a broad demographic, and, simply put, the ability and desire of many academics to marry their tourism and their scholarship. Thus, the field has embraced what Dennis Kennedy, according to the title of his influential book, has termed 'foreign Shakespeare'.[1]

Kennedy initiates his project with what remains a significant question: 'To what extent are western Shakespeareans prepared to acknowledge and understand that extreme kind of transculturalism [performance in Asia], especially when it violates accepted standards of interpretation?' (292). In order to measure the impact of performance far outside 'accepted standards of interpretation', Kennedy looks for a theory that will elucidate how Shakespeare operates in a variety of cultural, cross-cultural, transcultural, intercultural, and appropriated contexts, persuasively insisting that such a theory is 'much more important than linguistic analysis, textual examination, psychological assessments, historical research, or any of the Anglo-centered occupations scholars have traditionally valued and perpetuated' (301). Performance-oriented scholarship, then, provides an important capacity to challenge the traditional approaches that Kennedy lists, as well as to provoke a more nuanced understanding of those cultural practices in which Shakespeare now participates, wherever in the world they are situated.

Certainly, the prevailing trajectories for the study of Shakespeare in performance have impressed upon the field the global reach of the Bard. He is everywhere, yet he is especially in England, even if that very 'authenticity' is now almost always cited sceptically. Notwithstanding, I want to return to a more locally oriented elucidation of how Shakespeare 'operates' (to repeat Kennedy's figure), primarily in service of illustrating how easily predominant assumptions about the presence of Shakespeare are circulated

---

[1] The book's continuing relevance – and, indeed, its influence – is marked by the publication of a paperback version in 2004, more than ten years after the first publication of the book in hardcover format.

and deployed to account for every kind of performance – irrespective, it turns out, of the actual cultural setting and experience. When Kennedy promotes a more careful consideration of how Shakespeare 'operates', I understand that direction to refer to the relationship between performance and context: to understand motivations, engagements, impacts, and effects on specific and defined communities, across historical moments and geographical locations; to reveal new questions and concerns for the field; and, as he suggested, to challenge the 'accepted standards of interpretation'.

SHAKESPEARE IN AMERICAN COMMUNITIES

Within a recognition of the scope of global Shakespeare, it may be useful to question whether attention to performances worldwide in fact ever captures local practice(s) or recognises the formation of specific viewing publics. It is timely, I think, to explore production and reception parameters in the context of an expanded horizon for Shakespearean performance and, to do so, I turn to a territory that seems, in many ways, to fall out of sight in the face of authentic English and other 'foreign' performance. Thus, the Shakespearean performances examined in this essay are American, but still lie outside the usual frames of reference and situation for thinking about the presence of Shakespeare in both contemporary and historical moments. They occupy an interstitial space between the authentic and the foreign and, as such, throw into relief those exclusions that necessarily maintain what has become a definitive global vista for performance. This is not an essay concerned, then, with any of the major theatre companies or any of the renowned festivals that might be easily identified as imbricated in a traditional history of Shakespearean (re)production in the United States, nor is it about the import of British or even 'foreign' Shakespeares for North American audiences. Instead I look to a particular, if unexpected, geographical example so as to outline the grip of mainstream (national) critical discourse and to suggest how the comprehension of Shakespeare at a local level works to contradict an overdetermined presence for Shakespeare hailed by conventional approaches.

Scholars have, of course, long paid attention to the history of Shakespeare in certain parts of the United States, likely because, in Bristol's argument, 'the interpretation of Shakespeare and the interpretation of American political culture are mutually determining practices' (3). As a performance culture, this history has been recently vivified by the ambitious 'Shakespeare in American Communities' programme launched by the National Endowment for the Arts (NEA) in 2003, rather predictably on Shakespeare's putative birthday, 23 April.[2] This programme was designed 'to revitalize the longstanding American theatrical tradition of touring – bring the best of live theater to new audiences' (3) under the guidance of an impressive board (Harold Bloom, Julie Taymor, and James Earl Jones, among others) and honorary chairs Laura Bush and then-Motion Picture Association of America President and CEO, Jack Valenti.

In its 2007 programme report, the NEA commented:

> Throughout most of our history, the majority of Americans from every social class and various ethnic backgrounds knew his most famous speeches by heart. Only in the 20th century did Shakespeare's relationship with the American public begin to change. His plays gradually began to be regarded as high rather than popular culture. The once universally accessible dramatist had become our most sacred dramatist – to whom most audiences were not able to relate. (3–4)

Evidence for this assertion is not provided in the programme description, although it is one made commonly enough and one that Lawrence Levine effectively interrogates in his important *Highbrow/Lowbrow: The Emergence of Cultural Hierarchy in America*. What is relevant here, however, is the deployment of this historical narrative, where Shakespeare, who has previously belonged to 'the people', is instated, in the twentieth century and beyond, as the property only of a cultural elite. Thus, the 'Shakespeare in American Communities' programme description adopts an almost evangelical tone in 'introducing a new generation of Americans to the greatest writer in the English language' (3).

As a measure of immediate success, the NEA reports that the programme has in its first four years 'brought superb live theater to more than 1,700 towns across all 50 states, reaching new audiences that have little opportunity to experience live, professional theater' (3). This rhetoric, while admirable in its aims, assumes that Shakespearean performance must be imported to audiences who are without much in the way of cultural opportunity, and it is premised on this singular view that claims a popular Shakespeare of the nineteenth century (entertainment for the masses) and a high art Shakespeare in the twentieth, the subject today of scholarly enquiry rather than of theatrical excitement. In other words, then, in many ways this NEA initiative takes as exemplary Kennedy's argument for the need to turn away from traditional, academic

---

[2] All quotations about the Shakespeare in American communities programme are taken from the National Endowment for the Arts report, downloadable free of charge from http://www.shakespeareinamericancommunities.org or www.arts.gov, accessed 31 August 2008.

approaches, to prefer and promote Shakespeare in the theatre, since 'the once universally accessible dramatist had become our most sacred drama-tist – to whom most audiences were not able to relate' (4).

In the programme's first phase (2003–2004), the NEA supported six companies charged with the task of providing performances and educational activities throughout the country, with events taking place in every single state. All six companies came from urban centres, four of them from major theatre cities: The Acting Company (New York), Aquila Theatre Company (also New York), Arkansas Repertory Theatre (Little Rock, population 185,000), Artists Repertory Theatre (Portland, Oreg.; population 500,000), Chicago Shakespeare Theatre (Chicago), and the Guthrie Theater (Minneapolis, a theatre that opened in 1963 with a production of *Hamlet* under the direction of Sir Tyrone Guthrie). Enacting the desire to bring 'great' Shakespearean performance to audiences across America, the equation was straightforward: take established theatre companies and have them show their work to communities who do not otherwise enjoy the presence of Shakespeare. But this seemingly straightforward assumption is misleading. In fact, there is a disjuncture between this perception – and concomitantly, I argue, informed discussion of Shakespearean performances and the audiences that see them – and local realities that I describe here.

Although the Shakespeare in American Communities programme has grown and strengthened, it has done so only by acknowledging the existence of local Shakespeare companies. It transformed the initial trajectory of a national tour led by the six companies to a much more ambitious performance schedule involving about thirty-five companies each year. This expansion has largely been achieved through the creation, in 2004, of 'Shakespeare for a New Generation', a competitive grants initiative that has now supported the work of more than sixty-five theatre companies in the United States (National Endowment for the Arts 5). As the Shakespeare in American Communities project discovered, Shakespeare, in so many American communities, often already had a long-standing performance presence – already, then, challenging a national (and scholarly) perception about the nature of audiences for this theatrical work. This performance presence can be illustrated by the example of one such company, the Montana Shakespeare Company, and its relationship to this national incentive programme which has supported the company through the 'Shakespeare for a New Generation' funding initiative. Montana Shakespeare has received a grant in each of the five years that this initiative has made awards, success that has enhanced and expanded its engagement with local communities (through both performance and educational programmes).

MONTANA, SHAKESPEARE IN THE SKY

With its small population and surfeit of sky and space, Montana is, to most North Americans, a series of clichés rather than a place experienced first-hand. It is a state of calendar photograph scenery, cowboys, and country hoe-downs; it is an elsewhere from the largely metropolitan emphases of culture and thus from Shakespeare. It is remote both literally and figuratively from those cities that provided the theatre companies to launch the Shakespeare in American Communities programme. Montana has a total population of around a million people spread across an expansive geography that makes it the fourth largest state in the country; indeed, Norman Denzin, in his elegiac 'Performing Montana', opens by quoting William Kittredge's claim 'that the American West is an enormous empty and innocent stage waiting for a performance' (148).

But it is not, of course, a Shakespearean performance that either Kittredge or Denzin have in mind. For Denzin, 'Being in nature is a major part of my Montana self. To perform Montana is to shed a little bit of my Midwestern skin. These Montana performances teach my wife and me how first to see and then to love the mountains, the rivers, and the valleys; they teach us how to get outside ourselves and get back to a more basic way of life' (163). Yet, if this state is an elsewhere with the kind of regenerative potential about which Denzin waxes poetic, it is also a place where Shakespeare has, and continues to have, a history that contributes to the formation and operations of local identity. Ironically perhaps, it might be just the empty space that Peter Brook conjured up as a home for an imaginative and experimental theatre, one that is not burdened with the expectations of deadly theatre audiences for Shakespeare who sit passively in the dark mouthing along with the Bard's greatest soliloquies.

So, if Montana has any connotative value at all for Shakespeare, it might well be as a symbolic antithesis to an imagined, rather effete intellectual world that circulates, in some quarters, around the Bard. To take but one example, at a 2006 Washington fundraising dinner for Republican Senator (for Billings, Montana) Conrad Burns,[3] President Bush addressed the 200 dinner guests: '"I kind of like being on the same platform as Sen. Burns because he makes me sound like Shakespeare", Bush said, to

---

[3] Burns eventually lost his seat in the November 2006 elections, in part because of the significant

laughter' (Straub 7A). The President goes on to describe how Burns 'talks the language' of farmers and ranchmen, how they 'didn't need a dictionary or a Roget's thesaurus to figure out what he was saying', thus making Sen. Burns a real Montanan at the price of Shakespeare's, if not Bush's, propensity to obscure! Nonetheless, Montana has its own Shakespearean history, and this chapter, then, takes this counterintuitive locality as subject, not to make the argument for yet more diversification of geography in describing the production and reception of Shakespeare, but to understand better how fields of study expand yet remain within inscribed knowledge narratives, how certain geographies and histories 'naturally' support those narratives, and how, as a result, assumptions become sedimented and thus normative.

At first, then, I want to look at the recent and continuing history of Montana Shakespeare in the Parks, a summer touring company formed in 1973 that, for its 2008 calendar, planned seventy-four performances in fifty-eight different communities across Montana, northern Wyoming, and eastern Idaho. Each year the company produces two different shows for their summer tour and in 2008 offered productions of *All's Well That Ends Well* and *Macbeth* in support of its mission to provide professional theatre and Shakespearean educational programmes to communities across Montana and its vicinities, with an emphasis on under-served, rural areas.[4] Some of the performances take place in Montana's 'main' cities (a moot point since even Billings, the largest of them, has a population of about 100,000), but most of them take place in much smaller and obviously rural settings.

Montana Shakespeare in the Parks, significantly, has a more than thirty-five-year history and, although it has occasionally been noticed by academics (mostly through the company's function as an outreach programme for Montana State University-Bozeman), its only extended attention has come through the local Montana media that champion its productions and advertise its performance calendar. Occasionally the stories cover 'crises', such as in 2004 when the annual performances in Butte had been withdrawn because of a lack of local sponsorship; as Barbara LaBoe wrote in *The Montana Standard*, 'Butte doth protested so much that Montana Shakespeare in the Parks is coming this summer after all' (21 May 2004). It transpired that all the company needed was a $1,375 contribution from the Three Rivers Wireless Office to get Butte back on

---

national swing toward Democrat candidates but largely because of his ties to convicted lobbyist Jack Abramoff.
[4] This description of the company's goals for community outreach is drawn from materials posted on their website (www2.montana.edu/Shakespeare/) in 2006 and 2007, but no longer accessible.

the performance map and restore its annual Shakespeare fix (except, in fact, the audiences that year saw Molière's *Tartuffe* – not unusual since the company often has a non-Shakespearean play in its repertory). The scope of local reporting is, however, primarily to advertise the 'when and where' of the performances and to sketch in some biographical and other details about the actors involved in the year's productions rather than to provide critical interventions about the company's work.

But, of course, Shakespeare companies, resident or touring, are not unusual anywhere in North America. Rather, they are commonplace and the ground zero for an expanded Shakespeare in American Communities programme, an effect of the marketability of Shakespeare, his persistent place in high school and college curricula, and his usefulness to theatre companies in generating profits to underwrite other productions and per-formances. So it is not my purpose to examine Montana Shakespeare in the Parks as somehow representative of this phenomenon (if, indeed, it is), but rather to look specifically at how the particularities of the company's annual summer tour were disseminated in an article that appeared in the *New York Times* in July 2004 – and how we might read that representa-tion in and against customary Shakespeare discourses.

Jim Robbins authored 'In Montana, Shakespeare in the Sky', a piece that first appeared in the *Times* on 18 July 2004 and was subsequently republished in a number of the country's other major newspapers. Reporting from 'Birney, Mont.', Robbins began:

On a perfect summer evening, in the middle of what even many Montanans refer to as the middle of nowhere, ranchers and others from a hundred miles away or more made their way past this tiny town and drove half an hour more on a rutted, boulder-studded pink gravel road that winds through green mead-ows and pine forests to the top of an island in the sky called Poker Jim Butte.

It is live theatre, Montana style – not in the round, but on top of the world, recognisably the state of Denzin's description, once again evoked by way of echoes of *A River Runs Through It* and so many other movie images that, for most North Americans, are how we 'know' Montana. This is not a 'Shakespeare in the Park' performance that bears much resemblance to the definitive New York Public Theater's Shakespeare pro-gramme in Central Park, after all. In fact, Robbins's article repeats all those Montanan stereotypes, so that they might cumulatively pique our amazement that these performances happen at all:

Sometimes the lack of barriers causes problems. Dogs and cats have wandered on to the stage, and once three errant ducks waddled into the thick of things, interrupting a dramatic moment. It has rained, the skies have cast thunder and lightning and props have fallen.

And

> Only once in the troupe's 32 years did the show not go on at Poker Jim, which is federal land and, according to at least one local yarn, got its name because ownership of the butte once changed hands in a poker game.

About Birney, a place at the intersection of two unpaved roads, with the Northern Cheyenne Indian Reservation to its west, the Custer National Forest to its east, and no proximate Montanan town (Billings is more than 100 miles by road), Robbins observed:

> The troupe's visit is a major event in this town of 13 [...]

> 'This is our one shot at culture all year', said Butch Fjell, [the] husband of [Birney's postmaster, Laurel Fjell], and they make the most of it. Not only is the play an important cultural occasion, but the injection of 10 energetic actors into a quiet ranching town is also a treat – families offer beds for the actors and make potluck suppers to share after the play ends.

It would be easy, obviously, to point to the strategies Robbins uses to stress the differences between Birney and major metropolitan centres in the United States, between this audience and a theatre audience, between nature and culture, between expressions of community in this rural setting and the anonymity and isolation of people in 'real' cultural markets. The article revels in its own premise of 'How can this be?' and stages a kind of complicity with an imagined *New York Times* readership whose own cultural identities find this as extraordinary and charming as the author clearly does. In other words, Robbins takes himself as Shakespearean audience in the context of urban-based assumptions about theatrical performance and can only marvel at how 'foreign' this experience in Montana is. What his description reveals, I suggest, is, in fact, a 'local' Shakespeare marked by sites of difference from received discourses of production and reception.

One site of difference is predicated by way of the composition of the audience, made up of Birney's full population of thirteen and other 'locals' (Robbins suggests this draws on a 100-mile radius – probably conservative, since Montanans are well known for travelling two or three hundred miles to catch a high-school basketball game). The locals are, as an interview with company member Bill Pullman suggests, ranch families, Indians, and Hutterites (McIvor), a demographic far outside the most inclusive understanding of who goes to see a Shakespeare play, even when that is cast as a popular audience (in the case, say, of Shakespeare's Globe in London). Moreover, as another site of difference, there is the relationship of that audience, over time, to the Shakespearean production: as Robbins outlined this history,

'The people of Birney have probably seen more Shakespeare than 99 percent of the people in New York City', Mr. Jahnke [the company's artistic director] said. One evening here, he recalled, as he listened to two cowboy-hatted ranchers compare a Malvolio they had seen six years earlier to the one they had just seen, he shook his head and said, 'Where in the hell am I?'

This is, it seems to me, a remarkable point. What does it mean to have the kind of audience building, insider knowledge, and rare continuity that this Montana Shakespeare in the Parks annual summer tour provides? This audience not only defies an appropriately shaped knowledge of who goes to the theatre, and especially of who goes to see Shakespeare, but perhaps also enjoys a special expertise derived precisely from the intersection of the plays, the performers, and the place. Gary Jay Williams once asked whether it was possible to imagine 'a world without Shakespeare' (78); is it possible for urban audiences, I wonder, to imagine this world with Shakespeare? However those questions are answered, what is important here is the invisibility of the history of the company and the history of its audiences to national discourses around Shakespeare – whether in the intention and motivations of the NEA's 'Shakespeare in American Communities' programme or within a premier and influential print publication like the *New York Times*.

The task, as I think of it now, is to uncover and elucidate what might be 'foreign Shakespeare' within a terrain – North America – that seems otherwise overdetermined in its relationship to, and promotion of, Shakespeare-as-culture. When Montanans experience these performances as culture, what does that, more broadly cast, come to mean? When we read about these same performances situated in a bucolic language that insists on Montana's iconic place in geography, how do we understand the production and performance of Shakespeare's iconic place in history? This approach adopts what John Tulloch has suggested is 'the live theatrical event as a matter of occasion and place in the "now here", "inescapably local", and fragmentary yet also contextual and "interconnected"' (39). Its precise situatedness and the relationship of that to the contextual Shakespeare environment – and any possible interconnectedness – might reinvigorate a scholarly comprehension of Shakespeare's presence, whether this is prescribed nationally or globally. Locality may be one way that global Shakespeare loses its imperial will. As Martin Orkin has put it for a very different local project,

> Shakespeareans and their publishers within Europe and North America have no difficulty exporting Shakespeare or work on Shakespeare to whatever market within or beyond their own geographical domain may be interested. As well as questions of profitability, this entails, presumably, a metropolitan assumption that knowledge of the Shakespeare text and its by-products are, beyond the provenance of the metropolis, worth disseminating. But if the assumption is that such epistemologies are, in a culturally beneficent way, exportable, the reverse should also be true. Presumably, knowledge may be benignly imported. (3)

An import/export paradigm is perhaps untenable for a Montanan Shakespeare project, but it is the reversal of the usual understandings of market that I think important here. The practices of the Montana Shakespeare in the Parks programme and its continuity of engagement with specific audiences in non-traditional localities and spaces reconceptualise production–reception paradigms that are otherwise uncontested.[5] As previously indicated, the Montana Shakespeare in the Parks programme has been successful in garnering 'Shakespeare for a New Generation' funding, allowing the company to significantly expand its programming through this educational imperative. The creation of a 'Shakespeare in the Schools' programme by the company, supported by the NEA monies, has allowed the expansion of its performance calendar and contributes to the mandate of the new grant which is 'to support performances and related educational activities designed to deepen the appreciation and understanding of Shakespeare for participating students' (6). On the one hand, the success of Montana Shakespeare in the Parks refutes customary and received assumptions about Shakespearean performance; on the other, it marshals those same assumptions in support of its local work. If this history of Shakespearean performance created in Montana belongs to the audience in ways that identify and celebrate particular local communities and the continuity of those communities in their engagement with Shakespeare, then my next example elucidates Shakespeare's role in the making of local community and speaks directly to more usual accounts of Shakespeare in nineteenth-century America, especially as they are cited in much more contemporary promotions of performance.

---

[5] In this way, then, Poker Jim Butte lays bare the specificities of the definitive North American example for this genre, New York's Central Park and its history within the New York Public Theater repertory.

If the geography of Montana instates a paradigmatic status in contemporary fantasies of the Wild West, the state's history is perhaps even more freighted by this particular mythology. Especially in this context, it is surprising to discover a wealth of evidence about the place and popularity of Shakespeare in Montana more than one hundred years ago, and I want here to turn my attention to one specific locality, Butte. First, I should like to supply a few details about a town that is not well known to Shakespeare scholars, if to anyone in North America or elsewhere (although certainly this would not have been the case a century ago). Butte is located in south-western Montana and today has a population of around 35,000. At the end of the nineteenth century and into the first decades of the twentieth, however, Butte was a much more important place – famous, even, and for three things: it was widely known in America as 'the richest hill on earth' (the town is built on an extraordinarily rich deposit of copper), 'the Gibraltar of Unionism' ('where nearly every working person from theater usher to hoist engineer belonged to a labor union' (Murphy xi)), and as a Western frontier town with an open attitude towards liquor, gambling, and sex. Mary Murphy describes Butte as 'an exemplar of the rush into an urban, industrial age' (xiv) – remarkably, the town's population multiplied thirty times between 1880 and 1916 from about 3,000 to more than 90,000, 'making it the largest metropolis in the five-state region of the northern Rockies and plains' (xiv) and, at that time, one of the fewer than one hundred cities in the US with a population of more than 75,000. In this history of unprecedented growth and in the context of a predominant mining culture lies the town's multifaceted relationship to Shakespeare, illustrated here through two examples of specific performance cultures.

The first comes not from the records of Butte theatre, but in a rather different 'performance' setting through the history of one of Montana's longest-enduring women's clubs. The West Side Shakespeare Club was founded in 1899, holding its first meeting on 2 February of that year. Its inaugural president, Mrs Julia Winston Sheehy, led the group of seventeen women members under a mission statement of 'The mutual improvement of its members in literature, art, science, and the vital interest of the day'. The Club met every two weeks and followed a regular 'order of the day' as set out in their printed programme for the year's events:

Business Session 8 to 8:30 PM
Reading 8:30 to 9:30 PM
Paper and Discussion 9:30 to 10:00 PM

Each member is expected to answer Roll Call by a quotation.

In its first year, the members met thirty-nine times, with thirty meetings devoted exclusively to Shakespeare and the others mostly designed as social events (including an annual dinner). Each meeting was hosted by one of the members and organised by another. The first play given full discussion was *King John*: 9 February 1899 saw readings of Acts 1 and 2 with Mrs Georgie Nuckolls providing the paper, 'Character Sketch, King John'; 2 March saw readings of Acts 3 and 4 with a recitation by Mrs Nuckolls; and 18 March the reading of the final act and a discussion of a 'lesson' provided by Mrs B. Winifred Dickson, 'Constance, the Woman and Mother' (West Side).

In the Club's second year, the membership grew to twenty-five members – nineteen married women and six unmarried – and they launched the year's programme with a detailed study of *King Lear* including papers in different weeks about Cordelia, Regan and Goneril, and, finally, King Lear himself. Discussion of *Anthony and Cleopatra* included a paper on 'Egyptian Literature and Architecture'. The meeting on 2 April 1901 started the group's investigation of *Hamlet*, as well as indicating some of the diversification of interests the Club would now begin to pursue:

April 2, 1901
Reading Act I of *Hamlet*
'Prince Hamlet'   Edith Maloney
Discussion of the Women Writers of the XIXth Century

April 9, 1901
Reading Act II of *Hamlet*
'The Women of *Hamlet*'   Lida Lewis
Discussion of the Natural Resources of Montana

(The programme also indicates a quotation to guide the evening's events: ''Tis the mind that doth make the body rich' – Petruchio to Kate, 4.3.)

The Club celebrated its tenth anniversary in 1908–9 with the programme suggestion, 'It is good to rub and polish our brain against that of others.' Membership had dipped a little (it was now back in the low twenties, from a high of more than thirty[6]), and the programmes begin to

---

[6] Murphy suggests that membership in this and other women's clubs was by invitation (140).

include an 'In Memoriam' section as well as a list of non-resident members – women who had moved away from Butte but who obviously had continued to send their annual dues to the West Side Shakespeare Club.

By the end of this first decade the Club had expanded its interest to other drama and literature, often to focus discussion on contemporary political and social questions – for example, *Peer Gynt* as a prelude for a discussion on the suffrage debate – without ever neglecting Shakespeare: a meeting on *Othello* included a paper on Desdemona alongside a discussion of 'laws affecting women'. By the 1920s, when Butte was at its most prosperous and lively, the Club cast its net even wider: for the 1921–2 season, they started with Shakespeare's sonnets, but later weeks did not directly address the Bard, opting instead for discussions of psychoanalysis, Montana authors, and 'Women's Place in the Business World: Our Changing Standards'.

The West Side Shakespeare Club endured until December 1984, when the last records note a membership of only five, but eighty-five years of handwritten minutes show how much Club members produced, performed, and achieved in that time. The Club clearly offered a place of welcome, continuity, and interest not just for middle-class women (very much a minority population) but also, as Murphy has noted, for 'the most financially secure of the working class' in Butte (139). One programme records the fifty-year membership of Mrs Tennis – a woman who had also served as President of Marian White's Arts and Crafts Club, another Butte women's organisation that had a larger and more diverse membership with various divisions, including a literature section and a drama chapter devoted to putting on plays. This latter club was also instrumental in providing a scholarship programme for deserving women at Montana Tech as well as regular invitations to artists and lecturers, including the artist Marian White, who gave the club its name.[7]

I could not find any evidence that the women of the West Side Shakespeare Club ever attended the theatre as a group, but they were active in encouraging the movie theatre to offer a programme for children on Saturday afternoons, often gave donations towards the costs of lecturers and musical evenings (in 1913 Miss Nettie O'Donnell was invited

---

[7] There are also other examples of Shakespeare-based women's clubs in Montana. Elizabeth Greenfield's article describes the forty-year history of the Shakespeare Club of Great Falls, memorialised in a sketch by Charlie Russell (perhaps the most coveted artist of the American West) of the Club's 1902 'Midsummer's Night's Dream' festival that featured a menu only of foods mentioned in the play itself: 'pea soup, cold tongue, nut sandwiches, honey sandwiches, corn mayonnaise, squash pie, punch, grape ice, fairy cake and coffee' – review in the *Great Falls Daily Tribune* 18 May 1902, reproduced in Greenfield (53).

to talk about her recent trip to Stratford-upon-Avon, an event that was covered by the *Butte Daily Miner*), and made a donation each year of '2 good books' to the Butte Public Library. In other words, Shakespeare was a founding occasion for defining and elaborating their place in the world; it was Shakespeare who gave them common ground to forge identity, to understand change, and to promote a middle-class sensibility in a town where capitalist values drove very different interests. An extended reading of their programming might show the effects of Shakespeare for these women writing the local for themselves. Of course, that these women did not apparently go to the theatre fits with an emergent middle-class sensibility at the end of the nineteenth century: Americans believed that Shakespeare 'off the stage', as A. A. Lipscomb announced in 1882, was far superior to Shakespeare on the stage (Levine 73). This is not to say, however, that Shakespeare was not part of the Butte theatre scene.

My second example is approximately contemporary to the inauguration of the West Side Shakespeare Club. In January 1899, Mr and Mrs Daniel E. Bandmann appeared at Butte's Grand Opera House to present a Shakespearean performance. The first half of their bill presented Hamlet, Gertrude, and Ophelia (with Mrs Bandmann receiving praise for her 'clever' doubling), followed by an interlude from the orchestra, and a second-half performance of Macbeth and Lady Macbeth. The review in the *Daily Miner* noted that there was 'only one disappointing feature about Mr. and Mrs. Bandmann's appearance, and that was what they did was of such excellence that it did not satisfy the appetite of the audience. It was too much like giving the audience half a dozen oysters on the half shell followed by a little turtle soup, and trying to make those who had partaken believe they had just dined' (3 January 1899: 6). The report goes on to advertise an upcoming performance by Mr and Mrs Bandmann at the Grand Opera House in *The Merchant of Venice*: 'as Shylock, Mr. Bandmann is generally reputed in the theatrical world as the peer of all. This evening the people of Butte will be given an opportunity to get some idea of the great tragedian's interpretation of that master part'. Bandmann was, by 1899, an actor with more than forty years' experience in Shakespearean performance – typical, and perhaps one of the better examples, of many actors who toured the USA with versions of Shakespeare for the vaudeville circuit – and he was indeed noted for his rendition of Shylock.

Born in 1840, Bandmann was a German Jew who debuted as a Shakespearean actor at the Court Theater in Neu Strelitz when he was just eighteen. He left Germany for the USA in 1863 and performed across the country, apparently seamlessly switching to English-language performances. Indeed, Bandmann might be considered an early example of a global commodification of Shakespeare; in 1886, he published *An Actor's Tour: or Seventy Thousand Miles with Shakespeare*, a memoir describing his travels and performances of Shakespeare in Australia, New Zealand, India, China, Singapore, and Hawaii. But even for an actor with such a track record with Shakespeare in venues across the world, Butte seemingly appealed to him in ways that places in the other 70,000 miles had not. Around the time of the Grand Opera House performances, Bandmann bought land in the Blackfoot River valley, close to Butte, and eventually retired from the stage to become a gentleman farmer there.

What is notable about the Butte Grand Opera House performances of Shakespeare by Bandmann and others is that they appear as one in a wide variety of entertainments available in any given year – operas, comedies, farces, minstrels, novelties, burlesques, hypnotists, and an apparently popular booking in the late nineteenth-century West, Ben Hendricks, 'the only recognized and legitimate Swedish dialect comedian'.[8] Versions of Shakespeare, often accompanied by a lecture by the lead actor, were but one type of performance that passed through town and was characteristic of the nineteenth-century enjoyment of his plays as 'lowbrow', as Lawrence Levine has described it in his remarkable account of the emergence of cultural hierarchy in the USA.[9] How Butte's theatre calendar and other regular 'performances' (including the 'At The Theater' column that appeared in each Sunday's *Daily Miner*) operated on this entertainment/culture axis was one of the ways that Butte made and negotiated itself locally and in the world.

These two nineteenth-century illustrations signal here the complexity of Shakespearean performance, even or perhaps especially in this little-known venue, which underpins the much more general assertion of Shakespeare as a playwright for 'the people'. Certainly, the task at hand is not simply invested in the recovery of Shakespearean performance in Butte as either an appendix or a challenge to Levine's book, even if, in Butte, as in other American cities, Shakespeare was one place where different experiences of culture were enacted and experienced. Rather, I want to suggest this

---

[8] The types of entertainments listed here are drawn from study of the performance calendars for the Butte Grand Opera House and for Ming's Opera House in the state capital, Helena, in the appropriate time frame.

[9] Nineteenth-century North American touring performances typically included 'lectures' that served as a showcase for a celebrity; they were not lectures with critical content of the kind the West Side women would have had on their programme.

history and geography as another way of framing a discussion of how we think of Shakespearean performance in its widest sense and in the context of the communities it engages. This focus is on how Shakespeare serves the local, rather than how the local and the global (and all points in between) serve a voracious disciplinary appetite for Shakespearean interpretation. The commitment of the women of the West Side Shakespeare Club reveals how flexible and appropriate an embodied study of the Bard might be in the imagination and formation of identity in a world where capital would always trump culture. Here his citation was specifically in service to the conception and practice of middle-class sensibilities in a culture that had altogether other ambitions.

The argument, then, cannot always, and certainly not necessarily, be drawn around how local knowledges expand and refine our understanding of the Shakespeare industry both inside and outside the academy. Instead, a critical focus might more productively examine the production and reception of Shakespeare as it has been, and continues to be, a series of practices through which communities create and experience themselves. As the motto for the West Side Shakespeare Club defined and translated it, to convene around Shakespeare was 'to be prepared for life' (*tempori parendum*). This objective, it seems to me, instils a much stronger sense of agency for those varied audiences of Shakespeare in the nineteenth century – as well as those audiences in today's Montana – than critical discourses or cultural policies have yet allowed for.

Orkin has described the need to trace the ways 'in which local knowledges might be a factor in either the critical reception of the contemporary Shakespeare production, or subsequent critical readings of Shakespeare's original text' (4); so it is that Shakespeare in Montana, in the past and in the present, might rewrite or at least revise some of the common assumptions brought to bear on the hegemonic Bard and his presence and place(s), both literal and figurative, in contemporary North American culture. Shakespeare in Montana is all about the making and maintaining of local knowledge but this practice, too, is a kind of foreign Shakespeare, even in the English-speaking world. To take up Kennedy's appeal for a theory of how Shakespeare 'operates', then, scholarly enquiry must reanimate the questions and priorities that have applied, perhaps too easily and rather monolithically, to thinking about performance. 'Shakespeare in American Communities' makes the claim that it 'continues to reach across the whole eco-system of American theater' (6), and few, if any, would deny that Shakespeare alone achieves that kind of reach. My intention with the examples from Montana is to expand our understanding of how Shakespeare has 'presence' in specifically local contexts, to see how Shakespeare 'operates' outside conventional production and reception paradigms. What comes next, I think, is the expansion of the field of study to engage the whole range of eco-systems that deploy Shakespearean performance so as to forge, challenge, and promote distinct and local knowledge. In this way, we might eventually produce a more comprehensive account of the heritage of this Western canonical author and understand much more fully how his cultural status is so consistently reproduced.

I would like to thank Ellen Crain at the Butte Silver Bow Public Archives for her interest in this project and her helpful guidance through the excellent collection housed there. Citations from the Butte *Daily Miner* and from the records of the West Side Shakespeare Club are drawn from materials held in their collection and consulted in March 2006. I am also indebted to the staff at the Montana Historical Association archives in Helena, Montana, for their assistance with provision of the Bandmann volume as well as records for Ming's Opera House in Helena, also consulted in March 2006.

WORKS CITED

Bandmann, Daniel E. *An Actor's Tour: Or Seventy Thousand Miles with Shakespeare.* New York: Brentano Brothers, 1886.

Bristol, Michael D. *Shakespeare's America, America's Shakespeare.* London: Routledge, 1990.

Denzin, Norman K. *Performance Ethnography: Critical Pedagogy and the Politics of Culture.* Thousand Oaks, Calif.: Sage, 2003.

Greenfield, Elizabeth. 'Shakespeare "Culture" in Montana, 1902'. *Montana: The Magazine of Western History* 22.2 (1972): 48–55.

Kennedy, Dennis. *Foreign Shakespeare: Contemporary Performance.* Cambridge: Cambridge University Press, 1993.

LaBoe, Barbara. 'Protests Prompt Shakespeare Company to Put Butte, Mont., Back on Tour Schedule'. *Montana Standard* 21 May 2004. Factiva. 14 February 2006.

Lan, Yong Li. 'Ong Keng Sen's Desdemona, Ugliness, and the Intercultural Performative'. *Theatre Journal* 56 (2004): 251–73.

Levine, Lawrence. *Highbrow/Lowbrow: The Emergence of Cultural Hierarchy in America.* Cambridge, Mass.: Harvard University Press, 1988.

McIvor, Mary Cochrane. 'Pullman & Shakespeare in Montana'. 3 June 2002. http://www.billpullman.org/stage/MontanaShakespeare003.htm, accessed 7 September 2008.

Murphy, Mary. *Mining Cultures.* Urbana and Chicago: University of Illinois Press, 1997.

National Endowment for the Arts. *Shakespeare in American Communities.*
July 2007. http://www.shakespeareinamericancommunities.org, accessed 7
September 2008.

Orkin, Martin. *Local Shakespeares: Proximations and Power.* London: Routledge,
1995.

Robbins, Jim. 'In Montana, Shakespeare in the Sky'. *New York Times* 18 July
2004: 26.

Straub, Noelle. 'Bush Urges Montanans to Support Burns'. *Helena Independent
Record* 28 March 2006: 7A, 9A.

Tulloch, John. *Shakespeare and Chekhov in Production and Reception: Theatrical
Events and Their Audiences.* Iowa City: University of Iowa Press, 2005.

West Side Shakespeare Club. Archival records. Butte Silver Bow Public Archives.
Butte, Montana.

Williams, Gary Jay. 'Queen Lear: Reason Not the Need'. *Theater* 22.1
(1990–1): 78.

CHAPTER 13

Finding local habitation: Shakespeare's Dream at play on the stage of contemporary Australia

Kate Flaherty and Penny Gay

The Australian artist Arthur Boyd's etching *A Midsummer Night's Dream I* is harrowing and grotesque. Its subject is the Act 3, scene 1, union of the 'transformed' ass-headed weaver, Bottom, with the fairy queen, Titania. The work presents an indecipherable turmoil of grasping limbs and flailing hooves. The faces of the characters are nearly impossible to descry: Titania's head is thrown back and Bottom's face is darkly crowned with demonic curling horns rather than donkey's ears. The work freezes and frames a momentary Australian imagining – European folkloric characters transplanted in and transformed by a bewildering alien environment. Everything seems double.

Boyd's image provides a matrix of useful associations for a discussion of *A Midsummer Night's Dream* in Australia. First, it is at once iconically Australian and iconoclastic, for it bears similarity to Goya's 'Caprichos' – the catalyst for Jan Kott's famously iconoclastic essay 'Titania and the Ass's Head', which has in turn produced a tradition of stage interpretations that dare to dabble in the dark side of the play, particularly in its implicit and explicit sexual violence. Australian theatre programmes for this and other plays by Shakespeare attest to the enduring legacy of Kott's vision. One of the things this chapter seeks to do is to problematise an Australian enthralment to second-hand Eurocentric ideological approaches to the play, and to explore some of the tensions that arise from imposing an imported ideological aesthetic on the living, embodied, culturally porous medium of theatre. Secondly, Boyd's etching raises for consideration the operation of magic and power in relation to gender and class in the play: discourses which, through performance, are permitted to fuse with the exigencies of the cultural moment. By focusing upon these points of intersection between the play and contemporary Australian culture, the present essay identifies and critiques the various Australian cultural projects in the service of which the *Dream* has been employed.

A MIDSUMMER NIGHT'S DREAM IN AUSTRALIA

Following the move from imitation-English productions of Shakespeare – epitomised in the John Alden Shakespeare Company's repeated touring revivals of its luscious Victorian-style *Dream*[1] – to a more recognisably Australian acting, speaking, and production style in the 1970s, *A Midsummer Night's Dream* gained a prime position in the local imaginary. From the decade 1988 to 1998 it was Australia's most popular play, given no fewer than twenty-six separate professional productions (Milne 65). It is conceivable that this prominence reflected the changing organisational structures and ideological approaches of theatre companies. *A Midsummer Night's Dream*, by virtue of its ensemble nature, is much less of a star vehicle than the tragedies (or comedies such as *The Merchant of Venice*), which figure prominent lead roles and which were the most popular plays in Australian Shakespeare productions up to 1960.[2] The very features that made the play less obviously appealing in the nineteenth century could, moreover, be seen as contributing to its increasing popularity throughout the twentieth when, in the wake of the Berliner Ensemble, ideas of the actor as a worker gained currency.

Accordingly, *A Midsummer Night's Dream* was the perfect vehicle for an experimental, self-consciously performative ensemble production such as Peter Brook's of 1970. In light of Brook's influential production, which toured Australia in 1973, we conjecture that the contemporary Australian popularity of the *Dream* can be partly accounted for by the cultural permeability of the play's magic and by the possibilities of subversion of authoritative hierarchies that the play offers. Magic in dramatic narrative can either maintain and restore existing structures of authority, or subvert and overthrow them. In *A Midsummer Night's Dream*, both functions are evident. The present essay analyses the idea of magic in performance – where it is both transformational and metatheatrical – to lead an investigation of how the play's structures of authority and strategies of subversion have been staged recently in the Australian context.

---

[1] John Alden's production of the play (1951, 1959) was an unembarrassed imitation of Tyrone Guthrie's 'Victorian fantasy' production of 1937, which starred Vivien Leigh and (Australian) Robert Helpmann as Titania and Oberon. Alden, like his twentieth-century predecessors, tactfully offered 'traditional' visual styles with modern touches. See Golder and Madelaine, esp. the chapters on Asche (Richard Madelaine), Wilkie (John Golder), and Alden and Olivier (Penny Gay).

[2] As Golder and Madelaine point out (15), in the early and mid nineteenth century, *A Midsummer Night's Dream* was thoroughly eclipsed in popularity by the tragedies in general, and by *The Taming of the Shrew*, *The Merry Wives of Windsor*, and *The Merchant of Venice*.

Hailed by Katharine Brisbane as 'a great original interpretation' (Brisbane), Brook's *Dream* was seen by many as liberating the play from the sentimentally decorative accretions of Victorian stage tradition. Brook replaced skipping, gossamer-winged child-fairies with adult trapeze artists and tumblers. Perhaps even more importantly in the Australian context, Brook saw the 'mechanicals' as a kind of touchstone for the truth that can be conveyed beyond the success or failure of illusion in theatre. At the conceptual core of Brook's approach was metatheatre, which, by provoking dual awareness of both the dramatised situation and the framing theatrical situation, activates the human capacity to experience contradictory emotional responses simultaneously.

Australia has a long tradition of utilising clown-like working-class figures to provoke contradictory emotional responses. The highly theatrical 1994 film *Muriel's Wedding* is an outstanding example of an Australian sensibility that can blend derision of a clown-like character with sudden pathos and fierce identification. The films *Strictly Ballroom* (1992) and *The Castle* (1997) also blur the boundaries between broad farcical derision and passionate identification with working-class 'battler' characters (who all have seemingly impossible 'dreams'). This proclivity to extol the working-class clown as representative artist is also part of Australia's international popular profile, the obvious icon of the Australian artist/artisan being Paul Hogan, whose years prior to Hollywood fame were spent as a construction worker and rigger on the Sydney Harbour Bridge.

Another precedent for suggesting that Australian culture has a uniquely configured relationship with the 'mechanicals' is the play by Tony Taylor and Keith Robinson called *The Popular Mechanicals*. Premiering at Belvoir Street in Sydney in 1987, 'Pop Mex' took the mechanicals from *A Midsummer Night's Dream* and expanded their offstage story – hence the witty subtitle, 'a play without the play'. The play presented a brilliant confounding of accustomed 'high' and 'low' culture categories. It retained large portions of Shakespeare's play but blended them with vaudevillian song, dance, and puppetry set pieces, Elizabethan bawdry, and contemporary references. The piece provoked identification in the Australian context by its irreverence. It centralised the margins and hence challenged the ostensible hierarchies both within the original play and in Australia's relationship to Shakespeare. Furthermore, it satirised theatrical activity – both amateur and professional – and in doing so echoed the self-reflexivity of Shakespeare's play. The Popular Mechanicals were clowns of the kind with which Australian popular culture has a natural affinity – ambitious, contradictory, unwitting bearers of wisdom: 'In a way, because they are clowns, they automatically have an innocence and naivety. They drink raspberry cordial. They also have grand emotions. They're either depressed or over-excited, there's nothing in between' (Keith Robinson qtd in Hessey 18). It is therefore plausible to suggest that there is, in Australian culture, a ready-made place for a character such as Bottom. In many Australian productions of *A Midsummer Night's Dream*, Bottom occupies a similar place in the cultural strata to other fiercely loved Australian clowns. While far from representing the current experience of most modern Australians (particularly theatregoers), 'sweet bully Bottom' the worker calls up a collective reverence for the image of the blue-collar sage.

The way that *Dream* engages with such features of the Australian cultural context seems almost to bring Brook's project full circle. While in reaction to English nineteenth-century snobbery Brook pleads the innate dignity of the actor/artisan, Australian audiences are likely to side with the actor/artisans from the outset and to see the courtly set as the cultural 'other'. At a simple level, this can be accounted for by the common characterisation of the mechanicals as distinctly Australian workers or labourers. In most productions, the mechanicals appear to be Australian in a way that other characters, with their Old World hierarchies, are not. The mechanicals are often attired in labourers' clothes, specifically navy blue Bonds vests, King Gee stubbies shorts and Blundstone boots. These items of clothing have their original use in the context of labouring work, but Bonds shirts and Blundstone boots have also, because of their affordability, become the popular attire of university students and artists. It is also common for the mechanicals to wear football colours by way of either scarves or jerseys. This adds another layer of identification with the almost ubiquitous Australian love of sport. Associated with this is the notion of the Australian male as essentially a 'larrikin', playful, disrespectful of authority, fonder of the company of his 'mates' in the football team or military company than of interacting with the puzzling world of women.[3] Thus, in many productions, the mechanicals provide a matrix of associations with Australian culture, yielding a gratifying and unproblematic combination of worker and creative identities. It is therefore not surprising that it is the mechanicals with whom Australian audiences quickly identify and who contribute enormously to the sense of ownership of the play by the audience.

---

[3] For further discussion of the idea of the likeable 'larrikin' persona that male Australian actors often utilise in Shakespearean roles, see Gay.

Naturally there are limits to these broad assertions, which serve more as a hypothesis than as a conclusion about the cultural currency of the mechanicals in Australia. What remains is to examine the particular nuances of the mechanicals' cultural status and parallel issues of authority and subversion in recent Australian productions. Featured briefly are Jim Sharman's 1982–3 production for Adelaide's Lighthouse Theatre Company and Richard Wherrett's 1989 production for Sydney Theatre Company. At greater length we discuss Glenn Elston's outdoor production for the Australian Shakespeare Company, which has appeared in Australian cities over the past fifteen years; the Sydney Theatre Company's all-Indigenous 1997 production directed by Noel Tovey; the Bell Shakespeare Company's 2004 regional touring production directed by Anna Volska; Benedict Andrews's 2004 production with Company B at Belvoir Street, Sydney; and the 2007 production by the Sydney Theatre Company's ensemble The Actors' Company, directed by Edward Dick. Despite having the play in common, these productions offer explicitly divergent approaches to its magic and contribute differently to the discourses of power and subversion in the Australian context.

Jim Sharman, when asked to comment on his 1982–3 production for Adelaide's Lighthouse Theatre Company, expressed a debt to Brook's production:

I'd always wanted to produce *Dream* – ever since I saw Peter Brook's production in the early 70s, and it's taken all the time since then to feel I could approach it freshly. Of course, you really can't – a director comes to such a play with accumulated influences. It's the sort of play that's entered into theatrical mythology. (Prerauer)

Sharman's ensemble included Geoffrey Rush as Theseus/Oberon, Gillian Jones as Hippolyta/Titania, and John Wood as Bottom who, like all the other mechanicals, doubled as a fairy by sprouting mechanical wings. Utilising a cast of only thirteen, the production was praised for its economy as well as for the kinds of resonance it made available between the 'two worlds' of the play through role-doubling. Praise for the production certainly echoed praise for Brook's, lauding it a double triumph, 'liberating *A Midsummer Night's Dream* from conventional notions of faery dreaming [and] … liberating and purifying the text' (Harris). Descriptions of the production design (Sue Blane) suggest a clear intention to locate the world of the play in a recognisably theatrical domain: '[A]ll the world's a dream on a pearl grey stage that is goldenly melting into a star-studded void. The grand stairway that dominates the stage climbs up and lurches right with all the improbable theatricality of an old MGM musical' (Ward). Thus, 'the magic of theatre' was given a conspicuous place in the production's aesthetic, echoing Sharman's own particular enduring contribution to popular culture as the co-creator of *The Rocky Horror Show* (1973).

Richard Wherrett's 1989 production for the Sydney Theatre Company (STC) was notable for distinguishing itself both from the 'faery dreaming' of the early twentieth century and from Brook's radically minimalist aesthetics. Unlike Sharman's production, which was described as located 'out of any definable time or place except the bizarre dreaming that can occur in any of our heads',[4] Wherrett's offered a concrete location. Attuned to the sensibilities of the city in which it was performed, Wherrett's was an urban *Dream*, set largely in a 1980s dance club called 'The Wood', with Bottom (Luciano Martucci) as a confident young suburban aspirant to urban cool. The production abounded with recognisable local and contemporary cultural references, and Brian Thomson's set achieved an adroit blend of 1980s brashness and decadence with counter-culture punk:

This is indeed a feast for the eyes. On one side a vast circular bed of violet tulle, mismatched on the other with a quaint grassy knoll. Up behind is the globe, with the southern hemisphere conspicuously inverted. Inside it throbs the dance party club lit by an idly turning mirror ball. Two golden arcs, one a slide, the other a ramp, complete the moonlit scene [...] (Evans)

The dualities encoded in the design also pervaded the characterisation, which explored 'the notion of people leading double lives: conservative by day, uninhibited by night' (Payne). The role-doubling permitted this deliberate nuance from Wherrett: '[F]or me Oberon is the same person as Theseus. He changes his name and he changes his clothes and he goes out and parties all night' (Richard Wherrett qtd in Payne). The magic of Wherrett's dream world, therefore, comprised a distinctly late-twentieth-century Sydney form of carnivalesque inversion. Not surprisingly, in this version of topsy-turvy, recreational drugs had a role to play in the enchantments.

'DEALING WITH THE SKY': THE AUSTRALIAN
SHAKESPEARE COMPANY

Glenn Elston's outdoor Shakespeare productions for the Australian Shakespeare Company began in 1988 with *A Midsummer Night's Dream*

---

[4] The events of the play were apparently dreamt by the Athenians, suggesting that the dreaming mind itself is magical (Harris).

performed in Melbourne's Royal Botanic Gardens. Classified by some as 'rough theatre', lacking in vocal subtlety (Milne 68), Elston's productions are lighthearted in tenor, invite audience participation, involve physical stunts and laser lighting effects, and draw dependably large audiences every summer. They generate a socio-cultural space that differs from that of indoor theatre events and even from most open-air theatre. Geoffrey Milne has speculated that, as a consequence, Elston's productions draw audience members who would never usually attend the theatre (Milne 69).

The Australian Shakespeare Company performers cultivate a distinct two-way connection with audience members. This dynamic is facilitated by a playful and open responsiveness to unforeseen contingencies and evinces something of the Company's view of 'the magic of theatre'. The outdoor context makes Elston's productions vulnerable to uncontrolled variables such as weather, wildlife, and technical hitches. Yet, instead of blocking out these interruptions and accidents, the actors exhibit an energetic ability to incorporate unexpected events, even to transform them into meaningful moments within the world of the play. Most commonly the marriage of fictional moment with accident produces a comic effect. During a 1993 performance, for example, the lovers' escape to the forest was accompanied by the noisy drone of a low-flying plane. Lysander, played by Guy Pearce (more recently the star of films *Death Defying Acts* 2008, *Memento* 2000, *L.A. Confidential* 1997), looked up at the plane – by now the focus of audience attention – and said to Hermia (Jane Longhurst) 'That'll be your father out looking for us!' What might have been a distraction ended by drawing the audience back into the world of the play.

While Richard Fotheringham has noted the seemingly intractable division between sport and the arts in Australian culture,[5] this playful, improvisatory style of performance seems to bridge it. The spontaneity and dynamism of Elston's *Dream* come as a charmed and perpetual novelty to the modern audience accustomed to forms of art in which all 'effects' are highly managed. And in this respect the production cultivated something of the open-ended excitement of the outdoor sporting contest. Ross Williams, as Bottom, had a rapport with the audience that won him

---

[5] 'The superior importance of sport in modern culture has led to a system of preferred values that venerates sport as an activity which is spontaneous, expresses ideas and ideals through action, conceals effort and pain, is structured but unpredictable, and which has unplanned resolutions but with results that can be objectively and empirically measured. In contrast, theatre is supposed to be artificial, verbal rather than active, given to exaggerating effort and suffering, predictable, and with contrived, pre-planned conclusions, and judged by non-empirical (and therefore rather dubious) standards of "taste" and "technique"' (Fotheringham 1).

near-heroic status by the end of the play. His gifted extemporising and
his ease in the role made him seem closer and more 'real' to the audience
than the other characters. While the courtly set, and the higher fairies,
were comically preoccupied with their own dilemmas, Bottom and Puck
were preoccupied, first and foremost, with getting the audience's attention. Williams regularly integrated references to contemporary popular
culture – in this case, the ubiquitous American model. In 'The ouzel-
cock' Williams swaggered casually along the front of the stage as if with
a microphone singing his 'number' to a Frank Sinatra melody. Titania
awoke and contributed to the conceit, supplying 'cuckoo, cuckoo,' from
behind him in the manner of a coy backing chorus. Bottom's performance was met with enthusiastic applause from the audience to which he
responded in a smug American accent, 'Thank you. You've been beautiful.' Having effectively styled himself as the popular visiting entertainer,
Bottom seemed, rather than dismayed, glad to be deserted so that he
could soak up the limelight alone.

'THE STORY SHALL BE CHANGED': SYDNEY THEATRE COMPANY, 1997

In 1997, in the cultural programme leading up to the Sydney Olympics,
Noel Tovey directed an all-Indigenous cast in a production of the *Dream*.
Tovey identified resonance in the relationship between the *Dream* and
the Dreamtime: 'In Aboriginal culture, all the ritual stories are about
the Dreamtime, a time when humans and animals were the same thing.
So it's not really strange to our culture to have a man turned into an ass'
(STC). The production opened with the courtly set wearing Elizabethan-
style garments made in plain white calico.[6] While the neck ruffs and
doublets and farthingales gave a distinctly Tudor profile, the plain
whiteness of the fabric worn by Aboriginal Australians with bare feet
on a red-earth coloured floor accomplished a striking relocation which,
in itself, seemed magical.[7] The fairy world departed from Elizabethan
dress code. Puck, played by Laurence Clifford, wore a muddy-coloured
head-to-foot body-suit of tassels which, combined with his humorously
camp characterisation, implied the spirit of pantomime. Tessa Leahy as
Titania and Glenn Shea as Oberon each wore a body-suit with a serpent

---

[6] The source of KF's comments on this production is the STC archival video (recorded 25 September 1997), viewed on 22 November 2005 courtesy of company archives.
[7] The production was designed by Andrew Raymond and Julie Martin and lit by Tony Youlden.

streaking across the chest to the shoulder and a billowing cape. Amongst the other fairies were kangaroo and lyrebird sprites. Digital images projected onto the backdrop featured Australian landscapes and a winding Rainbow Serpent. The music and sound effects, composed by Sarah de Jong, combined Tudor court sounds of the virginal and percussion with didgeridoo and clicking sticks, effecting a surprisingly seamless and utterly new concoction. The intermingling of cultural categories accomplished by the production's aesthetics meant that its magic seemed just beyond cultural classification: various, hybrid, and alive. However, the hybridity of the production met with censure from several reviewers, whose pleas for more 'authentic' and more identifiably distinct cultural products revealed, as Emma Cox has pointed out, essentialist notions of cultural identity.[8]

The rigid authority structures of Duke Theseus's Athens were evident from the outset. There was a ceremonial stiffness about the speech patterns and movement in the initial scenes that implied a sense of oppressively imposed order. Many of the actors, particularly Gary Cooper who played Lysander, spoke with a formal, English-inflected accent. At first glance, the effect of the pale Tudor garments worn by the characters seemed aligned with the effect achieved in the Indigenous artist Julie Dowling's 2003 painting *The Paper Dress*, which depicts a young Aboriginal girl in a stiff, frilly paper prototype of a dress – a practice garment, with all that this implies. The characters' Aboriginality, not to mention vitality, seemed subsumed by the blank and oppressive machinery of British theatrical and cultural traditions.

If Tovey's selection of Shakespeare as the vehicle for proving the merit of Aboriginal talent implied (in some reviewers' opinions) too much reverence for Shakespeare, then the use of Elizabethan garments could be seen as reinforcing the problematic Eurocentricity of the endeavour. Although not for Tovey, for many non-Indigenous Australian commentators these choices proved a source of chagrin. However, this is a theoretical stance that ignores the subversive presence of the particular actor's body; it formulates an ideological construct without taking into account the participant, and potentially subversive, corporeality of the actors. The following discussion offers an account of how Deborah Mailman's particular vitality in performance undercut this theoretical overlay.

[8] '[T]he keen receptive focus on Aboriginal/European opposition might only be partly the result of Tovey's stylistic choices; it may also reflect an essentialist understanding of cultural and racial difference' (Cox 23).

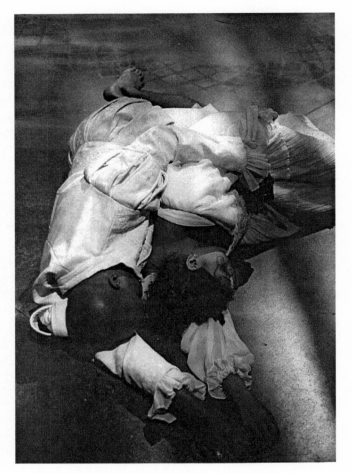

9. Helena (Deborah Mailman) and Demetrius (Tony Briggs) asleep in Act 4, Scene 1, of Noel Tovey's all-Indigenous 1997 production of *A Midsummer Night's Dream*, Sydney Theatre Company, in association with the Olympic Arts Festival.

Deborah Mailman's Helena at all points strongly signalled that the apparent enthralment to European cultural traditions would not be lasting. She undermined and exploited structures of cultural authority from within: from within sixteenth-century English drama and even from within an Elizabethan bodice and farthingale. Mailman's costume seemed not to inhibit, but rather to augment and impel her physical energy. It did not prevent her wrangling playfully with Demetrius or wrestling with Hermia. Mailman's angry departure from the suddenly besotted Lysander

(2.2.140) was particularly effective: she spun and stormed away, her sway-
ing white skirts accentuating her decisive movement down the dark cor-
ridor as Lysander looked long in amazement.

Palpably in command of her attire, Mailman was even more the master
of the language of the play. She utilised the stage space and the language
with confidence, as part of her own stock of creative resources. In particular, her easy use of her own Australian accent permitted her to exploit
the full expressive range of Helena's speech. The first laughter from the
audience came on her riposte to Hermia's comment on Demetrius:

HERMIA: I frown upon him, yet he loves me still.
HELENA: O that your frowns would teach my smiles such skill! (1.1.194–5)

Mailman spoke this line with dry Aussie sarcasm, almost as an aside:
'O that ya frowns'd teach my smiles such skill!' Within the rigid pattern-
ing of the language, Mailman, through tone and facial expression, com-
municated with utter bluntness; it would be hard to imagine a colloquial
phrase that could better express Helena's frustration at that moment.
The pithy tightness of the riposte gave the impression of irreverent frank-
ness, both towards the supposedly beleaguered Hermia and towards what
the audience may assume to be the outdated seriousness and sanctity of
Shakespeare's verse. In this way Helena deftly performed an Aboriginal
and Australian rebellion against the structures of cultural authority
within and around the play.

As the action of the play progressed, Mailman's performance of Helena
continued to subvert the dynamics of abjection and cruelty of which the
character is often a partially confederate victim. Helena's speeches in Act 2,
scene 1, harbour a disturbing tendency to self-abasement. Yet, in performing this self-abasement with comic energy and hyperbolic force, Mailman's
Helena wrested for herself a paradoxical potential to command the scene.
Her resourceful rhetoric of 'self-abasement', combined with her compel-
ling physicality, amounted to a performance that overturned the ostensible
power dynamics of the scene. A stiffly formal Demetrius, played by Tony
Briggs, seemed feeble and put upon, oppressed by Helena's superior vitality
and conviction. His threats were delivered as desperate but ineffectual bids
for power over her. 'Run where you will,' taunted Helena, as she, laughing, grabbed and tickled him so that he was forced to struggle against her
embrace, 'the story shall be changed: / Apollo flies, and Daphne holds the
chase' (2.1.230–1). Mailman convincingly rewrote the trope of romantic pursuit, on her feet, and in defiance of the Petrarchan model with all its implicit
violence.

'LOCAL HABITATION': THE BELL SHAKESPEARE
COMPANY, 2004

The Bell Shakespeare Company's *Dream* cast of nine directed by Anna Volska in 2004 exhibited an athletic agility and energy similar to that of Mailman's Helena and the Elston *Dream*. This time the roles were trebled: the actors who played the young lovers and the mechanicals also played the fairies, who took the form of half-human half-animal creatures. Their whirrs and clicks and scuttling, tumbling entrances in dim light denoted a new location: a forest, or more precisely, an Australian bush-clearing. They were uniform in appearance, dressed in baggy grey knee-length suits which suggested simultaneously small nocturnal marsupials and mythical creatures.[9]

While not being the dark or macabre creatures of Jan Kott's vision, these fairies were disconcerting. They belonged to Australian native bush lore rather than to European tradition, and they recalled the tricksy and sometimes frightening creatures from children's books such as Mem Fox's *Possum Magic*, Dorothy Wall's *Blinky Bill*, and May Gibbs's *Snugglepot and Cuddlepie*, and Indigenous Dreamtime stories which attribute distinct personalities to Australian animals. In this way the fairies retained the essence of childhood fairytale, but re-located it within a recognisable Australian tradition.

Volska's production implied that the mischief and shape-shifting possibility of the fairy realm, once ignited, exploded the mundane hierarchies of the human court. This is because, by Act 3, all of the humans had changed into fairies and would change many more times before the play was over. Their protean ability, combined with the imaginative collaboration of the audience, established a pattern of metamorphosis whose vital energies perpetually destabilised the rigid determination of social structure. All participants in the theatrical event were sustained in constantly changing relation to one another. The lovers became the fairies, and then the workers, then the players and then themselves as actors helping each other dress on stage to become the lovers once again. Theseus's later appearances were inflected with Oberon's charisma, and Philostrate revelled in hinting that we had met him before in another guise. The social stratification of the play was dismantled by the constant revelation that all were actors first, and, rather magically, lovers, mechanicals, and fairies as the situation required. All were primarily (hard-working) Australian artisans of the stage.

[9] The production was designed by Jennie Tate.

'DIFFICULT PLEASURE': COMPANY B, 2004

If the treatment of magic by the Volska and Elston productions exhibited an emphasis on popular and broadly accessible modes of entertainment, the 2004 Company B production implied a pointed counter-intention. Benedict Andrews, who directed the production, has become recognised in Australia for his brand of European intellectualism. Citing Barrie Kosky amongst his influences, Andrews claimed that for him 'difficult pleasure is entertainment' (Iaccarino). *A Midsummer Night's Dream* was Andrews's Shakespeare directing debut and considered by many an uncharacteristic choice for him. The seeming clash of Andrews's artistic profile with the play was used for publicity: 'A director with a penchant for works about life's dark side has taken on Shakespeare's sunniest play' (Low).

Despite this promise of something new, the Company B production echoed previous approaches by drawing heavily upon Jan Kott's 'darker' vision of the play. The first pages of the Company B programme quote the essay 'Titania and the Ass's Head' from Kott's 1965 work *Shakespeare Our Contemporary.* The fairy-world of Andrews's vision certainly bore traces of what Kott imagines as 'Titania's court consisting of old men and women, toothless and shaking, their mouths wet with saliva, who sniggeringly procure a monster for their mistress' (Kott 182). The result of Andrews's elaborate Kottian visual aesthetic was that it performed a muting effect upon the play. The characters, rather than feasibly driving the action of the play, often became spectacles of abjection. The fantastical was transmuted from supernatural kinds of power possessed *by* characters, to dark, subconscious appetites under which they laboured. The rulers of the fairy realm exercised a dubious, diluted, and cruel dominion. Oberon (Socratis Otto), his bare torso wreathed with a razor-wire tattoo, seemed bitter and damaged, hauling himself along the ground like a lizard. The minions of Titania (Helen Buday) were lumbering masked old men in tutus, and her union with Bottom was a public spectacle of bestiality and bondage.

Andrews's production intentionally disputed the accessible and communal pleasure popularly associated with the play. There was a cryptic opacity to the production which inhered in the modes of acting – highly stylised vocabularies of gesture, uneven patterns of verse speaking, and inexplicable stunts. Several of the actors slipped out of this rigidly codified mode into more engaging naturalism from time to time. Such moments of purposeful speech alternating with highly self-conscious chanting and recitation created the unevenness observed by one reviewer, Stephen Dunne:

It's bitsy because it's uneven – in performance terms, with some actors more attuned to the work and the direction than others [...] Andrews is rescuing a play that doesn't need rescuing, and the play's textual strengths and emotions are made remote and uneven by uneven acting and flashy 'look-at-me' directorial invention.

As much as this production sought to defy the 'niceness' historically associated with *A Midsummer Night's Dream*, it bore an uncanny resemblance to the Victorian penchant for spectacle. The production evinced what it probably saw as a post-modern pastiche: enthralment to eclecticism and stylistic possibilities rather than a cohesive and communicable vision of the play. However, Andrews's dual commitment to the aesthetics of voyeurism and expressionistic modes of acting left little scope for the innate power of the language to do its work. In a similar vein to Beerbohm Tree and Charles Kean, Andrews appeared to strive to elicit astonishment more than any other emotion from his audience.

While the aesthetics of Company B's *Dream* were radical and inventive, its social and gender politics were deeply conservative. The serious because plausible cruelties that litter the play lost their particular force as a consequence of being enlisted and elaborated for shocking effect. They became extravagant spectacles of cruelty insulated by a smugly sophisticated frame. Spectacles of female self-abasement were at the heart of the entertainment. Hermia seemed in a submissive trance in Act 1 as her father tore open the collar of her dress to publicly deride the love-token necklace given her by Lysander. Rita Kalnejais's Helena (in stark contrast to Mailman's) responded to Demetrius's violent threats (2.2) with infantile pliancy. She began removing her clothes and lifting up her schoolgirl skirt to show him her underwear. Demetrius then pushed her to the ground and groped her while pinning her throat with his hand and finally spitting at her. Still she remained submissive and even delighted when both men turned their affections to her.

Andrews's production imposed upon the play a distinct conceptual frame, which suggested elements of voyeuristic spectacle, German Expressionism, and Brechtian Epic Theatre. Such frames interpreted the play's magic from the top down – as a montage of surprising impressions, a startling sound and light show of dislocated caricatures. It used Shakespeare's play as an arbitrary platform on which theatre could be re-mystified and hence removed from the living particularities of the time, the place, and the crowd in attendance. In this sense the spirit of the endeavour might be interpreted as somewhat patronising: rather than responding to Australian cultural contingencies, foisting on the

Australian audience another version of 'high culture' in the wake of the rejected model of British imperialism.

The disjunction between Andrews's articulated emphasis upon the language of the play and his production's obscuring of its poetic force highlights a detectable tension within contemporary Australian theatrical practice. On one hand, we observe a well-grounded confidence and excitement about the potential for Shakespeare's play to speak to the immediate context. On the other hand, we observe an anxious drive to exculpate the play – and perhaps Australian theatrical activity – from the charge of easy pleasure, by importing models from Europe. This might be read as a new incarnation of Australian cultural cringe, one that simply looks further east on the European continent for the stamp of respectably rigorous and contemporary ideological approaches to theatre.

'WHAT CHEER MY LOVE?': SYDNEY THEATRE COMPANY, 2007

Recourse to the cultural authority of European ideological models of theatre was also evident in the 2007 production of *Dream* by the Actors' Company of the Sydney Theatre Company. The British director Edward Dick was brought in to direct the ensemble in a production which, by foregrounding its imported ideological orientation, muted the polyphonic energies of the play to a large extent and inhibited its capacity to speak to a specifically Australian audience.

The pre-set sequence took place in the ruins of an imposing neo-classical structure with an earthen floor.[10] The setting was European post-war (any war) rather than Australian post-settlement. The entire cast was on stage, working silently as artisans – weaving, sewing, welding, etc. The blankness of the 'workers'' expressions and their utter lack of interaction with the audience, combined with the rigid proscenium arch of the Sydney Theatre stage, gave a sense of meaningless monotony. Eventually the workers began to leave the stage with their work implements and re-entered in evening dress, clearly suggesting an early-twentieth-century European period – the men in white shirts and black tailcoats, the women in mermaid-profile dresses with long gloves and fur stoles.

In this context, the most cohesive aspect of the production was the choice to centralise Hippolyta's story. Hippolyta is given very few lines

---

[10] The production was designed by Ralph Myers. The Sydney *Daily Telegraph* critic commented that it 'suggests the remains of perhaps a civil war or a reign of terror. According to director Edward Dick, the lovers' story in *Dream* can only work if they are fleeing something terrifying.' The reviewer found this to be unnecessarily 'heavy symbolism' (Smith).

by the play but she carries, as a character, significant imaginative force in its dramatic workings. There is the implicit legacy of her suffering – in Theseus's very exposition he 'wooed [her] with his sword, and won [her] love doing [her] injuries' (1.1.16, 17). Moreover, as Philip C. McGuire has pointed out, Hippolyta greets Theseus's question 'What cheer my love?' with an enigmatic and therefore malleable silence. Through choices of staging this silence can be endowed with a diverse range of meanings. There is scope to interpret that silence as aggravated by what Hippolyta has just witnessed in the treatment of Hermia – a scene of disenfranchisement and degradation of a woman (and yet another conquest) by a circle of powerful men. Edward Dick undoubtedly gave Hippolyta's silence this specific force.

Pamela Rabe made a striking figure as Hippolyta – seeming a head taller than all the others and dressed in clothes of an earlier generation. She wore a fitted jacket, a skirt to the floor, a red muff, and a long black veil which was removed after she was obsequiously ushered in. The coolness between Hippolyta and Theseus was unambiguous from the outset. When he had finished his opening speech, an attendant held a card for Hippolyta to read from. She read slowly, vacantly, with a thick eastern European accent, stumbling over the word 'solemnities' and asking the attendant how to pronounce it. Hippolyta seemed little more than a hostage. She was palpably horrified by the treatment of Hermia in the subsequent scene and tried to comfort her. Ignoring Theseus's bluster, she made a grand and solitary exit through the upstage double door.

The dynamics of the imperial relationship between Theseus and Hippolyta were clearly perpetuated through the relationship between Titania and Oberon (the roles were doubled, as is now usual). Oberon was vindictively predatorial, and his assault on Titania was unambiguously malicious. It was hard to see what had brought them into harmony for the play's final blessing of the bride-beds. Likewise, a minimal reconciliation between Theseus and Hippolyta was effected through Theseus's new treatment of the lovers in Act 4, scene 1. As the lovers stood in the 'rain' which cleansed them of dirt from the floor of the set, Hippolyta and Theseus came to look at them as if they were an art installation. The separate high status of royalty was maintained, and Hippolyta seemed to soften a little towards Theseus as he overruled the intemperate courtier Egeus. In the final scene, while the other aristocrats watched the play within the play with a kind of unreserved and light good humour, Hippolyta, positioned to face the audience so that we might register all her responses, watched Bottom's performance, transfixed. The sincerity of Hippolyta's 'I pity the man' cut across the derisive tone of the other characters' commentary. Ultimately, however, she remained a powerless outsider: a refugee at sea amongst cultural and gender politics that she could barely comprehend.

The aristocratic European world thus depicted had little readable connection to Australian society. By contrast, the mechanicals were noticeably localised. Flute wore a local team's football jersey and socks. John Gaden as the tailor Starveling offered another version of his iconic 1930s gentle working-class Aussie grandfather. Most notably, Peter Quince became Miss Quince (played by Helen Thomson), who brilliantly channelled 'Kath', from the Australian hit television series *Kath and Kim*, in voice, mannerisms, and malapropisms. Kath is the working-class aspirant to culture and style, an energetic member of her local outer-suburban community, a character who would be completely committed to putting on a play but nervous about getting it right in high-culture terms. Local meanings were here readily available – Australian amateur 'little theatre' in the 1930s was a ubiquitous cultural phenomenon – but the director chose not to connect them with the play's aristocratic hierarchy.

Instead, Edward Dick's decision to foreground the busy and ostentatiously humble community of artisans at the play's beginning (ultimately tedious though it was to the audience) resonated with the ideology underlying the STC's Actors' Company. This group was founded by artistic director Robyn Nevin in 2005 on what is popularly understood as the ensemble principle of Stanislavski's Moscow Arts Theatre, and in resistance to the English repertory theatre model which involves artistic hierarchies and 'stars' playing the major roles. This deliberately articulated swapping of one outdated European model for another might be seen as symptomatic of a new artistic crisis of confidence in Australian theatre. It may also explain the recent fashion in productions of *A Midsummer Night's Dream* for 'rescuing' Shakespeare from its Australian popularity. Perhaps making connections with the present and/or the local is now seen as a cultural liability that jeopardises the production's international and cosmopolitan artistic status. Unfortunately, the effect of this apparent exertion of effort to attain international credibility often results in a production that offers cultural and temporal pastiche made bland by lack of cultural locus.

The significance of the Company's gesture of rejecting celebrity and hierarchy is somewhat negated, furthermore, by the Australian fetish for national and particularly international heroes ('Kath and Kim' among them, maintaining the nation's affection for their clowns). For this reason, the existence of the Actors' Company alone, regardless of how roles were distributed from one show to the next, directly fuelled the national appetite for stardom. At the same time, the Company distanced itself from such a populist project by laying claim to the sanctioning cultural authority of European models of theatre. This tension between the star-centred populism crucial to sustaining an audience-base in Australia and the tendency to try to bolster international artistic credibility by importing ideological models and expertise from Europe typifies the dilemma experienced by many of Australia's larger arts institutions. It raises the question of whom we are playing for. Are we playing for world attention and thereby reverting to the nineteenth-century assumption that the artistic cutting-edge is elsewhere – be it London or Berlin – or are we playing to speak about and to ourselves as Australian audiences?

A Midsummer Night's Dream, with its interest in the magical spirits inhabiting the natural world and its focus on working-class heroes (and their right and ability to make art), has earned a popular place in Australian culture, so much so that, as we have demonstrated, a neo-colonial 'European' perspective is at times invoked as a corrective. Arthur Boyd's iconic etching, the starting point for this consideration of Australian *Dream*s, suggests a way forward. Earthed in the Australian psyche, it makes a new reality through hard-wrought fusion with Old-World imaginings. Likewise the work of making Shakespeare speak to its performance context evolves most richly when it evolves from the ground up: in Australia, a land inhabited by dreams and dreamings, strange animals, carnivalesque urban centres, and outside them not a 'wood' but the Australian bush.

WORKS CITED

Brisbane, Katherine. *The Advertiser* (Adelaide) 9 June 1973. Cuttings book, archive of the State Theatre Company of South Australia.
Cox, Emma. 'Negotiating Cultural Narratives: All Aboriginal Shakespeare Dreaming'. *Southerly* 64.3 (2004): 15–27.
Dunne, Stephen. 'Bit Players the Stars in a Post-Punk Garden of Dreams'. *Sydney Morning Herald (SMH)* 23 July 2004: 14.
Evans, Bob. 'Glitter Outshines Substance'. *SMH* 11 December 1989: 92.
Fotheringham, Richard. *Sport in Australian Drama*. Cambridge: Cambridge University Press, 1992.
Gay, Penny. 'Recent Australian Shrews: The "Larrikin Element"'. *Transforming Shakespeare: Contemporary Women's Re-Visions in Literature and Performance*. Ed. Marianne Novy. Basingstoke: Palgrave, 2000. 35–50.

Golder, John, and Richard Madelaine, eds. *O Brave New World: Two Centuries of Shakespeare on the Australian Stage.* Sydney: Currency Press, 2001.

Harris, Max. 'Sharman's Risks Pay Off in Dream'. *The Bulletin* June 1982: 44.

Hessey, Ruth. 'Shakespeare Gets a Co-Byline'. *SMH* 19 November 1987: 18.

Iaccarino, Clara. 'The Whiz-Kid Who Won't Be Making It Easy'. *Sun-Herald* 18 July 2004: 27.

Kott, Jan. *Shakespeare Our Contemporary.* Trans. Boleslaw Taborski. London: Methuen, 1965.

Low, Lenny Ann. 'Dreams of an Explosive Imagination'. *SMH* 19 July 2004: 12.

McGuire, Philip C. 'Hippolyta's Silence and the Poet's Pen'. *New Casebooks: A Midsummer Night's Dream.* Ed. Richard Dutton. New York: St. Martin's Press, 1996. 139–60.

Milne, Geoffrey. 'Shakespeare under the Stars: A New Populist Tradition'. *Australasian Drama Studies* 33 (1998): 65–79.

Payne, Pamela. 'Dream of the Future'. *SMH* 8 December 1989: 2.

Prerauer, Maria. ' "Dream" Becomes a Reality'. *The Australian* 5 May 1982: 11.

Shakespeare, William. *The Norton Shakespeare: Based on the Oxford Edition.* Ed. Stephen Greenblatt, Walter Cohen, Jean E. Howard, and Katharine Eisaman Maus. New York: W. W. Norton & Company, 1997.

Smith, Gary. 'Fantasy Crashes to Earth'. *Daily Telegraph* (Sydney) 28 August 2007: 45.

STC. 'Making an Ass of Themselves'. *SMH* 12 September 1997. Cuttings book, archive of the Sydney Theatre Company.

Ward, Peter. 'All the World's a Pearly Stage'. *The Australian* 27 May 1983: 8.

CHAPTER 14

'Haply for I am black': Shifting race and gender dynamics in Talawa's Othello

Lynette Goddard

YVONNE BREWSTER'S PRODUCTIONS OF SHAKESPEARE

One expectation of British black theatre companies is that their main endeavour should be to produce plays by black playwrights, rather than endorsing the status of the British theatre canon by mounting plays from the European classical repertoire. Since the late 1980s, however, Talawa, Tamasha, Tara Arts, and Temba have mounted revivals and adaptations of plays by Shakespeare and other canonical European male playwrights, including Bertolt Brecht, Anton Chekhov, Henrik Ibsen, Federico Garcia Lorca, and Oscar Wilde.[1] The question that keeps arising in relation to these productions is whether a black (or Asian) director's approach produces new perspectives on these well-known plays. Tara's Artistic Director Jatinder Verma certainly believes so and coins the term 'Binglish productions' ('Challenge' 194) to refer to black British versions of European plays that make 'a deliberate attempt to confront the specificities of a particular theatre text with the different specificities – in time, place and cultural sensibility – of its performers' (Verma, 'Transformations' 58).

Binglish theatre is different from multi-racial productions (usually by institutions like Shakespeare's Globe, the Royal Shakespeare Company, and the Royal National Theatre) that maintain a conventional world view

---

[1] Talawa produced Shakespeare's *Antony and Cleopatra* (Liverpool Everyman and Bloomsbury Theatre, 1991), *King Lear* (Cochrane, 1994), and *Othello* (Drill Hall, 1997), as well as Oscar Wilde's *The Importance of Being Earnest* (Bloomsbury, 1989) and John Ford's *'Tis Pity She's A Whore* (Lyric Studio, 1994); Tara Arts mounted *Troilus and Cressida* (Contact Theatre and Battersea Arts Centre, 1993), *A Midsummer Night's Dream* (Lyric Hammersmith, 1997), *The Merchant of Venice* (New Players Theatre, 2005), and *The Tempest* (Children's Tour, 1993; also Tara Studio, 2007 and Arts Theatre, 2008) and Asian versions of Nikolai Gogol's *The Government Inspector* (1989), Georg Büchner's *Danton's Death* (1989), Pierre Augustin Beaumarchais's *The Marriage of Figaro* (New Players Theatre, 2006), and Henrik Ibsen's *An Enemy of the People* (2006); Ruth Carter reworked Federico Garcia Lorca's *Yerma* to *A Yearning* (Birmingham Repertory Theatre, 1995), and Deepak Verma adapted Émile Zola's *Therese Raquin* to *Ghostdancing* (Lyric Studio, 2001) for Tamasha Theatre Company; and Temba revived *Romeo and Juliet* (Young Vic, 1988) and Henrik Ibsen's *Ghosts* (Lyric Studio, 1991).

by 'integrating' performers of colour as 'pseudo white', where they might typically speak in Received Pronunciation (RP) and have no attention drawn to their ethnicity as informing the interpretation of the production. By contrast, Binglish productions are usually presented by independent black theatre companies and draw on the cultural heritage of the performers by incorporating black and/or Asian languages, music, movement, costume, and imagery to create performances that 'challenge the dominant European imagery of theatre' (Verma, 'Challenge' 198).

The expectation that black theatre companies will present interpretations of European plays informed by the cultural heritage of the performers is a common one, corresponding with what the post-colonial critic Helen Tiffin terms a 'canonical counter discourse' that aims 'to invest them with more local relevance and to divest them of their assumed authority/authenticity' (qtd in Gilbert and Tompkins 16). However, Yvonne Brewster OBE (Founding and former Artistic Director of Talawa from 1985 to 2003) resists the idea that black directors should adopt a race agenda or aesthetic when approaching the European plays, and she sought to produce them 'straight' on the basis that they are good plays that are as much a part of her cultural heritage as a Caribbean migrant to Britain as plays by black playwrights are. Brewster's formidable personality is reflected in her resistance to stereotypical expectations of black (women's) theatre. Five years after co-founding Talawa in 1986, she decided that the company would shift focus from black plays to produce classics from the European canon, the first of which was Oscar Wilde's *The Importance of Being Earnest* in 1989, followed in 1991 by *Antony and Cleopatra*, which was the first of three productions of Shakespeare. In an interview with Naseem Khan, Brewster argued for the right to tackle European plays without being required to render them 'black', and she condemned negative responses to her work as stemming from myopic and stereotypical expectations that black versions of Shakespeare would somehow be 'hip', 'cool', 'ethnic', or 'exotic':

Because it's an all-black production, critics expected (she exploded) a kind of zingy sappy snappy approach, an Afro rap musical, a Tony and Cleo. They said, as if it was an accusation, 'But you relied completely on [the] text.' Of course I did. Shakespeare is not a bad writer, I said. It's dangerous to feel you can't do the plays as Shakespeare wrote them. But oddly enough, it's the English who feel you've got to do something with Shakespeare. As black actors, you can do versions – like *Trinidad Sisters* (instead of *Three Sisters*) and *Playboy of the West Indies*. That's cool. But if you do it straight, you're treading in areas you don't have a right to be in. (Khan)

Brewster's *Antony and Cleopatra* (Liverpool Everyman and Bloomsbury Theatre, 1991) was the first British Shakespeare production to combine an all-black cast (African, Caribbean, and Asian) and a black director. She was attracted to directing the play because of its strong woman's part and sought to reclaim the role of the Queen of Egypt by casting a black actress as Cleopatra. In a pre-production interview, Dona Croll explained how she would bring something new to the role to distinguish her portrayal from those presented by white women: 'White actresses play her as a sexy queen. I play the politics and the power. Any woman who runs a country, turns it round from famine to feast and seduces Roman emperors is not a blonde bimbo. She is somewhere between Maya Angelou and Tina Turner' (Birkett).[2] The main criticism of the production came from reviewers who felt that more could be done to mark it out as a 'black' interpretation. Jeffrey Wainwright recognised that these criticisms may stem from 'assumed stereotypes' that a black 'approach to the European classics will produce radically new perspectives and references to surprise us' or use 'newly exciting, uninhibited acting styles [...] and less naturalistic staging which we think in some vague way might draw upon "ritual"'. Yet he still concluded that 'as a conceptual re-interpretation Yvonne Brewster's production is disappointing. Indeed, so straight is it in Helen Turner's unremarkable design, that one suspects the point is to confound our suppositions as to its colouring'.

The publicity material for Brewster's production of *King Lear* (Cochrane, 1994) emphasised the significance of Ben Thomas being the first black man to play the role on the British stage in 125 years, since Ira Aldridge's one-night-only appearance in Hull in 1859.[3] However, Brewster was adamant that the multi-racial cast was otherwise insignificant to understanding the production: 'The casting wasn't colour blind (colour blind is not to see the colour of the person) but non-racially constrained' (qtd in Schafer 134), which meant that performers of differing black and Asian races could be cast in the same family (playing the leading roles of Lear and his daughters Regan, Goneril, and Cordelia, as well as Edmund, Edgar, Kent, and the Fool) without any intention for meaning to be made from this. The cast members used various black/British accents, such as Liverpudlian-inflected RP for Cathy Tyson's Regan, cockney for Diane Parish's Cordelia, and Caribbean for Mona Hammond's Fool and David Webber's Kent. So, although no specific changes were made to

[2] See Rutter for a detailed assessment of the significance of this production in reclaiming the role of Cleopatra from a history of stage and film whitewashing.
[3] See Schafer for a detailed analysis of Brewster's production of *King Lear*.

Shakespeare's text, the production resonated with ideas of a provocative Binglish practice that uses the cultural background of the performers to evoke the sounds of culturally diverse contemporary Britain.

Debates about black interpretations of Shakespeare come to the fore when the race or colonial plays are mounted, where the expectation of a 'black'-informed production is paramount to figuring these sometimes controversial plays for a contemporary context. Brewster mounted productions of Shakespeare's plays primarily to create opportunities for black performers to play roles in which they would rarely be cast on the main Shakespeare stages (such as Antony, Cleopatra, King Lear, and his daughters). However, her production of *Othello* (Drill Hall, 1997) exemplifies how the casting of black performers can impact on how we understand characters in these plays and thus the political motives of the director. Brewster used colour-conscious and gender-aware casting and characterisation to refigure the racial and gender dynamics between the characters in Shakespeare's quintessential race play.

TRANSFORMING RACE

Brewster's production of *Othello* was framed in relation to prominent issues of the era, such as the Gulf War conflict and the O. J. Simpson murder trial, which were used as a backdrop for an exploration of contemporary racism. The publicity material indicates an express aim to allude to the ill-fated interracial relationships that are thought to have resulted in the death of a white woman, such as that between O. J. Simpson and Nicole Brown[4] and between Diana, Princess of Wales, and Dodi Al Fayed.[5] Brewster likens Othello to other modern men of colour who have had military influence, such as Idi Amin, Saddam Hussein, and Colin Powell, and she wanted to show that 'American football legends and Gulf War

---

[4] O. J. Simpson was acquitted of the murder of his ex-wife Nicole Brown Simpson and her friend Ronald Goldman after a high-profile police chase and arrest in 1994 and lengthy televised criminal court case in 1995, though a jury unanimously found him liable for the wrongful death of Goldman and battery of Nicole Simpson in a civil case in 1997. The O. J. Simpson case has since become somewhat of a motif for productions of *Othello*, particularly in the USA.

[5] Dodi Al Fayed's father Mohammed Al Fayed and other conspiracy theorists have notoriously claimed that Princess Diana and Dodi Al Fayed were killed because of their interracial relationship, imminent engagement, and the possibility that Princess Diana was pregnant with Dodi's child, which might mean that the future King of England would have a Muslim stepfather and a half-Muslim step-sibling. On 7 April 2008, the High Court jury of the Diana Inquest returned a verdict of 'unlawful killing, [due to] grossly negligent driving of the following vehicles and of the Mercedes'. They ruled out claims of a conspiracy between the royal family and MI6 to assassinate the Princess of Wales. See www.scottbaker-inquests.gov.uk/ for further details and transcripts of the hearing.

generals are not the first black men to achieve military or sporting success in white society only to be ruthlessly dispatched by the same establishment that built them up' (Talawa, *Othello* publicity).[6] The production was particularly informed by the comparisons between Othello and 'The Athlete' presented in Austin Clarke's essay 'Orenthal and Othello', in which he convincingly shows parallels between Othello and O. J. (Orenthal James) Simpson, such as highlighting the striking similarity of words used to describe 'The Athlete' – 'he took her youth, her freedom and her self-respect' – with the lines in *Othello* – 'Your daughter, if you have not given her leave, / I say again, hath made a gross revolt, / Tying her duty, beauty, wit, and fortunes / In an extravagant and wheeling stranger' (1.1.132–5). Clarke draws explicitly on Frantz Fanon's ideas about race and psychology to argue cogently that, although written almost four hundred years apart, the resemblance between these two speeches demonstrates the endurance of biological racism towards black men who are 'both victims of a racial epidermal schema'.[7] O. J. Simpson's story was suggested in Ben Thomas's slightly American-accented Othello, and this allusion was reinforced by the use of police-siren sound effects in the modern-dress production, evoking the high-profile police chase after the sportsman failed to appear to answer to the charge of double murder against him.[8]

Talawa's production of *Othello* opened in October 1997, just over a month after the death of Diana and Dodi in a Paris car crash on 31 August 1997. The issue was so sensitive that Brewster wrote to Julie Parker and the Drill Hall management to allay their concerns about possible references to the late Princess, reassuring them that 'no "quasi" characterisation of the Princess of Wales will be presented or [...] indeed any direct or indirect references to her will be made' (qtd in Jonson 312). However, Princess Diana's story is implied by the depiction of Roderigo as a lovesick foppish press paparazzo in desperate pursuit of pictures of Othello and his new wife. Reviewers also pointed out the resonance of a blonde-haired Desdemona, costumed in

---

[6] O. J. Simpson's 'fall from grace' was completed on 3 October 2008 when he was found guilty of all twelve criminal charges, including kidnap and armed robbery, pertaining to a botched robbery in Las Vegas in 2007. On 5 December 2008, Simpson was sentenced to a maximum of 33 years in prison, with the possibility of parole after 9 years. Judge Jackie Glass's pre-sentence summing up stressed that the verdict and incarceration were not retribution for Simpson's murder acquittal 13 years earlier. See http://edition.cnn.com/2008/CRIME/12/05/oj.simpson.sentencing/index.html#cnnSTCVideo.

[7] See Frantz Fanon, *Black Skin, White Masks* (London: Pluto Press, 1991), originally published in French as *Peau Noire, Masques Blancs* (Paris: Editions du Seuil, 1952).

[8] Production details are taken from my notes made from an archive video recording of the run (9 October–1 November 1997). References to line cuts and sound effects are taken from promptbook notations.

three-quarter-length army fatigues; Sam Marlowe described her as a 'Sloane Ranger in Barbour jacket and loafers', and Dominic Cavendish pinpointed that 'her wardrobe has a smack of the anti-landmine look about it'.

Brewster's production incorporated more black performers than would typically be seen in *Othello*, where he is usually the only black character in the play, although many productions have also cast black actresses as Bianca. Brewster cast black performers as Cassio, Emilia, and Bianca alongside Othello, which, as Elizabeth Schafer argues, 'transformed the play: Iago's racism is unforgettably underlined because not only was his wife, Emilia, black, but so was his rival, Cassio. So were most of the audience' (28). Iago and Roderigo were presented as two white men who use race as a basis from which to collude against the black men, heightening the force of their racially loaded descriptions of Othello's physical characteristics – 'the thick lips' (1.1.66) – and the speculated associated sexual behaviour of the 'lascivious Moor' (1.1.125). The racist undertones of Iago's statement that 'an old black ram / Is tupping your white ewe' (1.1.89–90) are amplified given that his wife is also black. However, the potential for a biologically reductive interpretation of Othello is unsettled by casting a black man as the innocent Cassio.

Brewster's multi-racial casting was a basis from which to undermine the racist assumptions of dangerous black men that are potentially embodied in the character of Othello. The casting of mixed-race actor Ben Thomas as Othello immediately unsettled the usual contrast between a dark black Othello and a pale white Desdemona, which impacted on how his disintegration from noble Moor to murderer might be understood in terms of race. Thomas's lighter skin complexion and slight build lessened the big dark black man/light white woman dichotomy, and Desdemona and Othello were presented in many ways as equals, with contrast neither in race nor age as apparent as they usually are. The early scenes portrayed them in a mutually tactile and lovingly playful relationship, clearly suggesting a sexual attraction that was expressed through touching each other on the bottom and stressing the innuendo of heading to the bedroom to consummate their marriage in Act 2, scene 3: Othello unambiguously flirted as he states 'Come my dear love, / The purchase made, the fruits are to ensue; / That profit's yet to come 'tween me and you' (2.3.8–10). Desdemona looked bemused and shocked when Othello publicly strikes her in Act 4, scene 1, and exasperated rather than fearful when he accuses her of being an 'Impudent strumpet' (4.2.79) in the next scene, defiantly answering back, 'If to preserve this vessel for my lord / From any other foul unlawful touch / Be not to be a strumpet, I am none' (4.2.83–5). Othello's threat towards her was reduced by cutting his premeditated line in Act 4, scene 1, 'Ay, let her rot and perish, and be damned tonight for she shall not live' (4.1.172), and his aside in Act 5, scene 1, 'Strumpet, I come! / Forth of my heart those charms, thine eyes, are blotted; / Thy bed, lust stained, shall with lust's blood be spotted' (5.1.34–6), where he implies that he is imminently going to murder Desdemona.

Discussions of whether a production of *Othello* challenges or reaffirms racist ideas about black men often centre on the deathbed scene (5.2) – described by Pascale Aebischer as 'a test-case for any production's attitude towards race, gender and violence' (136) – through analyses that explore how Othello kills Desdemona and her resistance (or not) to it. The bed in Talawa's production was simply made up of a duvet spread centre stage, on which Desdemona created space for Othello when he entered. His shirt was unbuttoned to show his bare chest, insinuating that he was about to make a sexual approach towards her, and she flirtatiously climbed on top of him and thrust her groin into his before he turned her over and straddled her. Desdemona did not appear to be aware that she is about to be killed and was given very little time to register what was happening, barely putting up a fight as Othello's mood abruptly changed and he quickly pinned her down on the bed to smother her. Their initial playfulness and equality in the bedroom scene reduced Othello's threat, and the dark violent black man stereotype was countered as the rapid change of mood in Ben Thomas's Othello also lessened the premeditated nature of the murder scene, making it appear as though he were having a moment of madness, acting beside himself and out of character.

The casting of a light-skinned Othello also troubled easy understandings of the motivation for Iago's hatred of the Moor and the usual distinction between these two key characters. Lois Potter observes, 'Most productions have traditionally showed a large, powerful but rather static Othello playing opposite a lighter, more mercurial Iago' (3), but the actors in Talawa's production shared a similar slim build and 'fair' skin, which unsettled ideas of a firm opposition between the black and the white characters. Othello, Iago, and Cassio were costumed almost identically in army uniforms, with their difference in status signified by Othello and Cassio wearing captain's hats and smartly pressed trousers, whilst Iago wore a red beret, combat trousers, and army boots; the comparative lack of medals on his shirt also signalled his lower rank and achievement. The mirroring of gestures in the actions of the main male characters emphasised the similarities between them as they stood around and saluted each other, blurring the differences between Iago, Cassio, and Othello, which consequently countered the possible readings of Othello's behaviour in primarily racial terms, of believing that he acts as he does because he is black.

The main criticism of the production was that the casting of black performers alongside Othello tempered the racism in the play and therefore failed to adequately justify how he is so easily taken in by Iago's scheming. Marlowe felt that the casting problematically 'weakens the sense of separateness that Shakespeare inflicts on his tragic hero [; ...] part of the reason that Iago is able to work so efficiently on Othello's psyche is the General's intensely isolated, and consequently vulnerable, position'. Marlowe's view is premised on the idea that the trajectory of the play hinges on the character of Othello being the only black man in a white society. But Brewster was keen to show that Othello is not isolated because there would have been other black people in that historical context too, whilst also poignantly reflecting the insidious ways in which racism works today. The black performers created a distinct community, emphasised by occasionally speaking to each other in Caribbean accents, making Iago's ability to manipulate Othello even more troubling as he is duped into murdering his wife despite being in a community of black people.

Iago was outnumbered as the only white man on stage in some scenes, and his jealousy towards Othello and Cassio was made obvious by his occasional exclusion from some of their discourse. Iago and Desdemona were a white minority in Act 2, scene 1, as they waited with Cassio, Emilia, and Bianca for Othello to return from war. Iago was visibly disgusted at Cassio's greeting of Emilia with a kiss on the lips, and the moment heightened his exclusion as Cassio spoke 'Welcome, mistress' (2.1.96) in a strong Caribbean accent as he scooped her into his arms. Iago's racism towards Othello could indicate that he also disrespected his black wife Emilia, towards whom he ironically directed his race-inflected humour and buffoonery as he banters with Desdemona: 'If she be black, and thereto have a wit / She'll find a white that shall her blackness fit' (2.1.131–2). However, this moment was not taken as a sign of disrespect as the three black characters playfully watched and laughed along with Iago's joke. Iago also demonstrated moments of clear affection towards Emilia. Immediately before she hands over Desdemona's handkerchief to him in Act 3, scene 3, he approached her from behind and they canoodled with each other, sharing a prolonged kiss, which could be read as evidence of his ultimate manipulation, but could also suggest some genuine mutual affection.

The casting of a black Cassio also underlines Othello's belief that Desdemona has been unfaithful to him, if he has internalised the racist idea that her marriage to him reflects a propensity for black men generally. Celia R. Daileader highlights that the romantic coupling of black men and white women is the dominant mode of representation of 'interracial couples from Shakespeare to Spike Lee' (*Racism* front cover), and the predominance of this point of view makes sense of Othello's jealousy. Iago's story of adultery thus worked as premised on racist discourses about black men, and the racist undertones of his gaze at Desdemona and Cassio as he plots his strategy were intensified by the way he and Emilia, sitting close together, mirrored Desdemona and Cassio on the other side of the stage whilst he delivered his cunning aside: 'He takes her by the palm. Ay, well said; whisper. With as little a web as this will I ensnare as great a fly as Cassio. Ay, smile upon her, do. I will gyve thee in thine own courtship. You say true, 'tis so indeed' (2.1.163–6). A reading of this moment as Iago's racist jealousy of Cassio's promotion was heightened by the audience seeing Emilia sitting next to him as he speaks. Her presence created an extra resonance, but she did not react to what he is saying, appearing not to hear as he delivered his lines as a soliloquy. However, Iago's later slow emphasis of the lines 'I do suspect the lusty Moor / Hath leaped into my seat' (2.1.276–7) and his vow that 'nothing can or shall content my soul / Till I am evened with him wife for wife' (2.1.279–80), whilst touching his own groin, ensured an overt expression of his jealousy of the possible adultery between 'the Moor' and his black wife Emilia, an army worker who was alone with Othello in many scenes. The sexual jealousy reading was manifested again in Act 3, scene 3, when Othello literally attacked Iago's sexuality by kicking him in the groin as he demands the 'ocular proof' (361) of Desdemona's disloyalty, and Iago's jealousy was apparent in Act 4, scene 1, as he sadistically gloated when Othello works himself up into a stupor and falls to the floor, whispering his lines 'Work on, / My medicine, work!' (42–3) straight into his ears before viciously kicking him down the stairs.

TRANSGRESSING GENDER

Several feminist critics have emphasised the interlocking discourses of race and sex in *Othello*'s coupling of a black man with a white woman.[9] Much

---

[9] See, for example, Joyce Green Macdonald, 'Black Ram, White Ewe: Shakespeare, Race, and Women', in *A Feminist Companion to Shakespeare*, ed. Dympna Callaghan (Oxford: Blackwell, 2000)

feminist criticism has focused on Desdemona, but, as Lena Cowen Orlin points out, work that examines how gender 'intersects with other categories of difference, like class, ethnicity, age and region' introduces the other female characters into the analysis, recognising 'Emilia and Bianca as critical to an understanding of Jacobean gender politics as is Desdemona' (6). Julie Hankey's account of productions of *Othello* on stage and screen also argues that recent interpretations informed by an 'alertness to questions of gender and ethnicity [... have] made Bianca's part much more prominent. She has, in effect, joined Emilia and Desdemona to make a trio of used and abused women' (227).

A gender-based analysis is as important to understanding the contribution of Talawa's production as a racial one, as, although Brewster claims to present Shakespeare 'straight' in terms of race, her productions invariably show an attentiveness to issues around gender. The Gulf War context was used as a backdrop for a rationale that 'challenges preconceptions of the role of women in the play, portraying the characters *Emilia* and *Bianca* as professional military women and *Desdemona* as the confident, loyal wife of the General' (Talawa, *Othello* education pack). The roles of these two black women were enhanced by placing them as army workers alongside the main male characters, a visible recognition of women's contribution to the armed forces and war efforts. Emilia was not presented as Desdemona's maid, so that a black woman was not seen waiting on a white woman, and the production provided a context in which Bianca was no longer presented as a whore. Emilia and Bianca, costumed similarly to the men in army trousers and bullet-/stab-proof waistcoat vests, were presented as professional black women who have independent careers alongside their marriages and relationships.

Emilia, given a context beyond simply being Iago's wife, was assigned some of the lines usually spoken by minor male characters (duke, senators, and sailors) and appeared in far more scenes than she usually would, often as the only woman on stage in the public world among men, which went against her usual placement primarily in the domestic spaces. Emilia does not usually appear on stage until Act 2, scene 1, but in this production she was present and vocal alongside the men discussing war strategy in Act 1, scene 2 and observing Brabantio's interrogation of Othello and

188–207; Barbara Hodgdon, 'Race-ing Othello: Engendering White Out', rpt. in *Othello: Contemporary Critical Essays*, New Casebooks, ed. Lena Cowen Orlin (Basingstoke: Palgrave Macmillan, 2004) 190–219; Rutter; Celia R. Daileader, 'Casting Black Actors: Beyond Othellophilia', in *Shakespeare and Race*, ed. Catherine M. S. Alexander and Stanley Wells (Cambridge: Cambridge University Press, 2000) 177–202, and *Racism*.

Desdemona in Act 1, scene 3. The idea of Emilia as a silent woman who only speaks out after Othello has murdered Desdemona was countered by her voice as an army woman whose presence ruptured the usually homo-social public arena. At the same time, her visible silence in many scenes, such as Act 1, scene 3, where she watched without speaking a word, poign-antly suggested her lack of agency as a woman in a man's world.

The other intervention Brewster made with the character of Emilia was to ensure that she was not seen waiting on Desdemona, removing any sense of the black woman as the white woman's maid. All of the lines where Desdemona requests Emilia's assistance were cut, and the only help she gave her was to unhook her necklace as she prepared for bed in Act 4, scene 3. Emilia entered the scene singing the willow song, after which she and Desdemona made the bed together, opened a bottle of wine to share, and then drunkenly sang the willow song together as Desdemona pre-pared for bed; their singing the song together made sense of it as a premo-nition of their pending murders, but they sang it merrily, rather than as a pensive lament. As Emilia did not act as Desdemona's maid, they were not presented as particularly closely allied before this scene, as Emilia's juggling of private and public spheres resulted in her loyalties being split between Iago, Othello, and Desdemona. Rutter highlights that, until this point, the 'men have been intimate, men have put their heads together and gossiped while women have kept aloof from each other' (142), but this is an important scene of female unity in the play, a 'women's scene, which privileges women's talk, women's bodies, women's thoughtful work upon the cultural imperatives that organize their lives' (145). This scene affirms some female camaraderie and paves the way for Emilia's reaction after the murder, where she pummelled her husband for his part in it and commanded the stage in defence of Desdemona.

Brewster's refusal to make Bianca the whore that she is usually por-trayed to be was significant in refiguring ideas of black women's sexu-ality and overturning stereotypical tendencies to cast black actresses in the role as a minority alongside Othello. Bianca's position as 'the most socially powerless of the play's three women' (Potter 186) was repudiated, and, like Emilia, she was present in the army arena in scenes in which she would not usually appear, playing a more integral role than usual as some of the minor male characters' lines were reallocated to her. Bianca first entered to announce the end of the wars in Act 2, scene 1, giving her a prominence that was quite different from her usual first appearance as Cassio's mistress when she is given the handkerchief in Act 3, scene 4.

Potter's suggestion that 'many [directors] are now taking Bianca seriously as a character rather than a comic floozie' (186) was reflected by cutting the line in Act 1, scene 1 that alludes to Cassio's wife – 'A fellow almost damned in a fair wife' (21) – and thus paving the way for depicting Bianca as a woman working in the army who has fallen in love with her colleague. The insinuation that she is a whore was removed by amending Iago's description of her as 'A housewife that by selling her desires / Buys herself bread and clothes. It is a creature / That dotes on Cassio; as 'tis the strumpet's plague' (4.1.92–4) simply to 'A housewife, that dotes on Cassio' (Talawa, *Othello* promptbook).

Presenting Cassio and Bianca in a mutual relationship also highlighted Iago's slurs as nonsense: for example, they stood wrapped in each other's arms as they awaited Othello's return from war in Act 2, scene 1. Act 3, scene 4 added a further depth to the mutuality of their relationship as they bantered fondly with each other, and the line where Cassio asks Bianca to copy the work on the handkerchief was removed, denying the possibility of reading him as a stereotypical black man mistreating his woman. Bianca's throwing of the handkerchief back at him and rebuff of his gestures of affection in Act 4, scene 1 therefore appeared to be the justified vexation of a woman who mistakenly believes that her partner has been unfaithful. Her accusation and anger remained momentary, however, as he pleaded for her acknowledgement that he is not guilty of an affair and tried to hug her; she initially shrugged him off before quickly acquiescing with an invitation for him to have supper with her. The following exchange with Iago maintained Cassio's warmth for Bianca by cutting more key lines, particularly his description of her as 'A customer' (4.1.117) – i.e., a harlot – and, indeed, it was Iago who carefully engineered the immediate rousing of laughter in the scene as he greeted Cassio. Cassio's resistance to the idea of marrying Bianca was presented as that of a love-shy, giggly young man who knows that she dotes on him, but is not quite ready for the commitment of marriage and, crucially, does not want to lose face in front of his comrade by revealing his mutual affection. The belittling of his relationship with Bianca that the text suggests was lessened further by cutting Othello's jealous asides, which frame the audience's perspective on the scene and enhance interpretations of this moment as Cassio disrespecting Bianca. In these ways, Talawa's portrayal alleviated the scene's potential contradiction of their construction of Cassio as a good black man who genuinely cares for Bianca.

When Bianca enters this scene and stands up for herself, Shakespeare offers a counterpoint to Desdemona's failure to stand up to Othello's angry reaction to her supposed infidelity.[10] As Evelyn Gajowski argues, Othello's mistaken belief that Cassio and Iago are discussing Desdemona suggests that Bianca could function 'merely [... as] a reflection of Othello's mistaken notion of Desdemona – paramour, courtesan, whore' (106). Thus, Brewster's refusal to present Bianca as a whore (for example, she was not wearing the scarlet dress in which many productions have costumed her) emphasised the error of his judgement. Brewster states, 'She denies being a loose woman and I choose to believe her' (Talawa, *Othello* education pack), highlighting that Iago is responsible for her being viewed as a whore and, as his entire role and character are built upon his being a liar, there is no need to believe him on this matter either. Bianca strongly defended herself against Emilia's charge of her as a strumpet in Act 5, scene 1, shouting, 'I am no strumpet, but of life as honest / As you that thus abuse me' (122–3). At the end of the play, she also played a key role in Iago's capture, 'Bring[ing] the villain forth' (5.2.282), perhaps as some retribution for what had been presented as his clear slander of her.

Kay Stanton notes that 'the highest number of uses of the word whore in a single work by Shakespeare, fourteen, is found in *Othello*' and suggests that it is possibly used 'in deliberate juxtaposition with "honest"' (94). All of the women in the play are at some point referred to as 'strumpets' or 'whores', such as when Othello asks Desdemona, 'Was this fair paper, this most goodly book, / Made to write whore upon?' (4.2.70–1), before unleashing his anger with denunciations of her as 'that cunning whore of Venice / That married with Othello' (4.2.88–9) and literally throwing coins at her as an indication that she is a whore on the line 'We have done our course; there's money for your pains' (4.2.92). Similarly, when Emilia speaks out against Iago's deceits, his ultimate slur is to call her a 'Villainous whore' (5.2.227). The word 'whore' is so freely used as a term of insult towards even the married women in the play that Brewster's refusal to make the unmarried woman a prostitute is a radical way of overturning the assumptions usually implicit when black actresses are cast in the role of Bianca. We might also conclude that as 'honest Iago' is a misnomer, given his propensity towards compulsive lying, so too are the women, judging by their behaviours, far from the whores that the male characters declare them to be.

---

[10] See Gajowski for further analysis of how Cassio and Bianca can be read as parallels to Othello and Desdemona.

NEW OUTCOMES FOR *OTHELLO*

Brewster's productions of Shakespeare for Talawa (as well as those by Tara Arts and Temba) have played a fundamental role in broadening the repertoire of black theatre in Britain, using black actors to bring these plays a modern resonance and relevance for new black audiences. Theatre critics were frustrated that Brewster did not bring them 'black Shakespeare', but, as can be seen from the analysis of *Othello*, the casting of mixed-race actor Ben Thomas was one of a number of innovations that underscored a race- and gender-aware interpretation that brought new perspectives to this well-known play. Pascale Aebischer, Virginia Mason Vaughan, and others have pointed out that a close reading of productions of *Othello* can be used to understand the racial discourse of the play and the racial attitude of the director.[11] Thus we might consider how the focus on racism, misogyny, and domestic violence in racial and gendered criticism of the play manifests itself as key concerns in a black female director's approach. Hugh Quarshie highlights that casting a black actor as Othello 'risk[s] making stereotypes seem legitimate and even true' (5), but concludes that black actors should continue to play the role in productions that use 'judicious cutting and textual emendation' to show that the character 'behaves as he does because he is a black man responding to racism, not giving a pretext for it' (18–21). Casting black actors as other key characters whom Iago exploits and/or manipulates certainly underscores such an understanding of Othello's behaviour as a response to contemporary and insidious forms of racism. Brewster's directorial decisions especially magnified the topicality of *Othello* for the contemporary identity politics of black women, a contribution to new outcomes for the play that can perhaps be summed up by recognising that a conventionally cast production leaves only white people alive at the end of the play. In this case, Talawa's casting of black performers as Cassio and Bianca meant that both a black man and a black woman lived to see another day.

Special thanks to Talawa Theatre Company, who generously gave me access to their archive material.

WORKS CITED

Aebischer, Pascale. *Shakespeare's Violated Bodies: Stage and Screen Performance.* Cambridge: Cambridge University Press, 2004.

---

[11] See Aebischer and Virginia Mason Vaughan, 'Introduction: Perspectives on *Othello*: Old and New', in Vaughan and Cartwright, 13–25.

Birkett, Dea. 'Dark Star'. *Guardian* 15 May 1991: 34.

Brewster, Yvonne. *The Undertaker's Daughter*. London: Black Amber, 2004.

Cavendish, Dominic. 'Review of Othello, dir. Yvonne Brewster'. *Time Out* 15 October 1997: 144.

Clarke, Austin. 'Orenthal and Othello'. http://www.talawa.com/article.php3?id_article=148, accessed 5 June 2006.

Daileader, Celia R. *Racism, Sexism and the* Othello *Myth: Inter-racial Couples from Shakespeare to Spike Lee*. Cambridge: Cambridge University Press, 2005.

Gajowski, Evelyn. 'The Female Perspective in *Othello*'. *Othello: New Perspectives*. Ed. Virginia Mason Vaughan and Kent Cartwright. London: Associated University Presses, 1991. 97–114.

Gilbert, Helen, and Joanne Tompkins. *Post-Colonial Drama: Theory, Practice, Politics*. London and New York: Routledge, 1996.

Hankey, Julie, ed. *Othello: Shakespeare in Production*. Second Edition. Cambridge: Cambridge University Press, 2005.

Jonson, David Vivian. 'The History, Theatrical Performance Work and Achievements of Talawa Theatre Company 1986–2001'. PhD Thesis. University of Warwick, 2001.

Khan, Naseem. 'Art of Darkness'. *City Limits* 16 May 1991. Talawa Company Archive.

Marlowe, Sam. 'Review of *Othello*, dir. Yvonne Brewster'. *What's On in London*. 22–9 October 1997: 53.

Orlin, Lena Cowen. 'Introduction'. *Othello: Contemporary Critical Essays*. New Casebooks. Basingstoke: Palgrave Macmillan, 2004. 1–21.

Potter, Lois. *Othello*. Shakespeare in Performance. Manchester: Manchester University Press, 2002.

Quarshie, Hugh. *Second Thoughts about* Othello. International Shakespeare Association Occasional Paper 7. Chipping Campden: Cloud Hill Printers, 1999.

Rutter, Carol Chillington. *Enter the Body: Women and Representation on Shakespeare's Stage*. London: Routledge, 2001.

Schafer, Elizabeth. *MsDirecting Shakespeare: Women Direct Shakespeare*. 1998. New York: St Martin's Press, 2000.

Shakespeare, William. *Othello*. The New Cambridge Shakespeare. Ed. Norman Sanders. Cambridge: Cambridge University Press, 1984.

Stanton, Kay. ' "Made to Write 'Whore' Upon?" Male and Female Use of the Word "Whore" in Shakespeare's Canon'. *A Feminist Companion to Shakespeare*. Ed. Dympna Callaghan. Oxford: Blackwell, 2000. 80–102.

Talawa. *Antony and Cleopatra*. Dir. Yvonne Brewster. 16 May–15 June 1991. The Bloomsbury Theatre, London, and The Merseyside Theatre, Liverpool.

　King Lear. Dir. Yvonne Brewster. Cochrane Theatre, London. 24 February–16 April 1994. Video. V&A Theatre Collections, London.

　Othello. Dir. Yvonne Brewster. Drill Hall Theatre, London. 9 October–1 November 1997. Video. Talawa Theatre Company, London.

Othello production archive, including promptbook, publicity, and education pack.

Vaughan, Virginia Mason, and Kent Cartwright. *Othello: New Perspectives.* London: Associated University Presses, 1991.

Verma, Jatinder. 'The Challenge of Binglish: Analysing Multi-Cultural Productions'. *Analysing Performance: A Critical Reader.* Ed. Patrick Campbell. Manchester: Manchester University Press, 1996. 193–202.

'Cultural Transformations'. *Contemporary British Theatre.* Ed. Theodore Shank. Basingstoke: Macmillan, 1996. 55–61.

Wainwright, Jeffrey. 'An African Queen'. *Independent* 30 April 1991: 14.

CHAPTER 15

British directors in post-colonial South Africa

Brian Pearce

Since the official end of the apartheid regime, several Britons have directed Shakespeare in South Africa, including Gregory Doran and Sir Anthony Sher (originally South African), Janet Suzman (originally South African), and Paige Newmark, who has worked in the USA and Australia, as well as South Africa. This chapter will discuss the various ways in which these directors have attempted to make Shakespeare relevant within a post-colonial context, in the process, on occasion, inverting their intended meanings through unfamiliarity with the historical context and the traditions of performance in South Africa.

Shakespeare is the most frequently performed playwright in contemporary South Africa, with productions mounted annually at Maynardville in Cape Town and at Mannville in Port Elizabeth. Shakespeare is also performed by a variety of smaller theatre companies, including the Actors Co-operative in Durban and Shakespeare SA, which, although based in the Eastern Province, tours more widely. Productions nowadays play to multi-racial audiences; however, one may still find a production playing to a predominantly white audience one evening and a predominantly black one the next, because, although divisions are no longer enforced, the country is still divided.

In trying to define what constitutes 'colonial' and 'post-colonial' in a modern South African context, one has to take into account the history of the country and the fact that throughout the colonial period British actors and theatre companies toured to South Africa. British actors also worked in South Africa with local actors. To a large extent, South African English Shakespeare productions were modelled on British productions, a situation that continued even after the boycott that affected cultural exchanges between Britain and South Africa during the apartheid period. With a few exceptions, including translations of the plays, South African Shakespeare productions continued to model themselves on British productions, although often those of twenty or thirty years earlier. The revolutionary work of directors like Peter Brook was not seen in South Africa, as it was in Australia in the 1970s: South Africans knew about British productions only by visiting London or through films and books. This lag between British and South African production styles meant that many of the latter were conservative in outlook and values; for example, South African white actors imitated British actors, with South African accents considered inappropriate in a Shakespeare production, although acceptable in a South African play.[1] After the end of apartheid in 1994, these rather old-fashioned Shakespeare productions persisted. Whether in modern dress or in period costume, they were performed predominantly by white English-speaking South African actors; if black actors *were* included in the productions, they were often in minor roles. It was Janet Suzman's production of *Othello* at the Market Theatre in 1987 that had broken the mould of racially segregated casting in productions of Shakespeare, although there had been earlier attempts.[2] Although in retrospect it may appear in some ways to have reinforced apartheid stereotypes, as Robert Gordon has argued (15–18), Suzman's 'radical production' nevertheless proved an important turning point (Loomba 148).

Hence, the situation in the 1990s, shortly after the end of apartheid, was one in which a highly colonial form of Shakespeare predominated. Shakespeare was a cultural icon, closely linked to the teaching of English in schools and used to entrench colonial values, including the superiority of English culture to other cultural traditions in the country.[3] The same standard works on the school syllabus tended to be produced, while numerous Shakespeare texts were totally neglected. How, then, would one

[1] Although this picture is fairly accurate, if only in general terms, it is also a simplistic one, for a number of teachers, professors, actors, and directors associated with Shakespeare were highly critical of the apartheid regime. In the apartheid state, any form of intellectual enquiry such as that represented by literature or theatre was bound to pose a challenge, and a number of South African Shakespeare productions were directly critical of the government; see Quince for an account of some challenging productions during the apartheid period. In conclusion he writes, 'Despite the appropriation of Shakespeare by the ruling classes as a "powerful signifier of conservatism" (Orkin *Drama* 235), therefore, despite the attempted depoliticization of the texts to stifle ideological dissent, theatre practitioners still managed repeatedly to recontextualize the plays in performance, thereby enabling these privileged vehicles for the recirculation of social energy to carry a critique deeply subversive of the dominant apartheid ideology' (157). One should also note that South African colonial productions during the 1970s and 1980s were often of a high professional standard.

[2] Rohan Quince, agreeing that John Kani was the first black actor in a major role in a major production, notes two previous productions that included black actors in otherwise white casts (email to author, 3 August 2008). It should also be noted that, prior to the Suzman *Othello*, there had also been all-black Shakespeare productions, such as *Umabatha* in 1970–2, which, although making *Macbeth* accessible to African audiences, reinforced racial segregation.

[3] See Johnson for an account of Shakespeare in relation to South African education.

define a post-colonial approach to directing Shakespeare in this context? First of all, it would involve some form of interaction or recognition of South African culture – for example, the use of South African accents and styles of performance, including dance and music. Furthermore, a post-colonial approach would involve a questioning of the play's authority and of a traditional (i.e., colonial) way of playing it. It might involve experimentation as a crucial aspect of the rehearsal process, instead of actors assuming certain outmoded ways of performing – a sense of spontaneity and risk-taking that would have been out of place in the Shakespeare productions of the past.

Titus Andronicus, the first Shakespeare production to benefit from the new cultural interchange following the apartheid years, was a curious choice of play. It had sprung to prominence in 1970 in a controversial Afrikaans production, translated by Breyten Breytenbach and directed by the German director, Dieter Reible, at the Hofmeyer Theatre in Cape Town, which was critical of the apartheid system (Quince 36). However, in Johannesburg in 1995, the play was virtually unknown. Gregory Doran and Anthony Sher's production, which played at the Market Theatre before travelling to the West Yorkshire Playhouse (Leeds), the Royal National Theatre (London), and the Almagro Festival in Spain (Thurman 30), played to full houses in England, but was poorly received in South Africa, both among critics and audiences, with the question of African and South African stereotypes becoming a major issue.

While its poor reception caused Sher a certain amount of disappointment,[4] the production was a curiously bad choice for South Africa in 1995, especially given the fact that Sher and Doran wished to draw direct parallels between the characters and situations of the play and South African politics. The previous year had seen the first democratic elections in the country after years of apartheid and civil violence; South Africans, black and white, were hoping that the new country would see an end to violence, rather than a return to it. Hence, a play that represents such extreme violence, produced with specifically South African parallels in mind, was not likely to be taken sympathetically: the bloodbath of *Titus* was one that the new South African nation was specifically trying

---

[4] See 'Poor Titus response' in the *Daily Dispatch*, and 'Sher play gets poor reception' in the *Evening Post* for a sense of Sher's 'disappointment'. As far as the controversy surrounding the production is concerned, Sher wrote a letter to the *Star*, saying, 'Angry? I'm delighted. The debate is up and running. Letters, public and private, newspaper articles and radio forums have produced a diverse, often surprising, always stimulating, range of arguments' ('A fond farewell'). However, in his and Doran's book on the production, Sher reveals his irritation at some of the reviews (205–9).

to avoid. In this context, Doran and Sher's production may have seemed to some not just to depict violence but actually to anticipate it, perhaps providing the kind of image of South Africa that English audiences and critics expected.

For another reason, too, the play was poorly timed. Immediately after any war, whether civil or international, societies are usually reluctant to confront drama that deals explicitly with violence or tragedy. In Britain in the period immediately after the Second World War, fairly light entertainment and escapist theatre, as well as poetic drama, found favour until the mid-fifties, when the new wave of realistic and experimental drama brought about a revolution. In 1955, Brook staged his famous production of *Titus Andronicus* at Stratford, with Laurence Olivier as Titus and Anthony Quayle as Aaron, a full ten years after the end of the war. If this violent play had been staged in 1945, the response to it might have been very different, especially if Brook had attempted to contemporise it and draw on stereotypical figures from the war for his characterisations.

Reviews of the Johannesburg production provoked a variety of responses.[5] For Digby Ricci, 'Such a bizarre, unthinking melange of styles is in no way suited to Shakespeare's masterly blending of genres and emotions and serves only to raise maddening questions, both serious and facetious, in the minds of bewildered audiences'; he concluded that '[t]his is a botched, insultingly unsubtle production' (82). Mark Gervisser's more positive review similarly felt that 'the conceptual underpinning of this production is often messy, often difficult to fathom' (84). Michael Billington, on the other hand, reviewing the London performances in the *Guardian*, concluded that 'its great virtue is that it's anything but a pale imitation of British Shakespeare. It puts the play into a specifically South African context and, even though the historical fit is not perfect, it confirms *Titus*' status as Shakespeare's first masterwork' ('Sher', 85).

The casting for this production was not 'colour blind' but, in fact, 'colour conscious': characters were cast according to racial categories, with the Romans presented as white Afrikaaners, the Goths as 'Coloured' South Africans,[6] and Aaron, of course, as a black man. Gervisser noted how the casting affected the interpretation of Aaron:

---

[5] *Shakespeare in Southern Africa* 8 (1995): 81–5 reprinted three reviews from the *Mail & Guardian*, which cover a spectrum of critical responses; references are to these reprints.

[6] The term 'Coloured' in South Africa refers to a specific group of people of mixed race (including Hottentot, Malay, and Dutch), who have their own cultural identity and even language (a dialect of Afrikaans); they originate from or live mainly in the Cape.

Sello Maake ka Ncube's performance of Aaron the Moor was troubling in a more rewarding way: using Shakespeare's language, he created an intensely powerful presence on stage; in his swaggering body and lilting voice there was sexuality and cold rage; one felt how he felt brutalised and fetishised. The point is that he is brutalised and fetishised by the very words he has to speak, for he is, after all, the product of a racist Elizabethan imagination. (84)

Mary Jordan described Aaron in this performance as 'a caged Iago, corroded and subverted by sexual suspicion. It would have helped enormously had one been able to hear or decipher one word he said.' Raeford Daniel wrote, 'The trouble is one often has trouble discerning what he is saying.' One wonders whether it is not a colonial stereotype of an African male, libidinous and inarticulate, that the actor's performance suggested, although the sexuality of the character is very much an attribute of Shakespeare's text.

One of the most controversial aspects of the Sher/Doran production was Sher's own interpretation of Titus, which was based on a caricature of a conservative, white, militaristic Afrikaaner reminiscent of Eugène Terre'Blanche, a man who, at the time, it was feared, could have unseated the whole movement towards reconciliation and peace in South Africa. Hence, the production tapped into some very real fears that South African audiences were experiencing. Furthermore, Sher tried to play Titus in a sympathetic light, cutting out the incident when he impulsively kills his son, Mutius, while working towards creating a feeling of compassion for the character (Thurman 33). In Sher and Doran's own account of the production, Doran explains this 'crucial decision [... to cut] the death of Mutius', asking, 'How do you find any journey for Titus to go, if he's barking mad to start with?' (111). However, inclusion of this incident prevents the audience at the outset from feeling any empathy for a character who later kills his own daughter. Sher's portrayal attempted to mislead the audience into feeling empathy for him.[7]

One of the crucial debates that the production raised concerned the question of accents. In his and Doran's account, Sher describes what happened at the Johannesburg auditions: 'Although we stress that we want to find a South African way of playing Shakespeare, practically every actor does his or her speech in an assumed English accent'; however, as soon as Doran 'encourages the actors to try again, using their own accents, their own

---

[7] Doran gives a further reason for cutting the death of Mutius: 'From a close study of the text, it seems that the death of Mutius might have been an afterthought, a late rewrite. It interrupts a conversation, and Marcus is given the clumsiest segue imaginable in an attempt to get back to the plot' (Sher and Doran 111).

energy, their own *centre*, they transform. Suddenly they become the actors who amazed audiences around the world on those Fugard tours, those Market tours – amazed audiences with their rawness, their passion' (45).[8] The production therefore used a variety of South African accents, with no attempt made to emulate 'Standard English'. However, as Natasha Distiller notes, these accents were often achieved self-consciously rather than reflecting the natural speaking voices of the actors. Far from presenting the case that Shakespeare should be acted in the accents of South Africans, the production appeared to exaggerate such speech patterns in a way that many resisted; Ricci, for example, found them 'offensively exaggerated' (82), and Distiller describes 'many of the main actors [...] putting on accents to do their earthy and authentic South African Shakespeare as much as they would be if they reverted to the English accents Sher and Doran decry as inauthentic' (4). Sher himself, as Distiller notes, did not use his own South African accent: 'Sher's Titus is an Afrikaaner; this is not Sher's native accent' (4).

Despite such reservations, Sher and Doran's production marked a turning point in the development of a post-colonial approach to Shakespeare production in South Africa, challenging prevailing South African notions about how Shakespeare should be spoken and provoking argument and debate about South African stereotypes and political readings in a local context. Thurman, for example, considers that the production 'distorted the society it aimed to mirror' (33), but there was something dialectically minded about it, a critical engagement with South African reality, rather than an attempt simply to mirror it. In exaggerating South African stereotypes, particularly white ones in a way that South African audiences and reviewers resisted, Doran and Sher were bringing South African culture into sharp critical focus, seeing characters in terms of how others saw South Africans as sometimes crude and unsophisticated, given to emotional outbursts, cruelty, and violence. However, Doran and Sher achieved exactly Brecht's ideal in his concept of dialectical theatre, where audiences are provoked to argue about the production and its meaning, rather than to accept it unquestioningly as an aesthetic experience.

---

[8] Natasha Distiller comments that Sher's thinking here demonstrates a 'standard colonial binary relation' between England and South Africa (3–4), with the production providing 'a vehicle for Sher as a white sometime-South African to search for an identity' (1). She concludes: 'What is being staged, then, is not an engaged contribution to post-apartheid South Africa, but a drama of self, a performance of an identity crisis, against a backdrop of a particular, and tiresomely familiar, binary conception of centre and periphery' (14).

Like the Doran/Sher *Titus Andronicus*, Paige Newmark's productions of *Twelfth Night* and *The Winter's Tale*, which played at the Grahamstown Festival in 2003 and 2005 respectively, raise similar issues about reflecting local context. *Twelfth Night* was set, with realistic detail in terms of costumes and settings, in the Eastern Province during 1850, with Illyria becoming Port Elizabeth. However, setting the play in a romanticised colonial context, accompanied by the strains of Beethoven's *Pastoral Symphony*, created a picture far removed from the harsher realities of colonialism: nineteenth-century Port Elizabeth was not a world of the leisured rich, love-sick aristocratic poets, wealthy sisters in mourning, or fun-loving knights, but one in which the Puritan values of Malvolio would have been more at home. However, in this production, Malvolio was presented, whether intentionally or not, as less moralistic than usual: more of a dandy or an aesthete than a Puritan. In this and other ways, Newmark's evocation of a nineteenth-century colonial world presented the audience with a purely idyllic romance, a fantasy of how modern colonialists might like to see their own history: tolerant towards black people (the characters in Newmark's *Twelfth Night* were colour blind to a black Feste, a black Viola, and a black Sebastian), aristocratic rather than struggling for a living, and non-moralistic instead of often strictly religious. However, settlers in the Eastern Province were drawn to a large extent from the English petite bourgeoisie and the working classes, as much victims of colonialism as colonialists themselves; the only upper-class representatives in the nineteenth century would have been a relatively small number of colonial administrators, church officials, and officers. Hence, by setting *Twelfth Night* in the context of a settler community, with references to Port Elizabeth and the local pub in Bathurst, Newmark was in danger of presenting his Grahamstown audience with a fable of their own history. This interpretative difficulty would not have emerged if Newmark had not specifically tried to locate the play in Port Elizabeth in 1850 and employed all the visual effects of costume and setting to support this reading. As it was, the production simply could not be read metaphorically, its own attempt at verisimilitude inviting the audience, very plausibly on one level, to enter into this historical fantasy world. This is a case of a British director not fully comprehending the history and conventions of the society he is evoking. In effect, Newmark superimposed an upper-class English society of 1850 onto the settler community of the same period.

In casting black actors as twins Viola and Sebastian, the production also allowed itself to be read in light of the notion that white people are unable to tell the difference between one black person and another. A more dialectically minded multi-racial casting, which could have given the production a rather ambiguous, post-colonial edge, might have been to cast a black actor as Malvolio in the midst of the very English colonial society: after all, a servant in a colonial realm in 1850 would have been likely to be black, and the play's class prejudice might then have found a parallel in racial prejudice. Another possibility might have been a predominantly black production, with Viola and Sebastian as white outsiders (i.e., new settlers) arriving from the sea. And, of course, the other option – of avoiding a historically specific South African setting – paradoxically would have allowed the director a much greater freedom in multi-racial casting.

Newmark often gives his productions a specifically African context: in his 2005 *Winter's Tale*, Bohemia became Azania, and Antigonus exited pursued, not by a bear, but a lion.[9] His 2007 *As You Like It*, which toured the Eastern Province and also played in Kwa-Zulu Natal and at the Grahamstown Festival,[10] turned the Forest of Arden into the southern African 'Forest of Mussina', sheltering characters who had escaped from a modern-day Zimbabwe, ruled by dictator Duke Frederick, who was modelled on Robert Mugabe. In pursuing this theme, black actors were cast as members of the ruling family, with white actors (for the most part) those who had already escaped from the court to the forest, although the actor playing Duke Frederick also appeared as Duke Senior. The production incorporated African phrases, music, and dance within an otherwise conventional production style. The danger was that the production trivialised the situation in Zimbabwe, as refugees from the dictatorship face a bleaker prospect than that offered in Shakespeare's play, while as yet there is no prospect of the dictator turning to a religious life. However, perhaps this is to interpret the production too literally, precisely the danger of a Shakespeare setting that is over-specific.

In contrast to *As You Like It*, with its localised modern Zimbabwean context, Newmark's 2007 *Hamlet* employed very obviously 'blind' casting techniques, while referring back to the conventions and context of the Jacobean theatre. Where *As You Like It* was updated and adapted, *Hamlet* was performed in the very original text of the First Quarto. As if

---

[9] In Tamar Meskin and Mervyn McMurtry's student production of *The Winter's Tale* at the University of KwaZulu-Natal in 2007, the bear became an African taxi called 'The Bear'.

[10] *As You Like It* and *Hamlet* were produced by 'Shakespeare SA', of which Newmark is the founding director; the company is a project of the Shakespeare Society of Southern Africa.

to emphasise the 'colour blind' aspect of his casting method, Newmark had Hamlet played by a white actor visibly older than the black actress playing Gertrude; Corambis (Polonius), played by a black actor, was also younger than Hamlet.[11] The discrepancies between the ages of the actors and those of the characters they played intensified the incongruity of their relationships, thereby seeming to signal that no meaning should be read into the multi-racial casting. Although no unintended meanings were suggested by the production, the overall quality of the performances was not sufficient to sustain the approach convincingly, and its veering towards the opposite of an over-specific reading made it difficult to see the contemporary relevance.

As these examples of Shakespeare productions in South Africa have shown, there is often a distinction between the interpretation and the performance of a text: the interpretation might be intended to be 'post-colonial', while the performance itself might actually serve to reinforce colonial stereotypes. On the other hand, a fairly conventional, traditional reading of a Shakespeare text, through its qualities as performance, might become genuinely post-colonial. I think that this was the case with Janet Suzman's production of *Hamlet* at the Grahamstown Festival in 2005, which later went on to the Baxter Theatre in Cape Town and the RSC Swan Theatre at Stratford-upon-Avon as part of The Complete Works Festival.

Suzman did not radically re-invent the play, adopt an eccentric reading, or try to localise the play too specifically. The actors wore modern dress, not suggesting any particular modern community, but with strong resonances of South Africa.[12] The casting was multi-racial, but not with any point being made about race: Suzman had adopted 'colour blind' casting methods,[13] a

---

[11] The talented black actor Sdumo Mtshali played Polonius (Corambis): one wonders why he was not cast as Hamlet.

[12] Michael Billington, describing it as 'a highly traditional *Hamlet* [...] given new life by the variety of the acting', noted that it 'evoke[d] South Africa's past in myriad ways': 'Denmark in this version is clearly a prison and Hamlet himself under virtual house arrest. When he explores the possibility of returning to Wittenberg, his exits are blocked by dark-glassed heavies. And when he puts on an "antic disposition" it is that of a political prisoner with blanket, prison mug and consoling recorder.' He also writes: 'John Kani [...] is an imposing and stately figure who carries with him the memory of countless Fugard productions: he even resorts, very tellingly, to African speech as Claudius vainly prays that "all may be well"' (Review). John Kani is identified with the struggle against apartheid: although not ever himself a political prisoner on Robben Island, he became a symbol of the plight of political prisoners to international audiences through his performances in Athol Fugard's *The Island* (1973). Hence, in *Hamlet*, he could very easily represent a former political hero who has become a dictator, as well as the father of a revolutionary, as Hamlet's father's Ghost.

[13] Suzman herself referred to her casting as 'colour blind' in a lecture she gave in Grahamstown on 2 July 2005.

10. The closet scene – 'Look here upon this picture' – in Janet Suzman's 2006 *Hamlet*, with Dorothy Ann Gould as Gertrude and Vaneshran Arumugam as Hamlet.

point emphasised by the fact that Hamlet was played by an Indian actor, Claudius by a black African actor, and Gertrude by a white actress, while Polonius and Ophelia were played by 'Coloured' actors. In this context, one could forget the issue of race, recognising that the actors were actors playing roles, a concept perfectly attuned to one of the major themes in the play and echoed in the production by a small inner stage: a stage within the stage. However, a careful look at her casting shows that the production achieved a very specific balance between different South African cultural elements. Following the original performances in Grahamstown and Cape Town in 2005, the role of Hamlet was recast for the production's 2006 re-staging, with Rajesh Gopie replaced by another Indian actor, Vaneshran Arumugam. This choice was unlikely to have been purely coincidental, especially given the interpretation of some of the other roles – for example, that of Claudius played by John Kani, with both director and actor aware of the parallels between Claudius and black dictators in Africa:

'Tyranny is also at home in Africa,' says Suzman. 'There's a tyrant just north of us in Zimbabwe.'Kani has reflected on Mugabe as a latter day Claudius.'There on our northern border is a man, once a good man, who wants to hold on to power even when it destroys both himself and his country.' (Blair 12)

However, although Kani was aware of the parallels between Claudius and Mugabe, there was no sense in which he attempted to model his perform-ance directly on Mugabe or any other dictator, a significant contrast to the way Sher approached the role of Titus in relation to Terre'Blanche and to the very specific parallels that Newmark intended between *As You Like it* and Zimbabwe.

Although the British reviewer Pete Wood did not draw any attention to Suzman's multi-racial casting, it would have been something South African audiences noticed. The racial categorisations, 'White', 'Black', 'Indian',[14] and 'Coloured', were imposed by the apartheid government, yet they have continued to be used in the post-apartheid period through the government Equity (affirmative action) Policy. The categorisations relate to different kinds of South African cultural identity and are therefore not simply a mat-ter relating to race. Suzman, in casting actors from three of the categories as Hamlet's family (or from all four if we include Polonius and Ophelia as his extended family), achieved something quite different from Doran and Sher in their production of *Titus*, where the three racial categories represented the conflict of opposing dynasties and one oppressed race. Doran and Sher's production related to the apartheid reality of the past, whereas Suzman's casting, ten years later, brought South African Shakespeare more into the post-apartheid world, where the mixture of races within a single social unit – the Danish court – is more probable and less inevitably divisive.

Suzman's setting was simple, a bare stage on a slight incline, with a small inner stage in the centre to create a level playing area, with a rounded black backdrop, against which the action took place. The setting helped to create a neutral space, allowing the metaphorical dimension of the play to find expression. This staging helped in Suzman's overall approach, not tying the play too literally to any one particular time or place or set of meanings, but allowing the text to have a more open-ended relationship with the contemporary South African context. Perhaps this production has initiated a new phase in post-colonial Shakespeare performance in

---

[14] The term 'Indian' in South Africa refers to those who in other countries would identify them-selves as 'Asian', 'Indian', or 'Pakistani': they are descended from those who came to South Africa before the division into Pakistan and India.

South Africa, where multi-racial casting avoids the dangers of directly representing history, while nevertheless referring to it.

Patrice Pavis's seminal *Theatre at the Crossroads of Culture* (1992) observes how we read contemporary performances of classical texts:

At the moment, the split between tried and tested classical values and modern values to be tested no longer exists; we no longer believe in the geographical, temporal or thematic universality of the classics. Their *mise en scène* opts for a resolutely relativist and consumerist attitude, which is postmodern since their only value now resides in their integration into a discourse that is obsessed neither by meaning, nor by truth, nor by totality, nor by coherence. (14–15)

While one might agree that there are no longer universal truths independent of culture, there are nevertheless human values that different societies have in common – even if they exist with subtle differences – and that classical texts allow theatre to explore. Shakespeare's relevance in South Africa today lies in the fact that his plays articulate questions relating to these values. This has nothing to do with Shakespeare in relation to the promotion of English literature or English cultural hegemony, but with the concerns of a contemporary, growing democracy and the need to examine questions relating both to cultural difference and to our shared humanity. Where colonial productions of Shakespeare inadequately referred to an English past, post-colonial productions of Shakespeare in South Africa, such as Janet Suzman's *Hamlet*, seem rather to refer to a more ambiguous and open-ended future.

WORKS CITED

Billington, Michael. Review of *Hamlet*, dir. Janet Suzman. *Guardian* 4 May 2006. www.guardian.co.uk/stage/2006/may/04/theatre.rsc, accessed 17 February 2009.
'Sher's "Titus Africanus" Hailed'. *Guardian*, rpt. *Mail & Guardian* 28 July 1995. Rpt. *Shakespeare in Southern Africa* 8 (1995): 84–5.
Blair, David. 'Shakespeare: The quintessential storyteller of Africa'. *Star* 24 April 2005: 12.
Bradshaw, Graham, Tom Bishop, and Laurence Wright, eds. Special section on 'South African Shakespeare in the Twentieth Century'. *Shakespearean International Yearbook* 9 (Abingdon: Ashgate, 2009).
Daniel, Raeford. 'Gone with the gore'. *Citizen* 31 March 1995: 21.
Distiller, Natasha. 'Tony's Will: *Titus Andronicus* in South Africa 1995'. Bradshaw, Bishop, and Wright.
Gervisser, Mark. 'What's wrong with relevance?'. *Mail & Guardian* 7 April 1995. Rpt. *Shakespeare in Southern Africa* 8 (1995): 83–4.

Gordon, Robert. 'Iago and the *swart gevaar:* The problems and pleasures of a (post)colonial *Othello*'. Bradshaw, Bishop, and Wright.

Johnson, David. *Shakespeare and South Africa*. Oxford: Clarendon Press, 1996.

Jordan, Mary. 'Shakespeare reconstructed'. *Business Day* 4 April 1995: 10.

Loomba, Ania. ' "Local-manufacture made-in-India Othello fellows": Issues of race, hybridity and location in post-colonial Shakespeares'. *Post-Colonial Shakespeares*. Ed. Ania Loomba and Martin Orkin. London: Routledge, 1998. 143–63.

Orkin, Martin. *Drama and the South African State*. Manchester: Manchester University Press, 1991.

Pavis, Patrice. *Theatre at the Crossroads of Culture*. Trans. Loren Kruger. London: Routledge, 1992.

'Poor Titus response'. *Daily Dispatch* 8 July 1995: 5.

Quince, Rohan. *Shakespeare in South Africa: Stage Productions during the Apartheid Era*. New York: Peter Lang, 2000.

Ricci, Digby. 'Titus Topples into the "Relevant" Pit'. *Mail & Guardian* 31 March 1995. Rpt. *Shakespeare in Southern Africa* 8 (1995): 81–2.

Sher, Anthony. 'A fond farewell – for now'. *Star* 12 May 1995: 10.

Sher, Anthony, and Gregory Doran. *Woza Shakespeare: Titus Andronicus in South Africa*. London: Methuen, 1996.

'Sher play gets poor reception'. *Evening Post* 6 July 1995: 12.

Thurman, Christopher. 'Sher and Doran's *Titus Andronicus* (1995): Importing Shakespeare, Exporting South Africa'. *Shakespeare in Southern Africa* 18 (2006): 29–36.

Wood, Pete. Review of *Hamlet*, dir. Janet Suzman. *The British Theatre Guide*. 2006. www.britishtheatreguide.info/reviews/RSC-CWhamlet-rev.htm, accessed 13 February 2009.

Shakespeare's audiences as imaginative communities

Christie Carson

All the case studies in this volume illustrate how meaning has been created by a particular community at a particular time, the plays transformed by the context in which they are produced. Throughout four centuries of Shakespearean performance history, the idea of a fixed community that responds to the plays as one audience can be seen to be both supported and disrupted by the vision of performance history put forward by this volume: while a study of Shakespearean performance can aid in our understanding of a community from the past, our understanding of that community must be complex and multifaceted. But what of present-day performances, of present-day communities? In considering this question, I want to address the role of Shakespeare in building identity through education, by examining the work of the education departments of the Royal Shakespeare Company (RSC) and of Shakespeare's Globe. Doing so will pose two related questions that go to the heart of the issues that this collection raises. First, can the notion of community continue to have its historical meaning in a world flooded by the work of political spin doctors, hard-selling advertising techniques, and email phishing – all of which manipulate the ideals of a homogeneous community – and by a range of resurgent forms of religious fundamentalism, which depend on extreme versions of those ideals? Second, and perhaps more essentially, can historically rooted performance criticism be a politically effective form of writing?

The links between theatre and politics, performance and democracy are, as Nicholas Ridout makes clear, at the centre of current ideas about performance emanating from performance criticism:

My focus on theatrical performance arises not out of any supposition that theatrical performance is the only proper object of performance studies, but because, in the discourses about democracy, issues of both participation and representation are often addressed in terms that point towards a 'special relationship' between democracy and theatre. (12)

In 'Performance and Democracy', Ridout tries 'to explore and contest this relationship' (12), but he begins the task by mapping out current definitions of the latter, pitting the US State Department decree that 'democracy is the institutionalization of freedom' against Jacques Rancière's much more contentious definition that 'democracy "is not a set of institutions or one kind of regime among others". It is, rather, "a way for politics to be"' (qtd in Ridout 11–12). In looking at the rhetoric that surrounds the RSC and the Globe's education work, I agree with Ridout on the usefulness of thinking 'about the relations between performance and democracy between the two poles of "institutionalization" [as defined by the State Department] and "insurgency" [as defined by Rancière]' (Ridout 12); however, in a somewhat simplified version of these opposing poles, I assume a model of institutional democracy that imposes structures, strategies, and practices of community involvement from an external position and a model of insurgency democracy that aims to encourage community groups to develop their own approaches. The 'institutional' approach is therefore envisioned as a top-down model of influence, and the 'insurgency' as a bottom-up model of social interaction.

Robert Shaughnessy's definition of the 'popular' further demonstrates the complexity of the idea of community action or involvement in the context of the rhetoric surrounding these ideas in the popular imagination:

The 'popular' is itself hardly a singular or uncontested term or frame of reference: seen from some angles, it denotes community, shared values, democratic participation, accessibility, and fun; from others, the mass-produced commodity, the lowest common denominator, the reductive or the simplified, or the shoddy, the coarse, and the meretricious. (2)

There have been many claims in different historical periods that Shakespeare's plays speak to an age with particular urgency, and this volume documents a sample of the range of times and places where that has been the case. However, in our post-post-modern digital age, I would suggest that language has become debased at the same time that cultural understanding has become ever more essential. The relationship between political rhetoric and Shakespearean rhetoric, I believe, is particularly important in the current historical moment when it is used to support educational policy and ideas about citizenship and shared values. As Shaughnessy maintains,

When the transmission and appropriation of Shakespeare are at stake, considerations of taste and aesthetic value are also bound up with inevitably vexed questions of cultural ownership, educational attainment and class, and with issues of who the desired and actual consumers of 'popular' Shakespeare may be, who these hope to include, and who they don't. (2)

In Rancière's 'insurgency' model of democracy, which in some ways can be mapped onto Shaughnessy's idea of the 'popular', 'a radically egalitarian principle prevails in which the only qualification to govern is that you possess no such qualification' (Ridout 12), making the only truly democratic model for 'the transmission and appropriation of Shakespeare' one that is disassociated from any institution. The idea of a popular democracy becomes interestingly problematic when it is applied to educational practices employed by the very institutional RSC and the somewhat less established (and establishment) Globe Education department.

The 'vexed' question of discussing the practices of teaching Shakespeare has its roots in the Bardbiz controversy arising from the Conservative government's imposition of the National Curriculum in 1988, a move undertaken in order to create, according to Kate McLuskie, 'a more flexible workforce who could more easily be directed by market conditions' (128). In her discussion of the controversy, McLuskie points out how the contradictions inherent in this debate have plagued every future attempt to publicly discuss the teaching of Shakespeare:

The Works, it is asserted, embody the finest and most complex poetry ever written but the stories are also assumed to speak directly to the human condition. His work is 'not of an age but for all time', yet it must speak particularly to the preoccupations of the twenty-first century. The work is transcendent and sublime, but it can also provide key skills of the post-industrial workforce. (McLuskie 133)

Ironically, as McLuskie points out, while John Major's Conservative government wanted a new flexible workforce, the Prime Minister's stated educational values were the embodiment of tradition: 'Knowledge. Discipline. Tables. Sums. Dates. Shakespeare. British history. Standard English. Grammar. Spelling. Marks. Tests' (Rosalind King qtd in McLuskie 129). The binary opposition between innovation, on the one hand, and tradition, on the other, which motivated politicians and, through the National Curriculum, influenced teachers, made it impossible to fulfil both of these mandates at the same time. It is hardly surprising, then, that the rhetoric surrounding the teaching of Shakespeare became increasingly political and problematic.

In order to address the current state of political rhetoric, as well as the current vision of Shakespeare in the popular imagination, it is useful to analyse two rhetorically rich slogans that attracted a great deal of media attention throughout 2008: the Olympic vision that came out of China – 'One World One Dream' – and the campaign refrain of Barack Obama – 'Change we can believe in'. The rhetorical strategies at play in these two examples can help to identify how the idea of community is currently being used internationally and how it may relate to the use of Shakespeare within a 21st-century education environment. Following this introduction to the language of democracy as seen through the idea of community, I will analyse the current vision of the role of Shakespeare in supporting and sustaining British (and particularly English) identity, as represented by the Stratford performance of Gregory Doran's 2008 RSC production of *Hamlet*, starring David Tennant and Patrick Stewart. In doing so, I hope to highlight a layering of meanings in the public domain that were generated by performance of this Shakespearean text within a particular geographic and cultural community.

To begin, then, with 'One World One Dream', the slogan for an Olympic Games the scale of which was unprecedented, it is interesting to question what world and what dream is being evoked. The demonstration of the unity of vision of the Chinese community was articulated in the Games' opening and closing ceremonies through the performance of military and faceless precision: a sea of bodies together creating a series of patterns, a visual rhetoric that both articulated harmony of movement and action and highlighted the impossibility, as well as the potentially detrimental nature, of individuality. Seeming to embody the 'institutionalised' model of democracy, these displays produced a vision of community that marks this nation as decidedly different from many other parts of the world, and yet the rhetoric is eerily familiar in the way it mimics so many recent advertising campaign slogans. It was particularly interesting to see the contrast between the Chinese vision of society and that presented by the London delegation in preparation for the 2012 Olympics: a London bus, surrounded by a diverse group of dancers dressed as Londoners of various kinds, complemented by the appearance of singer-songwriter Leona Lewis and footballer David Beckham. The strength of numbers working in harmony could not have been more clearly highlighted and contrasted than by the woeful inadequacy of the spectacle of Beckham kicking a single football across the field: the triumph of the lucky individual, the winner in the competitive capitalist game, was dwarfed by the sheer scale of the alternative vision of community that was represented in the stadium. Given the subsequent demise of the banking system that has supported this competitive world, the 'One World One Dream' slogan, as presented through this Chinese vision, now seems more complex, and the contrast between world views prophetic.

Like 'One World One Dream', Obama's 'Change we can believe in' slogan artfully negotiates both sides of the territory Shaughnessy lays out: it is equally vague, yet equally persuasive, partly because of, not despite, its lack of definition. The emphasis here is again on hope, since neither the nature of the 'change' nor the definition of who 'we' are can be clear. However, the 'we' has a historical precedent that the campaign consciously tried to evoke: the opening words of the Declaration of Independence, 'we the people',[1] are clearly the inspiration and also the justification for the use of this collective personal pronoun. The slogan moves towards the 'insurgency' definition of democracy but through the representation of 'the people' by the election to office of members of an elite, even if not institutional, group that will bring about the 'change' required, whatever it might be. It is interesting to note that both of these slogans imply an inclusivity that involves and invites anyone who is willing to 'believe', so that the art of rhetorical interpretation becomes an act of engagement in the building of a particular kind of community. The strength of both phrases lies in the fact that they can be adopted and adapted by any community to encapsulate 'shared values, democratic participation, accessibility and fun', while at the same time being both 'reductive' and 'simplified'. While the vision of democracy evoked is quite different, both slogans are quintessentially inspirational statements for aspiring populations, one about to move into a position of world influence and the other struggling to maintain its international influence and rebuild faith in its political systems.

The Royal Shakespeare Company's 2008 production of *Hamlet* provides an instructive example of how this international vision of democracy and change, as constructed in the popular imagination, was drawn into dialogue with the ongoing debate about the role of Shakespeare and Shakespeare's birthplace in English cultural life. In order to understand how Shakespeare is currently being 'performed' to help to engender a powerful vision of English cultural identity, it is useful to analyse the complex intermingling of meanings inherent in this production. The aim of this performative example is to provide a bridge between the overarching international dialogue about democracy and the very specific

---

[1] 'We hold these truths to be self-evident, that all men are created equal, that they are endowed by their Creator with certain unalienable Rights, that among these are Life, Liberty and the pursuit of Happiness.'

rhetoric currently being employed by the RSC and by Globe Education in their work with local community groups. The parallels that can be drawn between my initial politically motivated rhetorical examples and the vision of Shakespeare currently being propagated by the RSC and the Globe will help to highlight the pervasiveness of calculated Shakespearean ambiguity in this field.

With Michael Boyd as Artistic Director, and his work to develop a company influenced by the Eastern European institutional theatrical model, the RSC seems to be programming its seasons in a way that helps to support and further the cross-pollination of elite Shakespearean culture and popular ideas about democracy and culture. Gregory Doran's Dr Who *Hamlet* (as it has been nicknamed) provides an instructive example of the way an actor, a city, and a company can be transformed by the coming together of popular and elite culture. The *Stratford Observer* comments that 'since the opening of the RSC's production of *Hamlet*, the town's UK-based visitor numbers have risen and Stratford is enjoying what has begun to be described as "the David Tennant effect"' (Pecksen). Helen Robson, promotions manager at the Shakespeare Birthplace Trust, reports that 'she had seen a rise in the number of visitors going to see *Hamlet* and then wanting to learn more about the Bard'. She comments: 'I do think it's incredible that we have this celebrity culture that can have such a big impact on a town. He's one person yet he has had an effect on the numbers and types of visitors coming to Stratford' (Pecksen). The international celebrity culture, therefore, in this case, has had a very specific local impact.

Through the coming together of two powerful cultural icons, Shakespeare and Dr Who, it is possible to see a reanimation of the eighteenth-century cultural clash Christopher Baugh describes earlier in this volume. Baugh's notion that 'a sharp increase in popular tourism heightens an awareness of location and the distinctiveness of place' is essential to understanding Doran's production. In this *Hamlet*, as Baugh articulates, 'the *idea* of Shakespeare [becomes] a powerful catalyst for both generating and contemplating national identity'. Not only through the actors cast, but also through the accents used, this production negotiates between the establishment's use of the plays 'through their insistence upon degree, just laws and statutory order' and the popular audience's vision of the plays through 'Shakespeare's sympathy for and understanding of common people'. The Bard as sage and man of the people, at one and the same time, creates a powerful image. However, the new RSC vision of Shakespeare as seen through this production, like Dr Who, wears his infinite knowledge lightly, passing between ages and countries with ease. There is no challenge too great or culture too strange for Shakespeare/the Doctor to confront and overcome. Like the earlier political slogans noted, this vision of Shakespeare appeals both to a specific historically and geographically rooted community in England and to vague, simplified ideas about English international cultural influence. In the production, many levels of meaning at both the national and international level have combined to make Tennant a symbol of England, both in the past and for the future: two great English heroes, who are 'not for an age but for all time', coexist in the body of this slight Scottish actor. It is therefore not at all surprising, although disappointing, to discover that David Tennant both as Hamlet and as Dr Who speaks the Queen's English rather than employing his native Glaswegian accent.

Interestingly, the coming together of Shakespeare and the Doctor on the RSC stage marks the second meeting of these two icons in the company of David Tennant. In the last series of the television programme to star Tennant, the Doctor visited the Globe Theatre at Bankside. The real and very modern reconstructed replica theatre appeared in the time traveller's visit to the Renaissance period. As Martin White points out, this is the only time that the reconstructed theatre was populated by an audience pretending to be Elizabethan (171).[2] Ironically, the careful 'original practices' project of Shakespeare's Globe was in the popular imagination overridden by this filmic attempt to recreate a former reality. The 'reductive or the simplified' televisual realism of the programme helped to undermine the carefully researched experiments of the real theatre, altering the relationship between the Doctor, Shakespeare, and the historic Globe Theatre space in the international imagination. This strange coming together of meanings helps to illustrate the extent to which, one could argue, we have returned to an early modern vision of the simultaneity of time and action. In both the Dr Who episode and on the Courtyard stage, the past is present and the present is past in a way that helps to feed not only into an English sense of cultural identity but also into a sense of cultural heritage and international influence.

This confusion of myth and historical fact relates to another layer of meaning in Doran's production that has been largely overlooked: Patrick Stewart, who plays both Hamlet Senior and Claudius, also has a symbolic

[2] 'Clearly, we cannot expect modern audiences (nor would we want them to) to imitate their predecessors (the episode of *Dr Who*, set at the original Globe and filmed at the reconstruction, was the only time I have seen an audience perform in this way there).'

place in English cultural life. The generational divide that is at the centre of the play also manifests itself in the careers of its two stars: Stewart, whose plummy accent is accentuated, amplified, and endorsed in this production, represents not only an earlier tradition of acting but also a generation of British actors who temporarily fled to America to claim success. The reign of Captain Jean-Luc Picard as commander of the Starship Enterprise, over a number of seasons of *Star Trek: The Next Generation*, is mirrored but also challenged by the enduring power of the rejuvenating Doctor, whose on-screen career has spanned several generations and been embodied by ten (soon to be eleven) different actors.[3] The connection between the Doctor and Hamlet, as played by Tennant, an actor who stayed in the UK, continues to perform in theatre, and in particular values the performance of Shakespeare in Stratford, embodies both the conquering power of the English stage and Shakespeare's (and England's) enduring imaginative appeal and intellectual superiority. Stewart, like the parts he plays, must admit defeat and atone for his betrayal of the Shakespearean stage and his momentary lapse of cultural judgement. This complex and multilayered example again raises the question of how people access Shakespeare and the ideological questions this playwright raises about community, identity, and democracy in the twenty-first century.

Finally, then, how do these ideological questions relate to the work of the education departments of the RSC and Shakespeare's Globe? An increasing amount of work on pedagogy involves a self-reflexive sense of the power of the teacher in creating new meanings for Shakespeare. Ridout maps out, but also contests, what he considers the historical fallacy that sees a direct link connecting theatre, democracy, and education extending back to the Greeks:

This assumption involves a conviction that the line of inheritance has, indeed, been unbroken, and that when we speak of theatre and democracy we speak of the same things as did our forebears in fourth- and fifth-century Athens. What often disappears, where myths of this kind are in play, is history. (14)

Ridout uses the school hall, which at election time is transformed (somewhat theatrically) into the polling booth, as an example of the continued belief in the coming together of these three endeavours in British public life. Democracy is staged each election day in the educational establishments

---

[3] According to Wikipedia, citing news items and articles from the BBC, *The Economist*, and *The Times*, 'The programme is listed in *Guinness World Records* as the longest-running science fiction television show in the world and is also a significant part of British popular culture' (http:// en.wikipedia.org/wiki/ Doctor_Who, accessed 1 February 2009).

that propagate democratic ideals and also teach Shakespeare, and theatre studies has itself for some time modelled its pedagogic practices on the theatrical rehearsal process as a collective way of creating meaning. What proves interesting is that theatres have recently begun to emulate educational models of building communities around 'shared values'. Looking specifically at the current work with communities of the RSC and Globe Education, it is possible to see how rhetorical strategies that follow the two contrasting democratic models of 'institutionalisation' and 'insurgency' are being formulated.

It is important to point out that the education work of these two theatre companies is different in both scale and approach. The RSC's 'Strategy for the Education Department' states its aims as follows:

> The work of the RSC's Education Department is to deepen the understanding and enjoyment of Shakespeare for young people, up to the age of 19, regardless of ability and background. Our approach is to use creative learning methods adapted from the theatrical process, and to apply these to learning environments. ('Education Strategy')

The audience for this work includes 'Young people in education in the UK', 'Teachers and lecturers in the UK education sector', and 'Theatre educators' ('Education Strategy'). This is a quite narrowly defined audience in contrast to Globe Education's vision of its potential learning community. Patrick Spottiswoode, Director of Education, points out that Globe Education does not follow the traditional theatre education model, that of an auxiliary department working in support of the theatre to which it is attached:

> The Globe is unique among theatres, in my experience, in its commitment to education. From October to April, Globe Education has exclusive use of the stage so that all workshops and courses can include practical work in the theatre [...] The Education department is not answerable to the Marketing or Theatre departments. We do not educate for the box office. The Artistic Director and the Director of Globe Education are colleagues. (134)

While the audience that Spottiswoode describes initially sounds similar to the RSC's audience – 'schools and teachers; undergraduates, graduates and scholars; and the general public' (136) – the inclusion of the 'general public' is evidence of a different scale of work. This distinction between Globe Education and all other theatre education departments is supported by Spottiswoode's description of the development of the department 'from three full-time staff and a few freelancers in 1989 to twenty-three full-time staff, fifty freelance Globe Education Practitioners and two researchers on PhD studentships' (136). Despite recent dramatic expansion, the RSC's Learning Department cannot claim to match the scale of work undertaken by Globe Education, nor can it claim similar autonomy from the work of the theatre company to which it is attached.

Given the wide remit of Globe Education's vision of its purpose, my analysis of the work of these two education departments is selective, focusing primarily on work dedicated to drawing school-aged students into an active engagement with the plays in a way related to the needs of the curriculum but also fostering the idea of developing a community with 'shared values'. As a result, this analysis places a spotlight on two ongoing initiatives, the Shakespeare in Schools programme at the RSC and the work of the Southwark Community Projects at the Globe. While not absolutely comparable, both initiatives use a 'theatre-based approach' ('Stand up') and believe that this education work '[e]nriches the lives of young people because Shakespeare offers so many opportunities for learning about ourselves and the world we live in' ('Education Strategy').

The RSC's recent launch of a 'manifesto' to support the Shakespeare in Schools programme comes with the catchy slogan 'Stand up for Shakespeare'. The rhetoric here invokes both the political action of standing up for a principle and the act of engaged learning that the manifesto supports. Again, this clever and vague slogan is supported by carefully worded support statements that illustrate a thorough and perhaps even cynical knowledge of the treacherous nature of the terrain being navigated. The 'institutionalised' vision of democracy that a manifesto implies is contrasted with the active idea of a participatory practice that leans towards an invocation of the 'insurgency' model of democracy: 'Some 400 years after they were written, Shakespeare's plays are read and studied with undiminished interest all over the world, with every culture bringing its own distinctive perspective to his work' ('Stand up'). This opening sentence of the manifesto combines a belief in historical and cultural dominance, reinforcing the RSC vision of its work as seen in Doran's *Hamlet* production and giving a sense of national and even international influence. The notion that every culture can bring 'its own distinctive perspective to his work' tries to move away from a sense of cultural hierarchy, but in a way that clearly sets out, through the production of a manifesto, the primacy of the central perspective of the RSC.

The manifesto goes on to describe what it is that students are meant to get from their interaction with Shakespeare: 'Shakespeare can still speak to young people, inspiring them to articulate their feelings, develop their ideas and gain new insights into the world around them. It's no surprise that he remains the only writer studied by all young people in England and Wales' ('Stand up'). The emphasis on personal development in the first sentence aims towards a sense of universal appeal and experience. However, this idea is rather undermined by the somewhat surprising discovery that Shakespeare at the moment the manifesto was written was, in fact, compulsory in only two of the four nations of Great Britain. There appears to be an attempt to bind the nation's students and teachers together in collective action through the three imperative statements that accompany the manifesto: 'Do it on your feet', 'See it live', 'Start it earlier'. But, like the earlier political slogans, the vision of action put forward is consciously vague. These three statements could apply equally to any form of active learning, from drama to the teaching of science, history, or computing. The connection between Shakespeare and active learning is not clear, nor is the relationship between the aims of the manifesto and the practices of the Education Department.

The RSC manifesto was the product of a long consultative process entitled 'Time for Change', which seems to speak of grassroots involvement in educational practice. However, the nuanced and complex discussions of the knowledgeable education practitioners in the meeting I attended seem to have been lost in the simplified rhetoric of the manifesto. The fact that the RSC had staff signing people up to the manifesto on the streets of Stratford-upon-Avon on their open day and that Stand Up for Shakespeare cards were placed on every seat in the Courtyard Theatre during some performances again shows a tendency towards coercion rather than participation. In terms of the Education Department's practice, it is important to point out that the concrete idea, coming out of the consultation process, of creating a Learning and Performance Network that enabled a small number of schools to have an ongoing relationship with the company was upheld. The irony here, however, is that the political aims of the manifesto and the Education Department – to be inclusive, even universal, in the approach to Shakespeare's work without making Shakespeare compulsory through examinations – have had an impact on education policy, actually undermining the Department's work with individual schools in the long run. The recent change to the National Curriculum tests, with Shakespeare no longer compulsory for 11–14-year-olds, has resulted in many of the schools that were part of the Learning and Performance Network withdrawing from the programme, having found that they no longer need the RSC's help for this area of exam preparation. The careful tying of the work of the Department to the curriculum has resulted in an own goal – a result of the conflict arising from a grassroots movement of 'insurgency' working alongside an 'institutionalised' approach to policy change.

The Education Department's statement about this change reveals an interesting ambiguity, even defensiveness, along with the unusual use by the department of the personal pronoun 'we':

> We welcome the Government announcement about the removal of Key Stage 3 tests. Our hope is that this will enable more students and teachers to enjoy exploring Shakespeare's plays without the impending pressure of an exam [...] We look forward to welcoming you on to our KS3 focused INSET days and workshops. The content of these sessions will now support the wider needs of the KS3 English curriculum. ('Response')

The rhetoric employed by the manifesto resembles that of the Chinese Olympics: calculated vagueness used to dress up a thinly veiled political strategy. Unfortunately, in this case, the institutional aim of curriculum change actually made largely redundant the good practical work undertaken in training teachers and developing relationships with a small selection of schools across the country. Complacency about the influence of the company and this playwright's role in education, coupled with idealism about the dedication of teachers to the teaching of Shakespeare once it ceased to be part of KS3 compulsory examinations, resulted in an unpredicted outcome for RSC Education.

The Southwark Community Projects work of Globe Education is framed rather differently. This work comes out of the history of the local community and the strong political convictions of the project's founder, Sam Wanamaker:

> Globe Education's Community Projects are for the people who work, live and learn in the London borough of Southwark, the home of the Globe. We are committed to making Southwark a place where every member of the community can have and meet high expectations from Globe Education. ('Southwark')

This rhetoric reflects the hopeful and inclusive strategies seen in Barack Obama's campaign, and, like his campaign slogan, expresses a sense of mutual obligation and responsibility rather than a sense of being told what is best. This approach combines an appeal to 'shared values' and a belief that action should take place at the grassroots level, making clear that this department favours the 'insurgency' model of democracy:

> Community is a sense of belonging and the potential to be inspired together. The relationship between the Southwark community, Shakespeare's stories and the Globe is that we share this space, this air, these streets, these stories and the possibilities contained within the wooden 'O' as a common bond that

has the capacity to draw us together in the midst of our diversity. ('Southwark Community')

Like the RSC manifesto, this approach calls on history and geography, but in a way that is firmly rooted in the present and in the material world around the Globe.

The conviction of this approach comes, perhaps ironically, from a belief in the vague notion of 'shared values' (as opposed to a pragmatic approach to exams preparation), but it also reflects a commitment to the ideals of the project's founder: 'Our founder, Sam Wanamaker, passionately believed that the Globe should be rooted in its community and in the power of the arts as a force for change to transform communities. This inspires all of our work' ('Southwark Community'). This rhetoric presents a concrete strategy that addresses the needs of a current community that exists. This strategy closely mirrors the engaged community level approach that the Obama campaign employed so successfully and also reflects a similar belief in the shared responsibility of creating any new community. This belief is a direct reflection of the American founder's approach, which is rearticulated, as in the Obama campaign, by evoking the words of the Declaration of Independence: Fiona Banks, Head of Learning for Globe Education, in her description of the work of Globe Education, says that 'there are some ideas that are fundamental and some truths we hold to be "self evident"' (165).

Despite the somewhat idealised rhetoric of the Department, the work of the Southwark Communities Projects stands as testament to the Globe's dedication to these principles in practice. While Fiona Banks points out that '[a]ll programmes, of whatever duration, are bespoke and have the needs of the child at their centre' (158), Patrick Spottiswoode specifically highlights the work of Southwark Community Projects:

Southwark is a borough that is constantly in transition. We have been working to build a solid relationship with the community over the last twelve years [...] The Southwark Community Projects team has four members of staff who seek to involve every nursery, primary, secondary and SEN [special educational needs] school in a project over a three-year period, creating community ownership and pride in a theatre that inevitably has a national and international profile. (141)

One of the central projects of the Southwark Community Projects team is the annual *Our Theatre* project, which involves 'over four hundred students from Southwark primary, secondary and SEN schools' in a collaborative performance of one of Shakespeare's plays on the Globe stage. This collaboration and the annual *Concert for Winter*, which can involve up to fifteen schools in a Christmas celebration, truly provide a connection between the theatre and the geographic community in which it resides.

For many, the meaning of community involvement has been devalued by the use of notions of community-building for cynical purposes taken up by advertisers and politicians. Through conviction and addressing directly the destructive nature of this cynicism, Barack Obama has helped to instigate a new approach to the language that surrounds both community and politics. With another slogan, 'Restoring trust in government', his campaign spoke directly to the concerns of American citizens, making it clear that it is possible for individual action to have meaning. While it remains to be seen whether this political rhetoric will be followed up by a practical approach to involving individuals in the workings of the state, the work of the Southwark Community Projects presents an active and positive example of how the 'insurgency model' of democracy, with its 'shared values', can create a sense of community and belonging. The success of this model may well rely, as Susan Bennett argues, on a sense of historical precedent and geographic specificity:

> The new Globe is a reminder that when the first English public theatres were built at the end of the sixteenth century, the South Bank was a liminal space, exempt from the City's strictures and as such open to the full demographic of London's population as a 'liberty'. The contemporary Globe Theatre does not claim to be the real thing (it is not even on exactly the right site), but it is a quotation and a celebration of the advent of a public theatre that attracted a diverse and enthusiastic audience, mapping out new identities that eluded the City's surveillance. (84)

The collective community model promoted by Globe Education presents a possibility of cautious optimism because it is attached to an idea of shifting 'shared values' rather than to the more prescriptive outcomes and practices that an 'institutionalised' vision of democracy might entail. Looked at in this light, 'One World One Dream' and 'Change we can believe in' can both perhaps be seen as examples of a slow, steady approach to a new kind of democratic model that draws people together in a spirit of collaboration and trust rather than hostility and competition.[4] However, it is essential, as the education work of the RSC and

---

[4] There is a danger, as Rancière points out, of ' "democracy," legitimized by its "victory" over totalitarian regimes, abolish[ing] in advance any future political conflict in the name of a utopian consensus, in which dispute, disagreement, conflict – in short, the very people (the demos) after whom democracy is named – are made to disappear' (Ridout 19). The rhetoric of the two political slogans I have analysed has the danger of moving towards this post-democratic model of conflict reduction through consensus, whether from a top-down or a bottom-up model.

the Globe illustrates, to back up ideals with concrete practices that are historically and geographically rooted to develop trust and belief in a cynical population, to ensure that working practices do not become detached from the goals of their own rhetoric.[5]

The study of Shakespeare's role in developing, sustaining, and renewing identity across both time and geography provides a powerful testament to the aspirations of cooperation through language but also through performance and education practice. By addressing how Shakespeare has continued to function to bring diverse groups together in a spirit of collaboration and collective self-expression to develop 'shared values', it may be possible to understand a way forward in our increasingly challenging and diverse world. A critical understanding of the historical positioning of Shakespeare internationally might just have a small part to play in this essential struggle. The conclusion Banks presents about the work of Globe Education might go some way towards articulating an approach to a critical appreciation of the link between the rhetoric that surrounds ideas about community and the practices that embody and enable those ideals: 'But if our work is to be exciting, pioneering, rigorous, creative and worthy of the learners we serve, it must always be reflective, experimental, evolving. We must always be learning' (165). To have meaning, the relationship between theatre, education, community action, and democracy must be historically and geographically rooted; however, each rearticulation of the specifics of this relationship across time and space can inform an understanding of the role of Shakespearean performance in our own society. As the examples drawn here from educational rhetoric and practice illustrate, it is still possible to create meaningful community work. However, a critical understanding of what 'community' might mean at any given time to a particular society cannot be sustained

---

[5] While this book was in production, the RSC announced the opening of the Waterside Space, a new centre 'dedicated to education and community participation' (press release, 12 June 2009). Although this new initiative, coming at the end of the year-long 'Stand up for Shakespeare' campaign, indicates an important shift in practice to support the rhetoric around the ideas of community discussed in this chapter, it is significant that the press release quotes RSC Artistic Director Michael Boyd and Executive Director Vikki Heywood, but not Director of Education Jacqui O'Hanlon: it is therefore unclear whether it is the theatre company or the Education Department that plans to reach new audiences. In addition, Boyd's statement that the 'centre [...] reflects our *growing* commitment to family and community activities and our desire to connect people with Shakespeare and open up theatre-making to new audiences' (my italics) implicitly acknowledges that serving the local community has not previously been a company priority, as does Heywood's comment that the centre 'helps us offer more to life long learners and those outside formal education'. The full press release can be found at www.rsc.org.uk/content/8543.aspx, and further details about the RSC's work with schools, including a comment from the RSC's Director of Education, at www.rsc.org.uk/press/420–7852.aspx.

without concrete demonstration of the ideals of that community in action. Historically rooted performance criticism, therefore, has a role, perhaps even a politically effective role, in drawing attention to the changing nature of the relationship between Shakespearean – but also educational – text and performance, rhetoric and action. To avoid coercive democracy, it is necessary to understand and to rearticulate for new audiences the careful and often contentious processes of community creation both in the past and in the present. Shakespearean performance history and educational practices provide ample material for this important form of politically conscious writing.

WORKS CITED

Banks, Fiona. 'Learning with the Globe'. Carson and Karim-Cooper. 155–65.
Bennett, Susan. 'Universal Experience: The City as Tourist Stage'. Davis. 76–90.
Carson, Christie, and Farah Karim-Cooper, eds. *Shakespeare's Globe: Theatrical Experiment*. Cambridge: Cambridge University Press, 2008.
Davis, Tracy C., ed. *The Cambridge Companion to Performance Studies*. Cambridge: Cambridge University Press, 2008.
'Education Strategy'. *Royal Shakespeare Company*. www.rsc.org.uk/learning/4489. aspx, accessed 1 February 2009.
McLuskie, Kate. 'Dancing and Thinking: Teaching "Shakespeare" in the Twenty-First Century'. *Teaching Shakespeare: Passing it On*. Ed. G. B. Shand. Oxford: Blackwell, 2009. 121–41.
Pecksen, Jo. 'It's just what the doctor ordered'. *Stratford Observer* 28 August 2008: 1.
Ridout, Nicholas. 'Performance and democracy'. Davis. 11–22.
'Response to the Removal of KS3'. *Royal Shakespeare Company*. www.rsc.org.uk/ learning/7532.aspx, accessed 1 February 2009.
Shaughnessy, Robert. 'Introduction'. *The Cambridge Companion to Shakespeare and Popular Culture*. Ed. Shaughnessy. Cambridge: Cambridge University Press, 2007. 1–5.
'Southwark'. *Shakespeare's Globe*. *GlobeLink: Globe Education's online resource centre*. www.globelink.org/southwark/, accessed 11 January 2009.
'Southwark Community Projects'. *Shakespeare's Globe*. www.shakespeares-globe. org/globeeducation/southwark/, accessed 1 February 2009.
Spottiswoode, Patrick. 'Contextualising Globe Education'. Carson and Karim-Cooper. 134–46.
'Stand up for Shakespeare'. *Royal Shakespeare Company*. www.rsc.org.uk/standup forshakespeare/content/Home.aspx and www.rsc.org.uk/standupfor shakespeare/content/manifesto_online.aspx, accessed 11 January 2009.
White, Martin. 'Research and the Globe'. Carson and Karim-Cooper. 166–74.

Index

Plays by Shakespeare are indexed by title. Plays by other dramatists are indexed under the author's name. Individual productions are listed (as subheadings) in chronological order, referenced by name of venue, company, and/or director as seems most helpful.

Lightning Source UK Ltd.
Milton Keynes UK
UKOW051747211111

182463UK00001B/47/P